MT FUMAT
Castell del Rev
PUERTO POLLENSA
POLLENSA Nuestra Señora del Puig
PUERTO ALCUDIA
MT TOMIR
Caves of Campanet
LA PUEBLA
INCA
INISALEM
MARIA SINEU
anctuary of Bon Any
MONTUIRI
SAIDA
NAL Monastery of Cura PORRERAS
MAYOR
Sanctuary of San Salvador
POS DEL PUERTO
Santueri Castle
VALLGORNERA SANTAÑY
SES SALINES
PUERTO DE CAMPOS

CAPE FORMENTOR
BAY OF POLLENSA
ALCUDIA
BAY OF ALCUDIA
CAPE FA

Sa Canova CAPDEPERA CALA RATJADA
ARTÁ Caves of Artá
SANTA MARGARITA
PETRA SAN LORENZO Cañamel Castle
SON SERVERA
MURO
VILLAFRANCA PORTO CRISTO
MANACOR Caves of Hams
Caves of Drach
FELANITX
PORTO COLOM
CALA D'OR
PORTO PETRO
CALA FIGUERA

CAPE SALINAS

MINORCA

CABRERA

Toro
EN CASTELL
COLOM
CALA LLONGA
VILLACARLOS
CALA
Caves SAN BINIBE SAN PUNTA
Trepucó PRIMA
AIRE

140   150   Kilometres
N
90   Miles 100

FRANCE
MARSEILLES TOULON
BARCELONA
TARRAGONA
MINORCA
Ciudadela Mahón
Alcudia
MAJORCA
Palma
VALENCIA
IBIZA
CABRERA
Ibiza town
ALICANTE
FORMENTERA

The Balearics:
Majorca, Minorca,
Ibiza and Formentera

Travellers' Guide

The Balearics:
Majorca, Minorca,
Ibiza and Formentera

by Hazel Thurston

Jonathan Cape London 1979

By the same author:
From Darkest Mum
Let's Look at Ireland
The Travellers' Guide to Cyprus
The Travellers' Guide to Tunisia
Royal Parks for the People
The Balearic Islands

First published 1979

Text and maps © Copyright Helga Greene 1979
Maps drawn by Janet Landau
General Editors: Judith Greene and June Gordon-Walker

Jonathan Cape Ltd
30 Bedford Square, London WC1

British Library Cataloguing in Publication Data

Thurston, Hazel
    The travellers' guide to the Balearics. – (Travellers'
    guides).
    1. Balearic Islands – Description and travel –
    Guide-books
    I. Title   II. Series
    914.6'75'0483   DP302

ISBN 0 224 01645 8 (pbk)

    0 224 01718 7

Typeset by Computacomp (UK) Ltd,
Fort William, Scotland
printed in Great Britain by
The Anchor Press Ltd and
bound by Wm Brendon & Son Ltd,
both of Tiptree, Essex

CONTENTS

MAPS AND CHARTS

Acknowledgments

I have to thank the officials in the Tourist Offices of all three principal islands for the help and advice they were able to give me during my visits, especially as many of my inquiries fell outside the general run of their business. For the rest, a large proportion of my researches were conducted in the London Library, an institution upon which I have greatly depended throughout my working life as a mine of facts which, sometimes quite literally, lie below the surface of the countries I have visited.

Chart of Excursions

Town sights

Island	Major	Secondary
Majorca	*Palma* Cathedral, Episcopal Palace and Diocesan Museum Almudaina Palace Bellver Castle Monastery and church of San Francisco Vivot Palace Sollerich Palace La Lonja (Provincial Arts Museum) Consulado del Mar (Maritime Museum) Casa Consistorial (Town Hall)	*Palma* Harbour area Church of Santa Eulalia Montesión church Church of Nuestra Señora del Socorro Church of Santa Cruz and San Lorenzo chapel El Pueblo Español *Mercado* (covered market) Arab Baths *Rastro* (Flea market)
Minorca	*Mahón* Church of Santa María Casa Consistorial (Town Hall) Church of San Francisco Casa de Cultura *Ciudadela* Cathedral Casa Consistorial (Town Hall)	*Mahón* Carmelite Church and market Waterfront San Roque Arch Ateneo Museum Teatro Principal *Ciudadela* Bishop's Palace Churches Palaces
Ibiza	*Ibiza Town* Dalt Vila (Old Town) Cathedral and museum Puig des Molins Museum Punic Necropolis	*Ibiza Town* Waterfront Archaeological Museum Museo Taurino Museum of Contemporary Art

Out of Town

INTRODUCTION

The principal Balearic islands – Majorca, Minorca and Ibiza, with as an afterthought Formentera, that island beyond islands – form an archipelago, unified as a province of mainland Spain, and governed from Palma de Mallorca. Yet they are composed of so many contrasting characteristics, brought about chiefly by their individual climate, topography and history, that it is neither practical nor realistic to attempt to fit them arbitrarily into one literary portmanteau. In the arrangement of the subject matter of this *Travellers' Guide*, therefore, the relevant material, where it diverges critically from commonly applied rules and regulations such as relate to passports, currency, banking, postal services and motoring code, is set out under individual sub-headings. History and geography are the most important aspects treated thus.

The differences which will emerge from this comparative treatment will do much to explain why each island tends to attract distinctly different types of visitors, who as *aficionados* often return to the island of their choice year after year, to the exclusion of the others. At the risk of over-simplification, it may be claimed that Majorca is for sun-sea-and-sand addicts taking advantage of package tours and welcoming organized entertainment; Minorca may be said to appeal more to the taste of a staider class of tourist, looking for peace and a somewhat old-time tempo, while Ibiza provides colour and a way of life which has something operatic in its exuberance. And yet, like all generalizations, these assessments are easy to refute. Majorca possesses easily the most spectacular mountain and cliff-top scenery, in the crannies of which artists, musicians and diverse expatriates find seclusion. There are also central pastoral districts lying off the main roads, but served by market towns and churches which owe their existence to the reconquest of the island in the thirteenth century; these areas have retained much of the style of life of that period in their historic buildings and archaeological sites, not all of which have been disciplined for the convenience of organized sightseeing parties. Minorca, though boasting no more than a single main road between two fascinating and contrasting 'capital' cities, is studded with strange megalithic monuments which defy the speculations of the most informed of archaeologists; and in modern times great care has been taken not to impinge upon the island's natural beauty by over-development. Of the three islands, perhaps Ibiza, with its peasant and most 'un-European' native population, lives up to its superficial reputation most fully, yet bringing tremendous pleasure to sophisticated visitors. Formentera, because of its tiny scale, lack of salient physical features, and having no airport, is a place unto itself, rather remote, though in the process of being discovered by what may become a series of seasonal invasions difficult to absorb.

In placing descriptive information in juxtaposition, the hope is that comparison will make for clarity, for the reader either ensconced in an armchair or *in situ*, as well as prevailing upon increasing numbers of visitors to the Balearic islands to discover not only the hidden parts of the towns and countryside, but also to lure them towards exploration of a second or third island – perhaps not by committing themselves to an entire holiday on new ground, but at any rate by indulging in a short spell of island-hopping by sea or by air.

GETTING TO THE BALEARICS

Majorca

AIR

Palma airport is one of the busiest in Europe, with regular flights by the major airlines from western capitals and provincial cities, and from North Africa. Services to the Spanish mainland are frequent; direct to Madrid, Barcelona, Alicante, Valencia and Malaga (Iberia and Aviaco airlines) and to Minorca and Ibiza (Aviaco). A nine-hour service operates between Palma and New York.

British Airways operate a twice weekly service and Iberia Airlines daily flights from London-Heathrow to Palma; inquire about 'Poundstretcher' or other economy fares. A high proportion of the air traffic from Britain consists of charter travel taken up by tour operators, serving Luton, Gatwick, Birmingham, East Midlands, Newcastle-upon-Tyne, Glasgow, Cardiff and Bristol airports. Flying times range from 2 hours 50 minutes (Glasgow) to 2 hours (London-Gatwick).

Details of Spanish domestic flights – and reservations – are obtainable from Iberia Airlines, 169 Regent Street, London W1R 8BE (tel. 01-437 5622).

SEA

Steamship and car ferry services between the Balearic islands and the Spanish mainland, as well as inter-island traffic, are operated by the Compañía Trasmediterránea (London agents: Melia Travel Ltd, 12 Dover Street, London W1X 4NS, tel. 01-493 1985). There are regular weekday sailings to and from Barcelona, taking about eight hours, and three times weekly to and from Valencia and Alicante. There are more frequent sailings to Palma between July 1st and September 30th and during Holy Week. Cabins for from one to four persons are available, the more expensive having private toilets. Otherwise, seating accommodation may be booked in advance. The tariff for cars is based upon their weight.

From April to September a weekly car ferry service operates from Toulon to Palma, and during July and August from Marseilles.

RAIL

Information about travel from Great Britain to Barcelona, Alicante or Valencia is obtainable from leading travel agents, or from British Rail Continental Ltd, Information Office, P.O. Box 29, Victoria Station, London SW1V 6YL (tel. 01-834 2345). Reservations should be made well in advance, since there is no Spanish Railways office in the U.K., though couchette and sleeper accommodation through France may be obtained through the French Railways office at 179 Piccadilly, London W1V 0BA.

Spanish railway timetables, issued monthly, may be bought from B.A.S. Overseas Publications, 50a Sheen Lane, London SW14 (tel. 01-876 2131), price £2.20 including postage.

BUS

Though tickets on Spanish coaches and buses can neither be booked nor paid for in the U.K., advance reservations may be made in Spain. Details of coach services from Britain to Barcelona are obtainable from the Spanish National Tourist Office, 57–8 St James's Street, London SW1A 1LD (tel. 01-499 0901).

Minorca

AIR

Mahón's re-sited airport, 5 km. outside the town, is busy with direct flights from Europe, including numerous charter flights from British provincial airports. Frequent scheduled services connect all the year with Barcelona, Palma de Mallorca, Valencia and Madrid (Aviaco), while Iberia Airlines stop at Mahón on some of their London–Palma scheduled flights.

SEA

Regular three-times-weekly steamship services with accommodation for cars connect Barcelona and Mahón (11 hours overnight crossing). This service becomes a daily one (except Sundays) between July 1st and September 30th.

Ibiza

AIR

The airport is 6 km. from Ibiza Town. Numerous charter flights from London and the provinces cater for British package tours. Flying times range between 2 hours 5 minutes (Gatwick) and 2 hours 55 minutes (Glasgow). There are also frequent services from Nîmes and Paris, Frankfurt and Brussels, and flights to the Spanish mainland between Ibiza and Alicante, Barcelona, Valencia and Madrid.

SEA

Services include
Barcelona–Ibiza (11 hours) 1–4 sailings per week, according to season.
Valencia–Ibiza (8 hours) 1–3 sailings, according to season.
Alicante–Ibiza (8 hours) 1–3 sailings, according to season.
All these ferries are operated by Compañía Trasmediterránea (see p. 16).

CAR DOCUMENTS

British subjects no longer require an International Driving Licence when driving in Spain or the Balearics, provided they are not resident there and have a full U.K. driving licence.

A vehicle's log book must be carried, and a G.B. sticker displayed on a British registered car. Third party insurance is compulsory and a Bail Bond, which guarantees a cash deposit to a Spanish court of up to £500 in the event of an accident, is highly recommended. Insurance documents – the Green Card, providing insurance cover for the required area, and the Bail Bond – may be obtained from individual insurance companies, or through the British agents who specialize in Spanish tourist insurance: Trafalgar Insurance Co. Ltd., Trafalgar House, High Street, Leatherhead KT22 8AA (tel: Leatherhead 74422).

No car documents are required for customs clearance other than the car's registration book and insurance cover.

No one under eighteen years of age is permitted to drive a vehicle exceeding 75 c.c., while the minimum age for a motor cyclist (under 75 c.c.) is sixteen.

PASSPORTS AND CUSTOMS

Visitors must be in possession of valid passports. Visas are not required for passports issued by the governments of sixty-five countries. The exceptions, for the most part, apply to Iron Curtain nationals. If in doubt, inquiries should be made at the Spanish Consulate, 20 Draycott Place, London SW3 2SB (tel. 01-584 7405) on weekdays between 09.30 and 14.30.

Unaccompanied minors (under eighteen) must have the written consent of their parents or legal guardian for their journeys.

Customs regulations are approximately the same as on the mainland. No duty is payable on personal possessions, but when valuable articles are involved, such as expensive jewellery, cameras, field-glasses, sporting equipment, or even a portable typewriter, it might be as well, where possible, to carry proof of purchase, in case of any query on the return journey.

TRAVEL BETWEEN THE BALEARICS

AIR

Regular services operate between Palma–Mahón and Palma–Ibiza. There are no direct flights between Minorca and Ibiza, and Formentera has no airport. Services are run by Aviaco, and details are obtainable from the offices of Iberia Airlines.

SEA

Steamship services link Majorca with the two other principal islands and with Cabrera: the ships are comfortable enough, and carry cars (not to Cabrera). Services are as follows:
Palma–Mahón (10 hours) twice weekly.
Palma–Ibiza (7 hours) three times weekly (more frequent in summer).
Palma–Cabrera ($2\frac{1}{2}$ hours) Fridays only.
Ciudadela–Alcudia (3 hours) daily except Wednesdays.
Tickets are available from the following offices of the Compañía Trasmediterránea:

Ibiza   Av. Bartolomé Vicente Ramón, tel. 301650.
Palma   Paseo del Muelle, tel. 226740.
Alcudia   Lazareto 1, tel. 545342.
Mahón   Delagación de Aucona, Calle General Goded 27, tel.
             362954.
Ciudadela Delegación de Aucona, Calle Santa Clara 31, tel. 380090.
Bookings may also be made, and timetables provided, by that
company from their London agents, Melia Travel (see p. 16).
Reservations should be made well in advance during the summer
season.
     There is no direct sea or air communication between Minorca and
Ibiza.
     Ibiza–Formentera: on average there are four crossings from the
port of Ibiza on weekdays, and two on Sundays. (See p. 308.) Seas
may be rough. There is no air service.

TRANSPORT ON THE ISLANDS

RAIL

Whereas neither Minorca nor Ibiza has a rail system, there are two in
Majorca, separate and very different in character. One, the
commercial line, runs from Palma through the interior to Artá via
Inca; the other, narrow-gauge, line links Palma with Soller. For
further details of both, see p. 122.

BUS

On all three of the principal islands, country buses are the accepted
means of public transport. Their routes radiate from the capitals to
serve resorts, towns and villages. The buses run at regular, scheduled
intervals, the rule being, naturally, the further the distance the less
frequent the service. As an example, those serving the populous
coastal resorts on either side of the city of Palma may go as often as
every seven minutes, whereas less well patronized country routes
may justify no more than a twice daily service. All buses have their
scheduled stopping places en route, but their termini vary according
to the direction they are to take, the idea being to minimize
metropolitan traffic congestion. The official timetables designate these

termini. Bus stops are marked by a small 'p' sign for *parada*, as opposed to the 'P' which stands for car parking space.

GUIDED TOURS

All the popular sightseeing places on the islands are included in organized coach excursions from Palma, Mahón and Ibiza Town, as well as from main seaside resorts. Where justified (this means principally on Majorca) these continue throughout the winter season. Particulars may be obtained, and advance bookings made, at hotel reception desks, or through the tour operators' couriers which serve these establishments. Excursion coaches make a practice of collecting their complement of passengers from hotel foyers, and delivering them back at the end of the trip. Where detailed sightseeing is the object, itineraries should be scrutinized in advance, particularly in Majorca, where halts are sometimes limited to two per trip, a measure designed to relieve congestion and queues at specific venues. Hotels where visitors are on full board terms usually provide packed lunches.

TAXIS

City taxis are equipped with meters, beginning at a fixed charge, and displaying fares to specified adjacent resorts etc., but if the destination is not shown on the tariff card then a price should be agreed in advance. Fares for journeys beyond city limits usually have to be negotiated. In such cases the return fare may be charged – as for instance between the airport and city centre or resort hotel. A small surcharge may be imposed on fares to the docks, bullrings or football stadia – presumably not only to cover the disadvantage of a one-way hiring, but also for possible delay in transit. Charges remain the same, irrespective of the number of passengers carried. Each piece of luggage incurs a small charge, and waiting time costs extra.

Taxis, of course, are similar to private cars, and are therefore suitable for hiring for excursions, for which it is more than ever important for a price based on distance and duration to be agreed in advance – possibly through a hotel concierge or tour operator's representative.

CAR HIRE AND MOTORING

Some visitors bring their own cars to the islands, but these are in the minority. Self-drive car hire is the usual practice. Arrangements may be made after arrival, or previously through international car hire companies or the Spanish specialists; Melia Travel Ltd, 12 Dover Street, London W1X 4NS (tel. 01-493 1985). Hirers of motor bicycles, scooters and ordinary bicycles may be recommended by local travel agents, or information offices.

The average weekly charge for the smallest cars starts around 11,000 pesetas in the high season, inclusive of insurance and allowing unlimited mileage, but when the arrangement is to pay extra for mileage over a certain figure, the basic charge is lower. Cars may also be rented for a single day.

The rule of the road is to the right. Spain subscribes to the International Highway Code. Special attention should be paid to the following points:

Right of way is given to traffic coming in from the right, especially at roundabouts.

Unbroken lines in the centre of a road should never be crossed.

Three-point turns and reversing into a side street are forbidden in towns.

Side lights only should be used at night in built-up areas. Motorists are advised to carry spare headlight, sidelight and rearlight bulbs in case of failure.

Parking facing oncoming traffic is forbidden; also in narrow two- or one-way roads, near road junctions or entrances to public buildings.

Seat belts must be worn by drivers and passengers in the front seats of Spanish registered vehicles. When these are not fitted to a foreign car, and the visitors have reason to be exempt according to the laws of their own country, this regulation does not apply.

Children are discouraged from sitting in the front seat, although there is no law against this; if they do they must wear seat belts. Similarly, carrying babies on one's lap in the front seat is strongly discouraged, especially as doing so contravenes seat belt regulations.

Speed limits vary as follows: motorways 130 km. per hour, National Highways 110 km. per hour, other roads 90 km. per hour, towns and built-up areas 60 km. per hour unless otherwise specified.

Traffic lights are standard as in Britain, except that *two* red lights mean 'No entry'.

Some of the international road signs have Spanish words printed on them, e.g.:

Aparcamiento	Parking
Ceda el paso	Give way
Cuidado or *Precaución*	Take care
Curva peligrosa	Dangerous bend
Despacio	Slow
Desvio	Diversion
Dirección única	One-way street
Estacionamiento de automóviles	Car park
Estacionamiento prohibido	No parking
Lleva la derecha	Drive on the right
Lleva la izquierda	Drive on the left
Obras	Men working
Paso prohibido	No entry *or* No thoroughfare
Peligro	Danger

In the towns pedestrians should keep to their special crossings, which are marked *peatones*. The island police are more tolerant of minor misdemeanours than those of the mainland. Hitch-hiking, though not illegal, is discouraged.

PETROL

There are no petrol concessions for tourists. Four grades are available: 98 octane (extra), available at major petrol stations only; 96 octane (super); 90 octane and 85 octane (normal). Prices in 1978 were: extra 180 pesetas per gallon; super 166 pesetas per gallon; and normal 140 pesetas per gallon. These figures are for guidance only, as petrol is sold by the litre.

MAPS

Rough sketch plans are included in much of the readily available tourist literature, but the best and most comprehensive road map is issued by the Spanish branch of Firestone, and covers all the Balearic islands, as well as including a plan of Palma (scale 1:6,000). The general scale is 1:175,000. This map also includes an index covering the islands and Palma's streets, a practical legend and other useful information in Spanish and English. Inevitably there are discrepancies between the Spanish and Mallorquin versions of place names, but these are not too confusing.

This map is obtainable at stationers and newsagents in Majorca, or can be bought in advance in England. Edward Stanford Ltd, 12–14 Long Acre, London WC2E 9LP is the surest source.

Town plans of Mahón and Ciudadela figure in Minorca's tourist literature, while the Ibizan authorities publish a useful contour map of that island and Formentera (E.1:100,000). This has larger scale plans of the Old Town, San Antonio Abad and its environs, as well as Santa Eulalia del Río.

Map reading is made easier by an understanding of the common prefixes.

Avenida	Avenue, boulevard
Bahía	Bay
Cabo	Cape or important headland
Ca'n	Contraction of the Mallorquin *Casa d'En*, meaning 'House of … '
Ca's	Similar to the above
Cala	Bay, beach
Calle	Street
Camino	Road
Carretera	Highway
Paseo	Boulevard
Playa	Beach
Plaza	Square, place
Puerto or *Porto*	Port, harbour
Punta	Headland, point, smaller than a *cabo*
Puig (Mallorquin)	Mountain
Río	River
Son (Mallorquin)	Cf. the French *chez*; usually to denote a country estate, and invariably followed by the owner's name.

HOTELS AND RESTAURANTS

The names, addresses, categories and prices of all available accommodation are set out in leaflets issued annually by the Ministry of Tourism, and these are available on the islands or through the Spanish National Tourist Office, 57–8 St James's Street, London SW1A 1LD (tel. 01-499 0901). These up-to-date publications are the best means of prospecting possibilities before making bookings either independently or through a travel agent or tour operator. The islands are so popular that visitors are strongly advised not to leave their reservations to chance or incur unnecessary delay. Accommodation may be assumed to be heavily booked over festivals and during the peak holiday period lasting from late spring through to October.

As is natural in islands where a large proportion of the income derives from tourism, every type of accommodation is available, ranging from a five-star listing down to one star, followed by *hostales* and *residencias*, which are similarly graded, but only from three-star to one-star.

Just as certain resorts, especially those situated on the Bay of Palma, attract specific nationalities – French, West German, Scandinavian, British, etc. – some hotels in more polyglot neighbourhoods have come to be patronized by a similarly identifiable clientele. This trend may have come about naturally, encouraged by a proprietor who caters for his own people or be due to well-tried use by continental operators. In any event, the choice ranges from modern high-rise hotels, complete with every desirable amenity, to relaxed family establishments such as are (alas) no longer considered economic to build.

CATEGORIES AND PRICES

Prices and standards in each category are rigidly controlled by the government. The star rating of hotels as outlined in the official leaflets is specific. For instance, five stars promise air conditioning and central heating in all rooms, two or more lifts, several public rooms, bars, garages, hairdressers; all bedrooms will be equipped with a private bathroom, telephone, etc. At the other end of the scale, one-star hotels make do with permanently installed central heating but no air conditioning, with a lift obligatory only in buildings of five or more storeys, perhaps a single lounge or lobby; running water in bedrooms, sometimes cold only; and though some of these rooms may have a private W.C. the rule is one common bathroom to eight rooms. There should also be telephones in bedrooms.

Prices are quoted in pesetas, and are based on the maximum charge for two persons sharing a room. A separate price is given for *en pension* terms, consisting of three meals daily for a single person. (In certain instances a charge is made above the established maximum price for clients not availing themselves of at least one main meal a day.) Those hotels which have no single rooms are marked with an asterisk; and a supplement is charged for single occupation of a double room. Most hotels will, on request, make a reduction for children sharing their parents' rooms.

The tariffs must be displayed in the bedroom concerned, as well as listed at the reception desk. Where maximum and minimum rates are quoted under one heading, these will apply to summer and winter terms respectively. Quotations include taxes and service charges.

Complaints (if any) should be written in the Complaints Book which is required by law to be kept by the hotelier and produced on demand.

HOSTALES

These can be more like modest hotels than the family pensions of other countries. All of them must have adequate facilities and services to conform with their three categories. For example, a three-star *hostal* should have central heating, a lift in buildings of four or more storeys, and a lounge; at least 5 per cent of the bedrooms should have a private bathroom, and 10 per cent a shower, washbasin and W.C.; there should be a common bathroom between eight rooms, and room telephones. One-star *hostales* make do with cold running water in every bedroom, one common bathroom to each twelve rooms, and a public telephone only.

RESIDENCIAS

Residencia is the Spanish word for a hotel without a restaurant. Apartment-Hotels, Hotel-Residencias, Hostal-Residencias, Apartment-Residencias are permutations which speak for themselves, as long as one recognizes the modern trend towards self-catering. These establishments vary from the expensive furnished flat or suite to the equivalent of a British seaside flatlet. Many appear in the official lists, duly categorized from three-star downwards.

OTHER ACCOMMODATION

The introduction of caravan and camping sites has been resisted, though there are a few holiday villages and clubs mentioned in the text.

Certain tour operators have recently inaugurated cheap holidays consisting of air travel combined with basic (family-type) self-catering accommodation which is available upon arrival, but not specified in advance.

RESTAURANTS AND CAFÉS

Hotels which depend largely upon customers on package tours group these customers together at allocated tables for convenience when serving *table d'hôte* meals. Chance arrivals are usually ushered to a separate area of the dining-room, where they have an *à la carte* menu. In the first case, however, there is a choice of food, and strict meal times never seem to be enforced. Attention is paid to national tastes in the set meal menus, while a certain amount of local cooking is sometimes introduced as a contrast to the international food.

It may come as some relief that mealtimes have been adjusted to northern habits rather than the mainland Spanish, so that all meals, even in restaurants not connected with residential establishments, are at what Britons might regard as normal hours. There is no question of having to idle through the evening nibbling at *tapas* and drinking *apéritifs* before substantial fare is forthcoming. At the same time, late arrivals for lunch are never cold-shouldered, as in England.

Many seaside restaurants allocate space for visitors who bring packed lunches provided by their hotels. They are expected to compensate by buying drinks, or perhaps ice cream provided by waiter service.

PRACTICAL INFORMATION

TOURIST INFORMATION

The principal source of information in Britain is the Spanish National Tourist Office, 57–8 St James's Street, London SW1A 1LD (tel. 01-499 0901), where brochures and advice are readily available. Travel agents perform a similar service, and the good ones will indicate a choice of package tours likely to suit individual clients.

The addresses of the local Tourist Offices are listed under the towns in which they are situated; for Majorca under Palma, for Minorca under Mahón and for Ibiza and Formentera under Ibiza Town.

CLIMATE AND CLOTHES

Balearic weather generally may be described as typically Mediterranean, though moderated by sea on all sides and with substantial differences from island to island. The main consideration, of course, is temperature.

MAJORCA

The average temperatures as supplied by the Spanish Meteorological Office (in Centigrade) are as follows, the minimum reading being taken at dawn, and the maximum at midday.

	Max. °C	Min. °C		Max. °C	Min. °C
January	14	6	July	29	19
February	15	6	August	29	20
March	17	8	September	27	18
April	19	10	October	23	14
May	22	13	November	18	10
June	26	17	December	15	8

These figures may be supplemented by the knowledge that there are on average 286 days in each year when there is sunshine – no less than 146 of these being in the winter months, actually an average of five hours daily in winter as against ten hours in summer. Rain may fall on sixty-six days – though often in the form of sharp showers rather than a protracted downpour, except for brief spells in late autumn and early spring. Snow does not lie, except occasionally and attractively on the north slopes of the high peaks. Humidity, an important factor where comfort is concerned – remains constant at about 70 per cent throughout the year. The prevailing wind is south-westerly – but the greatest heat comes when it blows from North Africa. The temperature of the sea water seldom drops below 16°C.

MINORCA

Minorca's mean temperatures are lower than those of its Balearic neighbours, chiefly because it is more exposed and lacking in mountains to afford leeward shelter from its prevailing winds. It is not for nothing that the northern districts are known as the country of the Tramontana – in reference to the wind which blows across the Mediterranean from the Alpes Maritimes – and the southern half of the island is called by its inhabitants the Mitjorn, from their dialect word meaning south wind. It is obvious that this difference of climate has shortened Minorca's holiday season, so that many of its hotels close during the winter. Yet wind – or at any rate breeze – is no disadvantage in other months, especially for active people. Indeed this feature of the climate, which argues a welcome temperateness, is offset by meteorological statistics.

There is no snow, and no frost. All the year round mean temperatures at midday have been quoted as 17°C, but it perhaps gives a better idea to say that 8°C is the average for February, and 28°C for August. Rain falls about seventy-four days in the year, amounting to about 102 cms., the major part falling in winter; at other times there are only showers, which are quick to disperse. Further statistics for spring and summer months – in effect covering Minorca's season – count May as having eight sunless days; June, five; July, two; August, three; and nine in September. Good enough. Let no one but salamanders disparage Minorca's climate.

IBIZA AND FORMENTERA

Ibiza's hills protect the central and southern parts of the island in the winter, and the result is a more temperate winter climate than is enjoyed by the two larger islands. Frost is a rarity; however, in summer the thermometer may rise to 32°C. Rainfall is not considerable – a fact which is demonstrated by the presence of irrigation systems and the care which is taken to conserve every drop from the roofs of country houses and farm buildings.

Average daily maximum temperatures are as follows:

	°C		°C
January	14	July	30
February	15	August	31
March	17	September	29
April	18	October	22
May	22	November	18
June	25	December	14

In comparison with Ibiza, Formentera's climate is drier, and the land more exposed, so that the farmhouses have been built low to settle into contours, and fields are frequently protected against erosion by low drystone walls, sometimes no more than 50 cms. high. In many places where these measures are not possible the shallow soil has been blown away, exposing rocky outcrops. Twisted and bent trees, too, bear witness to what is endured in due season. The winter and early spring months are the windy ones, and those to be avoided by visitors with the tastes of salamanders.

Modern travellers do not need much advice about holiday clothes. In the Balearics winter things as we know them may be left behind; instead, those which we normally wear in an English spring or autumn may be supplemented by cardigans, pullovers, stoles or ponchos, so as to counter the distinct variations in temperature between sun and shade, open ground and shelter. In summer, anything goes for the beaches and sports areas, though a certain degree of formality is likely to be appreciated in hotels and restaurants at mealtimes and in the evenings; jackets and ties, for instance, for men, and for women long dresses or skirts if they so desire. The rest is common sense, because we all know by now that the bikinis and shorts which have become acceptable on the beaches would be out of place in churches or crowded shopping streets. Above all, Palma, Mahón and Ciudadela are capital cities, and not annexes of their coastal playgrounds. At risk of being accused of pessimism, we advocate the possession of a lightweight mackintosh, such as can be stowed in a tote bag and then hopefully forgotten.

On Ibiza and Formentera clothing need nowhere be formal. These are very much do-as-you-please islands, but new arrivals should take precautions against sunburn by covering up rather than stripping down.

HEALTH AND DRINKING WATER

Normally no certificate for smallpox vaccination is required, either for entry into the Balearics or return to Britain. If a T.A.B. injection and/or a cholera vaccination is desired as a safeguard against any possible outbreaks, these can be had from G.P.s or the British Airways Immunization Centre, Victoria Terminal, London SWI, tel. 01-834 2323, at a cost of £2 each, or free of charge on appointment at the Hospital for Tropical Diseases, 4 St Pancras Way, London NWI, tel. 01-387 4411. The T.A.B. innoculation is in two shots at intervals of from ten to fourteen days; the cholera vaccination is effective for six months only.

Visitors are frankly advised by the authorities not to drink tap water, but to keep a supply of mineral water in their bedrooms, as well as a bottle at table should they so require. At the same time, the point is made that there is nothing wrong with the water; just that its mineral content is unusual, and might not suit alien insides.

Much the same applies to food. Though great concessions are made to foreign tastes, notably in freshness of produce and the sparing use of oil in cooking and salads, any excess in eating unfamiliar and rich fare, such as sucking pig or shellfish, can have unfortunate results. The best advice is to go carefully and to arm oneself with a good recognized remedy for stomach upsets such as Diocalm tablets. If this does not do the trick, the local chemists are well used to such problems and others such as sunburn or minor accidents. It is as well to remember that no suntan oil or cream will protect skins exposed immediately and for too long a period to the full sun. Critical damage can also be caused not only to the skin, but by penetration of the sunrays very much deeper, which can produce sickness, headache and sometimes prostration. So take it easy at first.

Medical treatment is not free, so it is essential to take out an insurance policy to cover the duration of the holiday. Medical and hospital services are good, and in Palma there is also a regular all-night *farmacia* service, operated by rota; hotel concierges will be familiar with this. In cases of real emergency it is said that patients may be rushed to hospital by car with horn blowing and a white distress signal brandished from the window, the car being accorded similar precedence in traffic to an ambulance. Emergency medical service is always available from the Official College of Baleares Doctors, Paseo de Mallorca, (tel. 211229).

MONEY AND BANKS

The unit of currency is the peseta, which is composed of 100 centimos. Coinage is in denominations of 1, 5, 25, 50 and 100 pesetas, and notes of 100, 500 and 1,000 pesetas. Stallholders in country markets or the *rastro* may quote a price in the almost obsolete *duro*. A *duro* is one five-peseta piece.

Visitors to Spain are allowed to bring in pesetas to a limit of 50,000 and unlimited foreign currency, but on departure may take with them only what remains of this imported foreign money, plus a maximum of 3,000 pesetas. The easiest and safest method of carrying money is in travellers' cheques.

Banks normally close at 14·00, 13·00 on Saturdays. It must be remembered, however, that the Balearic islands observe the usual Spanish national holidays (p. 41) on which there is an almost complete shutdown of offices, shops, etc., including banks.

SHOPPING AND SOUVENIRS

MAJORCA

Though the island's produce is on sale throughout Majorca in every street of little shops and in larger complexes, it is always more fun to trace goods to their point of manufacture or, failing that, to the markets which operated long before the tourist boom. Many factories specializing in the production of leather goods, wine and spirits, wood and pottery articles, as well as the famous artificial pearls of Manacor, show visitors to their own sales areas at the end of guided tours of their production lines. These shops are regularly visited by the various coach tours, when an hour or more may be set aside for souvenir hunters.

The independent traveller, however, may glean greater enjoyment and, incidentally, wider variety from street stalls, where it is possible to find comparable goods, but unmistakably made by home craftsmen, displayed rather less blatantly. The Inca weekly market is the largest and most colourful of these open-air occasions, and has become popular with tourists, for whom special shopping excursions have been organized. The flavour of the country is to be captured unalloyed in Palma's huge covered market or *mercado* (p. 189), as long as it is realized that flavour is the operative word, because few concessions are made to the souvenir trade. This, however, is the place to go on the eve of departure for those of us who compulsively burden ourselves with choice vegetables, fruits, nuts, garlic, olive oil, saffron and suchlike on the homeward flight.

Though articles made of olive wood are for sale in quantity, it is worth searching out those that are not machine-turned and uniform, and above all not varnished. The requisite patina, especially desired in salad bowls, is best acquired by regular oiling during use. Some of the very thin and irregular bowls, complete with servers, have the most attractive graining.

Leather goods (and their factories) are located chiefly on the main road leading from Palma to Alcudia. This is the region of tanneries, discreetly hidden, but with their retail outlets convenient to the highway, beginning with the *fábrica* at Santa María. Coloured suede jackets and sports clothes are excellent buys, either off the peg or made to measure, as are shoes made at Binisalem and Lloseta – and, on another route, at Lluchmayor. Handbags, gloves, wallets, footwear, belts, spectacle cases and such smaller things, as well as good prestigious luggage, are temptations difficult to resist.

Good glass comes from Campanet, not far from Pollensa, also from Esglaieta, on the road to Valldemosa; attractive enamel ware, easy to pack, from Felanitx; lace from the mountain districts, especially Valldemosa and on the coastal route. The attractive pharmaceutical jars, such as were in use in the pharmacy at Valldemosa, together with wall plates and platters of antique design, tend to be imported from Valencia, but are intrinsically none the worse for that. Earthenware cooking pots, though bulky to carry, are unbelievably cheap. (The ethnic-minded cook who troubles to bring such things home may prolong their life by giving them a good boil in a larger receptacle and then a rubbing with garlic – unless this latter stage is ruled out by some British taboo.)

More sophisticated things are to be found in the Aladdin's caves of Palma's small shops. The artificial pearls of Manacor are to be described as part of the sightseeing programme on routes to the east coast (p. 242), but they shed their sheen over the smart jewellers shops here too. *Calle Santo Domingo*, leading from the northern corner of Plaza Cort towards Calle Conquistador, and rather unjustifiably lowered in tone by having been nicknamed 'Tourist Alley' is a good hunting ground for jewellery and watches; old prints and maps – reproductions of the finest work of Majorcan cartographers – are to be found in San Nicolás Street, not far to the north of here, and embroideries in both Santo Domingo and Calle Conquistador. Then there is a famous guitar maker with premises on Avenida Antonio Maura. At the other end of the financial scale, the Saturday flea market or *rastro* is recommended for idle exploration.

Shopping hours are flexible, but in general shops open from 08·00 or 09·00 to 13·00 or 13·50, then again from 16·00 to 19·00 or 20·00. Many close on Saturday afternoons, though food shops are often open for a few hours on Sunday mornings.

MINORCA

It becomes clear very soon after arrival in Minorca that ostentatious commercialism is not a characteristic of the island. This is shown by the relative scarcity of souvenir shops. That does not mean that there is not a great deal to buy, but it is necessary to search out mementoes to take home or give as presents, either by going direct to the island's factories and workshops to see their products at source, or by locating them in specialist shops. Reference to the section on agriculture and commerce (pp. 57–9) will lead the visitor unerringly to Ciudadela and Mahón for jewellery, both principal towns, and Alayor for shoes, San Luís for model boats, and Mahón for gin, liqueurs and leather goods. Household articles made from olive wood or glass are likely to have been imported from Majorca – and many of the more conventional souvenirs, such as embroideries, lace, and dolls faithfully presented in local peasant dress, may come from Spain.

IBIZA AND FORMENTERA

In islands which have been slow or perhaps unwilling to depart far from the peasant image, local handicrafts must be the most rewarding of buys – not that the search for them will present any difficulty here, because a representative selection of the island's products are on display in the booths of the Dalt Vila in Ibiza Town, as well as all round the island in markets and small shops. At the higher price levels there are leather goods, including sheepskin from the Portinatx district, and some attractive jewellery of consciously barbaric design copied from the *emprendadas*, the heirlooms of the peasant families. Hand-embroidered blouses and shirts are attractive and easy to wear, while a wealth of hippy-style garments are for sale in the markets and boutiques – not all of them cheap. In the lower price ranges there are sandals, straw baskets and rough pottery – some reminiscently Punic in design – as well as ornamental and useful carved wooden domestic articles. Then in the Dalt Vila, on the way up to the cathedral square, beyond the booths at the entrance gate, are the studios of artists of many nations engaged upon all manner of crafts. Their living may partially, at least, depend upon passing trade, so no hesitation need be felt in having a look round at whatever is on show at the end of the narrow alleys and in the tiny patios of the houses piled one on top of another. Here one may be welcomed in many languages, and though the artists are unlikely to be Ibizan, it is certain that the subjects or their work will reflect what we see around us on the island.

Formentera does not seem to have much to offer in the way of individual native crafts. Presumably the people, whose life has been hard, have been too hedged about by the problems of survival to evolve an indigenous art.

TIPPING

Tipping is in general practice, though one is unlikely to encounter rudeness if it is overlooked − for instance, when one first arrives at a hotel, not having acquired small change in Spanish currency. As a rough guide, an extra 5 pesetas or so should be given to the porter at the airport or the docks in addition to the fixed charge payable on each item of luggage. The porter handling baggage at the hotel should get another 5 pesetas, and when the doorman performs a special service, for instance calling a taxi, he would expect something in the nature of 5 to 15 pesetas. The chambermaid might be given 10 pesetas for each day of a stay, and the hotel porter at the desk, according to how much use has been made of his services, would probably deserve something over 100 pesetas a week. These suggestions, of course, do not apply to cases where an inclusive price has been charged already, though it is a good policy to be generous when some special service has been tendered.

Taxi drivers are rather more exacting as to their 'rights'. The rule should be about 5 pesetas as the tip for a 50 pesetas fare, but about twice that amount for a longer journey, and proportionately more for long sightseeing trips on which waiting around is involved.

Though a 10 per cent service charge is added to restaurant bills, it is customary to augment this by some small amount, especially if the meal has been good and well served. In bars, the odd loose change usually suffices. Nightclub and discothèque attendants would expect something like 25 pesetas above the 10 pesetas given to a cloakroom attendant. Then there are hairdressers: the average here is 30 pesetas plus 10 pesetas for the assistant, calculated on the basis of about 15 per cent of the total price. Cinema usherettes and attendants at bullfights should also be tipped. And to hand back 10 per cent of the price of a lottery ticket bought from a disabled street vendor is said to be lucky; at any rate it will call forth good wishes and blessings.

As for bargaining, don't, except in the *rastro*!

CINEMAS AND NIGHT-LIFE

MAJORCA

Though most of the seaside resorts have evolved their own night-life to suit the tastes of their clientele, Palma is undoubtedly the entertainment centre. We can go further, in nominating the Plaza Gomila in the Terreno district as its epicentre.

Entertainment varies from the formal to the uninhibited, for example from *son et lumière* to barbecue coach tours, which spirit parties to farmhouses (*fincas*) for evenings of good fellowship and eating and drinking, usually ending with dancing in the patio. Many restaurants and hotels all over the island have dance floors, and lay on gala nights with cabaret and discothèques, to which non-residents are welcomed, and a good many nightspots specialize in *flamenco*, though for a more authentic version of folk dancing and singing visitors are recommended to go further afield. Performances are staged in country places, such as Selva (p. 215), Valldemosa (p. 207) and La Granja (p. 203), as well as in La Lonja and the Casa Olivar in Palma itself.

Forthcoming concerts, ballet and theatre in Palma are advertised in the *Daily Bulletin*, and major productions are staged in the Auditorium on the Paseo Marítimo, while smaller cultural events favour the nearby Mozart Theatre. Appearances by visiting stars of international fame are by no means an exception, and this also applies to the world of pop music and general entertainment.

Palma has quite a few cinemas, most of which are air-conditioned. Films are usually dubbed or subtitled in Spanish, though the Rialto specializes in foreign films in the language of their origin, while the Sala Regina in Terreno shows straightforward English language films twice weekly. As a general rule, last performances begin at 21·00.

To sum up: entertainment tends to be cosmopolitan, and at all cultural levels, ranging from typical *bierkellers* and northern British club humour to folk dancing *fiestas* and serious art and music festivals, as at Pollensa (p. 224) in August of every year.

MINORCA

Until recent times Minorca was not notable for its night-life – presumably because the island attracted rather staid, unpackaged visitors. Mahón especially still appears to prefer a slightly old-fashioned image, and its visitors are recommended to go to Villa Carlos or San Luís for greater excitement. Much the same attitude to entertainment holds good throughout the island – the hotels usually providing the dance floors, and sometimes a discothèque. But one place of definite flavour is the Sa Cova d'en Xurio, at Cala'n Porter, which is in fact a troglodyte cave (see p. 303).

IBIZA

Nightclubs and discothèques have sprung up to meet demand, but one must expect them to be more cosmopolitan (though not necessarily more sophisticated) than Ibizan. This is in an effort to cater for the many nationalities who drift to the island, and who indeed sometimes remain in what to them has all the ingredients of a lotus-land. This feeling is shared by people from all spheres, from stars of the stage and screen, writers and ordinary holiday-makers to hippies.

SPORTS

MAJORCA
Tennis and golf

Long stretches of Majorca's coast, especially on either side of Palma, have been tailored into holiday playgrounds. Hotels have tennis courts, putting greens, swimming pools and similar facilities for their patrons, and in the majority of cases these are available to outsiders for a small fee. There are also specialist sports clubs for the more advanced or socially minded. Upwards of 150 pesetas an hour might be a fair charge for the use of a well-maintained tennis court. Golf is more expensive, but can be played at Son Vida outside Palma, at Costa de los Pinos on the east coast, at Santa Ponsa (9 holes) and Palma Nova.

Football

This spectator sport is well catered for. In fact football is something of a national mania, and the Majorcan team seems to maintain a fairly constant position in the Spanish second division. In the winter season the home team usually plays on alternate Sundays in the enormous Luís Sitjar Stadium on the outskirts of Palma.

Horse racing

There is horse racing (trotting) at the *carretera* in Soller and at the Son Pardo Hipódromo just off the Palma-Soller road, which doubles up as a speedway track. Races take place twice weekly in summer and once a week in winter. More countrified horse trotting events are staged near Manacor.

Other Sports

There is basketball and cycle racing at Palma's Velódromo, some not very sophisticated dog racing, and other facilities for roller skating, go-karting and ten-pin bowling.

Jai alai

Jai alai, a game similar to the Basque *pelota*, is played in what resembles a fives court. The *cesta*, a curved basket strapped to each player's wrist, is used for catching and delivering the ball at great speed, and a high degree of proficiency is achieved by the professional players, many of whom are recruited from the Basque country. Play usually goes on from 15·30 to 22·00.

Bullfighting

Mention must also be made of bullfighting, in spite of the controversy that this engenders. Palma's bullring, in the Plaza de Toros, is the third largest in Spain – that is, it is only surpassed by Madrid and Barcelona. It seats about 14,000. The season lasts from early April until the end of October, and bullfights take place on Sundays. Some tips might not come amiss: tickets may be bought about three days previous to the fight at hotel reception desks or from the Bar Rincón Taurino in Plaza Mayor. Do not leave bookings to chance, as there is great demand for seats. The *tendidos*, or segments of seating, are classified and graduated in price as *sol* (sun during part of the *corrida*, or programme) and *sombra* (shade), which can be calculated as beginning at the tenth numbered row or *fila*. All seats are reserved, but they are unpadded, so that it is wise to rent a cushion. And, incidentally, do not throw this into the ring in an excess of frenzy;

such practices, despite popular belief, are decidedly unacceptable. It would be well not to sit too close to the action unless you have already proved yourself as an *aficionado*. Useful guides on the subject, which raise bullfighting above the blood-letting image, and give it the standing of, say, cricket, are available in local stationers' shops. Try *Trim's Bullfight Guide*.

Riding and water sports

Though a certain amount of riding is available as at the rancho-type stables in Ca'n Pastilla, it will probably be water sports which will be in the forefront of the holiday maker's plans. Literally dozens of small harbours, many with a local *club náutico*, fulfil this need, and advice is readily available on such matters as boat hiring, local weather conditions and regulations. Where the beaches tend to be crowded, water skiing and the use of speedboats is banned within 250 metres of the shore in the interests of skin-divers, swimmers, airbed loungers and pedalo fans. Exceptions are made by the provision of a buoyed channel leading to the beach in question. Most of the coast is safe for swimmers, and without dangerous currents, though some care should be taken at one or two places on the north coast. The necessary equipment for various forms of water sport can be hired from waterfront shops.

Fishing and shooting

Fishing from rocks, jetties and small boats is very popular, and here again tackle and bait may be hired or purchased on the spot. However there is no game fishing, since the tuna run to no great size at this end of the Mediterranean. And, though a great deal of the shooting is the preserve of local landowners – many of whom shoot for the pot rather than as a sport, arrangements may be made for visitors – for instance to try their eye at wildfowling in the Albufera marshes. The close season is rigorously enforced throughout the island.

MINORCA
Water sports

Water sports are not particularly energetically organized, though the necessary equipment may be hired in the main resorts, and aqualung bottles filled at the Club Marítimo, Port Mahón. Yet the whole coast is full of natural advantages for those aquatic sportsmen who rely on their own resources. The rugged rocks and underwater caverns of the north coast make ideal hunting grounds for experienced skin divers and spear fishermen.

Fishing trips are best organized by direct contact with local fishermen at the various harbours and quays, and boats may be hired at Port Mahón, Cala Galdana and Arenal del Castell – to name some of the likely places.

For the spectator, yacht races in the Snipe class are held most Sundays in the season, and may be viewed from the terrace of the Club Marítimo, Port Mahón, to which visitors are welcomed.

Other sports

Football and trotting races usually take place on Sunday afternoons, as advertised in the local press. A form of curling, a game somewhat similar to the French *boules*, is played on a cement pitch at San Clemente. There are not a great many tennis courts – presumably because the glorious coast exerts such magnetism upon its visitors.

IBIZA AND FORMENTERA

Tennis, golf and riding

Depending upon their size, Ibizan hotels do their utmost to put their patrons in touch with the sport of their choosing – otherwise tennis courts may be booked at the club adjoining the football stadium in Ibiza Town. Mini-golf courses are laid out off the Avenida Doctor Fléming, San Antonio Abad, and at Santa Eulalia del Río, east of the church. Horses may be hired at both Figueretas and San Antonio.

Shooting

Ibizans have a passion for shooting (*la caza*), but this is not organized on British lines. The quarry may be songbirds such as larks or sparrows – anything which can be eaten; nevertheless the official close season for game – partridge, pigeon, quail, rabbits – is from October to February.

Water sports

Sea-fishing arrangements may be made through the Club Náutico on Ibiza Town waterfront, but the alternative is to arrange a trip with a local fisherman.

It goes without saying that all forms of water sport are catered for, and equipment may be hired at most sizeable resorts. Visitors requiring assistance, either as beginners or in developing some special skill – say in water skiing or underwater swimming – can get lessons at San Antonio Abad, Cala Llonga, Port d'es Torrent, Es Caná and possibly elsewhere.

Football and bullfighting

Football is very popular, though of no high standard, in spite of a good stadium having been built just off Avenida España on the way from Ibiza Town to the airport.

The other popular entertainment is bullfighting, and though the ring is small it generates great enthusiasm. However, in comparison with Palma's *corridas* these are minor affairs, and lacking in the ceremonial and expertise which do so much to compensate for the inevitable cruelties. Bullfights take place in the summer about once a month. Then, on Mondays from April to early October, spectators may be treated to bull-running in the arena – the point being for amateurs to try their luck and prove themselves against young animals and heifers, prior, hopefully, to making more dangerous appearances in the arena.

Other sports

Cycle and horse trotting races also take place in the football stadium, and are well advertised in the local press and on posters.

But while visitors rush around in the sunlight or chase their own dreams, they may happen to notice that the favourite relaxation of the Ibizan male appears to be a game of dominoes set up outside a convenient café or bar, while the dedicated paterfamilias may well elect to picnic or fish with his family on a Sunday – that is if he is not watching football on television. Nothing very energetic.

Formentera is even more relaxed, and does not bother with spectator sport; though facilities for full enjoyment of the sea are provided, especially for sailing and other water sports.

HOLIDAYS AND FEAST DAYS

PUBLIC HOLIDAYS

January 1st	New Year's Day
January 6th	Epiphany
March 19th	St Joseph's Day
Movable	Good Friday

May 1st	Labour Day
Movable	Ascension Day
Movable	Corpus Christi
June 29th	St Peter and St Paul
July 18th	Spanish National Day
July 25th	St James's Day
August 15th	Feast of the Assumption
October 12th	Christopher Columbus Day
November 1st	All Saints' Day
December 8th	Feast of the Immaculate Conception
December 25th	Christmas Day

FEAST DAYS

January 5th/6th	*Día de los Reyes* Epiphany procession in **Palma**. Waterborne arrival of the Magi.
January 16th/17th	St Anthony's Day. Ceremonial blessing of animals in towns and villages throughout the islands including **San Antonio Abad, and Ibiza Town**.
January 17th	**Ciudadela** celebrates the expulsion of the Moors in 1267.
February 11th	Celebration of Fray Junipero Serra's birthday at **Petra**, **Majorca**. Also local Almond Festival.
Good Friday	Processions throughout the islands. Notably *Cofradías* procession in **Palma**, torchlight march in **Pollensa**, procession of the Holy Burial in **Mahón** with *Geu* chant.
May 8th–10th	Christian-Moorish battle celebrated in **Soller**.
May 30th	Feast of San Fernando in **Formentera**; processions, dancing and folk singing.
June 23rd/24th	Medieval tournament at **Ciudadela** with jousting and 'armed combat'.
June 24th	Midsummer bonfires, Ibizan dances and *verbenas* at **San Juan Bautista**.
June 28th/29th	Water pageants at **Alcudia** and **Andraitx** port for St Peter's and St Paul's Day.
July 16th	Seagoing processions and nautical sports at villages throughout **Ibiza** to mark Feast of Our Lady of Carmel.

July 20th	St Martin cavalcades at **Mercadal**, **Minorca**.
July 25th	St James, patron saint of Spain. Festivals throughout the islands.
August 2nd	Christian-Moorish battle celebrated at **Pollensa**.
August 5th	**Ibiza Town** celebrates feast of Nuestra Señora de las Nieves with funfairs, dancing, sports and a dog show featuring the Ibizan hound (see p. 63).
August 7th–9th	Feast of Nuestra Señora de Gracia at **Mahón**. Cultural and religious events.
August 11th	Festival of Santa Cándida at **Lluchmayor** with concerts, dancing and fireworks.
August 15th	Feast of the Assumption. Special celebrations in **Majorca** at **Alaro**, **Andraitx**, **Puigpuñent**, **Porreras** and **Santa Margarita**.
August 17th	Horseracing and fireworks at **Alayor**, **Minorca**, for the feast of San Lorenzo.
August 24th	Celebrations of St Bartholemew at **Montuiri**, **Majorca**, with *Els Cossairs* dancing. *Jaleo* procession at **Ferrerías**, **Minorca**.
September 7th	Our Lady of Grace at **Mahón**. Horse races, concerts, processions, folk dancing.
September 8th	Our Lady of Jesus celebrations at **Santa Eulalia, Ibiza**.
September 9th	Pilgrimage to the Oratory of San Pedro Sagrado, near **Santa Ponsa**, **Majorca** (landing place of King Jaime 1 in 1229).
September 24th	**Binisalem** near Inca. Grape Festival – free wine.
October 5th	Bonfires and barbecues of special sausages, *butifarras*, at **San Juan**, **Ibiza**.
October 12th	Festival of the Pilar celebrated on **Formentera**.
November 4th	Celebration of San Carlos' day at **Santa Eulalia, Ibiza**.
December 3rd	Festival of San Francisco Javier, **Formentera**.
December 24th	Christmas Eve pilgrimage to Lluch Monastery.

All the interesting feast days are given in detail in a Spanish Tourist

Office pamphlet available at Information Offices. This is recommended reading for any visitors who might want to witness or take part in a *fiesta*. Dates should be checked with the Tourist Calendar issued each year by the Spanish Ministry of Information and Tourism in case alterations have been made to account for the coincidence of a Sunday with a particular saint's day.

POSTAL INFORMATION, TELEGRAMS AND TELEPHONES

All mail to Europe goes by air. Stamps are sold at post offices and also in *estancos*, or tobacconists, but it is usually easier to stamp mail and post it through one's hotel desk. Public letterboxes are usually silver-painted, with red and yellow bands. Post and telegraph offices are listed under the main towns on the islands, as also are telephone exchanges.

POSTAL RATES

	Internal	U.K.	U.S.A.
	pesetas	pesetas	pesetas
Letters	3	*19ₚ* ~~12~~ (up to 20 grammes)	40 (up to 20 grammes)
Postcards	2	8	36

TELEGRAMS
Compared with telephoning to the Spanish mainland, telegrams are cheap. The rate is 1 peseta per word plus a 15 peseta flat rate charge for an ordinary telegram. To send a telegram to the United Kingdom the charge is 15 pesetas per word, or if urgent 30 pesetas per word.

TELEPHONES
Many restaurants and bars have public call boxes in which *fichas*, or tokens, bought on the spot are used. The rate for telephoning the U.K. is 250 pesetas per minute, and for the U.S.A. 800 pesetas per 3 minutes.

WEIGHTS AND MEASURES

The metric system is used in Spain. Here are some useful equivalents:

WEIGHT   1kg. = approx. 2·2 lb.

FLUIDS	1 pint = 0·6 litres
	1 gallon = 4·5 litres

LENGTH	1 metre = 39·37 inches
	1 kilometre = 0·62 miles

AREA	1 hectare = 2·47 acres
	1 square kilometre = 0·39 square miles

CLOTHING SIZES

Men	*Suits*	British and American	36	38	40	42	46	
		Continental	46	48	50	52	56	
	Shirts	British and American	14	15	16	17		
		Continental	36	38	40	42		
	Shoes	British	7	8	9	10	10½	
		American	7½	8½	9½	10½	11	
		Continental	40	41	42	43	44	
Women	*Dresses*	British	10	12	14	16	18	20
		American	8	10	12	14	16	18
		Continental	40	42	44	46	48	50
	Shoes	British	3	4	5	6	7	
		American	4½	5½	6½	7½	8½	
		Continental	36	37	38	39	40	

ELECTRICITY

The usual voltage is 220 or 225 A.C., but some older properties still have 110 or 120 A.C. Hotel washbasins are usually provided with Continental-size electric shaver points. A.C. plugs are two-pin.

TIME

Normal Western European time is in force, that is, one hour ahead of Greenwich Mean Time. Spanish summer time, from early April to late September, is two hours ahead of G.M.T.

GEOGRAPHY AND GEOLOGY

The Balearic archipelago, which has no comparable near neighbour in the western Mediterranean, may be reckoned as consisting of fifteen islands situated from 80 to 300 km. (50 to 190 miles) east of the Spanish mainland, and averaging some 240 km. (150 miles) from North Africa. Their total land area has been calculated as 5,014 square kilometres.

MAJORCA

The capital, Palma de Mallorca, is also capital of the Spanish province which administers the other islands. Majorca is substantially composed of limestone, clay and marl, which argues that what is now dry land began at the bottom of the sea or a large continental lagoon. It has been deduced that the archipelago owes its emergence to enormous submarine upheavals caused by pressure upon ancient sediments, exerted by the weight of the land mass of what is now North Africa. The Majorcan mountains, contemporaneous with the Alps, are continuations of the mainland range which extends from Cadiz on the Atlantic coast of Spain to Cape de la Nao, north of the Mediterranean town of Alicante. At this point the mountains submerge, to reappear vestigially in Ibiza, and then in the spectacular precipitous chain of Majorcan peaks which begin with the tiny island of Dragonera off Majorca's south coast, then rear high as Mount Galatzo (1025 metres) and Puig Mayor (1445 metres) and, after a total length of 80 km., finally disappear abruptly into the sea at Cape Formentor.

Majorca has an area of 3,640 square kilometres, and is roughly the size of Cornwall, though more compact, with a measurement of some 100 km. from east to west, against about 75 km. from north to south. Barcelona is 208 km. to the north, and Algiers 282 km. south.

Since the width of the westerly mountain chain is only about 8 to 12 km., with nine peaks exceeding an altitude of 1,000 metres, the steepness of the mountains is inevitable. Prevailing winds from seaward leave white limestone bones of rock exposed, craggy and bleached, with cliffs which in many places drop 300 metres to deep water. Being so mountainous, much of the shore of the north-west coast is inaccessible, though a coastal road snaking along the contours high above sea level reveals the most splendid views, made all the more compelling by the provision of *miradores* as safe parking spaces, at selected vantage points. But wherever practicable the slopes are terraced for the cultivation of fruit and vegetables, and for the olive tree. There are occasional and sometimes perilous tracks and footpaths leading to the foot of the cliffs, usually immediately below small villages, but welcome exceptions come in the shape of the lush valley centred around Soller and its port, the purely scenic outlet of the Torrente de Pareis at La Calobra, and the newly developed (though colonized by primitive man) Cala de San Vicente at the northern end of the west coast.

A second and parallel mountain range outlines the east of the island, beginning in the south with a series of rolling hills. The scenery here is less impressive, and consequently less hostile. A comparable grandeur lies to the extreme north, beyond Artá, in a sequence of headlands almost completely unprovided with roads, and famous for limestone caves.

Between these two mountain systems there is a plain, known to the islanders as Es Pla, consisting of fertile, intensely cultivated land where the highest points are mere hills seldom reaching 500 metres but so remarkable when seen rising from level ground that almost without exception they have become sites for monasteries, calvaries and sanctuaries.

Taking into account the indentations of the east coast, with its alternations of *puntas*, or points, and *calas*, or coves (simply asking for development into tourist resorts), the Majorcan shoreline measures about 300 km. (186 miles). But the most important coastal features are undoubtedly the three magnificent bays which originally attracted shipping, and consequently trade and prosperity, to Majorca. They now receive foreign visitors in their legions. Palma Bay in the south, with the city at its centre, describes more than a semicircle facing the midday sun, while Pollensa and Alcudia Bays in the north have only a small promontory separating them. These look towards Minorca. Here, too, is the Albufera, the district of marshlands which, despite the fears of conservationists, has managed to put up some sort of fight against the developers.

There are no perennial rivers or other waterways, though numerous so-called torrents rush down well-worn courses after heavy rain. Much of the island's water supply is provided from seepage into natural underground reserves which traditionally were pumped to the suface by windmills. Electricity has now taken over.

MINORCA

On a clear day Minorca is within sight of Majorca, either from the
heights above the Bay of Pollensa or from that island's eastern tip,
which ends at Cape Farruch, with an intervening distance of only 40
km. (25 miles). This northerly position, open to winds blowing from
the direction of France and the Rhône valley, gives it a completely
different character. Much of the island consists of Miocene limestone
of the Tertiary period, and as such is a continuation of the Andalusian
mountain formations, though the north side of the island has harder
Devonian rock, similar to that occurring in Catalonia and Provence.
Some of the rocks of this northern half of Minorca – defined by a line
running from Mahón westwards, almost exactly along the route of
the main road through Mercadal and Ferrerías, but turning north to
the coast about 10 km. short of Ciudadela – are the oldest in the
Balearics (350 – 400 million years old). They were only joined to the
younger, southern half of the island to form its present shape in the
late Cretaceous period (135 to 65 million years ago), at the time when
the Alps were thrown up. The long inlet of Port Mahón was also
created then, at the point where the two halves failed to fuse together.
There is thus a division into two distinct geological regions which has
a noticeable effect upon the landscape and its agriculture.

The centre of the island is in the form of a low plateau, at its highest
between Alayor and Ferrerías, where Mount Toro, a landmark from
all directions, reaches an altitude of 357 metres.

The road connecting Mahón, the present day capital, with
Ciudadela runs across the centre the island, and may be taken as the
geographical and geological line of demarcation. To the north there is
rolling country, sparsely populated, ending in a very rugged coastline,
of which the principal inlet is the Bay of Fornells at its centre. The
land to the south, including much of the plateau, is cut into valleys by
winter rains, though productive farmlands have been established by
the removal of the stones which are such a characteristic of the
Minorcan landscape.

The island measures 50 km. (30 miles) from east to west, and 20
km. (12 miles) from north to south, while the coast has been estimated
at over 200 km. (130 miles) in length, allowing for the multiplicity of
bays and fiord-like creeks and beaches. These beaches are said to
number more than 120, though some, and these mainly in the north,
have no access roads.

Finally, the prime physical features, which have had the greatest of all influences upon Minorca's past, are the two harbours to which Ciudadela and Mahón owe their existence, and which, as we shall see, have sporadically brought the island into world limelight. Of the two, Mahón's is easily the more remarkable. It is justly claimed that as an anchorage Port Mahón is the finest in the world, with Pearl Harbour its only rival. This deep water inlet, penetrating inland for $5\frac{1}{2}$ km. and so narrow as to be easily defensible by cannon, was rated as being capable of accommodating every naval vessel in the world, and it is in a naval role that it played its part, and brought this otherwise insignificant little island into prominence, especially in the eighteenth and early nineteenth centuries. But now that the pattern of armaments has changed, and naval bases are less in demand, such a function has diminished almost to zero in favour of aircraft carriers and nuclear submarines, so that the echoes of glory and importance can only be revived by trips around the bay. In another parallel the creeks and beaches that once witnessed piratical raids are now wholly given over to visitors appreciative of sun, sea and sand, all to be enjoyed with a surprising measure of seclusion.

IBIZA

In topography, as well as in other respects, Ibiza and its dependant islands differ considerably from Majorca and Minorca, which are equally dissimilar from each other. When in ancient times the whole archipelago was known as the Gymnasiae – from the belief that its natives were either so ignorant or so hardy that they went naked even in winter – Ibiza was designated the most important of the Pityussae, or pine-clad islands. This appellation still applies to the island of Ibiza itself, though no longer to adjacent Formentera and its associated island of Espalmador, nor to the rocky offshore islets of Tagomago, Conejera and Vedrá.

To make direct comparison with the dimensions cited for Majorca and Minorca, Ibiza is 572 square kilometres (272 square miles) in area, only 40 km. (25 miles) across at its maximum (that is, from south-west to north-east) and is the closest to Spain of the three principal Balearic islands: a distance of 88 km. (55 miles) east. Majorca is almost equidistant: 85 km. (53 miles) to the north-east; and the coast of Africa is 220 km. (138 miles) away. The shoreline extends for 170 km., and the highest point is the Atalayasa de San José (475 metres), to the west of Ibiza Town.

Before modern developments, which tend to proliferate around the coast, the fortress town of Ibiza and the conurbation at its foot was for a time the only densely populated district. This is no longer so, since the growth of post-war tourism has turned San Antonio Abad in the west into a complex of hotels and ancillary establishments which cater principally for the package tour industry. Santa Eulalia in the east preserves its identity as a centre important to the country districts around it, with its old fortified church the nucleus to proclaim its historical role; the town remains unaffected by the adjacent development on this irresistibly beautiful section of the coast.

In contrast to the island's splendid shores, one of the most important topographical features is Las Salinas, the area of saltpans at sea level situated south of the town of Ibiza and beyond the airport. These occupy almost the whole of the promontory of that name, and are traversed by a causeway. Their commercial importance continues into the present time, though rather diminished since the ancient and medieval years, when their commodity made Ibiza a prescribed port of call for the trading nations of the whole Mediterranean and beyond.

FORMENTERA

Formentera is the fourth largest of the Balearic islands, and while its own offshore islands are less than 5 km. (3 miles) from the Punta de Portas, the southernmost tip of Ibiza, the sea passage from port to port is 17 km. (10 miles), and according to weather conditions can take as much as an hour and a half by scheduled steamer. Formentera is also the nearest of all the islands to North Africa. It measures 115 square kilometres, with a perimeter of almost 60 km. (37 miles). Nowhere is the ground higher than 197 metres, and its two hilly districts are at opposite ends of the island, with low-lying land, barely above sea level, in the middle. In fact, when viewed from the sea, the impression is of two separate islands, both bounded by cliffs. It follows that the scenery is surprisingly varied for such a small area; quiet pastures and cornlands level off to meet the sea, there to become dunes and shoals, or to terminate in pinewoods and bluff headlands. The plateau in the east is one of the most fertile districts.

The island is divided into three parishes administered from the capital, San Francisco Javier. From the visitor's point of view, too, the island may be regarded as three neighbourhoods: the east and west, which have the hills and cliffs and limited access to the shore, and the narrow low-lying waist between the two, where the beaches are to be found, both to the north and south.

POPULATION AND LANGUAGE

MAJORCA

Without causing offence, it can be claimed that Majorcans do not consider themselves to be wholly Spanish. History reveals the reason. They are islanders who were rescued from centuries of Moorish domination by Catalans of distinctly Frankish breeding, and not by Iberians from across the straits. At the same time, the period of Moorish rule lasted longer than it did in Catalonia, so that it can be assumed that the indigenous population acquired a strain of North African blood at least as significant as that assimilated by the inhabitants of Moorish Valencia. Be that as it may, Majorcans are credited with a high degree of individualism, commercial acumen and taste for the sea, all of which are absent from the make-up of the average sedate and land-loving mainland Castilian.

However Castilian, that is to say Spanish with the formal and courtly lisp, is the official language of the Balearics. School subjects are taught in it; it is the language of the administration, and newspapers are printed in it. But though it is used by some 95 per cent of the population, almost all Majorcans elect to speak native Mallorquin amongst themselves. Though this tongue bears closest resemblance to the Catalan language which is still in use north of the Pyrenees, and to a lesser degree to the dialect of Provence, it is a distinct language, rooted in old French but not easy to understand when overheard in the streets and market places. This will be no great disadvantage, even for visitors who speak no Spanish, since Majorca's popularity as a holiday playground has equipped its hotels with multi-lingual staff, and shops and restaurants naturally follow suit, providing the basics of northern languages sufficient for their customers to be served satisfactorily. But nowadays, since the decline in our national spending power, English is not always the most common foreign tongue.

Some Moorish words have also found their way into the language. These occur most generally in connection with agriculture, architecture, science and the arts – notably those skills in which the

Moors excelled. And the Moorish influence is also reflected in place names which have no Latin root, such as Binisalem, Almudaina, Atalaya, and in the quite common use of 'x', as in Andraitx.

In travelling around the island one may meet particularly swarthy individuals of the lower class. These are likely to be gipsies, who form a minority which has never been accepted by the authorities. Their presence as beggars and vendors of trinkets on the beaches is heavily discouraged, while efforts have been made to resettle them (rather uneasily) in a housing estate on the eastern outskirts of Palma. These people use a debased version of Spanish known as Cale, which has a sprinkling of Egyptian, Greek, Hungarian and even more outlandish words.

MINORCA

The Minorcan people are similar, but not racially identical with the Majorcans. Both climate and history has caused them to evolve on slightly different lines. The mixture of blood of which they are composed derives essentially from invaders and settlers; and it did not become wholly stabilized by the arrival of the Catalans in the thirteenth century, since the lower class Moors were allowed to remain on the island as labourers. The French and the British made their genetic contribution in the eighteenth century, though the letters of John Armstrong published in *The History of the Island of Minorca* in 1752 hint that any association made then fell short of actual marriage. He follows up this observation with a passage describing the debauchery of the British soldiery, which serves to emphasize his point. As further imbalance, the poverty of the island in the following century, before the national economy was supplemented by tourism, drove numbers of able-bodied men abroad – many to Algeria – in search of a livelihood.

Though the Catalan language was introduced during the resettlement of the land in the early part of the thirteenth century, totally replacing the Moorish Arabic which until then was in current use, a Minorcan derivative still exists in healthy form. This differs considerably from Catalan, and to a lesser extent from the native tongues spoken in both Majorca and Ibiza. However, as elsewhere, Spanish is the official language, so that visitors will have their best opportunity of hearing the island speech in markets and quayside bars or, better still, in full flood during the ceremonial orations which are an essential part of *fiestas*. As a postscript, some few English words have burrowed their way into the island vocabulary, such as *winderes*, for the Georgian-style sash windows which are completely foreign to Spain, and *saydbor* for sideboard, which inevitably conjures up a picture of heavily loaded dining-room furniture complete with decanters – of port, no doubt.

Ibiza and Formentera

The degree of racial admixture on Ibiza must be a matter for speculation, though it is likely to have been at its greatest during the period when the island was ruled by Carthage. Punic influences, as well as Punic remains, proliferate on the island even to this day. And it may not be altogether because the population has been predominantly peasant and maritime that many country people are swarthy enough in complexion to invite comparison with natives of North Africa.

As in Majorca and Minorca, Spanish is the official language, though it has made rather fewer inroads on the daily speech of the people, some of whom have failed to master what they must regard as an alien tongue. Even so, the islanders' Catalan is not pure; it has evolved into a distinct form known as Ibizenc which is punctuated with words owing little to the Frankish language. However, though some Ibizans may know no other tongue, the majority are content to use Ibizenc among themselves and to slip into Spanish when outside the family circle, or when transacting official business. Where the visitor is concerned, he will find that a smattering of Spanish as a *lingua franca* – a paradoxical term! – will be adequate even in country places. And anyhow the Ibizan tradespeople – and for that matter the Formenterans – have been quick to adapt themselves to the necessity for basic communication in the more common foreign languages.

The population of 3,500 or so on Formentera is distributed chiefly between the small port of La Sabina, which houses workers in the nearby salt industry – and San Farncisco Javier, the capital. (For reasons which will become apparent it is difficult to resist putting this title into inverted commas.) There are only two other villages of any size, though the recent tourist boom has brought about development along the edges of the island's beaches. Owing to colonization from Ibiza, there is no difference in racial types between the two islands.

AGRICULTURE AND COMMERCE

MAJORCA

History relates that Majorca's early prosperity was based upon the sailing trade, leading to Palma's traditional harbour at Porto Pi being superseded by the more convenient and central harbour installations integrated with the trading activities of La Lonja, the commercial exchange. Ensuing wars were responsible for trade recession, while no less crucial was the opening up of traffic with the Americas which shouldered the Mediterranean islands off the map. Revival of the sailing trade in the nineteenth century was eventually killed by the advent of steam, coupled with the loss of the Spanish colonies, so that from the end of that epoch Majorca inevitably became more inward looking. Consequently greater attention was paid to agriculture.

Until the influx of holiday-makers, which has increased the demand for country produce more than ten times, the island of Majorca was self-supporting. But nowadays a large amount of foodstuffs have to be imported. Yet as well as almonds, oranges and lemons, certain early crops find foreign markets, for instance early potatoes for England, and a quantity of dried fruit, particularly apricots and figs. The almost insatiable local demand for fresh fruit and vegetables has led to the extension of markets in town squares and streets, as well as in the great covered *mercado* of Palma. These have become a fascinating sight, representing as they do a true and undramatized version of the life of Majorcan people today, and the spontaneous interchange between town and country.

Systems of cultivation practised in Majorca are still based upon techniques inherited from the Moors, such as the building of drystone walls to form terraces for olives and horticulture and to counter erosion; and the introduction of irrigation in the form of *norias*, wells and channels which convey water where it is most needed in an island where rainfall is largely seasonal, but where underground water accumulates below the permeable soil. The *seguias* – cemented runnels serving villages and terraces on the western side of the island – are also typically Moorish in their channelling of spring and storm water into cisterns attached to houses and smallholdings. Harvests of one sort or another are thus able to follow one another without a break during most of the year.

The crop which makes the greatest impression upon visitors begins to show itself in early spring, when much of the island is covered by what looks like a billowing coverlet of pink and white blossom – pink for sweet almonds, white for the bitter variety. So extensive are these almond plantations that to see them to advantage it is advisable to search out high ground for a bird's eye view, or even to snatch a preview when arriving by air. The mass plantation of almonds dates from 1765 and since then expansion has been so great that there are now reckoned to be over 6 million trees in production. Eighty per cent of the harvest goes for export, and accounts for two-thirds of the total almond production of Spain. A tree will show profit some seven years after being planted. The green, velvet-encased nuts are usually gathered by women, and then the outer material is removed for milling, to extract the oil. The discarded shells make useful fuel. The almond kernels may be sold *au naturel*, roasted and salted, or made into dragées, nougat or other forms of confectionery and preserves.

There are few periods of the agricultural year when the Majorcan countryside lacks interest. Blossom follows blossom in almost uninterrupted succession: first the almonds in February, then oranges, lemons, mandarins, peaches and apricots. The corn harvest takes place in May and June; figs ripen in August and early September, as do grapes, and olives mature in September and October. Ploughing begins with the first autumn rains and transforms the face of the land.

Most of the farming activity is a delight to observe, and particularly so because even in these modern times minimal use is made of heavy machinery – due partly to high import tariffs but also to the intensive cultivation of catch crops in the limited space between lines of trees. One sees people and their animals engaged in techniques which have hardly changed throughout the ages. For instance, almonds are gathered by shaking them off the trees into sheets spread upon the ground. Similarly, green olives are beaten down from the branches by means of slender poles, while ripe black olives, are gathered by hand as windfalls. These are usually family, or, at most, local community operations.

Often the hollowed shell of a parent olive tree survives like some witch-ridden fairytale illustration, while suckers emerge from the stock in a cycle of renewal. Some trees, notably on terraces high above the north-west coast, are claimed to be a thousand years old. Thus the olive tree, so valuable as to have acquired innumerable myths and legends, is a provider of both fuel and oil.

Citrus fruits, the different varieties of which mature over a period lasting from autumn well into spring, are picked as they ripen, and not as a single crop. They may be seen to the best advantage in the sheltered *huertas* or fruit farms of the Soller valley.

Carob trees are less noticeable than the olive and fruit trees. The *algarrobas*, or St John's Bread, grow as individual specimens rather than in plantations. They too live for many years, and their beans are used not only as an important ingredient of cattle food, but also as a sweetener for manufactured products, and in the making of crude alcohol.

It is apparent that there has been a degree of movement away from the traditional system of land tenure, when vast estates belonging to important families with recognizably Catalan names were leased out to peasants and small farmers, very often on a system comparable to that of the now defunct English tithes. Many people now own their land, and for this reason many properties are small, a fact which also accounts for the continued use of mules, donkeys, horses and occasionally camels for work in the fields. Another is the animals' greater manoeuvrability, which gives them an advantage over powered machinery. And, as it happens, these archaic practices can contribute to the pleasure of the onlooker, who may well chance upon colourful cavalcades of families returning near nightfall from work in the fields and orchards, which are often situated at some distance from the towns and villages where they live. For here in Majorca, as in other Mediterranean countries that have lived in dread of raiders, the people tend to gather into protective communities rather than establish themselves directly upon their holdings; a trend initiated in Majorca by Jaime II in the course of his formation and settlement of inland market towns.

One traditional practice has caused remarkable modern changes of fortune. In the past it was customary for younger sons to inherit the worst and most impoverished of their fathers' land, for example, on the unproductive and rocky coasts. But tourist developments have transformed these previously negligible inheritances into plots of high capital value – thus completely overturning the established economic balance within families.

Because horticulture and cereal growing occupy land jointly with fruit trees their extent might well pass unnoticed, except possibly in the plantations of artichokes or melons – the more eye-catching crops. But in the district around La Puebla and Muró there have been extensive developments in drainage and land reclamation which now provide deep loam for the large-scale production of potatoes and other vegetables.

The wine-growing districts must not be forgotten; nor could they ever be by travellers on the main road between Palma and Alcudia. This passes through Binisalem, which is notable for the production of wine with a high alcoholic content. Vines are cultivated on terraces reaching high up the slopes of the *sierras*. The wine-producers on the main road below issue open invitations to passers-by to visit their establishments. Felanitx, in the south-east, has a comparable reputation for its flourishing vineyards, the speciality here being white wine.

Livestock farming and poultry rearing play an important part in the provision of food for the population, though this may not always be obvious to the casual visitor, for it is found to be more economic to stall-feed than graze the animals. The green fodder is thus cut daily and carried in panniers to the farms; small beasts of burden encountered on the road take on the appearance of walking haystacks. Corn crops are grown everywhere, and their yield is substantial, even though fields of any great size are the exception. Sheep and goats, when allowed to graze, are usually hobbled, and sometimes belled and herded, on land where boundary fences – if they exist at all – are not designed to be stock-proof.

MINORCA

Unlike the more populous island of Majorca, Minorca has never set out to capture tourists at the expense of traditional forms of commercial interchange. In fact, agriculture, industry and tourism are well-balanced – an achievement which encourages Minorcans to follow a proven style of life, and to remain staunchly individualistic. It follows that a large percentage of the people remain involved in the agricultural way of life which has grown up during past centuries. Owing to the accident of soil and climate, livestock farming with the accent on dairying has come to the fore, and serves markets for beef and cheese which extend far beyond the island's confines. Then, as an ancillary industry, tanning and the manufacture of shoes and other specialist leather goods yield a fair income. There has, therefore, never been very heavy pressure in favour of tourist development.

The shoe-making industry covers a wide spectrum, from high fashion in the Parisian market to workaday cowhide shoes soled with re-used motor tyres, which when run to ground in the lowlier shops and markets come as a boon and a blessing to active holiday-makers. Women's shoes are chiefly made in Ciudadela, men's in Alayor, and slippers in Mahón. For those visitors who stay long enough, and are quick off the mark, orders for made-to-measure footwear may be accepted and fulfilled according to promise – a luxury which elsewhere is beyond the means of most of us.

The periods of British occupation of the island may be credited with much that is beneficial to the agricultural scene. It was the far-sighted British governor, Sir Richard Kane, who set out to improve the stock of cattle – predominantly Friesian – and strains of wheat, by bringing in pedigree animals and seed corn from the British Isles. Hence the production of surplus dairy goods and succulent beef – so rare in Mediterranean countries – as well as the famous Mahonese cheese and, recently, the popular processed cheese and the ice cream which rivals that of Naples.

The climate lends itself to grazing, and the cattle are kept in fields walled by stones cleared from the ground. Though during the Middle Ages Minorca was famous for its wool, the sheep population has now declined, and is mostly relegated to the drier, hillier and less productive quarters of the island. The livestock is watered from cisterns which take pride of place in each complex of farm buildings. Mechanization has increased dramatically, considering that as short a while ago as the 1960s tractors were few and far between. Whereas in the mid-seventeenth century a certain John Armstrong, who described himself as a government engineer, estimated that two-thirds of the island's corn had to be imported, that figure must be far greater now, for the accent is on fodder crops for cattle – two of the most valuable present-day crops being red clover and lucerne, both comparatively drought-resistant. The bulk of these goes for silage.

Even in Armstrong's day all the olive oil consumed in Minorca had to be imported. In fact the only olive trees to be found are of the wild variety which bears no fruit and whose only use is as a soil stabilizer. Wine production, however, flourished in the eighteenth century, but lamentably was brought to an abrupt end at the close of the nineteenth by the dread phylloxera disease, though a very small quantity is once again being made in the neighbourhood of San Luís.

An industry for which the British may be said to be directly responsible is the distillation of gin. It happened that the occupation of the island coincided with the time when gin was the people's tipple in

Britain, and so in 1790, when the demand was created by other ranks garrisoned near Mahón, a local distillery was promptly established. It continues to flourish, employing a secret recipe which is passed from generation to generation.

In spite of the emphasis upon agriculture, and the full use of the land, it has been estimated that some 70 per cent of the island's manpower is engaged in the manufacture of shoes and jewellery – principally costume jewellery set with semi-precious stones. There are more than a hundred establishments so engaged – though this number includes small workshops and, to a lesser extent, piecework done at home. Buyers come from as far afield as Paris and other northern capitals, which demonstrates that the work, like other things Minorcan, is of a high quality.

To a lesser extent there is also interest in the building of model boats, and indeed of full-scale marine engines and fittings; and reproduction furniture made on the island – some of it decidedly Georgian English in style – commands good prices.

IBIZA AND FORMENTERA

Ibiza has always stood apart from the other Balearic islands, and indeed from Spain, and its patterns of trade show little affinity with those of its neighbours. This was true even in days gone by, when the only export of any consequence was salt. It still is, even when almost all the inhabitants are engaged in agriculture, fishing and, most recently, in the service trades.

The salt industry was probably founded by the Carthaginians, continued by the Romans and the Arabs, and then became the monopoly of important Italian companies, who shipped the mineral to northern Italy, where it was often bartered for wheat. The truth is that the Ibizans are reputed to have been so lazy about cultivation when a less exacting source of livelihood was to hand, with the sun doing most of the work, that the island fell far short of being self-supporting in food. Regulations had, as a consequence, to be enforced withholding cargoes from foreign ships that were not importing the grain essential for local consumption. Though native workers were employed in the salt works, the numbers forthcoming were inadequate, and they had to be supplemented by prisoners of war, to all intents and purposes slaves. The so-called 'red salt' of Ibiza was of the finest quality, and attracted a great quantity of French, Portuguese, Dutch and even Norwegian ships, many of them working fishing boats needing salt for the preservation of their catches during the long haul back to home ports. The salt pans, which still flourish, are situated in the south of the island. About forty are based on a lagoon into which the sea can be channelled prior to the evaporation process.

In Roman times, trade was based upon salt and, to a lesser extent, upon the export of *garum*, a too-tasty delicacy derived from the salted viscera of fish. Lead was another export, and also, rather more glamorously, murex, the ingredient prepared from certain molluscs and used for dyeing the imperial purple. The many amphorae which are continually being reclaimed from the seas around the island testify to the extent of trade with Rome. Arab historians confined their accounts of Ibizan exports to salt foremost, and then firewood and charcoal destined for North Africa. The fabled pines of the island were traditionally of exceptional value for shipbuilding, and are still used for that purpose, though on a reduced scale. Otherwise, junipers are the most common trees, or rather shrubs, though their wood is of little value.

A number of Ibizan peasants combine farming with fishing. When travelling around the island it is evident to the visitor that this is a country of small farms or *fincas*, each having its own white homestead. They are composed impartially of orchard, woodland, pasture and arable land put down to corn. The dispersal of farming was designed to spread the risk of the total loss of any crop in the event of naval bombardment or other attack from the sea. Ses Feixes, the market-garden area on the outskirts of Ibiza town, is one of the few parts of the island where intensive cultivation of any description is practised.

A feudal system of land tenure, the *aparceria*, is in decline. The word means partnership, and consisted of a verbal contract between the landlord, *l'amo*, and the *mayoral*, the tenant or sharecropper, which in practice meant a fifty-fifty sharing of crops and recognized expenses.

Formentera has saltpans that, as in Ibiza, are known by the generic name of Las Salinas. Their output is claimed to rival that of the larger island, as well as having contributed substantially to the island's income until sold to an Italian company in the late nineteenth century. Fishing and salt remain the traditional occupations, second to the growing of crops for internal consumption, though the production of the wheat that gave the island its name has declined. The sudden annual influx of tourists means that a very large proportion of food has to be brought in by sea from Ibiza and elsewhere, so that there is less chance than ever of this small island being self-supporting, except in salt. Commercial traffic is distinctly one-way.

FAUNA AND FLORA

Majorca
Fauna
Birds are shot in great numbers during the season between November and March, usually by landowners, as can be seen from the cautionary notices warning off casual sportsmen. The demands of the pot and a predilection for keeping the most colourful songbirds in cages account for the scarcity of wildlife here, as in the rest of the Mediterranean. It follows that the birds to be seen are usually migrants, which come in their hordes to find a temporary resting place on their long spring and late-summer flights between two continents. It is therefore the wilder and less accessible parts of the island to which we have to look for the free-soaring species: for hawks, which go unmolested on the island of Dragonera, where nature provides a copious diet of lizards; and for shearwater in great numbers off Pantaleu – one of the rarest of these being Cory's shearwater. Because of their nocturnal habits and their daytime inconspicuousness, nightingales are plentiful, which is something to be thankful for, as also for the occasional flash of a hoopoe across one's path.

Plans are still under discussion for the creation of a wildlife and nature reserve in the north-western *sierras*. In the meantime, however, one district that will be a certain delight to bird-watchers, and which to a large extent is protected by its essential intractability to development, is the Albufera, that area of marshes not far from Alcudia that plays host to a great variety of waterfowl – again many of them migrants – as well as myriads of insects, amphibians and reptiles. This is a hidden place, not penetrated by tourists, who would be deterred by claustrophobic areas of reeds (*phragmites communis*) reaching a height of two metres or more, and it takes perseverance and specialized knowledge to negotiate the maze of lagoons, channels and slightly raised embankments edged with tamarisk, in search of wintering duck. Teal, pintail and shoveller are common, as well as the willow warbler and chiffchaff from northern Europe. But it is in the migratory seasons, of course, that bird-watchers come into their own, and have the joy of observing such phenomena as sand martins arriving in phalanxes so solid as to warrant the use of the correct term 'a fall of birds'. More independent and conspicuous travellers are represented by egrets, flamingoes and the glossy ibis indulging in their own form of package tour, in company with lesser brethren such as whiskered terns, pratincoles and plover.

Birds of prey which may be seen on Majorca include the marsh harrier, the booted eagle, and the rare Eleanor's falcon with breeding grounds in the mountains, and a black vulture with an enormous wing span. Various plover remain on the island to breed, as does Savi's warbler, while its cousins, Cetti's warbler and the Sardinian warbler are permanent residents.

To return specifically to the Albufera, frogs, reptiles and insect life complete the live population of what is a very valuable ecological area, under sporadic threat from developers. But this portion of the island, as we have seen, possesses its own inherent defensive system, which is as well because the conservationist lobby on the island is far inferior to commercial interests.

Wild animals are scarce, and really only to be found occasionally in the highest mountains, where there are some wild goats and spotted civet cats; the best way of seeing them is stuffed in local natural history museums.

As a postscript to a rather depressing scene for naturalists, be it noted that Palma boasts a well-run animal refuge supported by voluntary contribution, chiefly by foreign residents.

Flora

It is the cultivated crops in Majorca which attract the eye far more than wild flowers. The almonds in particular go without further description, as do the orange and lemon groves, the olive trees, ancient relics as well as the scientifically cultivated, and the fruit trees in serried ranks. But great pleasure may be obtained from coming across wild freesias and narcissi in winter and spring, with great splashes of red poppies and yellow daisies later in the year, and more durable aromatic herbs such as marjoram, rosemary, lavender and thyme growing wild on rocky soil.

MINORCA

Since the island rises to no great altitude, the flora and fauna of Minorca contrast with Majorca's principally in the absence of alpine plants and animals. In fact, since much of Minorca is intensely cultivated, there is a comparative dearth of wild plants. Bird life differs very little from that of Majorca, especially since Minorca has its own Albufera of marshlands on the coast north of Mahón, which attracts a fair sample of migrants and residents.

Visitors particularly interested – especially those who can read Spanish – are advised to visit the Ateneo Museum in Mahón, where there is a good library as well as mounted specimens of birds, beasts and fish native to the island.

IBIZA

The plants and wildlife of Ibiza are of no outstanding interest, in that they conform to the usual Mediterranean pattern. However, the Ibizan hound or *ca ervissenc* makes up for this, in spite of its having been domesticated for many centuries. This breed of dog was reputedly introduced by the Egyptians or, some say, the Carthaginians. In any event, in its purest form it looks very antique, standing tall, loose-limbed and usually fawn in colour. In fact, all its characteristics claim it to be an archetypal hunting dog, capable of rivalling the fastest greyhound. Unfortunately true specimens are difficult to identify these days, particularly since foreign residents have tended to bring their own pets to the island, causing the inevitable miscegenation. The best chance of seeing the breed is in Ibiza Town, on August 5th, the Feast of Nuestra Señora de las Nieves, where in the course of a sports programme there is a special class for these unusual hounds.

HISTORICAL CHART

PERIOD	MAJORCA	MINORCA	IBIZA AND FORMENTERA
Prehistory (c.2000–1000 B.C.)	Cave-dwelling society develops into *talayot* period.	*Talayots*, *taulas*, and *navetas*.	Cave drawings.
Greeks, Phoenicians and Carthaginians (1000–123 B.C.)	1000–500 B.C.: trading posts established by Phocaean and Rhodian Greeks		
	400?–123 B.C.: Carthaginian domination.		480 B.C.: Carthaginian colonization begins. 217 B.C.: Romans under Scipio ravage island during 2nd Punic War.
		206–5 B.C.: Carthaginian general Mago winters on island, giving name to Mahón.	
Romans (123 B.C.–A.D. 450)			146 B.C.–A.D. 74: island an official ally of Rome.
	123 B.C.: conquest by Q.C. Metullus, Roman general. Palma and Alcudia founded.	123 B.C.: conquest by Romans under Q.C. Metullus. 47 B.C.: island surrenders to Pompey's son.	

PERIOD	MAJORCA	MINORCA	IBIZA AND FORMENTERA
			A.D. 74: loses ally status and becomes part of Roman Empire.
	A.D. 404: Balearics, previously part of Spanish province of Tarragonensis, granted separate provincial status.	A.D. 404: Balearics granted separate provincial status.	A.D. 404: Balearics granted separate provincial status.
	A.D. 425: major Vandal raid.	A.D. 425: major Vandal raid.	A.D. 425: major Vandal raid.
Vandals (A.D. 450–534)	A.D. 450: Romans abandon Majorca. Pirate raids.		
Byzantines (A.D. 534–707)	Balearics under Byzantine rule after Belisarius' defeat of Vandals in North Africa.		
Arabs (A.D. 707–1235)	A.D. 707–902: succession of Moorish raids.		
	A.D. 798: Charlemagne sends fleet to help islanders.		A.D. 798: Charlemagne's force takes Ibiza.
			A.D. 801: recaptured by Arabs.
		A.D. 859: major Viking raid.	A.D. 867: Moorish occupation begins.

PERIOD	MAJORCA	MINORCA	IBIZA AND FORMENTERA
	A.D. 903: Moorish occupation under caliphate of Córdoba begins. 1114: Pisan-Catalan crusade takes island but soon departs. 1116–1229: Moorish occupation.	A.D. 903: Moorish occupation under caliphate of Córdoba begins.	
	1229–30: Jaime I of Aragon drives out Moors and annexes island.	1232: Jaime I captures part of island by daring trick.	1235: island captured by forces from Iberian mainland. Becomes part of Jaime I's Kingdom of Majorca.
Kingdom of Majorca (1235–1349)	1276: Jaime I dies. 1282–1292: war between Jaime II and Pedro III, King of Aragon.	1286–7: invasion by Alfonso III of Aragon. Remaining Moors driven out or massacred. Island annexed to crown of Aragon.	
	1292–1311: Jaime II builds Bellver Castle. Progress on Palma Cathedral. 1311: Jaime II dies.	1292: island restored to Jaime II of Majorca.	

PERIOD	MAJORCA	MINORCA	IBIZA AND FORMENTERA
	1349: Battle of Lluchmayor. Jaime III dies. Pedro IV of Aragon incorporates island into his kingdom.	1349: incorporated into Aragon.	1349: incorporated into Aragon.
Aragon (1349–1492)	1391: country revolt. Jews killed in Palma.		
Spain (1492–Present day)	1521: peasant revolt drives out Viceroy. 1523: revolt put down by mainland troops. 1531–61: Saracen raids.	1535: Barbarossa, the Corsair, takes Mahón. 1558: Turks raze Ciudadela.	1529–30: Barbarossa winters in Formentera after naval victory off Playa de Mitjorn. 1543: Turkish invasion repulsed. 1554–85: construction of great city walls.
	1628: British landing repelled during Thirty Years' War.		
			1697: Formentera resettled by Ibizans after being uninhabited for 300 years.
	1704: Anglo-Dutch squadron off Palma.		1706: British fleet off Ibiza.

PERIOD	MAJORCA	MINORCA	IBIZA AND FORMENTERA
		1708: British force under Stanhope landed.	
	1713: French attack. 1716: Majorca loses title of kingdom, becoming a Spanish province.	1713: Minorca ceded to British by Treaty of Utrecht. 1708–56: British rule. 1756–63: French rule. 1763–82: British rule. Ended by successful Franco-Spanish expedition in 1782. 1782–98: Minorca under Spanish rule. 1798–1802: Last period of British rule. Nelson's visit.	
	1802: Treaty of Amiens confirms island as a Spanish possession. 1817–22: Liberal rising. 1880: beginnings of 'tourism'.	1802: Treaty of Amiens confirms island as Spanish. 1809: Admiral Collingwood based at Mahón.	

PERIOD	MAJORCA	MINORCA	IBIZA AND FORMENTERA
	1936–9 Majorca takes Franco's side in Civil War. Island bombed by Republicans based on Minorca.	1936–9 : Minorca supports Republican side. Rigorous blockade by Nationalists.	1936 : Ibiza and Formentera captured by Republican forces.

HISTORY

MAJORCA

PREHISTORY (c. 2000–1000 B.C.)

Clues to man's colonization of Majorca are to be found in cave
dwellings, usually in mountainous places such as those on the hillside
above San Vicente near the northernmost tip of the island. Such
primitive habitations are of two types; those used exclusively as living
quarters are circular with domed ceilings cut out of the rock, while
the equally important and contemporary funerary chambers are long,
with lateral rooms, not unlike the traditional earth mounds or
barrows which occur in England. One such burial chamber, discovered at Son Mulet between Lluchmayor and Campos in the south
contained numerous skeletons and ceramic urns in excellent condition. These remains have been dated as ranging from 2000–1700 B.C.

Balearic man progressed from inhabiting the cave and underground shelters, which had the basic advantage of sheltering him
from weather and wild beasts, and, as he became more secure,
families were grouped ·into communities. These villages were
provided with exterior stone defences and watchtowers, the lower
stages of which could be used as storerooms, tombs or possibly sacred
places where an elemental religion akin to Druidism may have been
practised, though no evidence of human sacrifice has been found in or
near these early sites. It is certain, however, that this emergent
civilization made use of bronze implements and household goods,
despite the fact that the Balearic islands were almost entirely deficient
in mineral resources. The discovery of ingots from this period has in
fact been taken as testimony to Majorca's position as a staging point in
Mediterranean mercantile traffic at an early period – a function which
was to be further developed by the Greeks and Phoenicians, and later
by the Romans.

The use of stone and the acquisition of techniques with which to
work it gave rise to ambitious building in the form of the megalithic
structures or *talayots* (towers) which remain a mystery to this day, but
which have attracted numerous theories, mostly contradictory,
advanced by archaeologists of standing. The puzzle is all the more
intriguing because these ancient monuments have no counterpart.
Their closest affinity is with the *nuraghi* of Sardinia, with a reminder

too of the dolmens and standing stones of ancient Britain, the Channel Islands and Brittany. No light is shed on either their origin or purpose by early visitors to the island – neither by the Phoenicians, nor by the Greeks nor the Romans, all of whom had their complement of historians. It must be conceded that these structures requiring great technical skill to put together without benefit of engineering or use of mortar, have outlasted all knowledge of the processes involved.

Majorca has fewer megalithic remains than Minorca, whereas Ibiza has none – an interesting pointer to the relative size of population on the three islands in prehistoric times. Majorca's most complete ancient settlement, known as Capicorp Vey, has the advantage of being well studied and documented under the auspices of the Institute of Catalan Studies, and it is maintained as a national monument. The prehistoric enclosure is situated a short distance off the minor road from Lluchmayor to Cape Blanco (p. 255). The buildings include as many as four *talayots*. The presence of a small chamber inside the majority of these structures yields no clue as to their function – whether it be watchtower, fortress, burial place, shelter for animals or food storehouse. Sa Canova, 10 km. west of Artá along the road to Alcudia (p. 253), is a comparable settlement, and equally easy to locate.

GREEKS, PHOENICIANS AND CARTHAGINIANS (c. 1000–123 B.C.)

It would appear that no measure of colonization was thought necessary by the mercantile nations which effectively dominated the Mediterranean for several centuries. The islands represented no source of wealth, neither were their people warlike nor a threat to communications. In fact, all that was required of the Balearics was that they should provide staging points and anchorages for ships in passage through the Mediterranean to Spain and beyond. The Phoenicians made use of the islands in the course of the long haul to British tin mines, while Greek traders knew Majorca as early as the eleventh century B.C. A few makeshift settlements were established about that time, probably first by the Phocaeans, inhabitants of a Greek city state on the coast of Asia Minor who, having been displaced by the Medes and Persians about 600 B.C., were to found Massilia (later Marseilles). Before this re-routing the Phocaeans engaged in island-hopping passages via Sardinia and the Balearics to

Spain, where they made landfall at Calpe, on what is now the Costa Blanca. But according to Strabo, the historian and geographer of the Roman Empire, when writing in the first century B.C., the first Greek traders to use the Balearics were Rhodians. Subsequently the Greeks developed the mainland base of Emporion, now Ampurias, on the Costa Brava, and thus they escaped head-on collision in the Balearics with the Carthaginians who, by about 520 B.C., had taken over the interests and widespread mercantile activity of their parent nation, the Phoenicians.

The city and empire of Carthage is believed to have been founded in 814 B.C. by the legendary Tyrian-Phoenician princess, Elissa, who is better known to us as Dido, nicknamed 'the Wanderer'. At that time the Phoenicians, established at the fabulous ports of Tyre and Sidon, and along the coast of Asia Minor, were in the process of being ousted and destroyed by the Assyrians. Much of the story of the birth of this great Carthaginian empire is legend, fostered by the imagination of classical writers and developed in epic film and grand opera. Yet truth must underlie the fiction. At about this time recorded history was beginning to take over from unwritten legend. In any event, from beginnings as small as an offshoot of Phoenicia, Carthage grew rapidly until she controlled all the commercial interests in the western Mediterranean that had been the perquisite of her forebears. In particular, Corsica and the Balearic islands became Carthaginian dominions. Though the story continues to be a mixture of legend, conjecture and fact, it is believed by some that the redoubtable Carthaginian general, Hannibal, was born in Majorca – or rather on its offshore island of Cabrera. The explanation is that his father, Hamilcar, diverted his ship to a Majorcan port when his wife went into labour during a voyage to Spain, and they put ashore in order that she might be safely delivered. Incidentally, both Ibiza and Malta make claim to the honour. However, what is an undisputed fact is that Majorca was of value to the Carthaginians, and was provided with garrisons designed not only to man strongpoints on trade routes but also to act as recruiting pools for military operations against Rome. Balearic mercenaries skilled in the use of slings formed an important part of warring armies, used both by the Carthaginians against Rome and, later, by the Romans themselves.

These Majorcan slingers are mentioned in the works of a learned chronicler, Don José Quadrano, who was a prominent figure in the Catalan literary revival of the nineteenth century. He describes early visitors to Majorca being driven from Majorcan shores by a hail of stones. These famous warriors were armed with slings made of leather with two cords, capable of firing stones the size of tennis balls. The missiles, carried in a pouch, were dispatched by a whirling of the sling, and found their target accurately at a range of up to forty paces. Boys were trained in this martial art by having their daily rations lodged high in the branches of trees, so that the food had to be shot down before it could be eaten. The name of the islands, the Balearics, is derived from the Greek verb, *ballein*, meaning 'to throw', which testifies to the reputation of the natives. These mercenaries were singularly unmercenary, preferring a standard ration of women and wine to gold as payment for their services, a system which met with the favour of their alien employers. They formed an important part of the advance guard in Hannibal's army when invading Italy from across the Alps, and were at a later stage employed by the Romans after they took over Majorca.

ROMANS (123 B.C. – A.D. 450)

Carthage may be held responsible for the Roman occupation of the islands, in that after the fall of the Carthaginian Empire in 121 B.C. her dominions passed to Rome. After the end of the second Punic War in 202 B.C. Rome was determined to conquer and hold the Iberian mainland in order to withstand invasion from the west. As Roman strategy was thus concentrated on subduing Spain for eighty years, the Balearics enjoyed a large measure of freedom. But during this time the islanders were engaged in piracy and harrying Roman settlements on the mainland, so the Senate was eventually forced to move against them. Complete conquest was achieved by Quintus Cecilius Metullus in 123 B.C. despite resistance by the redoubtable slingers, which was offset by his inspired counter-measure in protecting his ships with hides to cover the more vulnerable timbers. In due course he was fêted in Rome, being accorded a Triumph as well as the addition of 'Balearicus' to his name.

Though the accent was now on military occupation rather than on the use of trading facilities, some attempt was made to settle the island, and the cities of Palmaria (Palma) and Pollentia (Alcudia) came into being, swelled by the introduction of some 3,000 colonists brought from Spain and Rome. These arrivals are estimated to have formed about 10 per cent of the total population, and to have been responsible for large-scale viticulture, leading to the export of Majorcan wines, despite the report by Diodorus Siculus that the slingers drank to excess. Diodorus also reported that prior to the arrival of the Romans no use had been made of olives or their oil.

Some authorities favour a site near Colonia Sant Jordi as being one of the principal early Roman settlements – the theory being based on the discovery of sunken wrecks and scattered amphorae on the seabed. Unfortunately, however, Roman remains are few, owing to the depredations of the Vandals who filled the power vacuum following the decline of the Roman Empire. The theatre near Alcudia and the bridge at Pollensa are the only remains of importance which survive from the period of Roman domination.

During this time the Balearic islands formed part of the province of Tarragonensis (Tarragona) on the mainland of Spain. It was not until A.D. 404 that separate provincial status was granted, but by that time the Roman Empire was already in decline, its power dissipated by unwieldy areas of conquest and by leadership problems.

VANDALS (A.D. 450–534)

In 425–6 the island of Majorca suffered a devastating raid by the Vandals, who with the Visigoths and other northern barbarians were passing through Spain on a migratory route from the Baltic to North Africa, where they were to be defeated about a hundred years later. With the collapse of the Pax Romana on the European continent, the Romans abandoned Majorca and the other Balearics, and by A.D. 450 the islands were left to their own devices. By that time Christianity was flourishing under the suffragan bishop of Tarragona, but this was no protection against the Vandals who, though themselves Christians subscribing to the Arian heresy, were primarily concerned with martial conquest. They completely dominated the islands from 465 to 534. Little is known about that period. In fact, even methodical Roman historians and other writers appear to have ignored the Balearics, as though they were beneath their notice. We do know, however, that during occupation by the Vandals much that was civilized from previous centuries was 'vandalized' – destroyed – without any ordered system being substituted. The sites of two basilicas dating from c. A.D. 300 have been identified, one near Manacor, and the other not far from Porto Cristo.

It is clear that with the removal of the central authority of the

Romans the islands became increasingly dissociated from the Iberian peninsula, which, under a new monarchy created by the Visigoths who were established in Barcelona, was taking shape as what was to become Spain. In effect, the Balearics gradually began to assert their own identity, separate from their Iberian kinsmen, in a tendency which can be discerned to this day. It was about this time, with the slackening of government by outside powers, that Majorca became open to piratical incursions. To protect her people from these raids settlements were moved a few kilometres inland, behind the ports which served them and the watch towers built to warn of threats from the outside world. The twinned ports and towns of Puerto de Andraitx and Andraitx, Puerto de Soller and Soller, Puerto de Campos and Campos, with their outposts on high places, are living reminders of these perilous times.

BYZANTINES (A.D. 534–707)

Changes came with the rise to power of Belisarius, the great Byzantine general acting for Justinian, ruler of the Eastern Roman Empire from Constantinople. He routed the Vandals in North Africa in 533, defeating them by sea and land and wresting from them Carthage and other North African possessions. What is now Tunisia was incorporated into the Byzantine Empire in the spring of 534, and with North Africa went the Balearics. They were to remain more or less Byzantine until the beginning of the eighth century, and during this period of government by Greek officials, commercial connections were developed with Constantinople, and military strongpoints set up for the defence of trade routes. Majorca had slipped back into her traditional role.

ARABS (A.D. 707–1229)

In North Africa the seventh century was marked by the gathering momentum of Arab raids, which were to result in invasion and consolidation of power on a scale scarcely rivalled by the Romans. At first the Balearics were largely unaffected, until crisis was heralded by the landing in Majorca in 707–8 of an Arab naval expedition. The result was widespread devastation, though for the time being the objective was plunder rather than conquest. The enemy retired laden with booty in the form of treasure, slaves and ships.

Close relations with Byzantium languished in the eighth century, leaving the islands vulnerable to attack, especially after the Moors, having launched their invasion of the Iberian peninsula in 711, completed their conquest of Spain in 716. They were well on their way to forming their new-found Spanish possessions into the civilized and sophisticated state that came to be known as Al-Andaluz. The Balearics were largely ignored, except for spasmodic raids from Spain. These reached a particularly vicious climax in 798, when the islands were sacked. The situation was grievous enough for the islanders to appeal to Charlemagne for assistance – hopefully, since the great Frankish Emperor was at that time engaged in a struggle for possession of Barcelona. In response, Charlemagne launched a fleet charged with protecting the islands against raiding Saracens. However, efforts to remain isolated were doomed to failure. Once the irresistible force of Moorish ambition was firmly directed against the islands, they fell to a fleet commissioned by the Emirate of Córdoba.

The history of these early medieval centuries is confused by the fact that contemporary Moorish and Christian authorities tend to contradict each other, employing a combination of romantic legend, literary licence and wishful thinking rather than remembered or recorded fact. It is clear, however, that the Balearics were by then completely dominated by the Moors of the mainland. During this period they appear to have enjoyed a certain measure of prosperity, leading to the establishment of trading links with both Africa and Moorish Spain. This situation was encouraged by the fact that the Moors were prey to factional disputes within their own ranks, with the result that the offshore islands, to which little importance was attached, came successively under the domination of rival Moorish leaders, notably the Emir (later the Caliph) of Córdoba from 902–1015, and the Emirs of Denia from 1015–75. At other times local government was carried on by a succession of Walis, or governors, based on the island of Majorca. Not until the eleventh century was that island proclaimed an independent emirate.

But even though the natives of the Balearics showed talent in adapting themselves to alien rule from whatever quarter it came, this state of affairs was not to be tolerated by the Christian powers of Europe. Outraged by Moorish raids on Sardinia and the Italian coast, as well as by attacks on Christian and Catalan Barcelona, a consortium of Italian city states headed by Pisa was sanctioned by the Pope to mount a crusade against the Balearic usurpers, the reason being that the islands made such an excellent jumping-off place for these tiresome raids. It was rumoured abroad that tens of thousands of Christians were at that time being held captive by the infidels in the islands. The expedition was commanded by an archbishop, and was fully equipped for engagements by sea and by land. This imposing crusading fleet sailed from Italy in 1113. Unfortunately, however, it overshot Majorca, to make a landing on the coast of Catalonia, where it was thought advisable to winter while drawing reinforcements from the nobility and transferring command to the Count of Barcelona, Don Ramón Berenguer III. When the operation was resumed, a landing on Ibiza was easily effected, though by this time Majorca and Palma were better prepared for attack. Palma's immediate coastal fortifications were found to be impregnable, and so each of the four metropolitan precincts had to be reduced in separate engagements composed of attack and counter-attack from landward. Victory was eventually celebrated by wholesale massacre of the city's Moorish population.

Though the crusading operation was prestigious, and to be acclaimed far and wide to the credit of Christendom, no attempt was made at consolidation, and the conquering heroes, satisfied by their material gains, returned to their homes, leaving the Moors to re-establish their rule. And, as it happened, Majorca then enjoyed a prosperous period under an enlightened ruler by the name of Abu Ibrahim-Ashak, during which agriculture and commerce flourished as never before. However, the death of this governor brought conflict over the succession, and civil war spread from Spain to Majorca, the result being successive maladministration by first the Almoravide and then the Almohad dynasties. The old chaotic way of life was resumed, the accent still being upon piracy and raids upon Christian possessions so that, predictably, the Christian states became increasingly incensed. Another clash was inevitable; it had only been postponed because of the action of some Italian city states in defying papal injunctions against trading with the Moors. This traffic applied specially to Palma, which became a sanctuary for Christians who had fallen foul of overlords of their own faith elsewhere.

By the middle of the twelfth century, forces capable of opposing the Moors in the Western Mediterranean were building up, the chief object being the unification of the Christian kingdoms of Aragon and Catalonia, which came about in 1150. In 1218 their titular head was Jaime I, King of Aragon, Count of Barcelona and Lord of Montpellier, who succeeded to these and other sonorous titles at the age of five. The confrontation over the Balearics came when the young king neared his majority, and was both able and eager to assert his manhood and sovereignty. The pretext for action was slight compared with what had gone before; only the occasion was critical. Following the seizure of a galley belonging to the Moorish Emir of Majorca, two Catalan ships were taken in reprisal. It so happened that at that time, in 1228, the young King was invited to a banquet in Tarragona, where, doubtless by design, the menu contained many Majorcan delicacies, including some specially succulent olives. To make their point clearer, the King's host, Pierre Martell the famous navigator, and other members of the nobility, regaled him with stories of the rich potential of the Balearic islands. Jaime's imagination was fired, and before he left the table he had committed himself to driving the Moors out of those islands which lay close offshore and were an everlasting cause for humiliation.

In less than a year the expedition was ready. It was supported by the Church in Rome and was proclaimed a crusade. When in September 1229 the fleet took to the sea it was composed of 150 ships carrying about 16,000 men and 1,500 horses, enlisted chiefly from Tarragona, Barcelona, Narbonne, Marseilles and Genoa. Only the Aragonese nobles stood apart, preferring to reserve their resources for a future mainland operation aimed at a total reconquest of the Moorish kingdom of Valencia – in fact to driving the usurpers from Spain. The nobles who headed the various contingents had committed themselves to the enterprise on the usual undertaking that when victory came they would be rewarded by grants of land proportionate to their contribution in men and arms. The King himself sailed at the head of the invasion force. This is the point where, in the opinion of the majority of Majorcans, the history of their island begins.

THE RECONQUEST (1229)

The original plan had been for the troops to land at Pollensa in the north-west so that the central plain could rapidly be occupied while spearheads marched south upon Palma. However, a great storm blew up, carrying the ships further south to San Telmo, west of Palma and surrounded by mountains. After a vigil and prayers to the Virgin Mary, Jaime set foot on the small island of Pantaleu, from which he surveyed the interior, and judged it to be too rugged for full-scale disembarkation. His next move was to dispatch two of his most trusted Catalan noblemen charged with reconnoitring in search of a more favourable landing place to the east. Santa Ponsa, midway between San Telmo and Palma was the choice. Though the movement of the fleet along the coast was shadowed by Saracen troops, who themselves were impeded by the difficult terrain, the landing was effected before full strength could be brought up by the enemy. A decisive battle was fought on the day following the landing, that is, on September 11th, 1229. The fighting was fierce, with Jaime himself taking a prominent part. At the end of the day the Moors were forced to retreat behind the walls of the city of Palma.

Though certain of the Muslim chiefs on the island, which had been divided into twelve administrative parts, submitted without much further delay, Palma itself was more stubborn. It was three and a half months before the city walls were breached. Furthermore, final resistance in the mountainous districts had to be overcome, so that it was a full year before the victorious king felt established enough to return to Catalonia. According to prior arrangement, large country estates belonging to Moorish overlords were made over to the nobles who had accompanied Jaime, and it is of interest that some of their names have survived to this day in the roll of landowners. The conquest of Minorca was left until 1232, and that of Ibiza until 1235.

KINGDOM OF MAJORCA (1230–1349)

By March 1230 the Reconquest of Majorca was complete enough for the new state to be proclaimed, in an instrument known as the Carta de Població. Its thirty-seven sections set out the powers of the government and the judiciary, and it is rated as establishing the most enlightened and comprehensive constitution of medieval days. Indeed, it can be claimed that as a result of the rule which ensued, a great deal that is excellent in architecture, systems of land tenure and cultivation, as well as social structure was introduced and has survived from that time until the present day.

Power politics pressed hard upon the Mediterranean scene during the thirteenth century. Along the western seaboard the kingdoms of France and Aragon were in fierce territorial competition. In fact, in 1256 Louis IX of France, known as St Louis, laid claim to Barcelona and its dependencies, as well as to the Balearic islands. The outcome was that Jaime I of Aragon, who had assumed the extra title of Jaime

I of Majorca, surrendered his rights to considerable parts of south-west France, while retaining certain Catalan provinces, including Roussillon and Montpellier. Reciprocally, Louis withdrew his claims on Catalonia and the Balearics.

After his death in 1276 it was discovered that Jaime I had bequeathed Aragon, Catalonia and his rights in Valencia to his elder son, Pedro III. The Balearics, Roussillon and Montpellier were to go to his younger boy, who became King Jaime II of Majorca. The innate rivalry between the brothers was expressed by their opposing alliances: Pedro III with the Sicilians, then in the ascendant as a Mediterranean power, and Jaime II of Majorca with the French. Initially Majorca revelled in having its own young king, but disillusionment set in when he elected to spend most of his time at Perpignan, which he named as his capital. This entailed leaving the island's affairs in the hands of the noblemen who had acquired their estates through his father's patronage. The potentialities of the local disaffection thus aroused did not escape Pedro III, who saw in it a means of securing the islands and incorporating them in his own inheritance. Plans for invasion were well advanced in 1282 when Pedro died, but they were soon taken up by his successor, Alfonso III, who promised on his father's deathbed that he would unite Majorca with the Kingdom of Aragon. The invasion proceeded.

Palma was captured without much difficulty; so, too, was the remainder of the island, the stronghold of Alaro being the last to fall. After Alfonso had proclaimed himself King of the Balearics he took Minorca, in 1287. However, atrocities committed in reducing outstanding pockets of resistance in Majorca had aroused a great deal of indignation, which spread from the island not only to parts of the mainland but to France and Italy, resulting in Alfonso's excommunication by the Pope. Pressure was now put on Alfonso to earn remission by returning the throne to his uncle, Jaime II. He died four years after his invasion of the island, when undertakings were well under way for Jaime to return to his kingdom – subject only to his admitting to being a vassal of Aragon and forgoing his title to his previous mainland possessions.

Majorca at last had a resident king. To his credit, Jaime II immediately set to work to stabilize the island and work for its prosperity. He built Bellver Castle as the key to the defences of Palma Bay, and as a link in a ring of coastal fortifications; he converted the Moorish fortress of the Almudaina into a splendid palace for his own use; and he developed agriculture and commerce generally by the creation of eleven market towns to serve as centres for the island's produce. Trade routes were opened up with the Levant, and commerce with North Africa began to flourish. Jaime also became the patron of Ramón Llull, one of the foremost scholars of the time, and an exponent of Arab and African culture. But far from the least of his achievements was the implementation of his father's dream of building a great cathedral in thanksgiving for the victory which had followed the stormy landing and the capture of Palma on the last day of the year 1229. Jaime II also proved exceptional in administrative matters, showing himself to be both far-sighted and democratic. He gave the island a currency and bettered the lot of agricultural workers by guaranteeing them a minimum wage.

Jaime II died in 1311 at the age of seventy-one, leaving his works as monuments to his greatness. As his eldest son, Jaime, had renounced his claim to the throne by becoming a Franciscan monk, Jaime II was succeeded by his second son, Sancho, who carried on his father's interests in matters of reform, trade and civil liberties. He also occupied himself with strengthening the fleet, which was in constant action against Barbary pirates. It was some loss to the island, however, that Sancho was asthmatic, so that much of his time was spent away from the capital on the healthy heights of Valldemosa, where a hunting lodge was enlarged and transformed into a more permanent and palatial residence. This entailed a measure of removal from central affairs. He died, childless, in 1324.

The crown then went to Sancho's ten-year-old nephew, who became Jaime III. A regency council took charge of affairs of state, and the boy king was hastily betrothed to the five-year-old grand-daughter of the King of Aragon, in the hope that this would forestall territorial claims upon the island kingdom. However, even after the marriage was celebrated there was no resolution of what had developed into a long-term feud. Upon succeeding to the throne of Aragon in 1336, Pedro IV, Jaime III's brother-in-law, sought excuses to justify seizure of Majorca. To that end he fabricated an accusation that Jaime III was involved in a plot to kill him, and on this pretext the Aragonese effected a landing in Paguera in 1343. Little resistance was offered, except by garrisons at Bellver Castle and Pollensa.

By the time Pedro IV had arranged his coronation as King of Majorca in Palma, Jaime III had fled the country. But he rallied his forces to make an attempt to regain his throne, having sold

Montpellier to France so as to raise funds for the offensive. The landing in Alcudia Bay in October 1349 went well enough, and Jaime marched south across the island at the head of his troops, encountering scorched earth tactics as he went. His army was met at Lluchmayor by superior forces, and after five hours of fighting the battle was over. The King died fighting. His son, another Jaime who was never to be crowned, was taken prisoner but eventually escaped. Though he nurtured dreams of regaining possession of the kingdom of Majorca, he was neither able to return to the island, nor to ascend the throne.

This was the end of the dynasty of Majorcan kings founded by Jaime I, famed as the Conquistador. Having enjoyed independent status for only 120 years, the Balearics came to be incorporated into the Kingdom of Aragon, and hence became part of Spain when Aragon and Castile were united in 1492, after the Moors were driven from Granada.

ARAGON AND SPAIN (1349 TO THE PRESENT DAY)

What is known by some as the Golden Age of Majorca began in 1343 with the take-over by Pedro of Aragon. This is something of a misnomer. A large proportion of the ancient monuments in Palma which impress the visitor owe their existence to the previous century, and directly to Jaime II. It is true, though, that after the fall of the Majorcan kings an age of exceptional commercial prosperity set in. This was marked by the spread of culture and learning, and the beautifying of public and religious buildings. The availability of wealth was due primarily to the rise in power of the kingdom of Aragon and the island's connection with it. Once more Majorca was identified firmly as a port of call on the trade routes of the Mediterranean. The emphasis on learning, allied with practical considerations, produced a school of cartographers that was to become famous all over Europe, and which contributed significantly to the various voyages of discovery that were then enlarging the known world.

However, at quite an early stage there were signs of a reversal of fortune. There were already indications that the island would become neglected, not only because it suffered in the classical manner from having become a satellite of Aragon – which meant that the proceeds of taxation were diverted to the mainland to pay for costly Aragonese overseas wars – but also because the whole pattern of trade routes was in the process of change. Though Genoese merchants remained in Palma, trading from the beautiful Lonja, or exchange, which still graces the waterfront, and the Venetians continued to use Palma as a port of call, the Pisans withdrew. Very soon the bulk of trade was limited to shorter communications with Catalonia.

Acts of God – floods, earthquakes and plague – beset the island on various occasions. The fall of Constantinople in 1453 put a stop to traffic with the eastern Mediterranean, which had flourished ever since the days of the Byzantine Empire. Then the discovery of the New World in 1492 removed the Balearics still further from the commercial map, as did the Portuguese discovery of a sea route round the Cape of Good Hope. And the final expulsion of the Moors from Spain severely curtailed Majorca's traditional trade with the North African ports, as well as having the effect of diverting an ever-increasing number of Corsairs – the famous Barbary pirates – to the high seas in the pursuit of Christian shipping in the Mediterranean.

One of the most obvious factors in the decline of Majorca's traditional trading activities lay in the marriage in 1479 between Ferdinand of Aragon and Queen Isabella of Castile. Under laws made by those powerful joint sovereigns, Majorca was excluded from a share in the booty that was arriving in shiploads from the New World. That ban was not lifted until 1778. In the meantime Palma was starved of foreign currency, and became of no greater consequence than a warehouse for the Catalans of Perpignan and Barcelona.

But while this gradual national decline was taking place, it is noticeable to students of the island's history that most of the limelight was directed upon cultural achievements, based on the life style of the Majorcan nobility, which was concentrated almost exclusively on Palma. The remainder of the island and its peasant population were ignored. Natural resources went undeveloped. The common people suffered, affected not only by neglect but crushed by taxation imposed by Aragon and, locally, by absentee landlords – grandees living the courtly life in Palma, and involving themselves strenuously in the accumulation and outlay of riches. Their country estates represented no more to them than sources of revenue to be spent and enjoyed in the city; there was little thought directed towards increasing the productivity of the land, and still less to improving the lot of their tenants – who had little contact with them except at secondhand, through the payment of the crippling taxation and rents that were collected by the Jews of Palma, acting in the dual role of land agents and bankers.

The results should have been foreseen – if anyone had bothered to look ahead. As early as 1391 the country people had risen, to form armed bands strong enough to march against Palma, where they invaded and sacked the ghetto, killing almost the entire Jewish population. Violent resentment was easier to express against the tax collectors than against the landowners, who had so little contact with their dependents.

One of the most critical periods for the Majorcan nobility came in 1521 with an insurrection of peasants and artisans. This time events had been influenced by mainland politics: Charles (the great Emperor Charles V), the grandson of Ferdinand and Isabella, had come to the Spanish throne in 1516, and had shown a total ignorance and lack of respect for his inheritance and his people. Without consultation with the Valencian *cortes*, or parliament, he had authorized the formation of an armed brotherhood known as a *Germania*, which, contrary to the young King's expectations, forthwith opposed authority and seized the capital.

This mainland movement was used as a blueprint by Majorcan peasants and artisans in January 1521. They succeeded in taking Palma, forcing the Viceroy to flee to Ibiza. The nobility, the chief target of what was primarily an agrarian rebellion, took refuge in Bellver Castle and Alcudia – the former being taken after three months, the latter managing to hold out for over a year, until relieved by Charles's forces, following their landing in Pollensa Bay, and a massacre of the rebels. By the spring of 1523 the Viceroy was able to return. He retook Palma by peaceful parleying, but while the situation was being referred to Charles he broke the armistice terms, and ordered the massacre of nearly five hundred of the rebel leaders. Though armed resistance had been put down, nothing was added to the stability of internal politics, nor to the well-being of the islanders.

During this period of weakness, Saracen raids upon the island became more frequent. Pollensa was attacked in 1531 and 1550, Alcudia in 1551, Valldemosa in 1552, Andraitx in 1553 and Soller in 1561. Palma's walls were strengthened against expected attack from seaward, though as it happened they were to be manned once only, and against a Christian enemy, following the signing of the Treaty of Utrecht in 1713 which ended the War of the Spanish Succession.

All these events militating against the once prosperous island were reflected in the condition of Palma towards the end of the sixteenth century. The population had declined; one-third of the city was uninhabited and crumbling into ruin. Trade with the Mediterranean ports was almost a thing of the past. Local government, such as it was, was carried out not by able men but, on the hereditary principle, by men who feuded incessantly with their rivals, and had little interest in the island except as a means of increasing their personal fortunes. In 1610 many Majorcans emigrated to the mainland to take possession of properties from which the Moors had been displaced.

Though drawing little benefit from its political connection with the mainland, Majorca found itself contributing not only in taxation but in manpower to Spanish enterprises. The islanders fought for Spain in Algeria, Italy, the Netherlands and Sicily – and recruitment was so heavy that in 1633 Philip IV pronounced that no more levies should be made for fear of leaving the island defenceless against invasion. It was too useful as an outpost. In fact in 1628, three years after the English attack on Cadiz in the course of the Thirty Years' War, British forces had made a landing on the coast east of Artá, only to be repelled. Further punitive attacks, this time by the French, were made in 1680, and again ten years later, though without much serious intention of invasion.

Majorca was drawn into mainland politics to a far greater extent during the War of the Spanish Succession, between 1702 and 1714, when the throne of Spain was contested by Philip V, sponsored by France, and the Archduke Charles of Austria, supported by the English and Dutch. The Spanish majority favoured the French claimant, though Catalonia and Valencia ranged themselves alongside the Archduke. Officially Majorca took Philip's side, even though popular support was for Charles. And when an Anglo-Dutch squadron under the command of Admiral Sir John Leake arrived off Palma demanding recognition for Archduke Charles, the Majorcan nobles proclaimed their allegiance to the Austrian cause, and the Viceroy of the island was compelled to sign an Act of Capitulation. The issue was bitterly contested throughout the island, leading to waves of persecution and banishment. But when the claim of Charles were seen to be failing, Majorca continued to espouse his cause, despite the dispatch of a French squadron in 1713 charged with enforcing loyalty to Philip. After engagements at Alcudia and Felanitx, and a short siege of Palma, Majorcan opposition was overcome. This led two years later to a revision of the administration of the island and the abolition of many of the privileges granted to its people. In fact, from 1716 Majorca forfeited the title of kingdom, becoming no more than one of the many provinces of Spain.

During the next important Continental war, that of the Austrian Succession, between 1740 and 1748, in contrast to neighbouring Minorca the larger island was comparatively unaffected, since her harbours were of no great strategic importance; and similarly she was able to remain uninvolved in the Seven Years' War between the French and the English, which resulted in the occupation of Minorca by alternate opposing forces. The Treaty of Amiens in 1802 confirmed the islands as a Spanish possession.

The nineteenth century was comparatively uneventful. Majorca stood apart from mainland affairs, though experiencing internal difficulties. A rising against the constitutional government took place in 1817, and a liberal confrontation with authority persisted until 1822, when the so-called Absolutist leaders were executed.

When the Spanish Carlist Wars broke out as a result of Queen Isabella II's succession to the throne, little impression was made upon Majorca, which in any event had closer ties with Catalonia than with the larger kingdom; though the island was at this time constantly hard pressed by drought and famine, bubonic plague and cholera. Except for an abortive rising at Manacor in 1835 in favour of Don Carlos, uncle of the Queen, no fighting took place on the island. These wars, which had so great an effect on the mainland, ended in 1878, at which time Isabella's son, Alfonso XII, was established on the Spanish throne.

Towards the end of the nineteenth century, Majorca began to flourish again in her traditional role, with the accent upon agriculture, and especially the cultivation of the profitable almond. There were to be few political changes in the circumstances of the island, which, outside the mainstream of events, minded its own business. And, looking back, there were already signs of Majorca's potentiality as a tourist haven. Many French refugees from the Revolution had found their way to the island; by 1837 a regular steam packet service between Majorca and the mainland came into operation; and about this time the rail system was built.

Conditions on the island remained peaceful until the outbreak of the Spanish Civil War in July 1936. As had happened in earlier conflicts, Majorca was ranged on the opposite side to Minorca. She supported the Nationalist cause, and provided an important base for General Franco. The island was several times bombed by the Republicans who were in control of Minorca, but the island's resources were turned over to the Fascists for the establishment of bases for naval and air operations. One abortive landing of the Republicans near Porto Cristo had little effect. Visitors to Majorca would do well to realize that the scars suffered by the Balearic islands in the Civil War have never fully healed. The shock to national pride, and the different loyalties involved, make these bitter years a most unacceptable subject for discussion, especially by foreigners. History dies hard in the islands.

MINORCA

PREHISTORY (c.2000–1000 B.C.)

It was assumed until quite recently that the first settlement of Minorca occurred in the Bronze Age, or second millennium B.C., and that the strange stone monuments which are literally scattered all over the island were erected at that time – their mystery being that they would quite obviously have exceeded the domiciliary needs of the primitive population. More than 1,600 such sites are listed, of which a few only have been thoroughly investigated. But should any conscientious visitor attempt to count them he will soon be discouraged because in the course of clearing the land for cultivation, past and present-day farmers have tended to put surplus stones to practical use, such as forming shelters for livestock, employing age-old structural techniques; enclosing well-heads; protecting trees from animals; or simply piling the stones out of the way in some odd, rocky corner, thus reproducing archaic pyramidical forms. Fairly recently, however, a new theory has gained ground, based on the scientific dating of animal bones and horns, some of which show signs of having been worked by hand. These, by their juxtaposition with fragments of human skeletons, postulate that man occupied the island as early as 4000 B.C. The animal remains, most of which have been found in the caves in the south of the island, where the rock is softer than that of the north, are identifiable as those of the antelope *myotragus balearicus* which has been extinct for many ages.

It is these prehistoric stone monuments which give Minorca its first taste of distinction from the other islands of the Balearic group. They are of three kinds: the *talayots*, the *taulas* and the *navetas*. *Talayots* are conical structures which may stand as high as nine metres, though in their original form they may have been taller still – with their upper stonework now missing. Some are solid, but the majority contain an inner chamber and sometimes an internal passage. Their purpose remains a mystery: burial may be ruled out because no traces of human remains have ever been discovered in their proximity. One possibility is that they functioned as watchtowers and defensive outposts; another that they were the residences of local chieftains or, quite simply, storehouses. Almost invariably the *talayots* form part of some ancient village complex. One of the finest and most accessible is the Torre d'en Gaumés, south-west of Alayor (p. 303). Another, Trepucó, between Mahón and Villa Carlos, has been fully documented by members of the Cambridge Museum of Ethnology, who excavated it in 1932–4 (p. 278).

Taulas and *navetas* do not occur in Majorca; in fact, the former are a unique feature of Minorca. Invariably they are situated near settlements already incorporating *talayots*, and it is usual for them to be surrounded by a horseshoe of standing stones all their own. Their form consists of a massive upright stone supporting a horizontal slab, making a giant 'T', and not, as at Stonehenge, a horizontal carried by twin uprights. It has been assumed that these mysterious monuments, the tallest of which stands about four metres high, had a religious significance – perhaps as a symbol of sanctity since its upper surface or table-top is protected from violation by its height and overhang. Some authorities also propose a link with the worship of heavenly bodies, or even with the bull, as in Crete. In general, and for practical reasons, it is no longer believed that they were sacrificial altars, nor that they could have acted as supports for other structures. There are seven complete *taulas* on the island, though the sites of more than twenty others have been identified. One of the most convenient to visit is the Talati de Dalt, situated slightly south of the main road from Mahón to Alayor (p. 288).

The *navetas* have equal, if not greater fascination though less mystery, since it has been established that they were funerary monuments. They were named for their similarity in shape to an upturned boat. Owing to careful restoration and maintenance of the site, the best example is the *naveta* of Els Tudons. The site is well signposted about 7 km. east of Ciudadela to the south of the main road to Mahón (p. 290). It can be entered through its west end, giving into a small antechamber and then two long chambers one above the other.

There are several other examples, though many of them, in common with *taulas* and *talayots*, are difficult to locate. In any event, these three types of structure give the only clues we have as to early man's habitation of Minorca.

PHOENICIANS AND CARTHAGINIANS (c.1000–123 B.C.)

Though it may be assumed that the Phoenicians, that great nation of traders, could hardly have by-passed Minorca as a port of call to break their voyages to the Straits of Gibraltar and beyond, there is little evidence to that effect, beyond the tradition that they named the island Nura. The Greeks left few traces of occupation; at least very little has survived besides some coins, pottery and figurines. These are in the keeping of the Mahón Museum. Equally, little is known of the period of Carthaginian domination, except that Mago, the general commanding the battered remains of the Carthaginian forces in the Second Punic War, is described by Livy, the Roman historian, as having wintered his army on the island in the year 206–5 B.C. during recruiting operations. Pliny the Elder, another Roman historian, asserts that Mahón, the capital, owes its name to a corruption of the Carthaginian general's name. The historical connection with Carthage was last heard of in 202 B.C. after the Battle of Zama, in present-day Tunisia, when the Carthaginians, led by Hannibal, were soundly defeated, and their overseas conquests – Spain, Sicily and the Balearics – were surrendered under the treaty with Rome, which put an end to the Second Punic War.

ROMANS (123 B.C. – A.D. 450)

There followed a period of Roman influence initiated in 125 B.C. by Quintus Cecilius Metullus, the Roman consul, who became incensed by the use of the Balearics as a haven for pirates and by the tactics of the natives who spied out the movements of Roman shipping before sallying out with impunity to attack, then withdrawing into their own roadsteads under the protection of their fortresses. The principal punitive expedition was sent first to Majorca and then to Minorca, which was rapidly subdued and occupied. The islands were incorporated in the Roman province of Tarragonensis.

A period of marked development was then enjoyed, activated by Roman competence in government. Even at such an early period

Mahón and Ciudadela adopted distinctive roles: Mahón as the administrative centre, and Ciudadela as the focus of agriculture and local trade. Roads were built as much for strategic purposes, to facilitate the rapid movement of troops, as for economic reasons. But while great events were afoot elsewhere, Minorca remained largely unaffected by events in the rest of the Mediterranean, except in 47 B.C., when the island surrendered to Sextus Pompey, son of Pompey, Julius Caesar's rival who had been killed in Egypt a year before. After that, peace again reigned on the island, and in A.D. 404, with the rest of the Balearic archipelago, Minorca was granted provincial status.

VANDALS AND BYZANTINES (A.D. 450–707)

The Vandal hordes arrived in the islands about the year A.D. 425, and remained for approximately a hundred years. This period of occupation witnessed intense religious persecution because, though the Vandals were Christian, they adhered fanatically to the Arian heresy, which set out to eradicate all other forms of worship. Their fervour explains the paucity of early Christian remains on the island. In A.D. 533 the Vandals of North Africa were overcome by Belisarius, the Byzantine general acting for the ruler of the Eastern Roman Empire based in Constantinople. Thus the Balearics came under Byzantine rule. Minorca was then known as Minorica, meaning the smaller island, and so it remained until probably the end of the seventh century and the departure of the Byzantine overlords. From that time the islands were free from any domination, though being Christian they looked to the mainland and Charlemagne for protection from the forces which were building up on the North African shore. The Emperor dispatched a fleet to assist them in 799. But little resistance was possible against a vicious Viking raid in 859, which caused such destruction that only a few early Christian churches have survived.

ARABS (A.D. 707–1232)

The period of Moorish domination of Minorca began after the invading Arabians had succeeded in establishing themselves securely on Majorca. This operation was heralded by sporadic raids which increased in frequency and eventually led to total occupation of the

Balearic archipelago. In 902 the islands were incorporated in the Emirate of Córdoba, which became a caliphate in 924. Then with the collapse of Córdoba early in the eleventh century, when the Moorish administration broke up into a collection of fractious states known as the *taifa* kingdoms, government was carried on by the Wali of Denia from his mainland stronghold midway between Alicante and Valencia. Subsequently, as in the other islands, the fanatical Almoravide and Almohade Muslim sects held sway. Thus far Minorca, though always somewhat isolated because of its situation beyond the other Balearics, had a history much in common with that of its sisters.

CATALAN AND MAJORCAN KINGS (1232–1349)

After Jaime I's spectacularly successful invasion of Majorca in 1229, the fate of Minorca was left in abeyance while he concluded his mopping-up operations against the Moors. It was not until 1232 that the Conquistador's attention was directed towards the further island. In any event, he had not stayed consistently on Majorca, but had retired to the mainland, content to leave the aftermath of conquest to the predominantly Catalan nobles who had manned and financed the expedition. This as we have seen, was mounted on the understanding that the spoils of victory, in land and property, should be allotted to them in due proportion to their contribution.

In due course, a strategy of extreme simplicity resulted in the capitulation of Minorca's Moorish governors. When in 1232 Jaime I of Majorca paid a return visit to his new realm, he had under his command no more than three galleys. With some effrontery, however, it was suggested that a false rumour be spread in Minorca to the effect that a vast fleet and army were assembled in Majorca ready for invasion. In pursuit of this stratagem, Jaime camped above Capdepera on the mountainous north-eastern tip of Majorca, the nearest point to Minorca. According to the chronicle written by the King himself, he was supported by no more than six knights, five squires, ten servants and a few local scouts. Nevertheless his galleys were dispatched to Minorca to demand surrender. These messengers were favourably received while the Muslim *caid* consulted his subordinates. Meanwhile, a vast ring of bonfires had been lit on high ground in Majorca, within sight of Minorca, 40 km. distant, to give the impression that an army of overwhelming size was poised ready for invasion. The result was that the Muslims were hoodwinked into capitulation, and first agreed to acknowledge themselves to be the lieges of the King by providing him − interestingly, in view of the present agricultural pattern of the island − with 10,200 kg. of fresh butter annually. Then, on being pressed further, they agreed to the occupation of Ciudadela and other strongpoints. In the previous context it is also interesting to know that when in 1269 a levy was made to help finance a crusade, Minorca was scheduled to provide 1,000 oxen and other cattle.

While Jaime I remained on good terms with the Muslim governor of Minorca, trade was re-established, and the island resumed its role as port of call on the Mediterranean trade routes. In subsequent years, however, the relationship deteriorated, the ostensible cause being a quarrel between the Muslim governor and Pedro III of Aragon − not his brother Jaime II of Majorca, who was the legal overlord. The grounds of the dispute consisted of a well-founded suspicion that the new Moorish governor of Minorca had divulged top secret plans to the Moors of North Africa when a fleet of Pedro's warships put in to Mahón in 1282, preparatory to an assault on Tunis. The struggle for power which was at that time raging between the two royal brothers was further complicated by Pedro's claim to Sicily, and the installation of his Queen on the Sicilian throne, a move which aroused the Church of Rome, headed by Pope Martin IV, against him, and resulted in a papally sponsored crusade against Aragon. Throughout these major events Pedro continued to resent the position of Minorca, so strategically situated between his Spanish possessions and Sicily. Not unnaturally in view of their enmity, Jaime II of Majorca sided with the French in the disputes between France and Aragon, and this led to the mounting of an Aragonese invasion of the Balearics, which was not abandoned on the sudden death of Pedro III in 1285, within a few days of his joining the expeditionary force. In pursuance of his father's plan the new young King, Alfonso III, succeeded in ousting his uncle Jaime from Majorca before returning to Catalonia in order to reassemble his forces for an assault on Minorca. The invasion force assembled at Salou on the east coast of Spain and, accompanied by Sicilian warships, set sail in the late autumn, having used Majorcan harbours on the east coast as jumping-off places. The first attempt at the invasion of Minorca, made in spite of indications that peace was negotiable, was launched at the end of the year, only to be driven back by foul weather encountered off Cape d'Artruch, on the west coast of

Minorca. Nevertheless, the impetuous young king deployed a smaller force to Mahón harbour, where he waited impatiently, though secure against weather and foe, for reinforcements. When after twelve days' delay these were not forthcoming, he landed a theoretically inadequate force on the north shore of the harbour and prepared for battle on the plain to the north-west of the town. There, despite being outnumbered more than four to one by the arrival of Moorish contingents from North Africa, Alfonso won a decisive battle.

On January 21st, 1287 the island was formally annexed to the Aragonese crown, under exceedingly harsh terms. The climax was the mass drowning of shiploads of impoverished and physically weak Moors – the elimination of the weakest section of the population. Ciudadela was immediately proclaimed the island's capital, as it had been under the Muslims (Medina-Minurka). The mosques and Islamic shrines were forthwith converted to Christian usage. Noblemen who had supported the Aragonese cause were allotted substantial estates, as were members of the important religious orders, Catalan settlers were introduced to take possession of other forfeited lands, and the great patrician houses of Ciudadela were handed over to merchants for the furtherance of their commercial interests. Then, after having been 'in the news' for a short space of time, Minorca sank once more into its traditional obscurity, deepened by the death in 1291 of Alfonso III in Barcelona, at the early age of twenty-five, four years after his departure from Minorca.

Soon, through papal influence, the Balearics were restored to Jaime II of Majorca. Most of his attention was concentrated upon the rehabilitation of the larger island, where one of his most beneficial works was the foundation of market towns. However, he similarly promoted inland Alayor as a Minorcan centre, as well as subdividing the island administratively into seven parishes and introducing weekly markets at Mahón, Ciudadela and Mercadal.

ARAGON AND SPAIN (1349–1713)

The sway of independent Majorcan kings over Minorca ended with the death in battle in 1349 of Jaime III. There followed a period of inactivity and general decline, owing to remote rule from Catalonia. The end of the fourteenth century was marked by agrarian risings and civic unrest on the part of townspeople. Severe depopulation was countered by the introduction of pardoned criminals from the mainland as settlers which had some beneficial effect as a remedial measure. The fifteenth century experienced growing rivalry between Ciudadela, the capital, and Mahón, the chief port – each of which had its own Universidad, or general council, acting as a local authority. More than once the two factions were in active confrontation, and this phase lasted as long as ten years. Rivalry still exists.

The following century saw the increased power of the North African Corsairs, especially those Turkish vessels commanded by the swashbuckling figure of Barbarossa, who harried Christians by sea and by land, wherever they were most vulnerable. In 1535, following his rout by the Emperor Charles V which ended in the capture of Tunis, the fabled hero withdrew his shattered forces, reassembled them, and after sailing into the roadstead at Mahón under false colours, made a successful landing. Despite desperate opposition and assistance from all over the island, the town was taken after three days' siege, but then only because the gates were treacherously opened by individuals who had previously bargained for their personal immunity. The resulting carnage was tremendous, and much treasure as well as human booty was carried away immediately. No attempt was made to hold the island as the Corsairs were exclusively raiders. The result of this disaster caused Charles V to strengthen Mahón's fortifications. He employed Juan Bautista Calvi, who was also responsible for the construction of the fortress of Ibiza, and whose further contribution to Minorca's defences took the form of Fort San Felipe, to guard the approach to Mahón. Its existence deterred the Turks in 1558 when they raided the island, forcing them instead to descend in strength upon Ciudadela. Though gallant resistance was offered, the old city was sacked – in fact razed to the ground – and more than 3,000 Minorcans were transported to the slave markets of Constantinople (or Stamboul, as it had become), though a fair proportion were later repatriated through the intercession of the Holy See. These two major raids each had a devastating effect on an island with an already sparse population. Lesser raids, always hit-and-run affairs, continued during the seventeenth century. In fact, Minorca played a dual role, its shores and harbours being employed both for sallies against foreign shipping and as targets for attack.

ENGLISH AND FRENCH (1713–1782)

Very soon, however, Minorca was to make a reappearance in world affairs – quite simply on account of its possession of a unique deepwater channel capable of development as an ideal naval base. The early eighteenth century saw the outbreak of the War of the Spanish Succession, in which England and the Netherlands came in behind the Austrian claimant, the Archduke Charles, while France espoused the cause of Philip of Anjou, grandson of Louis XIV. Fighting in the Low Countries raged, where the British forces were under the command of the Duke of Marlborough, while operations spread to Italy and Spain. An expeditionary force under the command of Major-General James Stanhope was landed on Minorca in the autumn of 1708, with the co-operation of Admiral Sir John Leake, the senior naval officer serving in the Mediterranean. Both saw the necessity for equipping Mahón as a naval base. Ciudadela was taken with the minimum of resistance, and Fornells shortly afterwards, the invasion being helped by the predisposition of the Minorcans to support the Austrian cause. Though Fort San Felipe, overlooking the entrance to Mahón's harbour put up a stubborn resistance, the fighting was over in a fortnight, and with very few losses. The Treaty of Utrecht, which brought the war to a conclusion in 1713, gave Minorca to the British.

The island acquiesced fairly easily in British rule, the chief cause of contention being the transfer of the administration from Ciudadela to Mahón. The older city remained, and remains, the island's ecclesiastical capital. Much of the credit for good relations was due to the island's first British governor, Sir Richard Kane, who had served under Marlborough in the Netherlands. His concern for the welfare of the island embraced a wide field, but perhaps his most lasting achievements are the improvement of agricultural and horticultural produce by the introduction of good strains of stock and seed and, more obviously, the construction of the central road which connects Mahón, the new capital, with Ciudadela, the old.

In assessing the profit and loss to the island incurred by alien British rule, it must be realized that the new regime did not seek to impose a new pattern of administration, which remained much as it had been under the Aragonese monarchy. The island was divided into five *terminos* or counties, based on Ciudadela, Mahón, Mercadal, Ferrerías and Alayor. Each had a 'bench' of magistrates, the Jurats, who were responsible for local government and acted in liaison under the governor of the island. These magistrates represented the four estates – landowners, merchants, artisans and peasants – and had the power to convoke a Universidad (general council) of twenty-four members, elected annually.

The first phase of British occupation of Minorca lasted for over forty years, only to be terminated by a surprise attack by the French in 1756, in the course of the Seven Years' War. In a sense the success of the invasion surprised the French themselves, because their commander, the Duc de Richelieu, had originally intended first to subdue Fort San Felipe. Instead, not possessing the relevant maps, they made landfall opposite Cala Santandria, a few kilometres to the south of the entrance to Ciudadela harbour. The landing of some 12,000 men went unopposed by the citizens of Ciudadela, and the campaign then developed into a land attack upon Mahón, for which the town was unprepared. Spasmodic fighting continued for almost a month while the besieged British awaited reinforcements which were never to materialize, for when Admiral Byng, who had been sent to the rescue, found that he was outnumbered and outgunned, he retired to be eventually courtmartialled at Portsmouth and executed by firing squad. Byng's execution, generally held by historians to have been unjust, led to Voltaire's famous dictum, '*pour encourager les autres*'. The beleaguered British, meanwhile, had no choice but to capitulate.

The government of the island was then assumed by France. The French dominion lasted until 1763, the year of the Treaty of Paris, under which Britain regained Minorca in exchange for ceding to Spain Cuba and the Philippines – both of which had been captured during the course of the war. When fighting broke out afresh between France and Britain in 1778, the British garrison on Minorca was greatly depleted, so that when Spain entered the war against Britain the following year the native Minorcans could no longer be regarded as reliable. When a joint French and Spanish expedition was mounted against the British, the operation met with success, and Fort San Felipe was the only strongpoint capable of determined resistance. The siege lasted six months, until the blockade so weakened the British garrison that it surrendered in February 1782.

SPANISH RULE (1782 TO THE PRESENT DAY)

Minorca now came under the rule of Spain. One of the first acts of the new regime was to demolish Fort San Felipe. The island settled back into its traditional preoccupation with internal affairs, and world politics for the moment took second place. Of great interest was the establishment of a separate bishopric for Minorca at Ciudadela, though there was the customary heated divergence of opinion over which of the rival towns should be honoured as the primate's seat.

But the island was not yet done with the British. It was to be elbowed by them into prominence once more on account of its strategic position in the Mediterranean. Once the Napoleonic wars were in full swing, together with Gibraltar Mahón was destined to become an important naval base. A landing was effected in November 1798 under General James Stuart, whose tactics involved the taking of central Mercadal, the link between Ciudadela and Mahón – the latter no longer being protected by Fort San Felipe. The boast was that not a single English soldier was lost in the whole operation. There followed the short period of British rule of which British visitors to the island are most constantly reminded, during which it is possible that Admiral Lord Nelson stayed at the villa now called Golden Farm, or Villa San Antonio, which overlooks the port of Mahón. That visit, made much of in legend, could have lasted no more than five days, and disappointingly for embroiderers of the historical tapestry, Lady Hamilton was not with her lover at that period.

Minorca was restored to the Spanish crown in 1802, under the provisions of the Treaty of Amiens. By 1809, when Britain, Portugal and Spain were allied against Napoleon, Admiral Lord Collingwood, who had served under Nelson at Trafalgar, made Mahón his headquarters. Though the military presence on the island had been removed, some of the inner harbour installations had been retained as a naval base, and the admiral resided at El Fonduco, a mansion overlooking the roadstead, which is now a hotel.

On the whole Minorca was quiet during the nineteenth century, subdued mainly by poverty. Many of the native population were forced to emigrate in search of a livelihood. But it was during the Spanish Civil War that the island once more asserted its independent spirit. Though Majorca opted for the Nationalist cause, the Minorcans were in favour of the Republicans, with few dissenting voices. Though inevitably there were incidents on either side, Minorca emerged comparatively unscathed, beyond enduring a rigorous blockade. In the end the British were instrumental in negotiations which resulted in the comparatively peaceful handing over of the island to General Franco's forces in February 1939, just one month before the official conclusion of the war. As with the other Balearic islands – and the Spanish provinces – these events rate as recent and painful history, and do not bear discussion, even after the lapse of time and the great changes which have taken place in the interval.

IBIZA

PREHISTORY (c.2000–1000 B.C.)

Ibiza's early history has left a profound and lasting mark on that small island. Unlike Majorca and Minorca, it has few neolithic monuments in the form of *taulas*, *talayots* or *navetas*, though some cave drawings in the Sas Fontanallas caves on the west coast hint at occupation in prehistoric times. Opinions differ over their age, but it is generally considered that the island's population originated on the mainland, and that settlement was brought about by Ibiza's convenient location as a port of call and trading centre for the Mediterranean maritime nations.

CARTHAGINIANS (c.1000–123 B.C.)

In early days the Pityussae, or pine-clad islands, midway between the mainland and Majorca, would have been used by the Phoenicians as a stopping place on their trade route from their home ports of Tyre and Sidon to Gades, the early name for Cadiz, on the Atlantic coast of Spain, which was one of that sea-faring people's principal commercial centres. But it is the Carthaginians who made the enduring impact upon this small island.

Some authorities give 480 B.C. as the date of organized colonization of Ibiza by this breakaway group of seamen, traders and empire builders who surpassed their Levantine ancestors in the creation of a civilization all their own. However, a trading post appears to have been established on the Isla Plana, which is now joined to the mainland on the north side of Ibiza harbour, about the seventh century B.C. In confirmation Diodorus Siculus, the Greek historian who was responsible for forty books embracing the history of the world, states uncompromisingly that the first such settlement was effected in 654 B.C. However, it must be remembered that he was writing in the first century B.C., and might possibly have got his dates wrong. In any event, by the third century B.C. Ibiza held an important

position as a link between the mother city of Carthage and her
Spanish trading posts; in fact the island was rated the third most
important Carthaginian possession, that is, inferior only to
metropolitan Carthage itself and her imperial settlements in Sardinia.
And it is of interest that the island retained her importance even after
the destruction of Carthage and the conquest of Sardinia by the
Romans.

During the Punic Wars Ibiza remained loyal to Carthage in
resisting the Romans, and Livy recounts how a Roman invasion force
commanded by Scipio Africanus launched an attack from Spain in
217 B.C. and, failing to take the citadel of Ibiza, ravaged the country
before retiring in possession of considerable booty. (This argues an
accumulation of wealth in the villages and outlying districts, and
hence in the country as a whole, as it may be assumed that a large
proportion of treasure and goods must have been held safely in the
embattled capital.) Such wealth would have been the result of years of
domination by the Carthaginians, during which time they developed
and exploited mines and saltpans, while disseminating their own
knowledge of agriculture, fishing, building and manufacturing
techniques. A fair estimate of the status of Ibiza in Carthaginian times
may be deduced from the extent of the Punic *hypogeum*, or
necropolis, in the Puig des Molins (Hill of the Windmills) between the
old town and Figueretas Bay, only a short walk from the citadel's
walls. This rocky eminence is riddled with catacombs, and continued
to be used until well into Roman times, probably until late in the third
century A.D. Its scale, and the number of tombs it housed, is so large –
well beyond the needs of an island with a small population – that is
has been suggested that the dead, and perhaps the dying, were
transported here from far afield so that their bodies should rest in
ground which was considered to be so sacred and so pure that it was
free from all corrupting agents. Most unfortunately, the major part of
the site of the necropolis has been built over in the interests of tourist
development, and what remains is far from imposing except to
scholars conversant with what is hidden or destroyed. However,
compensation is to be found in the splendid museum adjoining the site
(see p. 328), where the finest and most beautiful collection of Punic
remains in the world are on display.

Towards the end of the Second Punic War, when the Romans were
indisputably in the ascendant, the island was not tempted into
disloyalty, and is said to have welcomed Mago, the Carthaginian

general, to her shores, and to have provided him with much needed supplies, weapons and replacement troops. Yet it is remarkable that when Carthage succumbed to Rome in 146 B.C. and was totally destroyed, Ibiza emerged without experiencing either defeat or destruction. She quietly became a recognized ally or surrogate of Rome, and retained this position even after 123 B.C. when Majorca was captured by Quintus Cecilius Metellus.

ROMANS (146 B.C. – A.D. 450)

All the same, Roman influence made itself felt, notably in the creation of good roads and aqueducts – one which survived as late as 1791, linking Las Salinas with the city, and others in the neighbourhood of Santa Eulalia and Santa Gertrudis. As a recognized ally of Rome, Ibiza had its own constitution and mint. Ibizan coins have come to light on widely dispersed sites, giving an indication of the scope of the island's trading interests, which depended upon grain and salt. No taxes or military levies were imposed by the Romans, and this privileged immunity was continued until A.D. 74, when Vespasian granted blanket municipal rights to all cities in alliance with the Roman Empire. Where Ibiza was concerned, this actually implied relegation from her hitherto independent position as a confederate state, and the island became subject to taxation in line with other Roman colonies. In the last century preceding the birth of Christ, when the great split between Julius Caesar and Pompey shook the Roman Empire, Ibiza – in contrast to the other two Balearic islands that had given in to the Pompeians without a struggle – remained loyal to Caesar.

VANDALS (A.D. 450–534)

The island was not spared the onslaught of the Vandals in A.D. 425–6, and appears to have suffered a similar fate to its sister islands. This is a period of history, lasting into the sixth century, which is almost without documentation, but the Vandals seem to have been responsible for the destruction of many Carthaginian and Roman works of art and architecture.

BYZANTINES (A.D. 534–707)

The Vandals, who had given their name to the Spanish province of

Andalusia, were defeated by the Byzantines under Belisarius in the first half of the sixth century and, in common with the other Balearic islands Ibiza was then included in the Spanish possessions of the Eastern Roman Empire based on Constantinople. The exact date of the Byzantine withdrawal is not known, nor its circumstances, though it is clear that when the occupying power's military strength began to decline, advantage was taken by the Arabs of North Africa, from the shores of which Ibiza was particularly vulnerable. In fact a major naval sweep of that part of the Mediterranean by the Arabs occurred about 707, and throughout the eighth century Ibiza continued to suffer devastating raids which grew in force and duration.

ARABS (A.D. 707–1235)

In 798 the great Emperor Charlemagne's forces wrested the island from the Arabs, but they recaptured it in 801. It was restored to the Frankish empire in 813, but after that date frequent incursions were suffered, and a major Arab invasion was foiled in 832. However, as a culmination of these see-saw events, the island was finally captured by the Arabs in 867. The usurpers were to remain in possession for five centuries, during which the Roman name Ebusus became the Arabic Yebisah. One major attempt at recovery for Christendom was undertaken in the twelth century, when a Pisan crusade blessed by Pope Pascal II assembled in Barcelona, where it wintered in 1113 preparatory to making a landing on Ibiza in the spring. The invasion was fiercely resisted by Muslim cavalry, but the citadel of Ibiza was seized in August of that year. It proved impossible to hold after its defences had been razed and since the major stronghold could not effectively be defended the crusaders could not hope to hold the island, and their forces dispersed.

The year 1116 saw the island once again firmly in the grip of the Arabs – this time the fanatical Almoravide dynasty which came from Morocco. There is little to be seen from the period of Moorish domination, with the exception of the irrigation canals in the horticultural district of Ses Feixes west of Ibiza Town and some fragments of wall (mainly on the hilltop Almudaina with its Tower of Homage) which were incorporated into the later massive defences of the Citadel or Dalt Vila. Place names containing the uncharacteristic letter 'x' are also reminders of that period of domination. The Arab, or what are loosely called Moorish, conquerors divided the island into five administrative districts: Alhaueth, Xarch, Benizamid, Portumany and Algarb. Later, after the Reconquest, they came to be known as Cuarton del Llano de la Villa, Santa Eulalia, Balanzon, Portmany and Las Salinas. Subsequently the number was reduced to four.

THE RECONQUEST (1231–35)

Though Jaime I's spectacular conquest of Majorca in 1229 was well established by the following spring, there was some delay in following it up by an operation against the Moorish usurpers of Ibiza, and even though the king had granted a Charter of Privileges to the entire Balearic group, Ibiza remained under alien control. Nevertheless, Jaime I was fully aware of his pledge that he would regain possession of every one of the islands. In 1231 an agreement was entered into with Don Pedro, the Infante of Portugal, and Nuño Sanchez, the Count of Roussillon, granting them the island, subject to the king's suzerainty, should they succeed in conquering it within a stipulated period. When the resultant enterprise failed, negotiations were entered into with Guillermo, Earl of Montgri, sacristan of Gerona cathedral and Archbishop-elect of Tarragona, promising him the island in the event of his taking it. De Montgri then solicited the aid of the two former negotiants. Each was to receive a third share of the island and a third of the town of Ibiza, while the noblemen concerned were to become feudal vassals of de Montgri. The authorization for the expedition, and the terms of settlement, are among the archives in Ibiza's cathedral.

The combined fleet sailed from Barcelona in 1235 according to plan. A landing was made from well within Ibiza harbour on August 8th, the plan being for machines of war to be assembled for the bombardment of the threefold lines of walls and ditches. Though the outer defences were taken without much trouble, the main and inner wall held fast, and the citadel was captured only after a siege of one month and seven days, and then, it is said, only as a result of the walls having been weakened in the course of fighting during the Pisan crusade of 1114. Another contemporary report gives credit to the disclosure of a secret passage on the Figueretas side of the citadel, which resulted in the storming of the heights from an unexpected quarter. As it happened, the consequences for the majority of the islanders would have been barely noticeable; the peasants remained virtual slaves, their lot only slightly improved by the transfer of power to Christendom when, according to previous agreement, the land was subdivided by the allotment of two shares to de Montgri and one to each of his principals. Subsequently Don Pedro relinquished his share, which consisted of the Santa Eulalia neighbourhood, to King Jaime, and it has been assumed that his portion of Ibiza Town went to de Montgri.

CATALAN AND MAJORCAN KINGS (1235–1349)

When in 1286 Alfonso III of Aragon chased his uncle, Jaime II of Majorca, out of his newly founded kingdom, a mission was sent to Ibiza demanding allegiance. Always independent in spirit, the local government agreed, subject only to the new King coming to the island to receive homage in person. Meanwhile the government of the island continued to be conducted by a Universidad composed of two legislative houses, a general and a secret council. When Jaime II was restored to his kingdom of Majorca it was discovered that one Zafortesa, the governor he had appointed to Ibiza, was abusing his position by impounding the taxes of Formentera and converting them for his own benefit. He was forthwith excommunicated by the Archbishop of Tarragona. When Pedro of Aragon finally put Jaime III of Majorca to flight, thus terminating the independent kingdom of Majorca, the Balearics were finally incorporated into the Aragonese realm and granted important trading concessions, particularly in the Ibizan salt industry, which put the island once more on the commercial map of the Mediterranean.

ARAGON AND SPAIN (1349 TO THE PRESENT DAY)

During the following centuries, in fact, the island played a dual role in the shipping world, being at once the target of North African Corsairs and marauders, and its natives themselves preying on foreign shipping, sailing the *zebecs*, or local craft built of Ibizan pinewood.

In spite of a ring of watchtowers, Turkish forces penetrated the region around San Antonio in 1383 and carried away everything they could, including a great number of captives. And well into the fifteenth century the island suffered raids by Arabs, Turks, and even Frenchmen, all of whom moved in rapidly, seized whatever was to hand and withdrew before help could be brought in from the town or neighbouring districts. By the time of the fall of Constantinople in 1453 the Turks were masters of the great part of the Mediterranean Sea. In 1536, the citadel of Ibiza was bombarded by a combined force of French and Turks before help could be mustered in the form of privateers by sea and cavalry by land. But a raid on the largest scale took place in 1543, in the form of a well-planned Turkish invasion, when 1,000 men were landed from twenty ships standing off Santa Eulalia. Though initially repulsed, they established a bridgehead at a second attempt, and went on to set up their cannon on the Isla de la Ratas in Figueretas Bay. Nevertheless, the attack was beaten back after a battle lasting four hours.

All in all, the pressures were so great that in 1554 Charles V, who had been elected Holy Roman Emperor in 1518, ordered the city to be encompassed by yet another set of walls. This work was entrusted to the military architect and engineer, Juan Bautista Calvi, who also strengthened Mahón. So ambitious an undertaking was this that it took thirty years to complete. By that time not only had the Emperor died, leaving his successor Philip II to carry on the work and to receive the credit, but the defences were already obsolescent, because in 1571 a Christian fleet under Don Juan of Austria had destroyed the Turkish fleet in the battle of Lepanto off the Gulf of Corinth, and so the massive defences were never tested.

Finally the fortress above Ibiza was completed in 1585, at a cost of considerably more than the estimated 50,000 ducats, half of which were contributed by the Archbishop of Valencia, Tomás de Villaneuva. It may be conjectured that this prelate's action in funding so much of the work may have influenced his later canonization.

The first decade of the eighteenth century brought a period of unrest and warfare on the mainland of Europe which was to have its effect upon all the Balearic islands, though preponderantly on Minorca, in the War of the Spanish Succession following the death in 1700 of Charles II of Spain. This degenerate king left no direct heir, though before his death he had nominated Philip, Duc d'Anjou, his successor. This candidate, being the grandson of Louis XIV, who was still on the throne of France at the time of Charles' II's death, was of course sponsored by the French. Britain and Holland, however, supported the claims of the Archduke Charles of Austria, brother of the Emperor of Austria – the fear being that a union between France and Spain would tilt the balance of European power in favour of France. When in 1706 the British fleet commanded by Sir John Leake made its appearance off Ibiza, as part of a sweep of the Mediterranean, the island took the hint and, in common with Valencia, Catalonia and (eventually) Majorca supported the Austrian claimant. The war ended in 1713, with the Treaty of Utrecht, when the death of the Austrian Emperor elevated the Archduke to the imperial throne, and the installation of the Bourbon candidate, Philip d'Anjou, as King of Spain effected the severance of that country and its islands from the influence of Austria, Milan and Naples. The record of their earlier adherence to the opposite cause did not earn the islanders favour with the Spanish monarchy, and in 1734 Philip V refused to restore certain privileges to the Balearics, though he did offer them a charitable payment, to be offset by their promise to bear arms for Spain in times of need. This explains the massive recruitment during the period of the Seven Years' War, between 1756 and 1763, when Prussia and England united against Spain and France.

The latter half of the eighteenth century was mainly one of peace and isolation, though the activities of Ibiza's own Corsairs continued for a time. One of the last engagements took place in 1806, when Antonio Riquer, with only a 72-ton ship at his command, boarded and took a 250-ton English brig which had a firing power of 12 guns. What is more, the battle raged in the channel between Ibiza and Formentera, giving Ibiza Town a ringside view of the David and Goliath contest. An obelisk in honour of the occasion has been set up on the quay.

By 1816, when an Anglo-Dutch fleet bombarded Algiers harbour, destroying a great number of ships before occupying the town, the Balearic islands were finally relieved of the threat of Muslim attack by sea – their principal dread throughout the centuries. The result was that little happened in Ibiza during the nineteenth century except certain improvements in communications were introduced. These, however, had small effect in lifting the shroud of remoteness that had descended upon the island. Ibiza, in fact, relapsed into being truly insular, and it was not until present times that it came into its own as a never-never land for expatriates and a once-a-year honeymoon haven for visitors.

In many respects, Formentera's history differs only slightly.

FORMENTERA
The Greeks named the island Ofiusa. Rather earlier in history it was populated, perhaps only seasonally, by Phoenicians and

Carthaginians. It is, however, the Romans who were responsible for its present name. Formentera is a derivative of the Latin *frumentaria*, meaning granary, as is the Catalan *forment*, the word for wheat. The name owes its origin to the fact that in Roman times much of the island's agriculture was devoted to the growing of corn to be used for victualling the Roman troops stationed on Ibiza, to which it was shipped for grinding in the mills of the Puig des Molins outside Ibiza Town.

There is little evidence of the Moorish conquerors of the Balearics having taken much interest in Formentera during their occupation. After the Reconquest, Guillermo de Montgri made it over to Berenguer Renart for settlement. However, security of tenure was never easy, since this outpost of Ibiza lacked natural defences. Thus it became recurrently the prey of invaders and pirates who not only raided it but used it as a haven from which to attack shipping and lands across the sea. The sixteenth-century Turkish *galleots* could be drawn up on to the sandy beaches when not in active service. One of the first recorded raids had been by Vikings in 859, but similar incursions persisted after the Reconquest. A very important naval engagement took place off the Playa de Mitjorn in 1529, when the fabled Barbarossa was returning from a sea battle in the Bay of Valencia. This battle won, he retired to Formentera to water and revictual his forces. By that time raids had continued at such great strength and so repeatedly that the native population had been evacuated to Ibiza, and the island remained uninhabited for 300 years, though some seasonal farming could be precariously carried on.

It was not considered safe to resettle the land until 1697, when it was parcelled out to Ibizans prepared to cultivate the land and to fish. The inhabitants of Formentera thus have no distinct identity in racial type, language or customs from the Ibizans. Almost to a man they have since the eighteenth century occupied themselves farming and fishing, and in the production of salt.

History made only a slight impact on Formentera in the eighteenth and nineteenth centuries, though mention is made of the island producing recruits for a very efficient militia. An eminent visitor in the person of the ever-inquisitive Archduke Luís Salvador came to the island between 1866 and 1888, and remarked upon the longevity of the population, attributing it to the simplicity of the way of life there. However, in the present century peace was disrupted by the capture of the island in August 1936 by Republican forces preparatory to their landing on the Ibizan south-east coast, but shortly after this Formentera settled down again to its insular way of life; that is, until modern trends overtook it. Tourist development was slow to be established, only becoming noticeable in 1972, with Playa d'es Pujols the first beach to come to be recognized as a playground resort. Water supply has always been a problem on the island, and has acted as a limiting factor in development.

CUSTOMS

The Balearic islands follow the Mediterranean pattern in their richness and variety of custom. The origins of many customs are lost in antiquity but normally there is a connection with the religious and historical festivals held in most towns and villages. It is at these events that the traditional costumes, fast disappearing in everyday life, can be seen.

The special feature of **Minorca** is the *jaleo*, officially translated as 'merrymaking on horseback', which is a reasonable description. A good example can be seen at Ferrerías at the Feast of St Bartholomew, on August 24th, which begins with a colourful procession of fourteen horsemen (*Sa Colcada*) led by a jester (*el flabioler*) mounted on a donkey and playing eighteenth-century music on a flute. A mass is said for the *caixers* (different estates of citizens) and rosewater is sprinkled over the congregation; then follows the fun of the *jaleo* with trick riding and horse racing. Alayor goes in for much the same excitement on August 17th, the feast of San Lorenzo, with fireworks thrown in. Other *jaleo* cavalcades are at Mercadal on July 20th, the feast of San Martín, at Villa Carlos on July 25th, the feast of Santiago (St James), and at San Luís on August 23rd.

A charming sight throughout the islands on January 17th, St Anthony's Day, is the ceremonial blessing of the animals in the market square.

The religious *fiestas*, when most of the customs can be seen, are on the great Christian days of Holy Week and Christmas. Most towns and villages have a special devotion to a saint and they also celebrate his or her feast day. The customs attached to these are local, differing considerably from district to district. However, there are several standard elements — processions, bonfires, singing — which go along with the special 'ingredient' in each area.

It has been claimed with justification that **Ibizan** folklore is more lively and spontaneous than that in the other Balearic islands. As an indication some country people — the women rather than the men — still wear an adaptation of the traditional costume for every day, and for Sunday occasions. This consists of a voluminous black skirt, a bodice, a coloured kerchief and shady straw hat — clothes well suited to extremes of heat and cold, and reminiscent of those of the Berber women of North Africa. Sometimes these are to be seen in more elaborate form on feast days and at country weddings, as well as in folk-dancing displays.

The full dress consists of the *gonella*, a long black pleated tunic worn with a bodice which has detachable sleeves and a double row of ornamental buttons. Aprons are tied around the waist. Shawls, too, are worn, and these come in many colours, though black, red or yellow are the most favoured, while, as in everyday life, the *cambuix* or headsquare can be topped with a wide-awake hat. The most unusual feature of the native dress is the *abrigai*, a small red cape slung over one arm, like that of a bullfighter. To gild what is already a flamboyant lily there is the *emprendada*, a massive piece of inherited jewellery consisting of loops of gold and silver filigree, coral or mother of pearl, worn as a necklace, and usually ending in a locket containing a picture of the wearer's name-saint or the patroness of her village. In contrast to all this finery, hairstyles are severe. The hair is brushed back from a centre parting and plaited, reappearing below the point of the kerchief, where it is beribboned with long streamers to accentuate its length. Though this dress is worn only on special occasions, young women may decide to get themselves up for lesser displays in white dresses held out by starched petticoats, the colour being provided by the *cambuix*, usually yellow.

The ceremonial dress of the men is equally striking: black worsted baggy pleated pants for winter, white linen for summer. These narrow at the ankle. A knife is secreted in the folds of a black or red cummerbund. White high-collared shirts are worn underneath black embroidered waistcoats with silver buttons, and the neckcloth is of silk. The finishing touch is a scarlet cap which is gathered into a black headband and points forward, like a cock's-comb, giving a revolutionary or bandit air.

Many of the traditional folk dances, such as *es caragol* (the snail) are warlike in the extreme. The dancers move in a giant spiral reminiscent of Greek island dances and, as part of the dance, young men fire their rifles into the air. Outside San Miguel's church one may see *es mac de fer trons* (the thunder-making stone), which was the traditional ritual venue. Household bonfires lit at farmsteads in celebration of the eve of San Juan used to be similar targets for uninhibited shooting.

The classical Ibizan dance is in two phases: the provocative *curta*, during which the woman executes figures of eight, followed by her beguiled partner, developing into the livelier *llarga*, during which the man leaps ardently after the woman, who is now in feigned retreat, but ready eventually to yield to coy surrender. In nuptial dances these figures are followed by the *dotze rodades* (twelve steps) and the *filera*, in which the bride is joined by bridesmaids who do their best, unavailingly, to capture the attention of the groom. The music for these dances is provided by instruments of antique origin which in design and ornamentation are peculiar to Ibiza: the *flauta*, made of oleander wood and beautifully inlaid; the *tambor*, or drum, usually played one-handed by the flautist; and giant castanets, *castanyoles*, carved from juniper wood. The majority of players are musically illiterate, so they play from memory, with improvisation. The traditional songs, the *cantandes* (*xacotes* in Ibizenc) are apt to be bucolic and bawdy – or they may by adapted to lampoon current events and self-inflated local dignitaries. In contrast, the *porfedi*, or battle hymns, are serious to the point of being inflammatory, and take us back to the times of alien incursions.

Special displays of folk dancing and singing are staged at 6 p.m. on Wednesdays and Fridays at San José, and also at San Miguel, usually late on Thursday afternoons.

The most impressive events in **Majorca** fall on the important dates in the Christian calendar – in Palma and at venerated religious sites. The Monastery of Lluch plays host on Christmas Eve to thousands of pilgrims who assemble to pay reverence to the presiding Black Madonna. In Palma on Twelfth Night, or *Día de los Reyes*, there is the splendid water-borne arrival of the Magi. They are greeted by fireworks and sirens and then the crowd forms itself into a cavalcade to proceed through the city streets.

Holy Week is of course a solemn period. In Palma the religious procession on Good Friday is composed of the *Cofradías*, various fraternities that are the heirs of the medieval guilds. Their representatives go barefoot and fettered, wearing penitential robes and inquisitorial hoods which cover their faces and make them an awe-inspiring sight in their anonymity. They bear litters representing the Stations of the Cross, and the only music is that of ceremonial drums. The penultimate group carries aloft a statue of the Blessed Virgin Mary adorned with Easter lilies, preceding the figure of the Christ Crucified. The slow procession forms up at the civil hospital, then winds its way towards El Borne and Calle Conquistador, finally reaching the Ayuntamiento in Plaza Cort. There it is received by the Captain of the Balearics, who has come in ceremony from his quarters in the Almudaina Palace. Later on there is a constant file of women placing mourning flowers at the foot of the Cross. This, incidentally is one of the rare occasions when Majorcan ladies may be seen wearing the graceful Spanish *mantilla*.

The torchlight procession on Good Friday at Pollensa is equally impressive. Then the much-revered images of Christ Crucified and the Virgin Mary are venerated at the foot of the monolithic cross on the hilltop Calvary above the town. This thirteenth-century cross is believed to have been thrown up by the sea at San Vicente, and to have been brought here by fishermen. When darkness falls the Christ statue is carried ceremonially down the steep steps to the parish church of Nuestra Señora de los Angeles in the central square of the town. Silence is observed, while the trail of flickering lights from torches and candles streams downwards. The procession is lengthy, composed of an adoring populace and a select retinue of town dignitaries drawn from the higher social estates, *señores y amos* (lords and masters), dressed in the distinctive robes and capes of their respective callings.

La Puebla is one of the best places to make for on January 16th–17th, St Anthony's Day, to witness performances of the folk dancers known as the *Canconers del Camp*, who gather around ceremonial bonfires known as *foguerons*. The music is made by tambourines and the *zambomba* or ancient drum, and additional entertainment is provided by the lively recitation of improvised verses which satirize local figures and parochial events, much to the amusement of those in the know. These recitations may be accompanied by music from archaic hurdy-gurdies, called *ximbombes*. The performers are in competitive pairs, and are known as *glosadors*.

July 25th is St James's Day, when the patron saint of Spain is honoured, and a public holiday observed, so that many events are staged in town and country locations, Muró, Santañy, Algaida, Calvia or Felanitx may be worth visiting then, as also La Puebla, which puts on a rural version of the bullfight.

Another category of events appears to be of pagan origin, celebrating the agricultural calendar, and especially the harvest. The different important crops all have their special days of celebration which perpetuate the Mallorquin pastoral heritage. For instance, a mammoth Melon Feast is staged at Villafranca in the autumn, and inevitably conjures up a parallel between human fertility and that most gravid-looking of fruit. It also goes without saying that the wine feasts at the end of September, especially those of Binisalem and its neighbourhood, have distinctly Bacchic overtones. Cultural events include the August Music and Painting Festival at Pollensa (p. 224) and the Spring Book Fair.

As well as these and the religious *fiestas*, Majorca also recognizes several important historical occasions, and marks them with enactments of glorious deeds. For instance, on September 9th there is a pilgrimage to the Oratory of San Pedro Sagrada, near Santa Ponsa, the landing place of King Jaime the Conqueror. On a far greater scale is the celebration on the last day of the year of the capture of Palma by that same national hero. On that occasion the staff of the original standard carried by Jaime I is borne ceremonially through the city streets to the music of brass bands and gunfire. Pollensa stages an exuberant mock battle between Moors and Christians to recall the events of August 1551, and similarly Soller acts out on May 11th and 12th the repulse of the Moorish landings which threatened port and town in 1651.

To parallel Majorca's celebration of her reconquest by Jaime I, **Minorca** commemorates the deliverance of Ciudadela from the Moors in 1267 by Alfonso III. These celebrations coincide with the Feast of St Anthony, on January 17th.

Ciudadela's most important annual event, however, takes place at the feast of St John the Baptist on June 24th. The festivities begin decorously on the previous Sunday, known as the *día des bé*, when, as part of a civic ritual which has remained unchanged since medieval days, invitations are issued to civic dignitaries and then to the populace – as if anyone in the neighbourhood needed such reminder. The fun really begins on the eve of St John, June 23rd, when a procession carries greetings or *caragols* to the mayor, proceeds in a cavalcade to the shrine of the saint before debouching into the main square, where a large part of the merrymaking consists of attempts to unseat the riders. On the following day, the actual feast of the saint, the cavalcade forms up again outside the Town Hall for a medieval tournament, which includes a form of jousting, the *juego de s'entortilla*, and 'armed combat', the *juego de las carotas*, in which missiles are hurled against wooden shields. This is followed by the even more perilous *el abrazo*, in which the combatants charge each other at headlong speed. Medieval dress is worn (without armour) defining the rank of the four classes of participants: the nobility, the clergy, the artisans and the peasants. Late that evening – very late – the celebrations end with a firework display.

Mahón is the place to be on Good Friday, to witness the solemn procession of the Holy Burial, when the silence of mourning is broken at intervals by the unique chant known as the *Geu*. The official mourners wear their traditional costumes and uniforms.

FOOD AND DRINK

Even gastronomically, there are distinct differences between the islands. The present tendency is for hotels to include one of more typically national dishes in their table d'hôte menus.

MAJORCA

In the Majorcan hotels they have learnt to modify Spanish cuisine, mainly by the judicious use of olive oil, in order to prevent that tummy trouble which for one reason or another has been known to plague many a foreign holiday. It is therefore to the restaurants that one must go in search of 'real' Majorcan food. An occasional foray into exotic cuisine is also possible, at least in Palma, where specialist restaurants – mainly in the Terreno district – can produce, say, the *rifstafel* of Indonesia, or excellent Chinese food above the level of ordinary take-away establishments. Then, at the other end of the gastronomic pole, there are ubiquitous fish-and-chip bars and, reflecting the importance of West German tourism, many specializing in *wurst*, and other types of sausage.

Incidentally, visitors who need to budget with care may be reassured by the fact that restaurants and bars are obliged by law to display their prices prominently. Also one set meal at an inclusive price must be on offer. A 'good food guide' is provided by the display of symbolic forks, five denoting the highest rating, one the lowest.

One difference in eating habits between Majorca and the Spanish mainland is of great importance: though it is not out of order to be served with meals right round the clock, late hours are not the norm. In fact, hotel meals correspond more or less to British timing, though their duration can be prolonged without signs of impatience on the part of the serving staff. This 'normal' time for beginning a meal therefore spares us over-indulgence in *tapas*, or aperitifs – those tasty titbits, such as olives, cubes of cheese, sausage, mussels, anchovies, mushrooms or peanuts – which can tempt the unwary into ruining their appetite for the meal to come.

Methods of preparation and ingredients being the same, the dishes are similar to those of the various provinces of the Spanish mainland. Yet certain differences emerge. A common factor may be detected in many Majorcan dishes, such as the tendency to serve meat mostly in made-up dishes, and the slap-happy use of tomato sauce which, however spicy, can become monotonous.

Specialities

There are several island specialities which can be recommended. None can be labelled as haute cuisine, but they are satisfying and make use of the good things from this area and the sea which surrounds it. One of these is *la sopa mallorquina*, which is something more than a soup, made by lightly frying then simmering an assortment of diced vegetables before pouring them and their juices into soup plates, each lined with a slice of very thin and possibly garlicky bread. Then there is the more ambitious *zarzuela de mariscos* — by its name betraying Moorish antecedents — made from chunks of crustacea and other fish cooked with tomatoes, almonds and garlic in *both* wine and brandy. *Caldera* is a more modest fish stew, made out of whatever is to hand, and *coca* an open flan filled with fish and vegetables. Eels served in garlic sauce are very popular in Majorcan households.

Shellfish, particularly lobster, crayfish or giant prawns (*gambas*) — served either grilled or with mayonnaise — are expensive, because there is an insatiable export market for them. But one safeguard against over-spending on such gastronomic delights in restaurants is the practice of weighing the fish at table once the customer has made his choice. Then, if the price is too high, he will have the option (if strong-minded enough!) of choosing some cheaper local speciality, such as octopus (*pulpo*), squid (*calamar*) or cuttlefish (*sepia*). Other alternatives might lie with red mullet (*salmoneta*), sole (*lenguado*), fresh tunny (*atún*) or the humble and absolutely delicious fresh sardine. Having chosen, one decides whether to have the fish cooked *a la plancha* (grilled), *a la romana* (dipped in batter and deep-fried) or *marinera* (poached in wine and tomato sauce).

Roast meat figures on many menus, but since we are accustomed to such a high quality in Britain, perhaps it would be more satisfactory to concentrate upon things which seldom find their way into our own butchers' shops, such as sucking pig (*lechón*) and baby lamb. Poultry is good and plentiful as well as tasty because much of it is free-range. Made-up meat dishes are also well to the fore on every menu. One is *el frito mallorquin*, a spicy fry-up of pigs' offal — far more delicious than any description can be; *sesos*, or brains are among some of its unidentifiable ingredients. Then there is *escaldums*, a chicken or poultry dish cooked with potatoes, and various pies with savoury fillings, accompanied perhaps by *tumbet*, which resembles the Provençal *ratatouille* in being composed of courgettes, peppers, onions and tomatoes 'sweated' in olive oil, but in this case including potatoes. Though not Majorcan, *riñones al Jerez* (kidneys cooked in sherry) can be strongly recommended.

The local Majorcan bread is crusty, and baked without recourse to the steam method which has lowered the standard of mass-produced bread in Britain, and driven so many cooks to baking their own. However, the absence of salt in the dough is a little strange to the British taste, though one quickly gets into the habit of supplementing it at table. Then there are various pastries and doughnuts, all with intriguing names. The queen of these must be the *ensaimada*, flaky and dusted with icing sugar, and resembling the English lardy cake. These may be bought in various sizes, the largest being huge cartwheels and packed in round boxes ready for export – even to Barcelona where, it is claimed, the water which goes into the mixing falls short of the ideal achieved on Majorca.

The most humble picnic food – and much that is luxurious – may be bought in *colmadas*, the equivalent of delicatessen shops. Here we may be reminded that the bulk of the population, especially schoolchildren, exist at midday on a ration of *pamboli*, which quite simply are hunks of bread dipped in oil and salt, possibly garnished with a little ham, tomato or other makeweight. *Bocadillos* are more elaborate sandwiches, and sausages of all varieties hang from the rafters – some to be cooked, some eaten raw. *Sobresada* is one of the most popular kinds.

Fruit there is in plenty, according to season, as any quick tour of market stalls will reveal. To follow fruit and cheese one might indulge in *turrón*, a type of nougat incorporating many good things, though this is more confectionery than dessert – originally a Christmas speciality. The best cheese, Mahonese, is imported from Minorca, and has the additional virtue of being suitable for drying and using in the manner of Parmesan.

Wine

The influx of visitors to Majorca has made it impossible to provide sufficient wine to meet demand, and a great deal has to be imported. There has also been a decline in production which can be attributed to a disastrous outbreak of phylloxera, that disease of wines which originated in the United States in the first half of the nineteenth-century and spread rapidly throughout the continent of Europe. It reached its climax in Majorca in 1891, destroying what had been a thriving wine export business to France, and by the time it had run its course many vineyards that could have been replanted with immune strains had been turned over to crops of another kind. So, whereas a traveller of 1811 named a great many vineyards growing Malvasia, Grio, Pampol and Muscadet grapes for white wine, and at Binisalem Banãlbufar, Inca and Son Berga grapes suitable for red, these days the principal wine-growing districts are centred around Sancellas, Consell, Inca, Binisalem and Santa María for red wines, and Felanitx, Manacor and Porreras for white. The sherry is not local, but is brought in from Jerez de la Frontera, its birthplace. The *manzanilla*, from San Lucar near Jerez, has an indefinable dry taste, and is worth seeking out here, as in Spain.

Several different sorts of liqueurs are manufactured, mostly sticky-sweet, the exception being a fiery *eau de vie* called *palo*, which is flavoured with crushed almond shells.

Spanish brandies in the middle price range are quite acceptable and comparatively cheap. An advertising impact has been made by the black bull of the Veterano brand, which looms obtrusively at many a roadside. Fundador is another well-known brand, and a third has the somewhat ironic name of Soberano.

One refreshing drink, common in Spain and enjoyed as a summer drink by visitors, is *sangría*, a glorified red wine punch containing mixed fruit macerated in brandy. It is best ordered for parties of three or more, since mixing in small quantities presents a problem. A cheaper and very popular drink here, as in Spain, is *cuba libre*, a mixture of cola and Bacardi or other white rum. Beware of being fobbed off with gin instead of rum, as this does not go down nearly as well.

All these wines and spirits, and many more, are available in supermarkets, and local ones can be found in the *bodegas*, the original wine shops, a great many of which can be discovered on the Palma-Pollensa highway, which runs through the heart of the wine-growing district. There are also several distilleries which keep open house for free sampling, and which are therefore compulsory – or compulsive – stops for motorists and coach parties.

Beer seems expensive compared with other drinks. And so, of course, are spirits imported from farther afield than the Spanish mainland. However, if you must have whisky you cannot go far wrong in sampling Dyc, the Spanish brand which is the result of research aimed at producing an equivalent to Scotch.

MINORCA

Travelling to Minorca from Majorca, the gastronomic climate
changes markedly. Here, because of the emphasis on cattle farming
there is excellent fresh meat available, and the preponderance of veal
on the menu is explained by the fact that in dairying country the
rearing of calves is less profitable than milk production.

Mahón cheese is known to be one of the best in Spain. It may be
eaten fresh, when it is still white, a few weeks old when it has begun
to turn yellow, or at a later stage of ageing when it is used for grating,
as with Parmesan. During the seasoning process each flat, square
cheese is suspended by a rope of native grass. Connoisseurs eat their
Mahón cheese with a knife and fork, unaccompanied by bread or
biscuit. It may be served following a recuperative interval between the
main course and the pudding, as is the habit in France. A recent
development is the production of El Cesario, a processed cheese,
which has become a valuable export. This consists of Mahón cheese
mixed mechanically with butter and other ingredients, the
conveniently wrapped triangular portions being packaged in round
boxes.

Excellent ice cream, made of real cream, is on sale everywhere.
The centre of this industry is at Alayor, where a go-ahead creamery
pioneered its production.

Another important source of good food in Minorca is the sea; in
fact the island has in the past been famous for the shellfish of its rocky
northern coast, as at Fornells. Unfortunately for visitors, however,
modern methods of refrigeration make it a practical proposition to
transport crustacea to mainland Spain, where there is an insatiable
demand. This makes it expensive at home, and scarce on restaurant
tables, even at Fornells. However, many lesser breeds of fish make
excellent eating, especially when newly caught and cooked in
traditional Minorcan fashion; some of these are *Meró a la parrilla*
(grilled rock bass) with mayonnaise, *gambas* (giant prawns) grilled or
boiled, grilled *calamares* (squid), *salmonete* (red mullet) *sole*
(lenguado), *atún* (fresh tunny) and the Mediterranean *denton*.

No mention of Minorcan gastronomy can omit the intriguing (if
notional) story of mayonnaise, the salad dressing which has
contributed so greatly to our cold tables. *Salsa mahonesa* undoubtedly
comes from Mahón, and though substantiated accounts of its origin
remain obscure, it is almost certain that it dates from the period of the
French occupation of the island. The most widely accepted story is

that one day when the great Duc de Richelieu was touring the island, he halted at a farmhouse in search of lunch and was dismayed to discover that nothing more elaborate than wine and a fresh salad was available. Nothing daunted, his chef explored the resources of the kitchen, and whipped up an inspired mixture of eggs, olive oil and lemon juice. Thus, it is claimed, mayonnaise was born, and introduced to France when the duke and his retinue were obliged to leave the island.

Though the French occupying power may be given the credit for this gastronomic delight, the English are responsible for something quite as important to visitors: Minorcan gin. At the end of the eighteenth century in England this was a working-class drink, and much in demand by British soldiers of all ranks. It was left to a Mahonese businessman in 1790 — twelve years before the British left the island for good — to obtain, somehow or other, a recipe which has remained a close secret within the firm of Beltran from that day to this. Minorcan gin, made conventionally from spirit flavoured with juniper berries, is almost indistinguishable from English brands. The normal strength is about 60 per cent proof. A stronger type, about 75 per cent proof, manufactured by the same distillery, goes, inevitably, by the name of Nelson. Another, newer distillery produces a gin called Xoriguer. The Beltran distillery is in full operation, and is a valuable exporter, not only of gin but of locally made liqueurs, three of which are Doria, Panchito and the medicinally named Estomacal. The firm is so fully productive that it issues an open invitation to visitors to the factory on the waterfront at Mahón, where uninhibited free sampling is not only offered but encouraged.

IBIZA AND FORMENTERA

Ibiza does not figure on any gastronomic map, except, of course, in having a reputation for locally produced food. Vegetable dishes and fish (especially shellfish) are therefore to be recommended to those who can get away from hotel menus offering international cuisine, the ingredients for which are apt to be imported. The liqueurs flavoured with herbs — *frigola*, *romany*, *hierbas* — are worth trying by people possessed of a sweet tooth.

One distinctly individual Ibizan speciality is the so-called *salsa para la fiesta de la Natividad*, or 'Christmas sauce'. In spite of its name, this is not a sauce, but a kind of punch with which to wind up the festive meal. Its main ingredients are eggs, ground almonds, chicken stock, biscuit crumbs, sugar and saffron – which gives it a distinctive flavour. The mixture is beaten over heat in a *bain marie* until it thickens. It is then drunk rather than eaten with a spoon. This conclusion to a heavy Christmas lunch surely argues a good lie-down in the afternoon.

Finally, on Formentera, that island of fishermen, because of three things ready to hand – fish, salt and sun – one may still see fish strung out on the branches of trees to dry. For those who do not find stockfish very palatable, its historical implications are more interesting. Before refrigeration was introduced on a commercial scale, this salted and dried fish was a valuable export to northern countries for consumption in the winter, and during the Lenten period of fasting.

INTRODUCTION TO ISLANDS AND ROUTES

The four following sections contain practical information specifically related to each of the principal islands, and not applying to the Balearics as a group. Accent is placed upon the capitals and their environs, with full descriptions of what is to be seen and the most convenient ways of visiting on foot all the principal places of interest. This is followed by descriptions of the features of less importance for more leisured travellers.

After the descriptions of the capitals come one of the most valued features of this series of guides: sightseeing routes aimed at taking in all the resorts, towns, villages, scenery and places of historic and archaeological interest in all directions. Where practical, these are round trips. Suggestions are included for the occasional detour, which will increase the distances of what are essentially single-day or shorter expeditions. Such diversions may entail the visitor taking advantage of overnight accommodation. Distances are given in kilometres. They are marked cumulatively along each route, the distances of the detours not being included but given in brackets.

MAJORCA

INTRODUCTION TO MAJORCA

The Phoenicians knew the island as Clumba, the Romans Maiorica, the Moors Mayurca, and present-day Majorcans opt for Mallorca. This version is pronounced Ma-york-a, that is with the liquid 'll' of the Spanish tongue, though it is here spelt in the anglicized way, representing more closely to the non-Spanish speaker the island's identity as the major of the Balearic group. Say what you prefer; it will not alter the pleasure, fun and interest you derive from exploring the island at greater depth than is possible when visiting only the well-publicized beauty spots. Though it needs some doing, it is still possible to step aside from the tourist currents into delightful backwaters, and to idle away the time after the traffic has moved on. Details will then emerge which might otherwise have been missed. Expertise will quickly be acquired in the use of normally busy roads, but only at times when traffic is not at its heaviest – and this applies to public transport as much as to car travel – and in learning to dodge the multi-lingual conducted parties (or cheerfully making use of them) as they throng some of the best-known halting places. It must be admitted that Majorca is a very popular island and the majority of visitors come to it for the elemental pleasures, but there is much more to it, as its own people know.

The author has taken her own advice: though the major roads are followed so that places of importance may be strung together into excursions, diversions have been indicated, and off-the-route possibilities suggested, while the overall descriptions of ancient monuments and scenic wonders have been punctuated with detail which, it is hoped, will make them come alive in their historical context.

As has been hinted, Majorca is a lovely island, but with a dual identity: extrovert and at the same time secretive; here and there somewhat flashy – but surely we have ourselves to blame for that – and elsewhere dignified and proud. Both aspects may be examined and enjoyed.

ANCIENT MONUMENTS AND MUSEUMS

Though Majorcan ancient monuments have been the subject of scholarly research and documentation, not much provision has been made for the ordinary sightseer in search of the prehistoric. In fact, with a few exceptions which have been charted on our tours, they are difficult to locate or, when found, disappointing. The same applies to early Roman remains and Christian basilicas, and even Moorish monuments. The truth is that the tides of succeeding civilizations have obliterated much that was good, beautiful and interesting, so that in general terms sightseeing begins with the thirteenth century, and is mainly reflected in fortifications, ecclesiastical architecture and palatial houses.

To some extent, however, the museums make up for deficiencies. And, though there is no comprehensive provincial or island museum, many historic places have annexes which serve as such, supplementing the evidence of times past presented in their own structure and appurtenances. For example, besides the episcopal museum adjacent to Palma's cathedral, there are collections assembled in such places as Bellver Castle, the Monastery of Lluch and the Maritime Museum in the Consulado del Mar; there is the art exhibition in La Lonja, and the more contrived and generally Spanish exhibits in the Pueblo Español. These, however, are by no means all; though some collections take a little searching out, owing to lack of publicity and erratic opening hours. Many of the provincial towns have their own museums, the best of these being the Archaeological Museum at Alcudia, followed by regional museums in such centres as Artá and Manacor, the Ethnological Museum at Muró, and the memorabilia of Fray Junipero Serra, lovingly preserved at Petra, his birthplace.

Though opening times vary according to special circumstances, the most likely hours are from 10·00–13·30 and 16·00–18·00. Some of the smaller museums are open only on specified days of the week, and less frequently in winter. Admission charges are low. Art exhibitions, especially those promoted privately, may be advertised in the English language newspaper, the *Daily Bulletin*.

TRANSPORT ON THE ISLAND

Rail

The original, commercial railway serves the interior of the island, and links Palma with Santa María, Inca, Manacor and Artá, while the other, and totally charming narrow-gauge line goes over (and through) the mountains as far as Soller on the west coast.

The former began with double tracks from Palma to Inca. It was British-built and equipped with rolling stock made in Birmingham and Manchester. The opening ceremony took place in 1875. Various extensions followed. But after the Civil War of 1936 a decline in the volume of traffic set in and closures continued into the mid-1960s, brought about by substantial improvements to the road network. A factor which contributes to the comparative inconvenience of rail travel is that since many of the central market towns are traditionally situated on rising ground, the stations intended to serve them had to be built some distance away, on the level. Level crossing barriers are non-existent, so that motorists must be on their guard for what is now very occasional rail traffic. The furthest distance – from Palma to Artá – costs 96 pesetas one way; from Palma to Inca the single fare is 28 pesetas.

The Palma to Soller line is quite another matter, though it has its terminus cheek by jowl with its senior and plainer sister. The ride can be rated as one of the most delightful short journeys in the world, not only because of the magnificence of the mountain scenery through which the train travels – or burrows – on its way to the sea. This light railway was built in 1912 at the expense of Soller's inhabitants, out of the proceeds of their then flourishing citrus trade. The first engine was made in Loughborough, Leicestershire. The line is now electrified, but studiously retains its old world charm, even in its station buildings. Another pleasure comes from the retention of the original first-class parlour coaches with splendid brass ornamentation and decorated armchairs – twelve to a carriage – which are greatly sought after. The journey takes about an hour, including halts at mountain village stations, and costs 40 pesetas first class, one way, and 30 pesetas second class. This trip can be extended by an equally antiquated but practical tram ride from Soller station to the port.

HOTELS AND HOSTALES

There is a very large number of hotels on Majorca, and though the following list is not exhaustive it gives a selection of the types of hotel and *hostal* to be found in most parts of the island. Telephone numbers are given in brackets.

Palma
HOTELS

Five star:　　　*Son Vida*, Castillo Son Vida (232340).
　　　　　　　(Swimming pool, golf, tennis)
　　　　　　　Fenix, Paseo Marítimo (23244). (Swimming pool)
　　　　　　　Melia Mallorca, Monseñor Palmer (232740). (Swimming pool, golf, tennis)
　　　　　　　Valparaíso, Francisco Vidal (280400).
　　　　　　　Victoria, Calvo Sotelo 125 (234342).

Four star:　　　*Bellver*, Paseo Marítimo 106 (231099). (Swimming pool)
　　　　　　　Palas Atenea, Paseo Marítimo 200 (281400).
　　　　　　　Racquet Club, Son Vida (230000). (Tennis)

Three star:　　*Alcina*, Paseo Marítimo (231140). (Swimming pool)
　　　　　　　Araxa, Alferez Cerda 22 (231640). (Swimming pool)
　　　　　　　Bosque, Bosque 15. (Swimming pool)
　　　　　　　Club Náutico, Muelle San Pedro (221405). (Swimming pool)
　　　　　　　Costa Azul, Av. Ingeniero Gabriel Roca 87 (231940). (Swimming pool)

El Chico, Monseñor Palmer (233740). (Swimming pool, golf, tennis)
Jaime I, Paseo Mallorca 15 (230643). (Swimming pool)
Majorica, Garita 9 (232840). (Swimming pool)
Nacar, Av. Jaime III 125 (222641).
Reina Constanza, Paseo Marítimo (237645). (Swimming pool)
San Carlos, C'an Morro 60 (230843). (Swimming pool)
Uto, Calvo Sotelo 633 (281300). (Swimming pool, golf)

Two star: *Atalaya*, Cabo Martorell Roca 14 (230640). (Swimming pool)
Brenco, Calvo Sotelo 217 (232347). (Swimming pool)
Capitol, Plaza del Rosario 8 (222504).
Horizonte, Vista Allegre 1 (230548).
Jumbo Park, C'an Tapara (238000). (Swimming pool)
Madrid, Garita 60 (233340). (Swimming pool)
El Paso, Alvaro Basan 13 (232740). (Swimming pool)
Rimini, Cabo Martorell Roca 66.
Virginia, Bellver 14 (233140).

One star: *Ayamans*, Camino Vecinal de Genova Porto Pi (234449). (Swimming pool)
Boston, Alcalde Fons (238067). (Swimming pool)
Colón, 21 de diciembre 93 (250245).
Infanta, Mulet 10 (232443).
Mar Bosque, Calvo Sotelo 110 (232644). (Swimming pool)
Palma Lar, Plaza Rosellon 21 (215517).
Pullmaniv, Juan de Saridakis (237745).
El Valle, Av. Calvo Sotelo 262 (234374).

HOSTALES
Three star: *Armadams*, Marqués de la Cenia 54 (230449). (Swimming pool)
Regina, San Miguel 189 (213703).
Santa Barbara, Vicario Joaquín Fuster 527 (274100). (Swimming pool)

Two star: *Abelay*, Capitán Castell 117.
Adalt, Alferez González Moro.
Archiduque, Archiduque Luís Salvador 44.
Navarra, Navarra 35.
Perú, Plaza Palau y Coll 18.
Rocaflor, Juan de Saridakis 8.
Villa Bonanova, Vista Alegre 2.
Villa Sea, Camino Vecinal de Genova 85.

One star: *Aglaya*, Vallori 1.
Alla, Antillon 235.
Baleares, Plaza García Orell 16.

Europa, Velásquez 12.
Florida, Av. Antonio Maura 18.
Héroes, Héroes de Manacor 88.
Holanda, Av. Calvo Sotelo 339.
Del Liceo, Av. Conde Sallent 5.
La Lonja, Tamoner 10.
Palma, Gral Barcelo 18.
Paraíso del Mar, Av. Calvo Sotelo 257.
La Paz, Salas 9.
Porto Pi, Av. Calvo Sotelo 428.
Scat, Industria 16.

Alcudia
HOTELS
One star: *More*, More Vermey (545505).
Panoramic, More Vermey (545484).

HOSTALES
Two star: *Ca'n Fumat*, Ctra. Puerto.

One star: *Posada de Verano*, Ctra. Puerto Pollensa.

El Arenal
HOTELS
Four star: *Cristina Palma*, Acapulco (262450). (Swimming pool, tennis)
Garonda Palace, Av. Nacional (262200). (Swimming pool)
Playa de Palma, Ctra. Arenal 11 (961940). (Swimming pool)

Three star: *Alegría*, Marqués de la Romana 1 (265100). (Swimming pool)
Aya, Ctra. del Arenal (260545). (Swimming pool)
Bahía de Palma, Ejército Español (264500). (Swimming pool)
Boreal, Sedal 11 (262112). (Swimming pool, tennis, golf)
Flamingo, Ctra. del Arenal (260645). (Swimming pool)
Latino, San Ramón Nonato 7 (260662). (Swimming pool)
Negresco, Playa de Palma (263162). (Swimming pool)
Paradiso, Perla 44 (260616). (Swimming pool, tennis, golf)
San Diego, Mirama 1 (263700).
Timor, La Perla (263136). (Swimming pool)

Two star: *Alejandria*, Ctra. Militar (262300). (Swimming pool)
Arenal Park, Padre Bartolomé Salva (261950). (Swimming pool)
Cosmopolitan, Av. S. Rigo-Las Maravillas (261100).
Encant, Amilcar 1 (260550).
Lancester, San Ramón Nonato (262400). (Swimming pool)
Marítimo, Ctra. del Arenal (260540).

               Orient, Urb. Las Lomas (261850). (Swimming pool)
               Sofia, San Ramón Nonato (261673). (Swimming pool)
               Vista Odin, Playa del Maravillas (262728). (Swimming pool)

One star: *Arcadia*, Cannas 25 (260064).
               Caribbean, Mossen Antonio M. Alcover (263550).
               Europa, San Bartolomé 16 (263400). (Swimming pool)
               Kilimanjaro, 18 de julio 47.
               Ondina, Ctra. Militar 539.
               El Pueblo, Misión San Diego. (Swimming pool)
               Tiuna Park, Villagarcia de Arosa 48.

HOSTALES
Three star: *Golondrina*, Amilcar 8 (261547). (Swimming pool)
Two star: *Don Pedro*, Zama.
               Juan Palma, Sitios de Gerona 7.
               El Mansour, Sitios de Gerona 38.
               Mar del Plata, Carretera Militar 584.
               Perú Playa, Las Parcelas.
               Son Sunez, Ctra. Militar 556.

One star: *Amic*, Av. Nacional 29.
               Aragón, Ejército Español 71.
               Baracoa, Asdrubal.
               Isel, Dido 12.
               Moya, Ctra. Militar 509.
               Royal, San Bartolomé 3.
               Xapala, Amilcar 15.

Bañalbufar

HOSTALES
Three star: *Mary Vent*, José Antonio 49 (610025).

Two star: *Sa Coma*, Sa Coma.

One star: *Baronia*, Gral. Goded 16.

Cala Bona

HOTELS
Two star: *Consul* (567652).
               Gran Sol (567275). (Swimming pool)
               Levante (567175).
               Levante Park, Ctra. Cala Millor-Cala Bona (567151).

One star: *Atolon*, Ctra. Cala Bona.
               Cala Bona (567271). (Swimming pool)
               Pergola.

HOSTALES
Two star: *Cala Azul*, Calle A 19.
                    Mar y Sol, Paseo Marítimo.

One star: *Capdemar*, Ctra. Cala Millor.
                    Nemo.

Cala D'or
HOTELS
Four star: *Cala Esmeralda*, Urb. Cala. (Swimming pool)
                    Tucan, Bulevard (657200).

Three star: *Cala Gran* (657100). (Swimming pool)
                    Costa del Sur, Av. Playa (236300).
                    Rocador, Marqués de Comillas (657051).
                    Skorpios Playa, Poligono 27 (657151). (Swimming pool)

Two star: *Ariel*, Av. de la Playa (657052).

One star: *Cala D'Or*.
                    Ses Putentes, Ctra. Calonge.

HOSTALES
Two star: *Cala Llonga*.
                    Oasis D'Or.
                    Trujillo, Cala D'Or.

One star: *Bienvenidos II*, Av. Tagomago 14.
                    Chico, Av. de la Playa.
                    Yuca, Santa Eulalia.

Cala Figuera
HOTELS
Two star: *Cala Figuera*, Cala Santanvi. (Swimming pool, tennis, golf)

One star: *Rocamar*, Juan Sebastián El Cano (653702). (Swimming pool)

HOSTALES
Two star: *Pontas*, Virgen del Carmen.
                    Ventura, Cala Figuera.

One star: *Baco*, Marina 33.
                    Can Jordi, Virgen del Carmen.

Cala Fornells
HOTELS
Three star: *Coronado*, Playa Cala Fornells (686800). (Swimming pool)

Two star: *Cala Fornells* (686950).

Cala Gamba
HOTELS
Two star: *Voramar*, P. de Cala Gamba 27 (260300).

One star: *Portixol*, Sirena 31 (271800).

Cala Mayor
HOTELS
Five star: *Nixe Palace*, Calvo Sotelo 537 (231841). (Swimming pool)

Four star: *Santa Ana*, Playa Cala Mayor (233640). (Swimming pool)

Three star: *Atlas*, Cabo Martorell Roca 21 (230940).
               Cala Mayor, Calvo Sotelo 525 (231340). (Swimming pool)
               Panoramic, Isabel Rosello (231144).

Two star: *Impala*, Son Matet (230443). (Swimming pool, tennis)
               Mercedes, Camino Son Boter (233247). (Swimming pool)
               Zenith, Teniente Mateu Gacias 8 (233047).

One star: *Condemar*, Calvo Sotelo 590. (Swimming pool)
               Gales, Calle 114.
               Vikingo, Camino Cala Mayor. (Swimming pool, tennis)

HOSTALES
Three star: *Acor*, Miguel Roello Alemay 68.

Two star: *Bell Amar*, Calle 267.
               Goyena, Calvo Sotelo 605.
               Mimosa, Suecia 9.
               Ponente, Calvo Sotelo 603.
               Tres Hermanas, Irlanda 11.

One star: *Carlos V*, Calvo Sotelo 213.
               Chipre, Calvo Sotelo 550.
               Villa Inga, Ctra. Son Toells 40.

Cala Mezquida
HOTEL
One star: *Pontinental*, Ctra. Cala Mezquida. (563596).

Cala Millor
HOTELS
Three star: *Borneo*, Urb. El Dorado. (567750). (Swimming pool)
               Flamenco, San Lorenzo (567305).

Sumba, Urb. El Dorado (567000).
Talayot, Cala Millor (567150). (Swimming pool)

Two star: *Alicia*, Ctra. Cala Millor-Cala Bona (567675).
Bahía del Este, Urb. Son Moro (567250).
Hipocampo, Urb. Son Moro (567201).
La Pinta, Urb. Son Moro (567253). (Swimming pool)
Playa del Moro, Urb. Son Moro (567045). (Swimming pool, tennis)
Santa María, Urb. Son Moro (567200).
Temi, Ctra. Cala Bona-Cala Millor (567829).

One star: *An-Ba*, Urb. Son Moro. (Swimming pool)
Don Jaime, Playa Cala Millor. (Swimming pool)
Morito, Urb. Son Moro. (Swimming pool)

HOSTALES
Two star: *Los Alamos*.
Eureka.
Marymar, Urb. Son Moro.
Pebar, Ctra. Cala Bona.

One star: *Ana María*, Ctra. Son Servera.
Arcadia, Po. Marítimo.

Cala Moreya
HOTELS
Three star: *Playa Moreya*, Av. Ciudad Manacor (570100). (Swimming pool)

One star: *Colombo*, Playa Cala Moreya.
Perla de S'llot, Calle y Esquina.

HOSTALES
One star: *Artigues*, Playa Moreya.

Cala Mondrago
HOSTALES
Two star: *Condemar*, Ctra. Santañi-Cala Mondrago.

One star: *Playa Mondrago*, Playa Mondrago.

Cala Murada
HOTELS
Two star: *Cala Murada*, Urb. Cala Murada. (Tennis)

One star: *El Torrente*, Urb. Cala Murada.

Cala Ratjada
HOTELS

Three star:	*Aguait*, Av. de los Pinos (563408). (Swimming pool)
	Lago Playa, Playa Son Moll (563058). (Tennis)
	Son Moll, Playa Son Moll (563100).
Two star:	*Cala Gat*, Ctra. del Faro (563166). (Swimming pool)
	Capricho, Ciscar (563500). (Swimming pool)
	Mar Azul, Cala Guya (563200). (Swimming pool)
	Regana, Av. la Guya (563862).
	Serrano, Son Moll (563350). (Swimming pool)
One star:	*Alondra*, Almirante Ferrandis (563566).
	Baviera, Rafael Blanes (563066).
	Bellamar, Bustamante (563493).
	Cala Literas, (553396).
	El Cortijo, Ramón Franco 53 (563255).
	Es Viñets, Cala Guya.
	Flacalco, San Andrés 17 (563558). (Swimming pool)
	Luz, Ctra. Cala Guya (563112).
	Saarland, Magallanes (563895).
	Samu, San Andrés (563313).
	Tampico, Leonor Servera 27 (563604).
	Tucan, Juán Sebastián El Cano (563392).
	Tulipan, Av. Manzanilla a Cala Guy (563250).
	Vaquer, Pizarro 17 (563146).

HOSTALES

Two star:	*Alfonso*, Almirante Cervera.
	Corona, Colon.
	El Golea, Plaza Queipo de Llano.
	Miravista, Leonor Servera 5.
	Palmera Playa, Triton.
One star:	*Alcina*, Av. de la Guya.
	Amor y Paz, Nereide 10.
	Club del Mar, Av. de América 29.
	Girasol, Reyes Católicos.
	Isabel, González Llana.
	Vista Verde, Monturiol.

Cala San Pedruscada
HOSTAL

One star:	*Ca'n Pedrus*, La Pedruscada.

Cala San Vicente
HOTELS
Four star: *Molins*, Playa Cala San Vicente (530200). (Tennis)

Three star: *Cala San Vicente*, Capitán Juergens (530250). (Tennis).
                Don Pedro, Playa (530050).

Two star: *Simar*, Capitán Juergens (530300). (Swimming pool)

One star: *Niu*, Playa Cala Berreras (530100).

HOSTALES
Two star: *Mayol*, Playa Molins.
                Los Pinos, Urb. Cala San Vicente.

One star: *Vistamar*, Cala Clar.

Cala Santañy
HOTELS
Two star: *Cala Santañy* (653200).

One star: *Pinos Play*, Cost den Nofre (653200).

HOSTALES
Two star: *Cala Santañy*.

One star: *Palmaria*, Playa Santañy.

Cala Serena
HOTEL
Two star: *Robinson Club Cala Serena*, Polígono 31 (657800).
                (Swimming pool)

Calas de Mallorca
HOTELS
Four star: *Los Mastines*, Cala Antena (573125). (Swimming pool, tennis)

Three star: *America*, Calas de Mallorca (573225). (Swimming pool)
                Los Chihuahuas, Cala Antena (573250).
                María Eugenia (573277).
                Samoa, Calas de Mallorca (573000). (Swimming pool, tennis)

La Calobra
HOTEL
Two star: *La Calobra*, Playa (517016).

Calvia
HOTEL
Four star: *Club Galatzo*, Urb. Ses Rotes Velles (686270).

Camp de Mar
HOTELS
Four star: *Gran Hotel Camp de Mar*, Playa (671000). (Swimming pool,
tennis)

Three star: *Lido*, Playa (671100).
Playa, Playa (671025). (Swimming pool)
Villa Real, Ctra. del Puerto (671050).

HOSTAL
Two star: *Villas Camp de Mar*, Ctra. Camp de Mar-Puerto.

Campos del Puerto
HOTELS
Two star: *San Juan de la Font Santa*, Ctra. Campos del Puerto (655016).

Ca'n Pastilla
HOTELS
Four star: *Alexandra*, Av. de los Pinos 73 (261642). (Swimming pool)
Gran Hotel el Cid, Ctra. Arenal (26050). (Swimming pool,
tennis)

Three star: *Almendros*, César 2 (260462).
Ambos Mundos, Polígono la Ribera (260746).
Leo, Polacra (264400).
Lotus Playa, Maestro Ekitai-Hau (262100).
Oasis, Bartolomé Riutort (260150). (Swimming pool)
Oleander, Playa (264850). (Swimming pool)

Two star: *Anfora*, San. A. de la Playa.
Apolo, Vigo 28.
Calma, Horacio 11. (Swimming pool)
Miraflores, Jabeque 4.
Perla, Horacio 29. (Swimming pool)
Pilari Playa, Av. Nacional.
Playa d'Or, Virgilio 50.

One star: *Balmes*, Bellamar.
Balle, Bellamar 1.
Bari, Virgilio 27.
Cibeles, Ctra. El Arenal.
Coral, Miguel Pallicer 22.

Covi, Lebeche 7.
Delfin, Av. Bartolomé Riutort.
Diana, Pio IX 3.
Don Quijote, Polacra 3.
Embat, Nansa.
Gala, Jabeque 7.
Rodal, Ctra. Arenal 67.
San Rafae, Singladura 4.
Trianon, Jabeque 5.

HOSTALES

Two star: *Marbell*, Plinio 4.
La Pedriza, Bartolomé Riutort 51.
San Antonio de la Playa, Llabrés Morell 2.

One star: *Excelsior*, Av. de los Pinos 42.
Maracaibo, Ctra. Can Pastilla.
Sabina, Ctra. Arenal.

Ca'n Picafort

HOTELS

Two star: *Columba Mar* (527025). (Swimming pool)
Exagon, Ronda de la Plata (527076). (Swimming pool, tennis)
Tonga, Ctra. Artá-Alcudia (527000). (Swimming pool)
Vista Park, Av. Romero (527300).

One star: *Africa Mar*, Av. Tria (527351). (Swimming pool)
Brisamar, Av. Colón.
Concord, Isaac Peral.
Farrutx, Av. Trias.
Haiti S.A., Ctra. Alcudia-Artá.
Mar y Paz, Jaime I.
Nordeste, Colón.
Santa Fe, Paseo de Colón.
Sarah, Pies Descalzos.
Sulta, Paseo Colón.
Yate, Vía Alemania.

HOSTALES

Two star: *Embat*, La Playa.
Flamenco, Av. Jaime I 23.
Galaxia, Av. Colón 48.

One star: *Apolo*, Paseo Colón.
Jaime I, Jaime I 23.
Jaime II, Jaime II.
Marbella, Cervantes.

Margarita, Av. Trias.
Yate Mar, Via Francia.

Cañamel
HOTELS
Three star: *Playa de Cañamel*, Urb. Torre de Cañamel.

Two star: *Caballito Blanco*, Torre de Cañamel (563850).

One star: *Caballito del Mar*, Urb. Torre de Cañamel.

HOSTALES
Three star: *Cuevas*, Playa Cañamel. (Swimming pool)

One star: *Retorno*, Playa de Cañamel.

Ca's Catala
HOTEL
Four star: *Maricel*, Ctra. Andraitx (231240). (Swimming pool, tennis)

HOSTALES
Two star: *Ca's Catala*, Ctra. Andraitx.

One star: *Dito*, Ctra. Andraitx.

Ciudad Jardin
HOTEL
One star: *Ciudad Jardín*, Isla Malta 170 (260007).

HOSTALES
Two star: *Bon Estar*, Minguella 13.
Del Francés, Minguella 8.
Sabela, Trafalgar 50.
Snipe, Las Rocas.
Son Ventura.

One star: *Bogambilla*, Isla de Malgrat 5.

Colonia de Sant Jordi
HOTELS
Three star: *Marqués del Palmer*, Ses Estanques (655100). (Swimming pool)

Two star: *Alfa*, Carabela.
El Coto, Molino 4. (Swimming pool)
Tres Playas, Urb. El Coto.

One star: *Cabo Blanco*, Urb. El Coto.
                   Lemar, Gabriel Roca 72.
                   Sur-Mallorca, Urb. El Coto.

HOSTALES
Two star: *Cristina*, Paseo de las Rocas 16.
                   Los Estanques, Colonia San Jorge.

One star: *Casa Chiquita*, Los Pinos 8.
                   Doris, Estanques 56.
                   Es Turo, Ingeniero Roca.
                   Martorell, Cervantes 2.

Coll d'En Rebasa
HOTEL
Two star: *Sagari*, Pasaje Las Rocas.

HOSTALES
Two star: *Cas Torrer*, Gonoy 21.
                   Salva, Fonoy 22.

One star: *La Cueva del Toro*, Arrecife 23.
                   Marinella, Trafalgar 23.

Costa de Los Pinos (Son Servera)
HOTEL
Four star: *Punta Rotja*, Urb. Costa de Los Pinos (567600). (Swimming pool, golf)

Deyá
HOTELS
Four star: *Es Moli*, Ctra. de Deyá. (Swimming pool)

One star: *Costa d'Or*, Lluch Alcari.

HOSTALES
Two star: *Mundial Ca'n Quet*, Ctra. Valldemosa-Soller.

One star: *Miramar*, Ca'n Olivar.

Felanitx
HOTELS
Three star: *Cala Gerrera*, Cala Ferrera (657650).
                   Playa, Cala Ferrera (657734).

One star: *Tamarix*, Cala Ferrera.

Formentor
HOTEL
Five star: *Formentor*, Playa Formentor (531300). (Tennis)

Illetas
HOTELS
Five star: *De Mar*, Ctra. Illetas (231846). (Swimming pool)

Four star: *Bonanza*, Ctra. Illetas (239745). (Swimming pool, golf)
                        Gran Hotel Albatros, Po. Illetas (233540). (Swimming pool)
                        Illetas, Ctra. Illetas (233545). (Swimming pool, tennis)

Three star: *Playa Marina*, Ctra. Illetas (237673). (Swimming pool)
                        Villas Bon Sol, Ctra. Illetas (233840).

HOSTALES
Two star: *Bella Playa*, Adelfas.
                        Nereo, Ctra. Illetas.

Inca
HOSTAL
One star: *Victoria*, Rubi 5.

Lluchmayor
HOTELS
Four star: *Maioris Palm*, Urb. Puig de Ros (263708). (Swimming pool,
                        tennis)

Two star: *Es Pas*, Valgorner. (Swimming pool)

Magalluf
HOTELS
Four star: *Antillas*, Playa (681500). (Swimming pool, tennis)
                        Coral Playa, Torre Nova (681948). (Swimming pool)
                        Flamboyan, Playa (680462).
                        Melia Magaluf, Av. Notario Alemany (681050). (Swimming
                        pool)

Three star: *Americano*, Urb. Eturba Polígono (680850). (Swimming pool)
                        El Caribe, Playa (680808).
                        Guadalupe, (681958). (Swimming pool)
                        Samos, Urb. Torre Nova. (680700)
                        Trinidad, Playa (681400). (Swimming pool)

Two star: *Don Paco*, Urb. Torrenova. (Swimming pool)
                        Dulcinea, Urb. Torrenova.

HOSTALES
Two star: *Florida*, Urb. Torrenova.
              Sur Este, Playa.

One star: *Villa Sol*, Torrenova.

Mal Pas
HOSTALES
Two star: *Mal Pas*, Playa.
              Playa Pins, Camino Manresa.

Manacor
HOSTAL
One star: *Jacinto*, Weyler 1.

Paguera
HOTELS
Four star: *Sunna*, Gaviotas (686754). (Swimming pool)
              Villamil, Ctra. Andraitx (686054). (Swimming pool, tennis)

Three star: *Bahía Club*, Ctra. Andraitx (686100).
              Beverly Playa, Rub. la Romana (686070).
              Carabela, Ctra. Palma-Andraitx (686276).
              Cormoran, Puchet (686650).
              Mar y Pins, Playa Paguera (696649).
              Nilo, Malgrat (686500).

Two star: *Bella Colina*, Bella Colina. (Swimming pool)
              Paguera, Luz. (Swimming pool)
              Playas Paguera, Ctra. Andraitx.
              San Valentín, Peral. (Swimming pool)

One star: *Carabela II*, Eucaliptus.
              Creta, Eucaliptus (686043).
              Don Miguel, Nogal 2.
              Platero, Gaviotas.
              Platon, Dragonera 7.

HOSTALES
Three star: *Venecia*, Rosal (686612).
              Villa Font, Villa Font (686095). (Swimming pool)

Two star: *Celo*, Gaviotas 23.
              Diamante, Palmira.
              Fortuna, La Luz.
              Linda Mary, Bella Colina.
              Villa Rosa, Malgrat.

One star: *Amistad*, Iglesia.
                Juan Mari, Olivo.
                Marchek, Ctra. Andraitx.

Palma Nova
HOTELS
Four star: *Cala Blanca*, Po. Duque Extremera (680150). (Swimming
                pool)
                Portonova, Po. del Mar 2 (681512).
                Punta Negra, Predio Hostalet (680762). (Swimming pool)
                Son Caliu, Playa (680162). (Swimming pool)

Three star: *Bermudas*, Po. Cala Blanca. (Swimming pool, tennis)
                Bolero, Av. Magaluf (680250). (Swimming pool)
                Honolulu, Av. Magaluf (680450). (Swimming pool)
                Santa Lucia, Duque de Extremera (681358).
                Tobago, Torrenova (680500). (Swimming pool)
                Treinta y Tres, París (681470).
                Trópico Playa, Paseo del Mar (680512). (Swimming pool)

Two star: *Don Bigote*, París (681162). (Swimming pool)
                Playa Palma Nova, Paseo del Mar.
                Son Matías, Av. Son Matías (681550).

One star: *Martínez*, Calviá.
                Morocco, Po. del Mar.
                Panama, Urb. Cas Sabones.

HOSTALES
Three star: *Pujol*, Po. de Cala Blanca.

Two star: *Gabarda*, Roses Bermejo 1.
                Garona, Hermanos Moncada.
                Villa Nova, Paseo del Mar.

One star: *Bélgica*, Jaime 1.
                Pinos Mar, Hermanos Moncada.
                Roberto, Jaime 1.

Portal Nous
HOTELS
Three star: *Bendinat*, Av. Bendinat. (Tennis)
                Fabiola, Las Flores. (Swimming pool)
                María Luisa, Caldentey (675600). (Swimming pool, tennis)

Two star: *Colorado*, Vaquer.

One star: *Savalon*, De Seguí. (Swimming pool)

HOSTALES
Three star: *Aguamarina*, Falconer.
              Portals, Av. América. (Swimming pool)

One star: *Villa Ampurdan*, Vaquer 8.

Porto Colom
HOTELS
Two star: *Cala Marsal*, Cala Marsal (575125).
              Las Palomas, Asunción (575152). (Swimming pool)

One star: *Estoril*, Ronda Cruceiro Baleares 7.
              Estoril, La Punta.

Porto Cristo
HOTELS
Two star: *Drach*, Ctra. Cuevas (570025). (Swimming pool)

One star: *Estrella*, Ctra. Porto Cristo-las Cuevas. (Swimming pool)
              Felip, Burdils 61.
              Son Moro; Ctra. Cuevas Drach.

HOSTALES
Two star: *Castell des Hams*, Ctra. Manacor.
              Neptuno, San Jorge 14.
              Santa María del Puerto, Ctra. Cuevas

One star: *Esperanza*, Navegantes 29.
              Grimalt, San Luís 2.
              San Marcos, Burdils 46.

Puerto de Alcudia
HOTELS
Three star: *Algebeli*, Urb. Las Gaviotas (545994).
              Ciudad Blanca, Urb. Ciudad Blanca (545100).
              Club Carabela, Ctra. Artá (545050).
              Golf, Montenegro 32 (545298).
              Sturno, Av. Dr. Davidson (545700). (Swimming pool, tennis)

Two star: *Astoria Playa*, Ctra. Alcudia-Artá. (Swimming pool)
              Condes de Alcudia, Zona Comercial Carabela.
              Lagomonte, Urb. Lago Menor.
              Maristany, Zona Comercial Carabela. (Swimming pool)
              Nuevas Palmeras, Av. Minerva.
              Reina del Mar, Av. Tucan. (Tennis)

One star: *Ca Toni*, Vía Almirante Moreno 20.
                        Vista Alegre, Vía Vicealmirante Moreno 22.

HOSTALES
One star: *Alcudia*, Ctra. Puerto.
                        Boccaccio, Av. Pedro Mas Reus.
                        Mar y Sol, Vía Vicealmirante Moreno 14.
                        Piscis, Ctra. Puerto.
                        President, Playa Aucanada.

Puerto de Andraitx
HOTELS
Two star: *Brismar*, Av. Mateo Bosch (671600).
                        Villa Italia, Camino de S. Carlos (671622). (Swimming pool)

One star: *San Marino*, Camino del Faro.

HOSTALES
Two star: *Acal*, Av. Mateo Bosch 14.
                        Bellavista, Av. Mateo Bosch 69.
                        Catalina Vera, Isaac Peral 55.

One star: Ctra. Cap de Mar 5.

Puerto de Pollensa
HOTELS
Four star: *Daina*, Tte. Coronel Llorca (531250). (Swimming pool)

Three star: *Capri*, Anglada Camarasa (531600).
                        Eolo, Ctra. Pollensa 10 (530152).
                        Miramar, Po. Anglada Camarasa (531400). (Tennis)
                        Pollentia, Ctra. Puerto Pollensa-Alcudia (531200).
                        Sis Pins, Anglada Camarasa (531050).
                        Uyal, Po. de Londres (531500).

Two star: *Raf*, Po. Coronel Llorente 28.

One star: *Bellavista*, Po. de Zaralegui 126.
                        Carotti, La Gola (531096).
                        Marcalma, C. Formentor Ang Ecónmo Torres.
                        Marina, Anglada Camarasa 57.
                        Panorama, Urb. Gomar.
                        Romantic, Ctra. Alcudia.

HOSTALES
Two star: *Borras*, Iglesias.
                        Luz de Mar, Méndez Nuñez 12.

Singala, Ctra. Formentor.

One star: *Corro*, Juan XXIII 68.
La Torre, Po. Coronel Llorente 84.

Puerto de Soller
HOTELS
Three star: *Eden*, Es Traves (631000).
Eden Park, Calle Lepanto (631200).
Espléndido, Marina Es Traves (631850).

Two star: *Mare Nostrum*, Marina.
Porto Soller, Urb. Satalaya.

One star: *Costa Brava*, Playa d'En Repic.
Marbell, Camino del Faro.

HOSTALES
Three star: *Es Port*, Antonio Montis (631650). (Swimming pool)

Two star: *Madrid*, Playa d'En Repic.
Monumento, Ctra. al Puerto.

One star: *Denis*, Es Traves.
Posada del Mar, Marina 58.

San Telmo
HOTELS
One star: *Aquamarin*, Playa.
Dragonera, Playa.
Elo, Punta Blanca.
Punta Blanca, Playa.

Santa Ponsa
HOTELS
Three star: *Bahía del Sol*, Av. Jaime I (680900).
Rey Don Jaime, (681654). (Swimming pool)
Santa Ponsa Park, (681562). (Swimming pool)

Two star: *Casablanca*, Vía Rey Sancho 11. (Swimming pool)
Piscis, Manzana 12.
Playa de Mallorca, Urb. Santa Ponsa.
Playas del Rey, Vía Jaime I 77. (Swimming pool)

One star: *Armando*, Av. Jaime I.
Miranda, Puig Blanch.
Playa Santa Ponsa, Puig des Teix.
Skal, Urb. Es Castellet. (Swimming pool)

HOSTALES

Three star: *Oeste*, Vía Jaime I.

Two star: *Bon Repos*, Vía Rey Sancho.

One star: *Coral*, Vía Jaime I.

S'Estany Dens Mas
One Star Holiday Villages:
> *Club de Mar* (570179).
> *Club Playa Romántica* (570122).

S'Illot
HOTELS

Two star: *Mariant*, Levate (570000).
                Punta Amer, Playa S'Illot (570170).

One star: *Playa Mar*, Playa S'Illot. (Swimming pool, tennis)

HOSTALES

Two star: *Bona Vista*, Llevant 4.
                Club S'Illot, Playa Moreya.

One star: *Mirgaym*, Olaya Moreya.
                Pinomar, Paguell 13.
                Sertonia, Levant.

Soller
HOTEL

One star: *El Guia*, Castañer 3 (630227).
                Soller, Romanguera 18 (630505). (Swimming pool)

HOSTALES

Two star: *Avenida*, Av. General Goded 32.
                Ferrocarril, Castañer 7
                Gran Vía, Plaza de América 2.
                Llado, José Antonio 102.

One star: *Bellavista*, José Antonio 78.
                Bibiloni, Ctra. Deyá 122.
                Las Golondrinas, Av. General Goded 61.

PALMA

Population 282,050.

Air and sea connections The modern San Juan Airport is 8 km. to the east of the city by a fast motor road, with good taxi, coach and bus services.

Airlines:

British Airways: Plaza Pío XII.

Iberia: Av. José Antonio 7.

Aviaco: Calle del Conquistador 42.

Shipping line:

Trasmediterránea Cía, Muelle 5 (the port).

Buses Buses depart and arrive at various points just off centre in the city, so as to avoid maximum traffic congestion. These places, and the buses' destinations are as follows:

From *Vía Roma 7* to Andraitx; Paguera; S'Arraco, San Telmo.

From *Archiduque Luís Salvador 50* to Bañalbufar, Estellencs; Galilea.

From *railway station* to Arenal; Ca'n Picafort; Cala Millor, Cala Bona; Cala Ratjada; Lluch; Manacor, Porto Cristo; Puerto de Alcudia; Puerto de Pollensa.

From *Av. Alejandro Rosselló 97* to Cala d'Or; Cala Figuera; Felanitx.

From *Plaza de España* to Cala Viñas; Magaluf; Puerto de Andraitx; Santa Ponsa.

From *Av. Alejandro Rosselló 34 to Inca.*

From Calle Aragón to Sa Cabaneta, Portol.

There is also a circular route which rings the city.

Rail The main railway station is in the Plaza de España (*Map* **3**), the Soller station adjacent to it.

Car hire A great many firms, often with sub-offices out of town, specialize in this business. Three of the best-known are:

Atesa: Plaza Pío XII, 8.

Avis: Paseo Marítimo 133.

Hertz: Edificio Mar, Paseo Marítimo.

Underground car parks

Plaza Mayor (entry from Calle Navarra).

Plaza Olivar.

Plaza Obispo Berenguer de Palou, off Vía Roma.

Yachts and cruisers for hire

Palcoa S.A. Edificio Mar, Paseo Marítimo.

Hotels See p. 123.

Information Subsecretario del Turismo, Av. Jaime III 10 (*Map* **14**). There is also an office at the airport. Guides and interpreters: Paseo Mallorca. The *Daily Bulletin*, the local English language daily newspaper, is also a good source.

Hospital Plaza Hospital. Off the northern end of Vía Roma (*Map* **6**).

Useful telephone numbers

Ambulance 230369.

Fire Brigade 251234.
Police 211221.

Central post and telegraph office Vía José Antonio 6 (*Map* **24**).
Central telephone exchange Vía José Antonio 4.

Theatres
Teatro Balear, Calle Zanguera.
Lirico, Plaza Libertad.
Principal, Plaza Weyler, below Plaza Mayor.

Cinemas *Astoria*, Navarra 13; *Augusta*, Conde Sallent 1; *Avenida*, Av.
Alejandro; *Borne*, Paseo Generalísimo 31; *Rialto*, San Felio 9; *Sala Regina*,
Teniente Mulet, Terreno.

Clubs
British Club, Calvo Sotelo 175.
British American Club, Solado Marroig 14, Son Armadans.
Asociación de la Prensa (Press Club), Paseo de Mallorca.

Banks Among many, with branches:
Banco de Bilbao, Plaza Virgen de la Salud 1.
Banco de España, San Bartolomé 40.
Hispano Americano, Syndicat 10.
Banco de Santander, Av. Rey Jaime III 38–40.

Consulates
Great Britain: Av. Jaime III 23.
France: Av. General Mola 43.
            Av. Argentina 115.
West Germany: Font y Monteros 64.
USA: Av. Jaime III 67.

Churches
Anglican and American Episcopal services at Church of St Philip and St James,
Calle Núñez de Bilbao, Son Armadans. Sundays 08·30 and 19·00; Wednesdays
11·00; Holy Communion 10·30.
Roman Catholic High Mass in the cathedral (*Map* **43**) at 10·30 Sundays.
(Confessions heard in English, French, German and Italian.) Also at Montesión
Church (*Map* **49**). Mass said in English at the Chapel of the Immaculate
Conception, Plaza Gomila, Terreno, Sundays 11·00.
Swedish Lutheran in Anglican Church of St Philip and St James, Sundays
11·00.
Evangelist Murillo 16. Services in Spanish, Sundays 11·00 and 19·00.
Christian Scientist Calle Mon. Palmer 23 (opposite Hotel Melia Mallorca).
Sundays 11·00, Wednesdays 17·00.
Jewish inquire at the Hotel de Mar, Illetas.

Museums and art galleries not listed in text.
Krekovics Museum, Son Fuestenet (2 km. from Plaza España). Ancient Inca
and Peruvian Art. April-October 11·00–13·00; 18·00–21·00 (not Sundays).
Mansion de Arte (Ochoa Museum), Calle Apuntadores 45. Primitive,
medieval Italian pictures and Goya etchings. 10·00–13·00.

Libraries
Biblioteca Publica, Calle Llulio. 10·00–13·00.

PALMA 145

Municipal Library, Ayuntamiento. 09·00–13·00, 17·00–20·00.
Special permission may also be given to consult the following collections:
Círculo Mallorquin, Luliana Archaeological Society, Conde de Perelada Library
in the Vivot Palace, and the episcopal library.

Sport

    Real ('Royal') Tennis Club, General A. de Montan.

    Racing (trotting) and speedway, Hipódromo Son Pardo, off the Soller road.
Weekly in winter, twice weekly in summer, including Sundays. Tote betting.

    Golf Son Vida (6 km.).

    Football Luís Sitfar Stadium.

    Sailing Club Náutico, Muelle de San Pedro.

    Jai Alai Fronton Balear, Paseo Mallorca. Continuous from 15·30–22·00.
Admission free.

    Bullfighting Plaza de Toros, Avenida del Architecto Bennassar. Sundays
17·00 (summer season only).

INTRODUCTION TO PALMA

The first glimpse of Palma de Mallorca – the name used by its citizens
– identifies it unmistakably as a capital, which indeed it is, in its role as
the political and ecclesiastical centre of the Balearic archipelago. The
fact that it has been preoccupied with commerce since an early stage
in its history is evidenced not only by its busy streets but by a wealth
of medieval architecture which owes its existence and survival to
mercantile prosperity. A second wave of culture is expressed in the
wide boulevards, arcades, plazas and pedestrian precincts where
shopping, eating out (and idling) are a pleasure.

This versatile city has shown itself capable of adaptation to the
requirements of tourism, which from beginnings in the early 1950s
has developed rapidly into a major growth industry of vital
importance to the island's economy. Many excellent hotels line Paseo
Marítimo – the elegant waterfront overlooking the harbour and
backed by the foothills of the north-western mountain range. The
majority of the historical buildings, associated with centuries of
lucrative trade, as well as with piety and thanksgiving in that they
testify to the deliverance of the islands from the Moors, are situated
near the water's edge, or else grouped within a well-defined medieval
quarter consisting of narrow streets lined by town houses, many of
which aspire to the dignity of palaces. This is the quarter which has
become the rendezvous for sightseers lodging elsewhere along the
coast, particularly in the resorts which spread out, like beads upon a

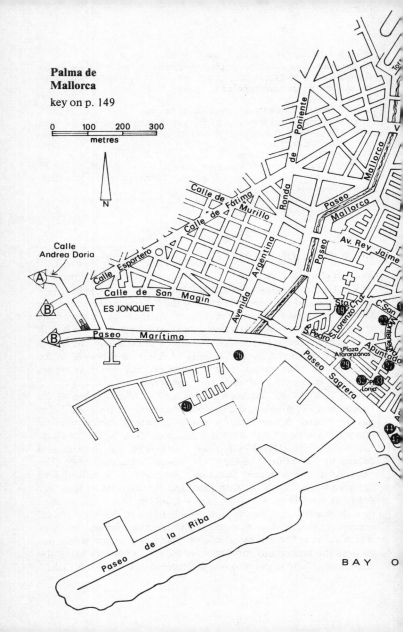

Palma de Mallorca

key on p. 149

0   100   200   300
metres

N

Calle Andrea Doria

ES JONQUET

Calle de Fátima

Calle de Murillo

Calle de

Ronda de Poniente

Paseo Mallorca

Calle Espartero

Calle de San Magin

Avenida Argentina

Paseo

Av. Rey Jaime

Sta. Cruz

C. San Monserrate

S. Pedro

S. Lorenzo

Apuntadores

Plaza Atarazanas

Paseo Marítimo

Paseo Sagrera

Plza Lonja

Paseo de la Riba

BAY O

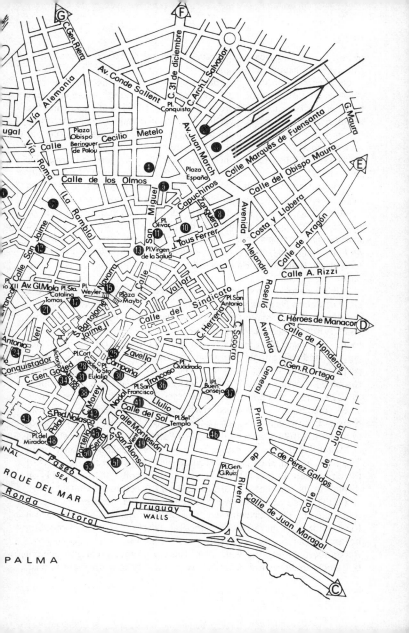

PALMA

string, to east and west of the city, and where there is direct access to the sea for all types of aquatic sport.

Owing to Palma's geographical situation, with a sheltered bay and deep water to the south, and level land surrounding it, the city was destined to become the natural point of arrival and departure for visitors, as it was in the past for would-be invaders. Approaches to towns from the direction of air terminals are apt to be uninspiring, and Palma's is no exception: it presents the usual conglomeration of waste land, billboards and indifferently landscaped terrain crossed by flyovers. The most noticeable feature is the proliferation of windmills – iron contraptions each associated with a cistern which, in the days before electrification, pumped underground water for use in suburban smallholdings. Few of these are in working order, and for the sight of the medieval and picturesque prototypes mounted on pointed stone towers new arrivals must await exploration of the flour mills or *molinos del Jonquet*; a few of these have been restored and are kept in trim above that part of Palma's old port which now serves as a yacht basin.

It is a loss to visitors arriving by air that they do not get their first sight of Palma from its sea approaches; this is most striking from the mail boats which make the night crossing from Barcelona in about eight hours, to arrive early in the morning. First come the steep, toothed peaks of the north-western *sierras* looming on the horizon – jagged and seemingly impregnable where they drop almost perpendicularly to the deep sea. The rocky island of Dragonera is rounded soon afterwards, to disclose a series of bays and inlets which, in 1229, set the scene for the reconquest of the island from the Moors. There are hints of sheltered harbours, above which small white houses stud the hillsides, before the cape of Cala Figuera is rounded, to reveal the full expanse of the Bay of Palma. Skyscraper hotels begin at Magaluf and continue on the fringe of every beach with only slight interruption until they crowd even closer together on the outskirts of the city. Then, in contrast to this brash modernity, Palma itself is on display in its combination of fairytale and functional architecture.

To the west, above the harbour or series of harbours, the city is dominated by the fourteenth-century castle of Bellver, but the central focal point is the pure Gothic cathedral, whose first stage of building began on the site of a Muslim mosque in the year following the Reconquest. Lining the waterfront there are other great and ancient buildings, massive and beautiful, which testify to a prosperous past,

Key to map of Palma de Mallorca

1 Sports ground
2 Soller railway station
3 Main railway station
4 Convent church of Santa Margarita (Military hospital) (p. 193)
5 Church of Santa Catalina (p. 180)
6 Provincial hospital
7 Church of the Convent of Santa Magdalena (p. 181)
8 Teatro Balear
9 Convent church of the Conception (p. 181)
10 Market (p. 189)
11 Former Convent of San Antonio (p. 181)
12 Church of San Jaime (p. 179)
13 Church of San Miguel (p. 180)
14 Tourist Office
15 Teatro Principal (p. 154)
16 Church of San Cayetano
17 Casa Berga (Palace of Justice or Law Courts) (p. 187)
18 Casa Belloto (p. 187)
19 Church of Santa Cruz and chapel of San Lorenzo (p. 179)
20 Sollerich Palace (Casa Morell) (p. 185)
21 Church of San Nicolás
22 Montenegro Palace (p. 186)
23 Telephone office
24 Post and telegraph office
25 Church of Santa Eulalia (p. 176)
26 Club Náutico
27 Casa Marcell (p. 187)
28 La Casa Consistorial (Ayuntamiento) (p. 188)
29 Consulado del Mar (Maritime Museum) (p. 166)
30 Vivot Palace (p. 184)
31 Casa Villalonga (p. 192)
32 La Lonja (p. 164)
33 Chapel of St George
34 Casa Oleo (p. 185)
35 Teatro Lirico

36 Monastery and church of San Francisco (p. 166)
37 Church of Nuestra Señora del Socorro (p. 178)
38 Arab Arch (p. 189)
39 Almudaina Palace (p. 160)
40 Club Náutico
41 Casa Maraqés de Palmer (p. 185)
42 Oleza Palace (p. 186)
43 Cathedral (p. 156)
44 Military post
45 Desbruill Palace (Museum) (p. 186)
46 Church of the Templars (p. 180)
47 Customs House
48 Episcopal Palace and Diocesan Museum (p. 188)
49 Montesión church (p. 178)
50 Casa Formiguera (p. 186)
51 Convent church of Santa Clara (p. 182)
52 Arab Baths (p. 189)

A route to El Pueblo Español (p. 190)
B route to Terreno District, Bellver Castle, Porto Pi Harbour, Andraitx (pp. 155, 171, 195, 199)
C route to San Juan Airport, El Arenal, Monastery of Cura (pp. 233, 234, 235)
D route to C.715, Manacor, Porto Cristo, Artá (pp. 242, 243, 245, 252)
E route to Inca, Alcudia, Pollensa (pp. 221, 226, 223)
F route to Valldemosa, Soller (pp. 203, 204, 209)
G route to Establiments, foothills of the sierras (pp. 231, 230)

For bus departure points see page 143
For parking areas see page 143

just as the hotels and tower blocks do to the present economy. Among the earliest are the Lonja, the fifteenth-century equivalent of a stock exchange, and the Consulado del Mar, the seventeenth-century Admiralty Court which now houses the Maritime Museum. The city itself, for the most part unseen, can be sensed, stretching far back into level and fertile country, well sheltered by the mountains and tree-clad slopes to the north and west.

HISTORY

Very little is known of the Roman occupation, when their colony of Palmaria was equal in status to Pollentia in the north of the island. Both these towns were destroyed by the Goths and Vandals, and what was to become the capital of the island was not to reassume a historical identity until the eighth century, when the Saracens invaded and renamed it Medina Mayurka. During the four centuries of Moorish rule the city was enclosed by four concentric walls, with its citadel, the Almudaina, functioning as the residence of the Wali, or governor.

When King Jaime of Aragon landed on the island in the autumn of 1229, he had at first intended to take Palma by storm before the Muslims, who had retreated behind its walls, could have had time to rally. However, unforeseen delays made a siege inevitable. The city was then bombarded by engines of war which recycled a variety of missiles including, it is said, the severed heads of Muslims who had been caught in the act of attempting to cut off the invading army's water supply. The assault reached its climax on the last day of December, 1229, when the walls were breached and the Christian army swarmed in, headed, it is rumoured, by the mystical figure of Saint George, the patron saint of Catalonia, resplendent in white armour. Chroniclers report that 20,000 Muslims were killed in the fighting. There was in fact a repetition of the wholesale massacre of the city's Muslim population which had been perpetrated in the Catalan-Pisan crusading operation of 1114–15.

The implementation of the Carta de Població – the written constitution – of 1230 created the basis for Palma's stability, and the city acquired further prestige upon the arrival of Jaime II, Majorca's own king, to take up residence in the rebuilt Almudaina Palace. With trade booming, the Catalan noblemen who had been granted country estates as recompense for their military services took advantage of the situation by moving in from the country to the city, where they involved themselves with shipping and commerce, and hived off a mass of their profits into the building of fine churches in thanksgiving and to the glory of God, while priority was given to the splendid new cathedral.

When in later centuries recession set in, the nobility reinvested in land, but made the mistake of adopting the role of absentee landlords more interested in levying taxes and collecting rents than in either the welfare of their dependents or the husbandry of their land. To a large extent popular disaffection was directed against the Jews who acted as agents, bankers and tax collectors. The Palma ghetto was sacked in 1391, and another rising of insurgents protesting their wrongs occurred between 1450 and 1452. There were further civil disturbances in 1521, when a peasant rebellion was fortified by Palma craftsmen who took up arms, occupied public buildings and forced the Viceroy to flee the country. He was strong enough to return two years later to enforce the rule of law. When a small party was admitted to the city for parley, power was seized treacherously, and the ringleaders of the rebellion executed. By that time, in the sixteenth century, Majorca's traditional markets had, for one reason or another, dwindled almost to the point of collapse, and one-third of the city was uninhabited and falling into decay. These were days of fear and uncertainty, made none the more comfortable by the rising power of the Church, invested in the Inquisition.

But human error and vagary were not exclusively responsible for the troubles of Palma's citizens. They also repeatedly suffered punishment by natural causes – in epidemics which further decimated the population, and recurred well into the nineteenth century in the form of yellow fever and cholera (1821, 1865 and 1870 being particularly bad years) and in earthquakes, and as if this were not enough, the city underwent what was perhaps its worst disaster in the flooding of La Riera, the seasonal torrent which flows down from the mountains to empty into Palma Bay. At the turn of the thirteenth century, the watercourse had divided the city roughly into two parts, the upper and lower, or east and west. Though Jaime II had recognized flooding to be a hazard, and had drawn up plans to divert the river, these had not been implemented. The consequence was that in October 1403 a great spate demolished a large part of the lower section of the city. The death roll amounted to more than 5,000, with, of course, a commensurate destruction of property. Though some subsequent measures were taken to control the river, it was not until 1623 that its course was turned, so that the flow was diverted into the moat outside the city walls. The river – dry in summer – is nowadays bordered by Paseo Mallorca until it reaches its outfall immediately west of the Club Náutico. Also, and of even greater interest from a town-planning point of view, the original course of the river has for a length of $1\frac{1}{2}$ km. been converted into two broad and dignified boulevards – Vía Roma (otherwise La Rambla) and El Borne, whose formal name is the Paseo Generalísimo Franco – which lead eventually to Paseo Sagrera and the waterfront.

The walls, too, had given trouble at various stages of history. Their original circumference encompassed an area containing the eventual site of the Almudaina Palace, the cathedral and some distance north. A second wall was added in the ninth century to take in much of the upper town lying to the east; and later, in the twelfth century a third wall was hastily erected to act as a defence against the Catalan-Pisan crusading operation. Though it was breached on that occasion, it was rebuilt by a Muslim labour force brought in from Andaluz immediately after the victorious Christians had retired from the island. During pre-gunpowder days these walls had been strong enough to withstand assault, except when there was treachery within the gates. However, in 1560 it was decided that they were inadequate, and should be strengthened. The fortifications were based on the original Moorish layout. The work continued sporadically for centuries according to the availability of funds, and it is ironic to know that the strengthened walls were to be manned once only in their history. This was in 1715, when the city withstood a siege for seventeen days only, in spite of its reinforced defence system (see p. 85). It is significant that by the beginning of the nineteenth century many of the walls and battlements were already crumbling – notably the seaward line.

These ancient and patched-up walls, which had contained and withstood so much action throughout the centuries, suffered ignominious demolition in 1873, when it was decided that they would be better removed so as to allow space for the growth of the city, and incidentally to make it more hygienic. This was done in the face of opposition by traditionalists. Present-day visitors may well search in vain for remnants of the old lines of defence; nothing is left that is of great consequence, with the exception perhaps of the Almudaina Arch to the south-west of the palace, and much of this is a reconstruction. However, it will interest dedicated map-readers to observe that the city's ring road, consisting of sections named variously as Avenida this and that, encloses the bulk of the older built-up area in a series of angles. This line defines the original outer fortifications. The seaward defences, too, have been almost entirely scrapped in a major scheme of land reclamation aimed at further protection against flooding, and as an extension of the port area. These works have created the Ronda Litoral which carries fast-moving traffic to seaward of the old quarter of the town, the cathedral and the Almudaina Palace to join, without interruption, the coastal trunk road leading west out of the city.

During the years when Majorca existed in isolation as a mere part of a Spanish province, lassitude set in. This was reflected particularly in Palma. The largest island of the Balearic group was far less affected by, and involved in, world affairs than Minorca, which was of considerable strategic importance to the warring European powers. Nevertheless, in spite of depression and poverty the eighteenth and nineteenth centuries had brought some improvement to Palma both in planning and in general smartening up. In fact, the concentration of the landed gentry in the metropolis, though it was at the expense of the countryside, caused the building and maintenance of a great many grand town houses whose architecture owed much to Italian taste and the Renaissance, and which are of inestimable value today.

In the same way that the bombing of cities in the Second World War in northern Europe created space for modern traffic-free development, the re-routing of the Riera presented the opportunity for reorganizing the medieval, haphazard pattern of the congested streets. The two new boulevards that were built were additionally provided with ornamental stonework, such as the fountain of Las Tortugas (the Tortoises) in what is now known as Plaza Pío XII, and a series of benches, as well as traffic islands with ample space for trees, shrubs and formal borders. El Borne was lit by gas as early as 1859, before the introduction of an electric power station in 1902, the year, incidentally, when the city's first hotel, the Gran, was opened. The hotel-building explosion was slow at the beginning, but was hastened somewhat by the inauguration of a fast steamer service to Barcelona in 1911, and – as a presage of the future – the first crossing of the channel by aeroplane from Barcelona in 1916.

THE OLD CITY

Though it is possible to become temporarily disorientated in Palma – usually because intriguing narrow streets tempt one to depart from a set course – the geography very soon becomes imprinted upon one's memory if one thinks in terms of boundaries. To begin with, there are the harbour installations to the south, alongside which the coast road pursues an uninterrupted course, overlooked by great buildings and, later, by grand hotels. The ancient town behind may be divided into two: known as the upper and lower. Reference to the map will show that these are contained by the tangential avenues created by the removal of the outer walls. The two sections of the town will then be seen to be separated by El Borne, which is a good example of traditional Spanish town planning with its trees and parterres and a double flow of traffic – not exclusively wheeled, because it is here that the evening *paseo*, or ritual walkabout, may be seen to advantage from pavement cafés and restaurants. El Borne continues north, becoming Calle San Jaime until, near the church of Santa Maddalena it meets Vía Roma, again with its central island, plane trees, flower stalls and ornamental shrubs. Incidentally, this thoroughfare's name is of recent origin, given to commemorate the island's allegiance to the Nationalist cause during the Spanish Civil War when Mussolini's air force was stationed near by. Two plaster statues of Romans stand guard at the south-eastern end. El Borne and Calle San Jaime meet at Plaza Pío XII roundabout, where the deeply arcaded Avenida Rey Jaime III (with banks, smart shops, and the Tourist Office) branches off westward, while in the opposite direction, by way of Avenida General Mola, one can reach the central Plaza Mayor by a flight of steps below the little-used Teatro Principal. The theatre backs on to this spacious pedestrian plaza, beneath which there is an equally roomy car park. From here onwards to the north-west and the south, the street patterns are irregular. Deep inside this quarter will be found the greatest number of the medieval churches and palaces which are such an important characteristic of this city. Though some sort of pattern radiating from Plaza Mayor may be discerned on the map, in practice this is difficult to follow. However, distances are not great, and no harm will come from blind wandering until some recognizable landmark is reached.

PRINCIPAL SIGHTS

Harbour

The bright, sun-drenched motorways and promenades bordering the sea are in direct contrast to the alleys of old Palma, though they show off to advantage the great buildings which overlook the harbour. The roads coming in from the east, from the direction of the airport and the mushroom growth of beaches such as El Arenal, pass little of distinction, so that for history, entertainment and scenery we should look westwards. Below the Almudaina Palace and the cathedral's terrace there is a park which has one corner given over to the armed forces directly in line with the mole and its Customs House (*Map* **47**). From this mole, not far from *La Lonja* and the *Consulado del Mar* — both trade-inspired — we come across groups of fishing vessels, with their nets and other tools of the trade spread out to dry or to be mended. This scene is always photogenic, though anyone in search of fresh fish must be up betimes, preferably between 6 and 7 a.m., when the boats come in to unload and disperse their many-hued catch to the markets.

The shoreline is broken by a second jetty, which forms one side of a basin for the Club Náutico (*Map* **26**); here there are also seafood bars and outdoor restaurants on the seaward side of the palm-shaded Paseo Sagrera.

The outfall of the occasionally torrential La Riera is immediately to the west, now that it has been safely contained within its embankments. Suburbia lies to the north, but the Santa Catalina district close to the shore is an old one, and well marked by the picturesque windmills of Es Jonquet which once provided the power for grinding wheat for the city. A few of these evocative old buildings have been preserved and contribute enormously to what even without them would be an arresting scene.

Beyond, continuing westward and then veering south, Paseo Marítimo continues for 3 km., past the Terreno district which has become an entertainment centre, for shopping, eating and drinking, and for night-life, with Plaza Gomila as its hub. In fact it is a sort of modernized Soho given over to junketings and holiday behaviour patterns. Its seaward boundary is an uninterrupted range of high-rise buildings, mostly hotels and apartment blocks, which cater for many different nationalities in and out of the usual summer season. At the back, and still dominating the scene, Bellver Castle stands on its pine-speckled hill.

The coast road leads on towards the Spanish naval station and to the docks, then to the harbour of Porto Pi (p. 195). This ceased to be of importance in the mid-fifteenth century, when trade came to be concentrated around La Lonja, necessitating the creation of more convenient harbour installations.

CATHEDRAL
(*Map* **43**.)
Palma's splendid cathedral, dedicated to the Blessed Virgin Mary, and known to Majorcans as La Seo, is one of the wonders of Gothic architecture, not only on account of its size and the beautiful golden sandstone from Santañy of which it is built, but also for its interior grace and lightness. These have been achieved by the provision of sturdy outer buttresses which take a great proportion of the weight off the pillars, so that these manage to be unusually slender as well as taller than average.

History
The origin of this cathedral goes back to the fateful September of 1229, when Jaime I's landing on the island might well have been turned to disaster by stormy weather (see History, p. 78). At that moment of crisis the King vowed that should his enterprise succeed he would raise a monument to Our Lady as a pledge that he would retain possession of a Christian kingdom which no previous Spanish sovereign had been able to hold. Following the success of the invasion and the overthrow of the Moors, he immediately assigned a corner of the Almudaina grounds for this purpose, so that foundations could be laid over the site of an existing mosque. This circumscription within what was then a walled city explains why the edifice is crowded so closely upon the palace. A beginning was made in the construction of the Chapel of the Holy Trinity, at the extreme east, and that work was sufficiently advanced for it to be consecrated in September 1269 by Palma's second bishop, in the presence of the King. Further work on the apse then had to be postponed pending the provision of embankments to seaward. These preliminaries were completed in 1327, making it possible for major work on the cathedral to be resumed, leading to the consecration of the high altar on October 1st, 1346. Work at this period was under the supervision of Jaime Mates, a Majorcan. From this time forward operations were hampered by

stop-go periods, owing to political uncertainty, wars and chronic shortages of funds; and sometimes architectural trial and error such as had beset some of the great Continental cathedrals, notably Beauvais, where collapses had occurred. The bays of the nave were not completed until the end of the sixteenth century, and it was another hundred years before the side chapels were added. After this, little remained to be done until the structure was shaken by earthquake in 1851, necessitating reinforcement of the west front. This resulted in the addition of two mock-Gothic turrets, which, unfortunately, obscured two rose windows designed to balance those at the east end. Alterations were made to the interior at the beginning of the present century, when Antonio Gaudí, an expert in the prevailing Catalan-Gothic revival, was commissioned to restore the cathedral to a more authentic Gothic appearance. He opened it up by fitting the choir stalls into the Chapel Royal, at the same time dispensing with the choir screens, which by their very definition had obscured one third of the cathedral, and the high altar, from the view of the congregation.

EXTERIOR

The best and indeed the only open viewpoint for the cathedral is from the south, or seaward side. Seen with a minimum of foreshortening, the proliferation of knobbly Gothic pinnacles at the apexes of the outer buttresses fits into a geometrical pattern, echoed by the similarly ornamented flying buttresses joining the roof high above the nave. Many of the tall, narrow window spaces between these buttresses are set at an angle, as in our modern Coventry cathedral, though in most cases these have been filled in with masonry, leaving the windows on a higher level to provide the interior with ample light.

The most important feature of this side of the cathedral is the ogival (or pointed) south entrance, known as the Portal del Mirador because it surveys the spread of Palma Bay. This imposing entrance was designed in 1389 by the sculptor Pedro Morey, who commissioned other artists to contribute to its carvings. The splendid Last Supper in the tympanum is by Jean de Valenciennes, while the surrounding decoration is attributed to Henri d'Allemand, and is typical of Flemish workmanship. The full-length statues of prophets and apostles in niches on either side of the doors are by Guillermo Sagrera, an important Majorcan sculptor who was in charge of work on the cathedral from 1420–47. It was originally intended that there should be fifty-five such statues, but only five were installed.

The Mirador entrance is seldom used. To enter the cathedral it is necessary to circle the west front by way of the pavement which separates it from the Almudaina Palace, passing a flight of steps at the top of which there is a plain memorial cross. Except for the carvings of the tympanum and the representation of the Virgin Mary, symbolically accompanied by sun and moon against a background of palm trees, the west front is disappointing, not only because of the difficulty of taking it all in without getting a crick in the neck, but also because it is apparent even to the inexpert eye that much of the decoration has suffered from the reconstruction which followed the nineteenth-century earthquake. The two flanking turrets, 62 metres in height, are an awkward addition to a façade in which everything but sculptural detail deserves to have been kept simple. The west door is used only on ceremonial occasions, public access being otherwise restricted to the Almoina portal.

This northern entrance is the work of Francisco Sagrera, son of Guillermo. The word *almoina* signifies almsgiving, and this door is so named because it led into a chapel used for that purpose. In the paved area outside, at one corner of the cathedral buildings, stands the square, solid bell-tower, 52 metres tall and one of the earliest and therefore typically Catalan features of the cathedral complex. It houses a set of nine bells, the oldest and heaviest named N'Eloi, which weighs 5,700 kg., is 2 metres in diameter, and was cast in 1389. When it was tolled in 1857 as a warning against impending storm its reverberations shattered much of the cathedral's stained glass. Sightseers are directed not through the Almoina gate but, by way of the entrance, to the Treasury, immediately to the west of the bell tower. Several rooms here are maintained as a museum, adjoining the cloisters.

Cathedral treasury
Hours 10.30–13.00; 16.00–17.30.
In addition to items which remain part of the living cathedral, many others of beauty and value are displayed in these rooms. They include thirteenth-century religious paintings of the Majorcan school, Flemish tapestries, bejewelled crucifixes, gold reliquaries fashioned from Inca treasure – which, as we all know and regret, was melted down by the conquistadors for shipment to Spain – together with ornate silver

candelabra, ancient manuscripts and books of plainsong; and much else besides.

Apart from this diversion, the first-time visitor to the cathedral would be well advised to make his way directly to the west end, where with his back to the great closed door, he may pretend that he has just stepped inside. This tactic guarantees maximum effect. The dimensions of the cathedral are astonishing. The space between this point and the high altar seems unbelievable in that the single-span vaulted roof is supported, as far as may be seen, only by fourteen octagonal columns of extreme slenderness. Their proportions, and the manner in which they branch out at a height of 21·5 metres to form the ribs of the roof invite comparison with an avenue of fronded palm trees. As a point of interest, Milan is the one Continental cathedral which possesses columns of a greater height.

Allied to the provision of maximum usable space, which has been described as the finest victory of mind over matter the Middle Ages ever achieved, there is the superlative lighting from the very high windows. But the most striking feature is the east rose window, which claims to be the largest in the world. The segments of its glass are red, blue, yellow, green and grey of singular purity, though of no great age. Another rose window lights the Chapel Royal, and there are two more in the apses of the north and south naves, as well as those two balancing, in the west wall.

To dwell on facts and figures: the cathedral is 121 metres long and 55 wide. The height of the central nave – nearly 44 metres – exceeds that of all but one of the great French cathedrals, namely Beauvais. The two lateral naves measure 29·40 metres in height, and the width of the central nave is more than half as much again as that of comparable medieval buildings. When looking upwards, it is of interest to be reminded that in the fourteenth century, when building funds were running low, the island's nobility paid for their individual coats of arms to be incorporated in the keystones of the vaulting, thus contributing to the cathedral's construction and at the same time ensuring their families a lasting memorial.

There are fourteen side chapels set in the north and south walls of the naves, in the spaces between the outer buttresses. That of Nuestra Señora de la Corona – third from the left when facing the Mirador entrance – contains relics brought from the monastery of Valldemosa after its dissolution in 1836; on the opposite side of the cathedral in the chapel of St Jerome there is the tomb of a grandee who fought in the Peninsular War and was a friend of the Duke of Wellington. The Iron Duke is portrayed standing in the background of the battle, but valiantly brandishing pennants. Two other chapels, dedicated respectively to Corpus Christi and St Peter, are at right-angles at the head of the north and south naves, level with the high altar. The sacristy is to the right of the chancel, while the chancel itself has now been extended into the Chapel Royal, to accommodate the high altar in its new open position arranged by Gaudí. The royal coats of arms are in evidence on either side, where Gaudí installed the 110 walnut choir stalls which were made in 1328 by Camprodon, the master woodworker and sculptor brought from Perpignan to work on the cathedral. He was assisted in his work by two Moors, who appear to have been involved, contrary to their hereditary faith, in making the intricate and beautiful carvings of animals and other figures on the arm rests. The altar, surmounted by Gaudí's unusual canopy, is marble and dates from the day of consecration in 1346. The chapel of the Trinity occupies the small space dictated by its apsoid form at the east end of the cathedral, and contains the tombs of Jaime II and III of Majorca. Though the practice has been discontinued, these were designed so that the remains they contained could be drawn out, as though from a filing cabinet, for inspection and veneration.

Other features of exceptional interest and beauty include the fifteenth-century tomb of Bishop Galiana in the Royal Chapel, the Baroque altarpiece and two pulpits or lecterns. Of these, that of the Gospels in Plateresque style was designed by Juan de Sales, an Aragonese sculptor, and incorporates scenes from the New Testament. Of special interest are the telamons (male counterparts of caryatids, those maidens who bear the weight of so many Greek buildings on their heads) − who in this instance carry much of the pulpits on their backs. Tapestries, paintings, tombs, church furniture, and a section of the original choir screen now set up near the Mirador exit deserve careful inspection.

Almudaina Palace
Map **39**.
There are several ways of reaching the Almudaina: from the direction of the old Portella quarter of the town, to the east, which means that both cathedral and palace are encountered rather too abruptly, and in

foreshortened perspective; by a flight of steps to the north leading from Calle Conquistador, and rounding the military headquarters; or, better still, from the terraced gardens known as S'Hort del Rei which have been fitted into the space to seaward which once formed the *ronda*, or outer perimeter of the fortress-palace. When approaching this way from the direction of Avenida Antonio Maura, which is an extension of El Borne, a pool of ornamental water acts as a reminder that in olden days the sea came inland as far as this, reaching the palace walls, and possibly enabling Arab sailing ships to discharge and take on cargo and passengers at what would have been the watergate of the palace, near where there is now a reconstruction of a wide-spanned Moorish arch. Steps lead from here to a higher terrace which runs under the lovely frontage of the building. Another flight of steps brings us to the foot of the plain wooden memorial cross and the pavement which separates the intricate west front of the cathedral from the more severe stone facing of the Almudaina. The first archway on the left is the one used by visitors; the further one is heavily guarded and out of bounds. Inside there is an office where tickets are issued for conducted tours. These set off at scheduled intervals, in the charge of a multi-lingual guide. Independent wanderings are prohibited.

HISTORY

Though it can be assumed that the Romans would not have ignored such a salient position overlooking the anchorage of Palma Bay, the Almudaina is known first as the fortress-cum-residence of the Moorish Walis who governed the island for more than six centuries. It consisted in their time of a complex of pavilions, buildings and service quarters dispersed in an area of some 20,000 square metres. At that time the sea came up to its southern walls. And though rather romantically we are inclined to refer to the present palace as Moorish, it was in fact almost completely reconstructed for the Majorcan kings soon after the Reconquest, after which it became the residence of Jaime II for the last twelve years of his life. It was taken over by the king of Aragon when Majorcan sovereignty was abolished, and this marked the beginning of many vicissitudes. After this time the whole palatial complex, once so richly endowed, was insufficiently used and suffered accordingly. Pedro IV of Aragon saw it as a safe place for housing prisoners, so as to remove that charge from the civic authorities. Dungeons, relics of the Moorish regime, are thought to exist beneath the King's Apartments, one part of the palace which is open to conducted parties. Later, Juan I gave house room to an alchemist in the hope that he would discover the secret of transmuting base metal into the gold which was in constant demand by the state. Brief visits were also made by Alfonso V, and then by the Emperor Charles V in 1541. More than three hundred years were to elapse before royalty in the person of Queen Isabella II again came to the island to take up brief residence. However, a range of grand rooms on the upper floor overlooking the harbour is presently maintained for the use of any visiting head of state – lately Generalísimo Franco, and now King Juan Carlos – while the very important and beautifully appointed State Apartments immediately below and the adjoining rooms known as the King's Apartments are open to the public. However, by far the largest proportion of the buildings is out of bounds; the Captain General of the Balearics occupies what were originally the Queen's Apartments, while a large portion of the palace is taken up by the Provincial Courts of Justice and Archives.

The architect to whom the work of reconstruction was entrusted was named Peter Selva, and it has been suggested that he was a native of this island, which would account for the 'Moorishness' of the overall design and some of its detail – a style in the midst of which he would have been nurtured – while concessions to Gothic taste would have been made for royalty accustomed to European courtly standards and the work of craftsmen of the first order. In pursuit of this policy, workmen and artists were brought to Majorca from the Continent, and were employed not only on the palace but on the cathedral and city churches – working, in fact, according to a system of priorities based upon available funds and the time factor.

Very few relics of the Moorish era have survived, and even these are in doubt, though the decorative ceiling of the loggia to the right immediately inside the courtyard has the best credentials. It has been claimed that two of the square towers flanking the entrances are original. But what look most Moorish of all, the slender arcades on the first floor overlooking the sea, besides being one of the most effective features of the place, certainly were part of the restoration, and could even be replacements for later and narrower Gothic fenestration.

In any case, Jaime II was a man of taste and dignity who knew how royalty should live, so that no expense was spared in the interests of display, comfort or pleasure. He was to be provided not only with a roof garden and menagerie, but also with an enviably sophisticated plumbing system. Peter Selva, who was also the designer of Bellver Castle – a completely different architectural concept – was assisted in the Almudaina by Francisco Campredon, the master metal worker from Perpignan to whom is attributed the angel which, rather like a weathercock, surmounts the central tower once known as the Tower of Homage. This was damaged by earthquake and lightning in the eighteenth century, after which it was considerably lowered for safety's sake.

The State Apartments
Hours 09·00–13·00; 16·00–18·00.

These rooms are intercommunicating, and though the original main reception hall has been subdivided into three, all are spacious, with flagged floors and vaulted ceilings, or tessellated with painted rafters. Each room has been provided with a well-chosen complement of furniture, correct in period though not from the original palace collection. Many of the Flemish tapestries and Spanish paintings depict classical battle scenes, and there are also portraits of the Spanish kings, which can be identified with entries on a fascinating and complex family tree demonstrating the lineage of the ruling house. The figures of two knights in contemporary armour stand guard on either side of the throne and its resplendent royal coat of arms. The adjoining King's Apartments are equally carefully furnished, and decorated with restraint.

Chapel of Santa Ana

There remains to be seen the beautiful Gothic chapel of Santa Ana, on the west side of the courtyard, beyond the Tower of Homage and the stairway leading up to the Queen's Apartments where the Captain General resides. This delightful little chapel, which has been well restored, is similar in design to the chapel of the Holy Cross in Perpignan. Though the entrance is Romanesque, the interior with its single nave is pure Gothic. Sculptured keystones are one of many fine features. The fourteenth-century reredos behind the main altar is the work of one Rafael Moger, and its side panels portray St George and St Vidal, a Catalan saint. The central panel is modern. A side chapel enshrines the remains of St Praxedes, a local saint martyred when, in spite of their acceptance as Mozarabs, the Christian population of

Palma suffered intense persecution towards the end of the period of Moorish rule.

Chapel of San Jaime

On the further side of the small Queen's Court there is another chapel, dedicated to St James and contemporary with Santa Ana's chapel, where it is known that Christian services were celebrated early in the fourteenth century.

La Lonja
Map **32**

The coastal road takes the form of an elegant boulevard, the Paseo Sagrera, west of the Almudaina Palace, on the further side of the extension to El Borne. This drive is bordered on one side by harbour installations and on the other by buildings of exceptional grace, and has, for good measure, a lovely shady central island as promenade. La Lonja is the first important building to landward.

History

The need for the equivalent of a chamber of commerce was recognized by Jaime I, and ground for that purpose was allocated as early as 1293. However, the site, which measures 40 metres by 28, was left unfilled until, in 1426, building began to go ahead in the creation of a multi-purpose centre for commercial transactions involving the marketing and shipping of commodities, all under the aegis of a tribunal qualified to settle whatever differences might arise. The initial architectural work was entrusted to Guillermo Sagrera, one of the brothers after whom the promenade was named, and who was at that time the master architect in charge of the building of the cathedral. He estimated that his new commission would take fifteen years to complete. Unfortunately, the expense of material and wages proved so heavy that, in spite of their wealth, the foreign merchants of Palma who had commissioned the project fell behind in their payments, and Sagrera found himself funding much of the work, and was eventually forced to sue for reimbursement. This combination of delay and frustration explains why in 1448 he obeyed with alacrity the command of King Alfonso of Aragon that he remove himself to Naples, there to employ his talents upon the Castelnuovo.

The work of finishing La Lonja devolved upon Guillermo's brother Miguel, who made himself responsible for much of its decoration.

The building, in all its beauty, was finished about 1456, not only its Gothic design but its detail being influenced by the Italian art of the Renaissance. Trading was immediately transferred from an adjacent small building, previously run by Genoese merchants, which was then converted and consecrated as the chapel of St George. At the same time, harbour works in the vicinity were enlarged, so that the less convenient facilities at Porto Pi to the west fell into disuse.

Following such rich and important beginnings, it is sad to realize that this gem of a building should later have deteriorated to match the almost total rundown of trade which was to beggar Majorca after the opening up of new sailing routes and creation of other allegiances. By 1809 it had sunk to being no more than a warehouse for the storage of corn. But at present, though there is no prospect of a return to its original function, the Lonja is securely maintained as the Provincial Arts Museum.

Provincial Arts Museum
Hours 10·00–12·00; 15·00–17·00.
This houses a collection of modern Majorcan paintings, together with fifteenth- and sixteenth-century altar pieces salvaged from country churches, and a few remains from the Roman town of Pollentia.

Exterior
The elegant façade, built of stone quarried at Santañy, is pierced by narrow windows and adorned with decorative and unmilitary battlements used in the Gothic tradition in secular building; it is punctuated by turrets and gargoyles, and given particular shape by four more substantial octagonal towers, one at each corner, which contain spiral staircases leading to the roof. The elaborate and beautifully carved entrance is from a small plaza at the building's eastern side, and despite this orientation strangers might well jump to the conclusion that this is a church.

Interior
The interior is simple in that it consists of a single hall divided into two naves of equal size and height by two rows of spiral stone columns – three to each line – of supremely delicate workmanship. Their nine arches spring outward from the columns without benefit of any load-bearing capital. These delicate, fluted columns and their branches are an obvious evocation of the palm tree, as a symbol of the

wealth and luxuriance of Palma's golden age. Light filters through carved Gothic windows.

Consulado del Mar
Map **29**.
A short distance to the west of La Lonja, and separated only by a small garden which contains a fountain and a reconstruction made from the original masonry of the sea gate of the port, we next come to the fine seventeenth-century building which functioned as the Admiralty Court. The façade is rather more elaborate than that of La Lonja, which it complements despite the difference in period. It has a loggia consisting of five arches on rounded pillars, and a balustrade overlooking the comings and goings to seaward. The fine coffered ceiling of the interior is perhaps the building's next most attractive architectural feature. Thorough restoration – some experts say too thorough – was undertaken in 1950.

MARITIME MUSEUM
Hours 10·00–13·00; 16·00–19·00.
Nowadays the Consulado del Mar houses the Maritime Museum, rather like a mini-Greenwich. It has on display navigational instruments and naval weaponry, charts, paintings of sailing ships and portraits of their masters, doing its best to perpetuate the memory of the splendid era when Palma was a power in the Mediterranean and the birthplace of some of the finest cartographers the world has ever seen.

Monastery and Church of San Francisco
Map **36**.
Except for its size, this most beautiful and celebrated of Palma's churches rivals even the cathedral, and should be placed high on the list of city sightseeing. The church and monastery are in the centre of the old quarter, a few blocks east of the Casa Consistorial and the church of Santa Eulalia.

HISTORY
According to the custom of the period, Franciscan friars accompanied Jaime I and his nobles on the expedition which resulted in the taking of Palma on the last day of December, 1229. Ancient documents record that three years later the brotherhood was granted land lying

outside the city walls, but that in 1238 they removed themselves to a more central site hitherto occupied by a Moorish soap factory. This was converted into church and monastery in time for consecration in 1244 by Ramón de Torrella, the first bishop of Majorca. Some rather insignificant remains of this first foundation are incorporated in what subsequently became the Military Hospital, not far from the Plaza España. The original buildings were made over to the nuns of Santa Margarita in 1279 in exchange for a house already in the ownership of the convent. When it was then proved that there was not enough scope for the growing Franciscan community, they were given a larger piece of ground, and the foundations of the present church were laid by Jaime II in 1281. Building began in 1286, when the Franciscans, despite their rule of poverty, and supposedly inspired by the activities of the rival Dominican order, embarked upon an ambitious architectural project, at that time out of all proportion to the needs of Palma's citizens. Fortuitously, it was at this time, about 1300, that the heir to the throne, Prince Jaime, surrendered his rights to the succession in favour of joining the Franciscan order, where he adopted the sonorous title of Fray Jaime de Mallorca. As a direct result, the concerns of the friars came more than ever under the patronage of his father.

Mass was first said in the new church in the autumn of 1317. At that date the roof was of wood, but after it had been heightened, enlarged and reconstructed in stone in the Gothic style, the church was reconsecrated in 1385. Some of the most famous master builders and stone workers of the time, and of succeeding centuries, were employed when further improvements and additions were undertaken, including the provision of chapels in the apse. These, together with the already existing side chapels tucked in between the buttresses, number twenty-three. Incidentally, it is in these chapels that a great many of the art treasures of the church – paintings, murals and sculptures representing the work of Majorcan artists – are to be found.

A thunderbolt demolished part of the south side of the church in 1480, and lightning also struck the west front and inflicted irreparable damage on two of the side chapels, as well as the choir gallery, so that these were out of commission until after 1621, when a major rebuilding scheme got under way. The nave was restored, but the choir was never returned to its original position, and the ossuary to which the mortal remains of the friars were consigned was built over as the result of a reduction in the ground plan. The lovely west front with its Baroque entrance, which was finally completed by Francisco Herrera, remains as it was in those days. The present nave measures 74 by 14 metres, and is more than 25 metres in height.

In the meantime the church and its community continued to function, while both the body of the church and its cloisters served as a burial place for the Majorcan nobility, and accordingly yielded substantial material benefit to the community. The memorials and tombstones that still exist, in stone and recorded in the archives, read like an edition of Debrett which was kept up to date until the early nineteenth century, when such interments were forbidden by law.

In 1490 the church of St Francis experienced the culmination of a bitter feud between two of Palma's ruling families, the Armadans and the Espanyols. So much blood was shed in the precincts that the church had to be closed pending reconsecration.

Throughout the centuries the church and monastery have been associated with famous and learned men of the Franciscan order, not least the Blessed Ramón Llull, whose tomb is one of the most important monuments, and Fray Junípero Serra, who was born in the country town of Petra and joined the order in 1730. He it was who sailed to the New World, where in course of time he was instrumental in founding the state of California and its early missions, and endowed the city of San Francisco with its name.

It must be remembered that the religious orders on the island were disbanded in the nineteenth century. The Franciscans were granted no grace or exemption, and the church and monastic buildings began to decay following occupation by various local government departments and scholastic establishments. In fact, bad conditions forced many of these bodies to vacate the premises, and portions were sold off to private persons. The Treasury was in use in 1885 as a prison. Not until 1906 was a college reassembled in the range of buildings on one side of the cloisters, and then, in the same year, the whole complex was at last returned to the Third Order of St Francis. It has since been declared a national monument, though it remains in the use and custody of the friars.

Exterior

The 'new' façade of the church, built in 1621, is particularly effective, with its plain dressed stone and the glorious doorway contributed by Herrera some seventy years later. It is pierced by a huge recessed rose

window, but the doorway is what takes the eye, enshrining as it does
the Blessed Virgin in Triumph, with the arch over her head supported
by two somewhat Grecian caryatids. Flanking her we can identify
Ramón Llull by the book in his hand, and on the opposite side Duns
Scotus, who too was a Franciscan. The space between the top of the
rounded arch and the rose window is occupied by St George and a
dying dragon, near which the date, 1700, is incised. St Francis and St
Dominic appear below, one reading, and the other accompanied by
his dog. The façade is crowned by a shallow tympanum, with a
balcony pierced by seven arches. These are matched by openings in
the flanking turrets added in 1733, in which are mounted badly
weathered terracotta statues of St Francis and St Dominic, the
founders of the two great orders of mendicant friars.

Whilst on the subject of the church's exterior, it is worth
mentioning that the view of its high Gothic western end is worth
seeking out by way of the Calle Troncoso. This aspect gives a glimpse
of the tall bell tower – more like a minaret with its cupola and
balcony, which seems to invite the *muezzin* and a call of the faithful to
prayer.

For the most part, the alterations undertaken from the end of the
seventeenth century were to the interior of the church, though it is
worth remarking that many of the most recent were to counteract
enormities of taste perpetrated in the past. As recently as 1950 a mass
of limestone plaster was scraped away to expose the old stonework.
Attention was also given to fenestration, resulting in the provision of
twenty-seven new windows, which transformed the appearance of
the nave, providing it with light entirely in keeping with the original
Gothic design. These were ceremonially blessed in 1960.

INTERIOR
The interior of the church demonstrates to a large extent what the
official booklet calls the 'delirium of Baroque', which though contrary
to the rules of simplicity and poverty observed by St Francis, gives
pleasure to most visitors. Unfortunately a general masking of the
stonework by rather casually imposed wood carvings in 1732, and the
addition of a red line of local marble around the walls, cannot be said
to be an improvement, however acceptable may be the reinstatement
of the choir to a position flanking the apse. The fifteenth-century choir
stalls, with their carved armrests, all bear the escutcheons of the

nobility – which may be taken as evidence of the close association of the early settlers and potential merchant princes with the various stages of the church's maintenance and development.

But this church is so crammed full of works of art and matters of interest that visitors would be well advised to buy the little handbook, translated into French and German as well as English, that is on sale at a small bookstall in the cloisters. Of all that is to be seen, the high altar is the most important. It is constructed in three tiers, the lowest being a priceless gold tabernacle with revolving doors. This is flanked by representations of Ramón Llull and San Domingo in niches. The upper sections contain sculptural groupings of saints executed in a wealth of decorative stucco, and culminating in a splendid St George in the act of slaying the dragon. The paintings behind the high altar were commissioned in 1635. The one in the centre is of topographical interest in that it depicts the Bay of Palma stretching out at the feet of the Madonna.

The next most important feature, since his spiritual presence seems to pervade all parts of the church, must be the funerary monument of the Blessed Ramón Llull. This was the concept of a member of the order who died in 1460, and also does much to perpetuate the memory of one of the most important Majorcans who ever lived. The effigy lies horizontally, facing outwards (rather precariously) above a line of pointed Gothic niches that were intended to contain allegorical figures of Grammar, Logic, Rhetoric, Arithmetic, Music, Geometry and Astronomy, the seven fields of learning of that great medieval scholar. In the event the niches were never filled, and certain other aspects of the monument remain unfinished. However, Ramón Llull's mortal remains in the sacristy miraculously escaped destruction by the fire which destroyed those of Fray Jaime, and they were subsequently taken from their vulnerable wooden coffin and transferred to a stone urn; this was cached beneath the pulpit until in 1492 the remains were transferred to an alabaster urn designed a few years earlier by Francisco Sagrera. This urn is now mounted on a plinth upon which the royal arms, those of the Llull family and an inverted crescent (to signify Ramón Llull's missions to the Muslims of North Africa) are emblazoned. For many centuries sporadic efforts have been made to forward the canonization of the great man, but so far these have met with about as much success as the schemes to complete his shrine. The rumour is that the processes towards canonization were countered by the Dominicans, who had failed to enlist Llull into their own order. Blessed he must be, however, in more than one sense.

CLOISTERS

The cloisters are another of the notable features of the foundation, having a prominent and long-standing function as an oasis of the peace and calm which is so much part of the daily life of members of the Franciscan order. They are reached through a side door leading out of the church on its right or south-east side, where a verger levies a small fee for the privilege of visiting them. It is on record that the layout of these cloisters was planned in 1279, though building did not begin until about 1314, by which time noblemen who claimed the privilege of burial there were already installed with their memorial tablets in what was to become one side of this lovely quadrangle.

Here again is Gothic at its best: a square of delicate filigree in stone forming an arcade which contains a deep, shaded ambulatory, and encloses a spacious garden with palm trees, pines and a well-head erected in 1652. A closer look will show that though three sides of the cloisters are uniform, the north side, which is the oldest, has alternate columns of different thicknesses, with similar variation in the decoration of their capitals. These pillars support another tier, forming a balcony which is roofed with tiles. From this level a good but foreshortened view of the bell tower can be obtained. The tower was heightened sometime after its erection in 1734, the idea being to increase its range of sound. The roof of the church is also tiled, though it is difficult to see from ground level. The west side of the cloisters was not completed until about two centuries later than the others, and it is noticeable that the octagonal columns here are rather heavier and less graceful than the earlier ones.

A seminary abuts one side of the cloisters. This was inaugurated and blessed by Cardinal Spellman of New York in 1952. There is also a small but interesting museum at first floor level, integrated in the church itself, but accessible by a staircase leading up from the cloisters. Here there are to be seen works of art for which there was no room in the body of the church, nor in the Treasury attached to it.

Bellver Castle

Bus To the main entrances from Plaza de la Reina, at southern end of El Borne. The Castle of Bellver – translated as 'Beautiful View' – is so much an integral part of Palma's defence system that in spite of being about 3 km. south-west of the city centre, and less from the sea, it has an immediate claim on visitors. Also, as its name suggests, it presents a bird's-eye view of the capital and its relation to the geography of Majorca. The ascent to the castle may be made either from the Plaza Gomila in the Terreno district, on the Calle Calvo Sotelo, or more circuitously, by the Calle Bosque, off the same road, but nearer Palma.

The 140-metre hill upon which the castle stands is a public park, scattered with pines, oleanders and natural vegetation. But since the immediate approach by about 1 km. of road or path is steep, and because public transport passes the park by, visitors who do not wish to walk far are recommended, especially in hot weather, to go by car, taxi or coach. The descent is quite another matter, by twisting paths which keep clear of the motor road.

History

Similar to many other major architectural works on the island, this castle was built by the second king of Majorca, who commissioned his trusty architect, Peter Selva, for the task, which was begun in 1309. The result is something totally different from the Almudaina Palace, for which Selva was also responsible, in that it has no Moorish connotations at all. In fact the plan of Bellver owes its inspiration to certain Catalan palaces, such as Perpignan, and similarly has been described as a perfect example of Mediterranean military Gothic. The circular design indeed is one foreign to Spain, and another rare feature is that the military and residential quarters incorporated within the castle walls are separate. This is one of the best preserved castles of its period.

The residential arrangement was important, since the stronghold was designed to be a summer residence to which royalty could easily repair to benefit from an open situation and cooling breezes. In fact, the asthmatic King Sancho took to using it in 1314 before it was properly ready. But very soon, as well as having an obvious value as a lookout post and stronghold, it came to be used for the housing of political prisoners and, later, ordinary criminals. Among the first to be incarcerated were members of the family of Jaime III, following his death in the battle of Lluchmayor in 1349. It also doubled as a place of refuge, most notably when, in 1391, it was occupied by Jews escaping from massacre in the Palma ghetto. It was to accommodate royalty once more in 1395, when King Juan of Aragon fled to the island with his queen to avoid the pestilence that raged at that time in Catalonia.

In 1408 the Carthusian prior to Valldemosa was appointed warden, and his successors remained in charge until 1717, when they were replaced by a governor appointed by the Crown. The castle and its park are now the property of the municipality of Palma.

Though seemingly impregnable, Bellver was sacked in the sixteenth century – not by the foreign invaders against whom it was built but in the course of the peasant revolt. During the War of Independence (1808–13) a number of French officers taken prisoners of war were transported to Majorca following the battle of Bailén, and though conditions at Bellver were deplorable it is known that the other ranks who were condemned to imprisonment on the island of Cabrera or in the hulks of Cadiz fared far worse. All the same, graffiti on the dungeon walls – names and initials and the odd cry of despair – paint a melancholy picture. The survivors were not repatriated until 1814. Two distinguished men incarcerated in Bellver deserve special mention. The first, the noble Austrian statesman, reformer and writer, Gaspar Melchior de Jovellanos, was exiled to Majorca in 1801 by Queen Maria Luisa of Parma, the notorious consort of Charles IV. He had been kept in custody at Valldemosa, but was moved to Bellver, where he managed to continue with his writings. A memorial plaque has been set into the wall of the little room where he worked. Then, perhaps more memorably from the British point of view, it was at Bellver that General Luís de Lacy was executed. Though born in Andalusia this soldier was a scion of the Irish rebel aristocrats, romantically known as the Wild Geese, who fled (or flew) from their native land to escape British vengeance. De Lacy fought for Napoleon until the war was directed against Spain. Thereafter he allied himself with the Duke of Wellington, himself an Irishman. Subsequently, after Napoleon had recognized the Bourbon Ferdinand VII as King of Spain the general was regarded as a potential menace, and was consigned to Bellver, where in 1817 he was executed by firing squad. A tablet near the entrance to the castle marks the spot. During the later nineteenth and the twentieth centuries, Bellver has been visited by royalty on the occasion of their stays on the island, though it has not served even as a temporary residence.

STRUCTURE

The central and main portion of the castle rises from quadrifoil fortifications built into the rock at the summit of the hill, and was provided with a dry moat. The inner castle is circular, equipped with four towers at cardinal points, three of them uniform, and the fourth and largest – known as the Tower of Homage – standing a short distance apart, and accessible by two arched bridges. This portion of the castle housed the garrison and the prison quarters – the lowest stage of which possessed no windows or doorways, but was serviced rudimentarily by a hole in its ceiling. Hence it is known as La Olla, or 'The Pot'. This and the other three towers, rounded on their outer sides, are completely functional and designed to provide fire power in every direction.

The palatial part of the castle is its core. The large, completely circular courtyard is open to the sky, and surrounded by two tiers of inward-facing arcades. The arches at ground level are rounded and Romanesque, and formed by sturdy pillars, while immediately above them there is a second circle of delicately pointed and interlacing stonework forming a shallower arcade. All the rooms lead directly from one or other of these two corridors. The largest halls are situated on the ground floor, while the private rooms occupied by royalty are on the upper level. At intervals, and by means of the towers set into the outer walls there is access to the roof terrace with its battlements, again uninterruptedly circular. Not only does this provide an unrivalled view far into the distance on all sides, but also an enthralling picture of the castle's design. One practical feature of the circular layout, which is aesthetically so satisfying, is that it was designed so that every drop of rainwater could be channelled inwards for storage in a huge central cistern. Without this provision the building would have been valueless as a fortress.

Besides their accessibility from the internally-facing open corridors, all the vaulted chambers communicate with each other, except where impeded by the stairs. There are very few outward-facing windows in the walls, and where these exist they are no more than slits, so that light comes mainly from the central courtyard which catches the sun at all hours of the day, and at the same time lies partially in shade, much in the same way as a bullring does.

Some of the castle's rooms, including the chapel, now serve as an archaeological museum, and contain, along with other exhibits, Roman mosaics from Alcudia, the site of Roman Pollentia. The Roman statues in the courtyard have been brought here from Raxa, where they formed part of the collection of Italian art made by Cardinal Despuig in Italy. But perhaps the most interesting feature here, since it evokes the medieval domestic way of life, is the kitchen, with its central great fireplace and chimney with four flues, enormous cooking pots and other utensils to match.

OTHER CHURCHES AND CONVENTS

Unplanned wanderings through the city's narrow streets and alleys are likely to reveal more churches than would be thought possible within such a circumscribed area. Any difficulty in seeing them stems from that same congestion: with very few exceptions an unobstructed view even of their façades – often flush with the street, and not necessarily definitively oriented – or of their belfries, is hard to come by. But nearly all these churches and convents are beautiful and interesting in their own right, as well as being an illustration of Palma's history, while the best of them merit deliberate searching out. Others are worth something more than a passing appraisal and some slight effort to place them within their historical context. Incidentally, the word most generally used for male monastic foundations, is more likely to be *convento* than *monasterio*.

At the time of the Reconquest of the island, all over the continent of Europe the sturdy Romanesque style of ecclesiastical architecture was giving way to the more elaborate and pointed Gothic, though the timing of the transition varied from country to country. Generally the Gothic style lasted at least until the fifteenth century. Where the Balearics were concerned, perhaps because they were off the map, it prevailed for some two further centuries before the influence of the Baroque began to be felt.

When Jaime I arrived in Majorca, one of his first considerations was to begin work on the cathedral which he had pledged to build in thanksgiving for divine assistance during his landings. The creation of lesser city churches was also in his mind, but had to be deferred. Meanwhile services for the Christian community could be celebrated in converted mosques. A massive programme of church building was not in fact initiated until well into the reigns of Jaime II and Sancho. The style of these new churches came to be known as Catalan-Gothic, because they owed not only their overall design but also their detail to foreign craftsmen imported from the court at Perpignan and further afield; some such were the Lombard stone workers of the fifteenth century, who played a decisive part in realizing the pointed Gothic arches and vaulted ceilings traditional to France and Catalonia. The cathedral is of course the supreme example, though others such as the churches of San Francisco, Santa Eulalia, Santa Cruz and Santa Margarita immediately spring to mind.

But not all of these are of one piece or period, and certainly not in their outward appearance. When fashion finally changed, and Gothic fell into disfavour to be replaced by Baroque exuberance, major rebuilding was not always deemed necessary. A transformation could be effected by the expedient of covering over the external brick or stonework of a façade and superimposing a wealth of ornamentation, frequently expressed in the form of a new portal. This became general practice – and can be seen to advantage in the churches of San Francisco and San Jaime. However, in special cases new churches came to be built in what was known as Balearic Baroque, to satisfy the newly acquired taste of patrons and subscribers who now, instead of being members of the court following, were for the most part prosperous noblemen and merchants conversant with Italy and the Renaissance. The form of these purely Baroque churches was distinct from what had gone before; it was usually rectangular with the nave ending in a single apse which could be wide enough to house as many as five side chapels, or which alternatively devoted its space to forming the background for a splendid high altar, as in the church of San Miguel. Besides ranges of side chapels on both sides of the nave, there was frequently a larger communion chapel, covered with a dome and lighted by its lantern – all contained by an outer cube of masonry. There could also be screened and balustraded galleries over the side chapels, and an open gallery of greater importance at the west end. The ceilings were barrel-vaulted and often painted, while profuse decoration in the form of painted and gilded plaster and woodwork incorporated heavenly figures, fruit and garlands of flowers. Montesión and Nuestra Señora del Socorro are instances.

Church of Santa Eulalia
Plaza Santa Eulalia; Map **25**.
This, the largest of the city churches, with the exception of course of the cathedral, was the first to be built after the entry of Jaime I into Palma in 1229, on the site of what until that date had been a mosque. Except for modern restoration work, mainly to the façade, and the addition of the belfry in 1894, the church is very much of a piece, the reason being that it was completed within the space of twenty-five years in the middle of the thirteenth century, and therefore escaped the stop-go phases of construction characteristic of later times.

The distinctive feature is its great size, 57 metres by 27, enclosing a nave with only two aisles and no transept, that is, with its roof extending unbroken over the entire ground plan. The feeling of space and lightness this concept provides is furthered by the fact that, rather unusually, not all the Gothic windows, set high on either side, have been blocked by masonry. The Gothic altar screen in the first chapel to the right is of special interest, while the ornate rococo high altar cannot possibly be disregarded.

Because of its very early foundation, this church has witnessed a great many historic and ceremonial gatherings from the time of Jaime II onwards. In 1435 it was the building selected for the mass 'conversion' ceremony and baptism of the Jews of the city. It had so happened that during Easter week the Jewish community of the time was accused of conducting a sacrilegious mock Crucifixion. For this they were summarily condemned to death at the stake. It was then ordained that the less painful ordeal by hanging could be bartered for if the Jews professed conversion and submitted to baptism. Clemency was thereafter extended to selected apostates, with the result that the community was not totally annihilated, though their synagogues were closed and their possessions sequestrated. Those who survived came to be known as Chuetas or Xuetas, and though they and their descendants continued to profess the Christian faith, it is known that many of them observed their traditional religion in secret. Nowadays, though staunch Christians, this minority remains somewhat apart from the other citizens of Palma, and have their own guild.

More in the field of gossip columnists is the story of how Ramón Llull, who has left his mark on many other parts of Majorca and its capital, in his profligate days pursued a married lady upon whom he had designs – one Ambrosia de Castillo – by riding his horse into the church when she was at her devotions. Unable otherwise to discourage him, the lady allowed her admirer to follow her home, where she bared her bosom to his view – those breasts which he had recently and so impudently praised in lyric terms. To his horror he now saw that they were riddled with malignant growths. This traumatic experience is reputed to have been the turning point in Ramón Llull's career, for soon afterwards he set his feet on a pilgrim's way which was to lead him through a lifetime of scholarly and practical devotion to the conversion to Christianity of the Muslims of North Africa.

Montesión Church
Calle Montesión; Map **49**.

As a change from Gothic architecture, but pursuing a train of thought on the subject of the Chuetas, those born survivors, we come to Montesión church, whose name is an obvious translation of Mount Zion. This shares the honour with Nuestra Señora del Socorro of being one of the finest Baroque churches in the city. Because it was built on the site of the synagogue that was destroyed in 1435, at the time of their mass conversion to Christianity, this has long been accepted as the place of worship for Palma's Chueta community.

This Jesuit church was begun in 1571, though not completed until 1683, when its richly sculptured façade and portal with spiral Solomonic pillars were added. The façade incorporates statues of Saints Ignatius Loyola and Francis Xavier, the two most famous founders of the Jesuit order, supporting, on either side, the central figure of the Virgin Mary against an intricate scroll pattern.

Adjacent to the church there is a school run by the Jesuits, based upon a reading room which existed as early as 1485, and which was converted to its present use in 1561. The courtyard contains a statue of a teacher from Valencia, Alonso Rodriguez, who was canonized in 1888 on the grounds of his sanctity and numerous good works. The cell he occupied, to the left of the entrace, has been turned into a communion chapel, and contains a wax effigy of the saint as well as his mortal remains.

The interior of the church itself is lit by elegant Renaissance windows above the balustraded and screened galleries. In the tradition of the Baroque period, the ceiling is barrel-vaulted and painted, while great use is made throughout of gilded woodwork and stucco. The altarpiece in one of the side chapels is considered to be one of the finest examples of Majorcan religious art.

Church of Nuestra Señora del Socorro
(Our Lady of Perpetual Succour); *Plaza Buen Consejo*; *Map* **37**.

Though roughly contemporary with the Church of Montesión, this church of Augustinian foundation is simpler, though it, too, has rounded arches forming side chapels, with balustraded galleries above. The most important side chapel is dedicated to San Nicolás de Tolentino; simplicity, however, ends with the cupola, which is supported upon arches and decorated with heavenly figures disporting themselves amidst luxuriant vegetation. The artist responsible was Francisco Herrera, who learned his trade in Rome and worked in Minorca between 1680 and 1690, before being summoned to Majorca to complete the façade of the church of San Francisco – whereupon he also decorated this chapel in a spirit of fantasy which, in effect, does little to detract from its originator's religious intention.

Church of Santa Cruz
(The Holy Cross); *Calle Santa Cruz*; *Map* **19**.
Once again this church is in the Catalan-Gothic tradition of architecture, and is easy to identify by its site on rising ground slightly inland between the Consulado del Mar and the re-routed Riera torrent. It is both apparent and well-documented that Santa Cruz was built in the fifteenth and sixteenth centuries from stone taken from the quarry drawn upon for Bellver Castle by Peter Selva. The dimensions of the single nave are imposing, and the altars resplendent with gilt. There are pictures, too, of saints painted by the Majorcan school of the late fifteenth century.

Much of the exterior, including that of the apse, is plain. This gives the church a fortress-like appearance which is enhanced by its square belfry and unusual pyramid roof. The high altar is at the west end of the church. It is from this point that we are led to an even more rare feature.

Chapel of San Lorenzo is situated immediately below the high altar. Except that it possesses a separate entrance and staircase leading down from Calle San Lorenzo, this might be taken for the crypt of Santa Cruz which happens to be rather later in date. Both, however, are under the ministry of one parish priest. While Santa Cruz is Catalan-Gothic, San Lorenzo is in the purer Gothic style and one of the first of such to be built in Palma under the patronage and direct supervision of the later Majorcan kings. It is unique in having survived unaltered. The characteristic stone roof and pillars are in scale with the building's small dimensions, and light is provided by equally small windows piercing the stonework of the apse and side chapels situated immediately above it.

Church of San Jaime
Calle San Jaime; *Map* **12**.
This single-naved church, founded by the early Majorcan kings, was

begun in the fourteenth century, but has patently been considerably altered, redecorated and embellished right up to the nineteenth – the most obvious change being the transformation of the façade from Gothic to Baroque, which occured in 1776. The figure of the patron saint, sporting the familiar emblem of the scallop shell of the pilgrim, is set above its portal.

Church of San Miguel
Calle de San Miguel; Map **13**.
Though this site, where a mosque stood until that moment, was consecrated on the very day of the capture of the city, so that a thanksgiving service could be held in the presence of the king, and though the work of reconstruction was well under way early in the fourteenth century, the belfry is the only part to survive from that early period. However, nothing could be a better reminder of victory than the beautiful painted statue of Our Lady of Health which accompanied Jaime I on board his flagship, and was presented to the church as part of the first consecration ceremony. It is in the chapel to the right of the nave, and steps to the foot of the dais upon which it is set are provided for the convenience of devotees.

Convent church of Santa Catalina
on east side of Calle de San Miguel; Map **5**.
This is yet another church founded by Jaime II, but it is one of the conventual properties whose future was in jeopardy after the closure of the monasteries in the nineteenth century – a period as cataclysmic as Henry VIII's dissolution of the monasteries in England some centuries earlier. Demolition was then on the cards, while evacuation and decay were inescapable. In this case, however, the building was restored in 1949 and declared a national monument. One special feature is the tomb of a Catalan nobleman who with thirty knights and three hundred men-at-arms landed on the island in September 1229 with his sovereign.

Church of the Templars
off east end of Calle del Sol; Map **46**.
The Knights Templar who participated in Jaime I's crusading expedition were granted land in the south-eastern corner of the city. However, that order of chivalry was dispossessed early in the succeeding century, following scandals which shook the political,

martial and ecclesiastical world. Their church, part of a larger complex of religious buildings, is now occupied by a charitable institution. The entrance and two side chapels survive in their pure Gothic style. Most of the early church, however, has been demolished or restored to the point of reconstruction. This is a great pity, since this was one of the few city churches executed in Romanesque style. Only a few carvings and the rounded arches of some of the side chapels echo the period.

Former Convent of San Antonio
Calle de San Miguel; Map **11**.
Some effort should be made to gain admission to this elliptical eighteenth-century chapel with its curved cloisters, almost opposite the church of San Miguel. It is a rare sight with its Florentine stylishness and its frescoes, which are unique in this part of the world. The custodian may be found in the vestry of San Miguel, and should unlock the door.

Church of the Convent of Santa Magdalena
at north end of Calle San Jaime; Map **7**.
The eighteenth-century church, built on ancient foundations, is distinguished by its lofty cupola. Here is preserved, in a crystal urn, the incorrupt body of Santa Catalina Tomás, the peasant girl from the mountains who joined this order of nuns in the sixteenth century. To the left of the entrance there is a small chapel fitted with a grille, through which the laity were allowed to communicate with the nuns.

Convent church of the Conception
north of Avenida Rey Jaime III; Map **9**.
This was formerly part of the town residence of the illustrious Zaforteza family, and has many features of interest, including the narrow pilastered Gothic windows known as *finestres coronelles*, which are the result of some recent restoration work aimed at uncovering and replacing features embodied in the original Gothic design. There are also some paintings in the cloister, a courtyard with Baroque decorations and, more importantly, the fifteenth-century convent refectory. Further details inside the church include a painted organ case on the north wall depicting Santa Cecilia. Tapestry hangings, specially commissioned for the refurbished church, are faded, yet rare in subject.

Convent church of Santa Clara

between Calle San Alonso and the Ronda Litoral; Map **51**.

Though the present buildings date from the seventeenth and eighteenth centuries this church was founded in 1256. Like that of the church of San Francisco – with whom after all Santa Clara had a close relationship – the belfry has a Moorish air. Silver decoration incorporated in the west entrance is a reminder of the art of the silversmiths in those days when precious metals came pouring in from Mexico, the result of Aztec works of art being melted down by the conquistadors for convenience in transport.

PALACES AND TOWN HOUSES

It is not at all a bad idea to think about Palma's great residences or *palacios* at the same time as the city's churches. For one thing, they have a comparable history; for another, they are to be located in the same quarters of the town, often cheek by jowl. They are thickest on the ground north and north-east of the cathedral, not far from the ancient Portella quarter which seems quiet and remote, except that there is one-way traffic in the narrow, paved streets, where the sun cannot penetrate for long past the carved timbers of overhanging eaves.

As befitting a city created by noblemen and rich merchants, the wealth of a family and its culture tended to be expressed in stone, not only by the public monuments it subscribed to, but by lasting evidence of a gracious and expansive style of life. Comfort and permanence were the criteria, and, in outward appearance at least, ostentation fell well behind. In fact, many of these mansions present an impassive and withdrawn aspect, relieved only by stylized detail in gateways and the few window openings which give upon the street.

Many houses owned by rich Muslims at the time of the Reconquest would have been constructed of tamped earth and baked clay bricks, but the Christian settlers favoured stone, out of which they could build their Gothic residences equipped with the narrow twin windows known as *azimez*. However, much of Palma was laid waste by fire in the sixteenth century, which meant that when the houses of the wealthy came to be rebuilt between 1650 and 1750 advantage was taken of the fashionable Renaissance trends which had been brought here from the Continent, and particularly from Italy.

Should one question the economics of this architectural revival at a

time of the island's recession, the answer is that though trading had
declined, the aristocratic families had reinvested their money in
property and were deriving sufficient profits from taxation and rents
to express their wealth in massive stone structures, ornamental
wrought iron, and carvings – all for beauty's sake. Columns and
capitals, arcades, and enlarged window frames and doorways
departed from the old narrow Gothic shapes, cloistered from the
streets.

The layout of the archetypal house, known by the title of the family
which owned it, and usually situated in a *calle* which similarly bears
that name, is surprisingly uniform. It can be taken as a rule that there
is a great arched gateway, often equipped with a wooden door on
pivots, which was destined to be enlarged in the late sixteenth and
seventeenth centuries to admit coaches, then taking over from horses
as the usual form of transport. Here, in the midst of what was in
essence part of the service area of the mansion there would be a
zaguán, or dismounting area, in advance of the square or rectangular
courtyard around which the house was built. These spaces are on
such a scale that one would hesitate to use the Spanish word *patio*,
which has developed rather unfortunate suburban connotations in
our country. Each is provided with a beautifully designed well-head
of stone with fine ironwork – an important piece of domestic
equipment – and usually some specimen exotic trees and flowering
shrubs, and sometimes a fountain. But the most striking feature of all
is invariably the stone outside staircase leading up to the first floor or
piso principal. The rooms at street level, in the shade of arches, were
essentially functional, comprising stabling, servants' quarters, storage
and other domestic offices. The upper rooms inhabited by the family
are out of sight, not only because they are raised above the domestic
scene, but also because they are screened inside a balustraded arcade
which may extend around the four sides of the quadrangle. There is
often a second storey, on a diminished scale but also provided with
some form of loggia, and roofed with tiles.

The halls of the *piso principal* communicate with one another, and
may have painted ceilings or be panelled in the red pine known as
llanyam vermell. There is often Baroque decoration of classical figures
and garlands of flowers and fruit, sometimes set in panels in damask-
hung walls. Contemporary furniture included seats upholstered in
leather or velvet and sturdy wooden chests for storing clothing. The
bedrooms were provided with fourposter beds, splendidly draped, and

the master bedroom usually had either access to a small chapel or its own altarpiece installed. Such altarpieces are of course very valuable. It is gratifying to know that of the houses which still stand and remain in private ownership, many have managed to preserve their original furniture and works of art.

Unfortunately many of these houses were vandalized and neglected in the nineteenth century so that little remains but their façades and bare bones. Yet quite a few remain in the possession of descendants of the families that have owned them for centuries, while others have been converted to uses more appropriate to this modern age. It follows that in neither category are they invariably accessible to the public, though good manners are such in this city that no objection will be made to visitors walking through the unmistakably medieval gateways in order to get a good view of the gracious buildings around their courtyards.

Before embarking upon any definite plan for exploring the *palacios* 'in depth', it would be best to consult the Tourist Office, for the facilities for viewing those open to the public vary from house to house, and according to season.

The following list of town houses begins with the most famous and important; these are also listed in the Palma itineraries (pp. 190–3)).

Vivot Palace
2 Calle Zavella; *Map* **30**.
Hours 9·00–13·00; 15·00–18·30.
This, more than most, merits its title as a *palacio*. It was built early in the eighteenth century by a Majorcan aristocrat, Don Juan Miguel Sureda Villalonga, who supported the French claimant in the War of the Spanish Succession, in opposition to the majority of his peers. Accordingly he was granted the title of Marques de Vivot upon the accession of the Bourbon Philip V, and this elevation resulted in the total reconstruction of his family's town residence. The palace follows the conventional practice of presenting a plain exterior to the world, its opulence being expressed in the courtyard with its red marble colonnade and the stairway that divides on its way to the commodious loggia and *piso principal*. The eight reception rooms – more of them than usual – are distinguished not only for their contemporary tapestries, furniture and paintings of the Spanish school, but also for their ceilings decorated with classical subjects by an Italian artist. The

library contains rare books, some rescued from the city's vanished Capuchin monastery, and also maps dating from the period when Majorcan cartographers stood high among their fellows.

Sollerich Palace or Casa Morell
22 Calle San Cayetano; *Map* **20**.
Hours 10·00–13·30; 16·00–19·00.
Another veritable palace, this building was begun in 1763 on the instructions of the Majorcan nobleman who had been created Marques de Sollerich and a grandee of Spain in return for his services to the monarchy. The alternative name is used because he died without leaving a son and heir, so that his estates descended through the distaff side of the family.

Though the entrance to this palace is from the *calle* to its west, it is unusual in actually looking out upon the street – in this case El Borne, near Plaza Pío XII, – so that it is worth reconnoitring on that side to view its beautiful loggia with round arches supported by slender Ionic columns and ornamental wrought iron.

The entrance on the opposite side leads into the traditional paved courtyard and to a staircase which, this time, begins as a double and then joins to form a single flight. The marble used throughout is reddish, and was quarried on the family estate near Alaro. Selected rooms on the *piso principal* are open to the public. These include a large reception hall with family portraits on its walls, a chapel equipped with a seventeenth-century altar and some attractively appointed bedrooms. Various documents concerning the ennoblement of the house's founder are on display.

Casa Marqués de Palmer
17 Calle del Sol; *Map* **41**.
This otherwise rather severe Gothic structure has mullioned windows with supporting caryatids, and crowning medallions which owe much to the Renaissance. One is dated 1536. The carved eaves of the roof which overhang the street, casting deep shadows, are a very interesting and substantial feature.

Casa Oleo
8 Calle de la Almudaina; *Map* **34**.
This is one of the earliest examples, since parts of it date from the fifteenth century, including a fascinating *zaguán* with its typical

Moorish-influenced ceiling. For some time this building has housed a collection of antiquities in the ownership of the Luliana Archaeological Society. Their sculptures are grouped in the courtyard. The building is not open to the public.

Oleza Palace
33 Calle Morey; Map **42**.
Built near the end of the sixteenth century, but with later additions, this great house is a balanced mixture of the Gothic and Renaissance styles of design. The courtyard is exceptionally large, and shows off to advantage the three Corinthian columns which spring from the first-floor balustrade as supports to the roof. The entrance hall is two storeys high. Flemish tapestries based on cartoons by Rembrandt hang upon the red damasked walls of the interconnecting reception rooms. The altar of the miniscule chapel attached to the main bedroom is believed to enshrine a splinter of the True Cross presented to a member of the family by Pope Gregory XVI.

Montenegro Palace
Calle San Felió and Calle Montenegro; Map **22**.
This is where Cardinal Despuig was born. His many treasures were willed to his nephew, the Count of Montenegro. These include an important library and numismatic collection. The fabric of the palace was badly mutilated in the nineteenth century.

Veri Palace
16 Veri Street.
This was built in the fifteenth century, but is now heavily restored following a period of considerable neglect.

Desbruill Palace
Calle de la Portella; Map **45.**
Hours 10·00–13·00; 17·00–19·00.
Entrance charge 50 pesetas.

This now houses the Museo de Baleares. Special features include typical overhanging eaves and wrought ironwork. Among the exhibits are Gothic pictures and retables in wood, and medieval pottery.

Casa Formiguera (*Map* **50**), in the same street, is one of the earliest of such houses still in existence.

Casa Bonapart
Calle de la Palma.
This is likely to have been in existence in 1411 when its owner, Hugo Bonapart, was despatched to Corsica by Martin V of Aragon, there to act as his regent. Napoleon Bonaparte is presumed to be a descendant. The house has been restored.

Casa Belloto
Calle Felio; *Map* **18**.
This has a rebuilt seventeenth century façade.

Casa Moner
Calle Felio.
Note the decorated window frames and lintels.

Casa del Marqués de Ferrandell
Calle de San Jaime.
This is now a hotel.

Casa Berga
Plaza Santa Catalina Tomás; *Map* **17**.
This is now the Palace of Justice or Law Courts.

Palace of the Marqués de Campofranco
Calle Pueyo.
One of the most magnificent.It houses priceless treasure, including a tray which is thought to be the work of Benvenuto Cellini.

Palace of the Marqués de Ariany
Plaza de las Atarazanas.
This is now a school, and has a gallery of seven arches overlooking the Paseo Sagrera.

Casa Marcell
Calle de Apuntadores; *Map* **27**
This has an exceptionally fine staircase.

March Palace
Plaza de la Reina.
This is worth identifying, in that it was built between 1940 and 1945

for Juan March, a Majorcan magnate of humble birth who became
not only a substantial benefactor but was also a collector of Spanish
old masters, a patron of present-day Catalan artists and a connoisseur
of many other art forms.

OTHER SIGHTS

Episcopal Palace and the Diocesan Museum
Plaza del Mirador; *Map* **48**.
Hours 10·00–13·00; 16·00–20·00 *summer*.
       10·00–13·00; 16·00–18·00 *winter*.

Across the small open space to the east of the cathedral we come upon
the façade of the episcopal palace, its austerity relieved by its golden
fabric and superb Gothic portal. The building is in the Gothic and
Renaissance styles – in fact, the mixture as before. Reputedly its first
phase of building began in 1238, while the façade was completed in
1616. Inside there is a porch with interesting rafters, leading to a
courtyard and garden equipped with a sundial of 1734, and with a
stylishly graduated staircase leading up to the principal floor – all
according to the traditional pattern. Another entrance to seaward
gives access to the part of the buildings which were once the bishop's
private quarters, but which are now devoted to the diocesan museum.
This contains a great many diversified exhibits garnered from sites
and churches in all parts of the island. A set of ground-floor rooms
looks out over the harbour, and it is amusing to compare the present
view with a striking painting of St George and the Dragon depicted in
action against this very background. Though religious paintings,
statues, manuscripts and items of church furniture predominate, there
are also antique tiles, coins from the days when Majorca minted its
own currency, Moorish carpets, and a variety of objects harking back
to prehistory. The sepulchral stone of Suleiman ben Mansour, who
died in the 357th year of the Hegira (A.D. 968) links up with the
medieval relics.

La Casa Consistorial or Ayuntamiento
(Town Hall); *Plaza Cort*; *Map* **28**.
This pure Renaissance civic building, with its three-storeyed façade
beneath overhanging eaves carved by Gabriel Torres in 1680, takes up
the entire south side of the small, irregular square which is the
traditional place of assembly for the citizens of Palma on ceremonial

occasions. The city's dignitaries were accustomed to taking their place on the great balconies upon which the windows of the first floor opened. This site was originally occupied by the Hospital of St Andrew, from which local government was conducted, but when by 1597 this had fallen into disrepair a new building was commissioned. This was completed in 1670.

Between the two front entrances there is a raised seat reserved, thoughtfully, for aged citizens. The covered inner quadrangle gives access to offices. However, the interior is of no great interest, since it was gutted by fire in 1884 and subsequently rebuilt. Part of the building now houses on its ground floor the municipal museum and public library. Priceless archives are kept on the floor above. Among these the principal treasure is a set of royal decrees dating from 1228 to 1717 – many of them beautifully illuminated. There are also some Roman statues, and pictures – not always portraits – of historical personages, beginning with Hannibal in his putative role as a native of Cabrera. The most valuable of the pictures is ascribed by some exponents to Van Dyck, and depicts San Sebastian's martyrdom.

The neo-Gothic Palace of Deputies in Calle General Goded close by contains on its ground floor a small arts and crafts museum.

Arab Arch
*Calle Almudaina; Map **38**.*
This is one of the few remains of the Moorish city's fortifications. As the east gate it marked the limit of the old town.

Arab Baths
*13 Calle Serra; Map **52**.*
These, with the arch mentioned above, comprise the only direct evidence of the Moorish occupation. The baths follow the standard design of a *hamman*, a vaulted roof held up by twelve horse-shoe shaped arches, lit from a small central cupola. This is private property and is kept locked, but the custodian and his key are to be found at 11 Calle Portella. A tip will be appreciated.

Mercado
*Plaza Olivar; Map **10**.*
Like other markets, this one should be visited early in the morning for tempting displays of the fruits of the earth and sea, laid out in abundance to attract the housewife's and the hotelier's custom. The

whole vast building is covered, and in spite of its modernity echoes the Majorcan architectural pattern. Strolling around here, especially through the aisles devoted to fruit, vegetables and fish, can be a delight even to visitors committed to table d'hôte meals. There is another, smaller, market opposite the Plaza de Navigación, on the far side of the Riera, west of the central city.

Rastro (Flea Market)

This is held on Saturday mornings, spreading along the avenues between Plaza San Antonio and the sea. Old clothes, bric-à-brac, and all manner of detritus can be turned over on the stalls, whether or not the intention is to buy. Incidentally, this is one of the few places where bargaining – complicated where Majorcan rather than Spanish is in general use – is part of the game. To increase the handicap, prices are sometimes quoted in *duros*, the island's obsolete unit of currency, rather than in pesetas.

El Pueblo Español
off Calle de Andrea Doria.
This very ambitious touristic complex is, of course, modern, though much of it is aimed at reconstruction of the past. Built mostly to the design of a mushroomed Spanish village, complete with towers and ramparts, it purports to reproduce typical Iberian architecture, an impression which is knowingly reinforced by copies of important mainland buildings. These in themselves form an architectural 'museum' beginning, chronologically, with a Roman theatre which is used for stage performances. Many hours may be spent here in unexacting researching of Spanish and Majorcan culture, folklore and cuisine – just as long as entertainment is the prime objective. Within this recreational complex a large amount of space is devoted to a conference hall equipped with all the aids of modern technology, but wherever possible retaining something of the classical style.

SIGHTSEEING ROUTES IN CENTRAL PALMA

There follow four practical and not too exacting routes for walkabouts in central Palma. These take in, respectively, the two most imposing and interesting buildings: the Almudaina Palace and the cathedral; La Lonja and the Consulado del Mar on the waterfront and the old quarter of the city which lies behind; the even more fascinating Portella district of tortuous old streets to the east, with its complement of palaces, fine churches and scant Moorish remains; and the more northerly area bordering on the shopping and commercial sectors of the city, where are to be found the church of San Miguel, among others, and the modern *mercado*, or market, which is wholly indicative of Majorca and its island produce.

Though only the principal sights on each route are pinpointed, a considerable number of lesser sights exist on the way or slightly off course, to be returned to perhaps on another day, when the major ones have been thoroughly explored and appreciated. Reference to the town plan of Palma (p. 146–7) and the coded description in the text will bring these to the attention of the sightseer.

Principal landmarks

Starting from the south end of Avenida Antonio Maura (the continuation of El Borne), take the steps, left, below the Almudaina terrace, turn left again and ascend the further flight of steps leading to the paved area which separates the Almudaina Palace (*Map* **39**, pp. 160–3) from the west façade of the cathedral (*Map*, **43**, pp. 156–60). When justice has been done to both of these magnificent buildings, retrace the route along the Mirador Terrace on the seaward side of the cathedral, to get to the episcopal palace, which houses the diocesan museum (*Map* **48**, p. 188).

From here take Calle Palau northwards, turning right into Calle San Pedro Nolasco, then second left into Calle Morey, passing at No. 33, the Oleza Palace (*Map* **42**, p. 186). Then after looking left into Calle Almudaina at the Arab Arch (*Map* **38**, p. 189) continue along Calle Morey to Plaza Santa Eulalia and the fine church of that name (*Map* **25**, pp. 176–7); immediately east of the Plaza Cort where stands the beautiful Casa Consistorial or Ayuntamiento. El Borne at its junction with Avenida Antonio Maura (Plaza de la Reina) can then be reached by heading back to turn right into Calle Victoria from Avenida General Goded, then left into Calle Conquistador.

Lower town

Continue southwards down El Borne before turning right into the coastal promenade and motor road, Paseo Sagrera. La Lonja (*Map* **32**, pp. 164–6) is the first important building on the landward side. Beyond this, but close by is the Consulado del Mar (*Map* **29**, p. 166).

By way of Plaza Ataranxaras, Calle San Pedro and Calle San

Lorenzo, the church of Santa Cruz (p. 179) which embodies the chapel of San Lorenzo (*Map* **19**) is to be found. This ancient quarter ends at Paseo Mallorca, which lines the Riera watercourse – the limit of the town in its middle historical period.

To the north of the church of Santa Cruz turn right into Calle San Felio, then left into Calle Cateyano for the Sollerich Palace, otherwise known as Casa Morell (*Map* **20**, p. 185). One of two alternative right turns here, out of Calle Cateyano, will discharge the promenader safely at the north end of El Borne, at Plaza Pío XII roundabout. This is an excellent point of reference for the shopping streets of Avenida Rey Jaime III, Avenida General Mola and Calle San Jaime, which run west, east and north respectively.

San Francisco and Portella Quarter

From Plaza Cort and the Casa Consistorial (*Map* **28**) take Calle Cadena into Plaza Santa Eulalia (*Map* **25**) beyond which and between Calle Campana and Calle Zavella stands the Vivot Palace (*Map* **30**, p. 184).

Returning to the north-east corner of Santa Eulalia, follow Calle Zavella into Plaza Quadrado, to come out at the north-west side of the church of San Francisco (*Map* **36**, p. 166–71), and enter it from the plaza of that name.

Calle Padre Nadal, opposite the west front, leads by a turn left into Calle Del Sol, passing on the left La Casa de Marques de Palmer (*Map* **41**, p. 185). Continue to Plaza del Templo to see the church of the Templars (p. 180). South-west of this point we come to Montesión church in the street of that name. Rounding the church into Calle del Viento and turning right into Calle San Alonso, we find, rather hidden, the convent church of Santa Clara (*Map* **51**, p. 182).

To the west, by way of Calle Serra, we reach the Arab Baths (*Map* **52**, p. 189). Turn north as if following the bend in a hairpin into Calle Portella (not to be missed) to reach Calle Morey and the Oleza Palace (see the first itinerary). From this street corner Calle Pedro Nolasco leads back to the north-east corner of the cathedral, and to the steps north of the military government headquarters, which descend to the level at the junction of Calle Conquistador and the Plaza de la Reina roundabout. Otherwise, by turning right up Calle Morey, and through the Almudaina Arch (first itinerary) one can look into the courtyards of Casa Villalonga and Casa Oleo (*Map* **34**, p. 185). This street joins Avenida General Goded just short of Plaza Cort.

Central Palma

From Plaza Pío XII follow Avenida General Mola into Plaza Weyler, continuing by Calle Navarre to view the east end of Vía Roma (La Rambla). Then retrace the route a short distance past the Teatro Principal (*Map* **15**, p. 144) and go up the steps which lead into the pedestrian precinct of Plaza Mayor. To the left, midway across the plaza, Calle San Miguel – a busy but not excessively modern shopping street, in spite of being the longest in the city – leads north. Halfway along we come to the church of San Miguel (*Map* **13**, p. 180) and then to the old convent of San Antonio (*Map* **11**, p. 181). Around the corner, Plaza Olivar serves the extensive Mercado (*Map* **10**, p. 189), which could come as a relief from church sightseeing. The Calle San Miguel has two more of these to offer in the shape of Santa Catalina de Siena and, beyond, the Military Hospital, a national monument in the form of the conventual church of Santa Margarita (*Map* **4**). A short distance further on Calle San Miguel reaches Plaza España and what was once the perimeter of the city.

ROUTES ON MAJORCA

By far the greatest number of visitors choose to stay within easy reach of Palma, and settle at the resort of their choice, somewhat less than 10 km. on either side of the city, which is on the shore of the benign, southward facing Bay of Palma. When planning routes, therefore, Palma has been taken as the starting place, though in the realization that if touring from outlying places is involved some adjustment will have to be made. This decision has also been reinforced by the fact that all important roads radiate, like the struts of a fan, from the capital city.

The island being so small – just about three times the size of the Isle of Wight – none of the suggested excursions is likely to take more than one day's comfortable driving, and in many cases less, though in one a break might not come amiss. This decision has been made in view of another practical consideration: accommodation is heavily booked – very often out of season as well as at the height of summer – so that it would be unrealistic to encourage readers to rely upon chance overnight accommodation, or even to hope to make advance reservations for single nights in a place where the hotel industry depends upon stays of a week, ten days or a fortnight's duration.

The Chart of Excursions (pp. 12–13) gives distances as the shortest one-way route from Palma. It will be seen from the diagram of routes on pp. 196–7 how easily any one of these could be linked with its neighbours to make an extended trip. The first five itineraries travel west, north-west and north from Palma, substantially clockwise, in quest of the most spectacular scenery and places of compelling historical and visual interest – though the shortest route through the foothills (No. 5) is more leisurely, almost domestic in its lack of drama. Following these, we chart two unexacting trips to the interior – each with religio-historic interest, before setting off for the north-east and east coasts in three separate itineraries, again arranged clockwise, describing the best sightseeing in those directions. The final trip, to Cabrera, is by sea.

Route 1: Coast west of Palma

The plan is to follow the westerly outline of Palma Bay, passing through a chain of resorts which does not begin to peter out until after Magaluf. Though these seaside places have certain differences and attract their own clientele in terms of nationality and spending power, such distinctions are not immediately apparent to the motorist bent on discovering the realities of the island. In general, this first stretch of coast consists of bays punctuated by rocky headlands which the main road cuts across, and backed by high-rise buildings and pine-covered foothills studded with private villas. Development schemes have not succeeded in obliterating reminders of thirteenth-century history.

The coastal road rounds Mount Galatzó, opposite the island of Dragonera, to embark upon one of the most breathtakingly scenic of its sections, high above sea level. The first possible mountain pass leading back to Palma is taken, making a round trip of 90 km.

Route Leave Palma by Paseo Marítimo or Calle de Fátima north of the Santa Catalina district, and continue in either case on the Avenida Calvo Sotelo, which becomes C.719 or the Carretera de Andraitx (Route Exit B). A few optional short detours are indicated. A new dual carriageway provides a faster, alternative route from Palma to Palma Nova. Beyond Andraitx the road is designated as C.710, and continues along the clifftops as far as Bañalbufar, soon after which the right fork, leading into the mountains, is taken for Esporlas and Palma. Total round trip 90 km. The right fork after Bañalbufar continues north-east to Valldemosa (9 km.) forming a link with Route 2 (p. 203).
Bus For Puerto de Andraitx depart from Vía Roma 7.
Museum Son Mas at Andraitx.
Dolphinarium Marineland at Portals Nous.

[4·5 km.] **Porto Pi.** Though nowadays it accommodates the Spanish naval station and the military zone of San Carlos as well as the commercial quay where Barcelona and Minorca-bound steamships and cruise liners berth, this medieval port, where King Jaime I anchored his fleet in 1229, was at an early period superseded by a harbour more convenient to the city. The fifteenth-century *Tower of Pelaires* and its fellow, which still stand, closed the harbour every night by means of a chain stretched between them.

[5–7 km.] **Cala Mayor** consists of a succession of small beaches in the Ca's Catala and San Agustín districts. For obvious reasons these are crowded during the season.

Majorca
Diagram of Routes

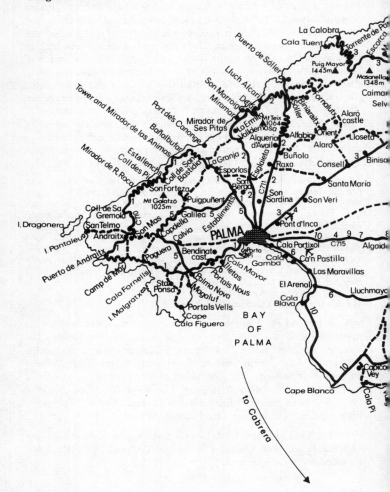

La Calobra
Cala Tuent
Torrente de Por
Escorca
Puerto de Sóller
Puig Mayor 1445m
Masanella 1348m
Caima
Selv
Lluch Alcari
Son Marroig
Deiá
Fornalutx
Sóller
Bunyolaraitx
Alaró castle
Miramar
Mt Teix 1064
La Ermita
Valldemosa
Alfabia
Orient
Lloseta
Mirador de Ses Pitas
Bañalbufar
Alqueria d'Avall
Alaró
Port des Canonge
Esglaieta
Buñola
Consell
Binisa
La Granja
Raxa
Estallenchs
Coll de San Bastida
Esporlas
Santa Maria
Coll des Pi
Mirador de R. Roca
Son Berga
C711
Son Sardina
Son Veri
Son Forteza
Mt Galatzó 1025m
Puigpuñent
Establiments
Coll de Sa Gremola
Galilea
Pont d'Inca
I. Dragonera
San Telmo
Son Mas
Capdella
Calvia
PALMA
Cala Portixol
Algaid
C715
I. Pantaleu
Andraitx
Porto
Can Pastilla
Puerto de Andraitx
Paguera
Bendinat cast
Cala Gamba
Las Maravillas
Camp de Mar
Cala Fornells
Sta Ponsa
Illetas
Palma Nova
El Arenal
Lluchmayo
Mogaluf
Cala Blava
I. Malgrat
Portals Nous
Portals Vells
Cape
Cala Figuera

BAY
OF
PALMA

Capico Vey
Cala Pi
Cape Blanco

to Cabrera

[8 km.] A right turn leads, in 1 km., to *Bendinat Castle*. The eighteenth-century castle was built in the grounds of the Moorish fortress where Jaime I is reputed to have eaten his first meal after his landing in September 1229; he was so elated with success that he praised the plain fare by crying '*Bendinat*' – the Catalan equivalent of *bien manger*.

A left turn at the 8 km. mark provides a short detour to **Illetas**. Developments on this wooded promontory linked by a network of service roads overlook the bay and its islets.

[10 km.] **Portals Nous:** the small beach and its surroundings have acquired greater importance and popularity since the creation of the *Dolphinarium*, on the left of the road.

[14 km.] **Palma Nova** is a highly developed resort on comparatively level land. Its sandy beach is often crowded. The *Club Náutico* is associated with its harbour. The town provides a wealth of souvenir and holiday goods, as well as entertainment night and day. The main road runs a short distance inland, and a side road to the right climbs (through the Sierra Burguesa (p. 231)) for 5 km. to **Calvia**. Palma Nova may be taken as the outer limit of Palma and its direct influence upon the coast.

[15 km.] A left turn leads, in 1 km., to **Magaluf**, one of the newest development areas and, in reality, a satellite of Palma Nova; here the coast turns abruptly south to form the western arm of Palma Bay.

[15·5 km.] A detour to the left off the Paguera road is to be recommended. It runs for 10 km. across the centre of the promontory to **Portals Vells**, 1 km. short of **Cala Figuera** and its lighthouse, before continuing round the headland from which there are splendid views overlooking the *island of Malgratx*, Santa Ponsa, and the south-west corner of the island with high mountains behind. Rejoin the main road north of Santa Ponsa. The additional distance is about 18 km.

[16 km.] **La Bataille Pass** On the right of the road a small chapel contains the *Piedra Sagrada* – the stone which served as an altar for the first mass to be said for the Christian invasion troops of 1229.

[17 km.] **Santa Ponsa.** The newest developments on the neck of the headland are served by good roads. A large stone *Cross* marks the site of the historic landing of 1229. The older parts of the town are at the head of the creek, and a secondary road leads from here into the foothills and on to Calvia (p. 232).

[23 km.] **Paguera,** with its two beaches, is a pleasant, small place, though quite lively; it has been 'discovered' by Scandinavian and German visitors. The pines give shade along the dunes of the shoreline.

Cala Fornells, 1·5 km. to the left, has excellent bathing from rocks and a tiny cove. The road to the right in Paguera leads to the mountain village of **Capdella** [5 km.]. Originally this neighbourhood consisted exclusively of great estates granted to Jaime I's followers, which were consistently well farmed during successive centuries.

[26 km.] **Camp de Mar.** The last beach before the main road climbs cross-country direct to Andraitx by the Coll d'Andritzol [4 km.], but the longer route is more scenically rewarding. Turn left uphill by a pretty road across the neck of a two-pronged peninsula.

[30·5 km.] **Puerto de Andraitx.** This picturesque harbour on the southern edge of a deep inlet 'twins' with inland Andraitx, and acted as the classical outpost of what was an important small provincial town. As such it bore the brunt of numerous piratical incursions. Nowadays the port has busy quays and moorings for yachts and fishing boats; there are beautiful views back towards the high mountains, and across the bay to a second lighthouse and further anchorage. There are modest waterfront hotels and bars, but not too many or too grand to detract from the charm of the place, which has drawn a complement of foreign residents, among whom sailing enthusiasts figure. The beach is small, but unspoilt coves are not far away. Fishing trips and boating excursions, around Dragonera island, for instance, are easy to arrange.

[36 km.] **Andraitx.** A most charming small town which has been saved from development by its distance from the sea. The Roman settlers called it Andrachium. Its buildings have a medieval appearance, mainly because many of them lean inwards over cobbled streets. From its hill the town looks south towards its protective port. The predominant colours are ruddy browns and ochres, matching the local soil, but some of the houses are colour-washed and faded by strong sunlight. Though the date 1729 is carved over the entrance to the *church*, the building dates from the thirteenth century, a period familiar to us from Palma's churches. Wednesday is market day, when villagers assemble from the countryside.

If there is time, it is a good idea to drive north for 0·5 km. up the valley, then to turn right for the great house known as *Son Mas*, built on the commanding site of what was once a Moorish castle. From its terrace, where cannons have been mounted to accent the strategic importance of the site, there is a fascinating bird's-eye view of the town. Son Mas and its courtyard stand up well to comparison with the town houses of the same date in Palma. Indeed, town and country houses often follow a similar design, and though the country ones may be on a larger scale, there is the same provision at ground level for horses and services in stalls and under arcades, a similar wellhead and grand staircase leading up to the *piso principal*. The museum at Son Mas is worth visiting, not only for its exhibits but because of the spacious rooms in which they are accommodated.

Continue north on the recently improved and always spectacular road which winds around spurs of the mountains on its way to the west coast.

[37 km.] At the crossroads a right turn leads in 9 km. by a tricky mountain road to Capdella while the left turn goes to San Telmo [7 km.]. This latter road makes a most enjoyable detour by way of the *Coll de S'Arraco*, through the village of that name, passing through country planted with citrus, olive and carob trees. The fishing village of San Telmo is immediately opposite the *island of Dragonera*, a great hunk of rock with the cliffs on its seaward and western side rising to 310 metres. Its isolated situation makes it a natural bird sanctuary. Though visitors are not exactly encouraged, the landowner (who maintains a remarkable garden and collects ornamental birds) is unlikely to oppose a peaceful landing. San Telmo boatmen will also put visitors ashore on the tiny island of *Pantaleu*, about half a kilometre offshore. According to the measure of Jaime I, who provisionally established himself here while his advance party spied out the land, it is a long cross-bow shot from the coast.

The little village of **San Telmo**, the most westerly in Majorca, fits firmly into the scene, where fishing boats find shelter from storms in a choice of coves. This outpost came into its own only after the Corsair peril abated. A *fort* was originally built in 1302, 1 km. to the south of the village, but its successor, still standing, is sixteenth-century, and its

structure embraces the village *chapel*. This took the fancy of the
Archduke Salvador, who preserved it for posterity. Public viewing is
limited to the feast day Pancretat (distribution of holy bread) on the
first Wednesday after Easter, when the villagers dance on what was
once the town threshing floor – an occasion which has overtones of
Sir James Fraser and his *Golden Bough*.

Returning to the main route, continue north from the crossroads
above Andraitx through pinewoods tumbling down spurs of the
mountain range, to reach what amounts to a tableland bordering the
shore, but where except in rare places the cliffs are too sheer to allow
descent even by the proverbial mountain goat.

[41 km.] The *Coll de Sa Gremola*, 400 metres above sea level,
provides the first of several viewpoints of a combination of cliff and
mountain. This stretch of road is comparatively new, as in the days
before tourism and sightseeing there was little demand for easy
communication.

[51 km.] *The Mirador de Ricardo Roca* is one of the compulsive
halting places for enjoyment of the scenery. There is no provision for
roadside stops other than in places such as this. A car park and steps
lead up to a terrace which offers an unobstructed view of the west
coast and the sea far below – very often stained deep colours by the
currents. Peasant lacemakers usually sell their work and other
handicraft souvenirs at the roadside, below the restaurant.

The road plunges into a short tunnel (*El Grau*) through the rock.

[55 km.] *The Coll d'es Pi*, immediately north of the summit of *Mount
Galatzó* (1,025 metres) is where the road twists inland to present a
view of Estellenchs far below. A restaurant is built out on a platform,
where eagle's-eye views can be combined with good eating.

[56 km.] **Estellenchs** is the only village on this section of the coast.
The surrounding terraces are planted with orange trees, and the
greenness and obvious fertility of the land is explained by the
existence of an irrigation system by which water from the mountain
is channelled through stone courses. The *church*, with its square
belfry is crowded upon by houses, which appear to be clinging to
each other for support in order to avoid being swept downhill. In the
church, the reredos of carved pinewood, bearing the marks of local

workmanship and materials, is exceptionally fine. A steep track leads down to sea level.

[62 km.] *The Tower and Mirador de las Animas*, above the Punta Verger, provides parking space and an observation platform. It can be seen that this was an obvious site for the sixteenth-century *watchtower*, built to stand sentinel against the Barbary pirates as well as to relay signals up and down the coast.

[63 km.] **Bañalbufar.** Here there is some respite from scenery of unmitigated grandeur. The village is essentially agricultural, with the land surrounding it neatly terraced in geometric patterns formed by walls of a height dictated by the gradients, and descending almost to the edge of the sea. Some are very high indeed.

The secret of the neighbourhood's prosperity is based upon a spring of water above the village. A copious supply is channelled down through water courses of ancient construction, and stored in individual open cisterns – each landowner having the right to a specific allocation. The vineyards of the adjacent *Baronia* manor house were once celebrated for their Malvoisie wine, of a Madeira type. Unfortunately the original vines perished as a result of disease, but an effort is now being made to reintroduce similar stock. This picturesque village suffered considerably early in this century from depopulation and drift from the land, but in compensation its old houses have become increasingly popular as second homes and among expatriates.

The road swings inland over the *Coll de San Bastida*, after which it is possible to reach the sea at Port d'es Canonge; there is, however, only a rough track.

[69 km.] Fork right away from C.710, which continues in the direction of Valldemosa, linking up with Route 2 (p. 204).

[70 km.] A side road comes in from Puigpuñent and the villages on the south-eastern spurs of the mountains.

[73 km.] **La Granja:** the evidence of its courtyard and fountains, and the channelling of water down through the gardens proclaims the Moorish antecedents of this elegant country house. In any case, the lands were once in the hands of Cistercian monks, and its name, meaning 'granary', suggests that it was then a farm rather than a monastery. It passed into the hands of the noble Fortuñy family in the middle of the fifteenth century, and is still owned by them. The house has a splendid balustraded terrace, where the roof is supported by beautifully proportioned lines of columns and arches. The aspect is southern, over the gardens, terraces and vineyards, through which water cascades from level to level, combining the ornamental with practical irrigation. Because of the steepness of the site, the house is unusual in having no more than one storey at its rear. Visitors are treated to the sight of traditional arts and crafts practised by country people dressed in peasant costume. It is also the venue for displays of folk dancing and singing.

[75 km.] **Esporlas** is a town built on two sides of a river bed. Drystone walls are a feature of the neighbourhood. Just outside the town a side road to the left leads to *Esglaieta*.

[82 km.] **Establiments.** La Riera, the course of which is at most times dry, runs to the right of the descending road.

[90 km.] Palma is reached at the junction of Vía Alemania and Avenida Conde Sallent, north of the Vía Roma.

Route 2: Valldemosa and Soller

The first objective is the Monastery of Valldemosa, in ideal mountain surroundings, looking back over Palma and the plain. Apart from its associations with George Sand, the eccentric French writer and intellectual, and her lover, Frédéric Chopin, this is a romantic place, evocative of a more distant past. On the further side of the mountain range we travel the clifftops, stopping to survey magnificent scenery from the occasional *mirador*, and pass through the village of Deyá, the home of many expatriate writers and artists, before going on to Soller in its valley of citrus trees, clustering around prosperous *huertas*, and the port which guarded it from barbarian raiders, and which is one of the most picturesque in the island. On the return journey to Palma there are a great many country houses to be seen, and two to be visited: the once-Moorish mansion of Alfabia, and Raxa, with its comparably fine gardens and ornamental water.

Route Take Calle de 31 Diciembre from Plaza Conquista, which is immediately west of the Soller railway terminus (Route Exit F). Fork left on the outskirts of the city away from the main road to Soller for the mountain village and monastery of Valldemosa. After crossing the watershed we join C.710 – the southern section of which is outlined in Route 1 – en route for Soller. The return to Palma is by the 400-metres-high Coll de Soller, descending by a series of hairpin bends to the plain and the straight run back to Palma, keeping in touch now with the miniature railway after it has burrowed through the mountains, (total 68 km.).

From Valldemosa it is only 9 km. south-west along the C.710 to link up with Route 1 near La Granja (p. 202).

Another possible, though longer, link route is to continue north-east on the C.710 from Soller to join up with Route 3 south of La Calobra (p. 217).

Train To Soller via Buñola.

At first the country is given over to almond orchards and studded with windmill towers, before it begins to climb into the sierra with orange groves, then olives in terraces and, eventually, pines and bare rock.

[10 km.] **Esglaieta.** Convenient parking is provided outside a roadside glass factory, where the processes may be observed from a gallery; close by there is a shop selling its products and other souvenirs. This is the last village before the ascent into the mountains. Crossroads lead left to Esporlas [5 km.] and right to Santa María [14 km.]. The direct road continues through rapidly changing scenery and a defile known as *S'Estret* (the narrow pass) deep into the mountains, and to a sudden and charming view of the monastery surrounded by its cypresses and well-watered terraces.

[17 km.] **Valldemosa.** The village is about 400 metres above sea level, and catches every breeze – sometimes rather too many in winter, but refreshing in summer – making this a pleasant district for country walks. The village is very attractive and clean, but crowded with visitors to the monastery – most of whom arrive by tourist coach. There are narrow winding streets and glimpses into patios gay with flowers. The modest *birthplace of Catalina Tomás*, Majorca's own saint, is open to the public. She was born in 1513, and in her girlhood worked as a servant in the great house of Raxa (p. 212), where she won renown for her sanctity and resistance to the attentions of the Devil. The parish *church*, built in 1254, but much altered, boasts a statue of Santa Catalina near its main altar.

A level roadway leads to the entrance to the monastery.

THE MONASTERY OF VALLDEMOSA

HISTORY

In 1311 King Sancho built himself a palace in the mountains for use as a hunting lodge, and to give him respite from the asthma which afflicted him at sea level. After his death the building was given to monks from Scala Dei, near Tarragona, for conversion into what was to become La Real Cartuja or royal Carthusian monastery. Very little remains of either the palace or the original religious buildings, which were rebuilt several times: in 1446 and again in the sixteenth and seventeenth centuries, at which later date the cloister of St Mary was added. By the following century, the growth of the community was such that a new church was called for. This was begun in 1737 and finished in 1812.

At that time the community was wealthy and completely self-sufficient. It housed some fifty monks, not counting numerous 'satellite' hermits attracted to the bare mountains behind. However, the buildings had to be abandoned in 1835 at the time of the suppression of the monastic orders, and though the Carthusians eventually managed to return from abroad to their mother house in Spain, they never regained Valldemosa. From that time forward, even to the present day, various parts of the monastery have been let as apartments to private individuals.

Only three years after the departure of the monks, a set of three cells were rented by George Sand, the *avant garde* French writer, for the accommodation of herself, two of her children, and her lover, Chopin. (At that time the island could provide very little in the way of alternative accommodation). Though the visit of the romantic pair lasted no more than ninety-seven days it has been fostered as a legend by the tourist authorities, and so accounts for the parties which flock to the site and make individual sightseeing exceedingly difficult. The facts as we know them are somewhat at variance with George Sand's own account, given in her book *A Winter in Majorca*, copies of which are prominent on the bookstalls here. But footnotes by Robert Graves, the English translator, rectify certain mis-statements, and a 'Refutation' in the form of an appendix written in 1841 by J. M. Quadrano does the same. In any event, the talented couple arrived here by accident, having failed to find rented accommodation in Palma upon their landing in Majorca. Their hope had been to gain some alleviation of the composer's chest trouble – which in fact was tuberculosis, a disease which was greatly dreaded at that time in view of its contagiousness, and mortality. This dread was expressed by the Valldemosan villagers, and reinforced by their disapproval of the lady's morals and her outrageous behaviour in other respects. It is quite clear that a running feud developed, greatly aggravated by the baleful nature of Solange, the younger child. Certain of her pranks might well have turned to tragedy instead of farce. One of the most trivial, but blown up beyond all recognition, concerned her insistence that fleas had been deliberately introduced into the roast chicken set upon their table.

Much of the story is funny as well as grotesque, and we may sympathize with the ailing Chopin in his frustrations, such as in getting his piano manhandled up the mountain in bad weather, and by washed-out tracks. Nevertheless, contemporary letters written by Chopin give little hint of persecution by the superstitious peasantry, and it has been established that he found time to write many of his finest preludes here, as well as put finishing touches to other works, in what, at least as far as scenery was concerned, should have been a place of the utmost tranquillity. But whatever the balance between truth and exaggeration, a tour of the three cells taken over by the party cannot fail to be absorbing. Though with the exception of the piano – which again proved recalcitrant – all their belongings were removed at the time of their departure from the island, a great deal has been reinstated, and the rooms are full of atmosphere. A nostalgic touch is provided by a fresh rose which is laid every day on the genius's piano. Much of the fascination, too, is provided by the cells themselves, which do not conform at all to the conventional and austere pattern of cubicles usually found in monasteries. Even when occupied by the monks they were arranged in roomy suites of three, opening upon beautiful, individual flagged gardens with running water, a terrace and balcony offering a splendid view back towards the Bay of Palma.

THE MONASTERY; THE PRIOR'S ACCOMMODATION
This is also open to visitors, and consists of four rooms, including a *library* of valuable original documents and books. And though when the community dispersed they were able to carry away all their own furniture and possessions with them, the present furnishings – lustre pottery, furniture, pictures, – are of the correct period.

Apart from the *cloisters*, which even in summer are so chilly that we can understand George Sand's complaint that they were 'full of ghostly terrors' (no doubt brought on by the February winds or Solange's practical jokes), one of the most fascinating parts of the monastery must be the ancient *pharmacy*, which has had its counters and shelves restocked with old pharmaceutical instruments and medicaments contained, mostly, in antique stoppered jars and phials. This pharmacy was still in use at the time of George Sand's occupancy, when the needs of the village continued to be ministered to by a survivor of the community. It did not close until 1912.

There is also a small municipal *museum*.

The *church* is neo-classical, cruciform and provided with a cupola. Its chief interest lies in its vaulted ceiling which is decorated with frescoes painted by Manuel Bayeu, the Carthusian monk who was brother-in-law to Goya. Other features include floor tiles, choir stalls and the *pietà* of the high altar, all of which are worth looking out for; while interesting vestments, reliquaries and other religious objects can be seen in the *sacristy*.

At the conclusion of the guided tour, visitors are led to an adjacent hall, designated as *King Sancho's Palace* to see performances of folk dancing and singing. Outside, on level ground, there are booths where native handiwork, particularly lace, is sold by girls dressed in the costume of the district, the most flattering part of which is a white wimple.

Fork left on leaving the village, to ascend in a short distance to the ridge and splendid panorama of the west coast.

[18 km.] Turn right on meeting the coastal road (C. 710) running north-eastward.

[21 km.] *The Mirador de Ses Pitas*: as with other regular viewpoints, this one has been chosen with care, and parking space is provided. A track above the road to the right leads to *La Ermita* (the Hermitage) traditionally inhabited by recluses who, however, developed a reputation for hospitality.

[21·5 km.] *Miramar*: this estate was one of the first of several to be purchased by the Archduke Luís (christened Ludwig) Salvador of Austria. The manor house of Miramar stands on the site of the School of Oriental Languages founded by Ramón Llull in 1276 (see p. 236) with the object of instructing thirteen Franciscans in Arabic, preparatory to their commitment to missionary work in North Africa.

The earliest surviving remains are a watchtower and portions of the cloister of Santa Magdalena, transferred here from the demolished Palma convent. The house contains a collection of furniture and ceramics – all in the Majorcan style.

The Archduke was a truly exceptional man. He came to Majorca in 1867 when he was only nineteen, and developed such a passion for the place, and for the west coast in particular, that he determined to preserve it for posterity. In fact, he was an environmentalist before that term was ever thought of. He was rich, the third son of the last Duke of Tuscany, and a cousin of the Austrian emperor. It is said that he developed an aversion for court life after the death of his mistress, a local girl, from leprosy. In any event, he immersed himself in his studies and learnt the Majorcan language, to become the foremost authority on the island's archaeology, history, topography, folklore and wildlife – all of which he recorded in scholarly works. One of these was a volume written to commemorate Ramón Llull's 500th anniversary. He developed a special devotion to this great missionary and philosopher, with whom he had a great deal in common. As an expression of these feelings he dedicated a chapel at Miramar to Llull, near the cave where this medieval scholar is thought to have retired for study and meditation in the thirteenth century. The Archduke was also responsible for the roadside hostelry where wayfarers were permitted to stay for a limited period, on terms reminiscent of youth hostels. This is now a hotel.

[23·5 km.] *Son Marroig* is the largest of the Archduke's manorial properties, and the one in which he chose to live. He landscaped the site, gracing it with terraces, statuary and a *belvedere* of Carrara marble. The house itself had been built in the sixteenth century as a fortified mansion, of which a square watchtower has survived. The graceful colonnade is a much later addition. The house contains the furniture, paintings and various collections made by the owner in the course of his travels and researches, and is open to the public. From the roadside there is a view of the rocky headland of *Na Foradada* far below, and the natural cleft or eye in it, in the safety of which Luís Salvador kept his yacht, the *Niké*.

[28 km.] **Deyá.** Soon after the road twists decisively inland to follow the outline of the *Punta Deyá*, the village comes into sight on a built-up conical hill rising from the small valley. Understandably in view of its picturesqueness and 'other world' atmosphere, Deyá has become a favourite resort among artists and writers, who have entrenched themselves in the traditionally built houses which line the narrow streets of cobbles and series of steps, and defy gravity by means of supporting arches thrown across the lanes. Robert Graves has for a long time headed the list of famous inhabitants of the neighbourhood who have involved themselves in local happenings and pursued lives of their own choosing. A steep track leads down to sea level. There is an excellent view of the mountains pressing in from the east, dominated by *Teix* (1,064 metres), the summit of which is more easily reached from the Valldemosa side.

[30 km.] **Lluch Alcari.** This hamlet similarly has become popular with painters, as an alternative to Deyá. It lacks direct access to the shore.

A succession of hairpin bends takes the road inland for a first glimpse of Soller, spread out upon the floor of a natural amphitheatre walled by mountains.

[38 km.] **Soller** is a very distinctive town, with its individual atmosphere based, it is suggested, upon commercial links with the south of France, to which its men traditionally emigrated with cargoes of oranges and lemons. Having made their fortunes as greengrocers, merchants and restaurateurs, they returned to enjoy a prosperous retirement. The place seems to have borrowed something of the character of a French provincial town. Latterly the fruit trade has been threatened by the rival produce of Valencia. Prosperity has declined since the time around 1912, when the community was affluent enough to build its own narrow-gauge railway across and through the mountains to the capital. This has been of great benefit in terms of trade, and now is a feature beloved by tourists. If closure comes about, as is threatened from time to time, it will be a severe loss.

There is a fine *square*, presided over by the *church of San Bartolomé*, and complete with cafés with outdoor tables, a fountain and plane trees – again more French than Spanish. Calle de Luna, leading from the square, and narrow like the others, is the best for shopping. Though fundamentally medieval, the church underwent a not very prepossessing face-lift at the turn of this century, and may now be classified as neo-Gothic. Inside there are two statues of note: one of the patron saint, executed by an Italian sculptor in the local dark marble, and the second a fourteenth-century Madonna.

EXCURSIONS FROM SOLLER

Puerto de Soller

Hard by the delightfully old-fashioned railway station, with its brass bell that is sounded five minutes before departure times (allowing just time enough to sprint up from the town square), and its intriguing rolling stock, we find the terminus of the tram which links town and port, 5 km. away, for the town of Soller turns its face from the sea, as though entirely occupied with the sheltered land which surrounds it. For this is another of the old towns which relied upon an outpost for warning and defence against attack. But reliance upon the coastal watchtowers and landlocked port was in one instance at least misplaced: when in May 1561 a raiding party consisting of 1,700 Corsairs landed and proceeded to sack the inland town. However, they were eventually repulsed by reinforcements summoned from strongpoints on the further side of the mountains. To balance the account, 418 Moorish heads were collected and placed on stakes for exhibition. That event is celebrated with great gusto on the anniversary of victory, in May of every year.

The port has great charm, and is spread out along a horseshoe waterfront served by the tram, which transforms the short but possibly dusty journey from Soller into something of a treat. Until recently the houses in the port were all occupied by fishermen and associated tradesmen, but those overlooking the quays have now become popular with visitors, and at ground level have been converted into shops, some with flats above. Bathing facilities are limited, owing to the lie of the land, but the harbour is a lively place, deriving as much of its popularity from the pleasure of travelling by Heath Robinson train and tram from the heart of Palma as from its sheltered waters.

Fornalutx

This is one of several delightful villages set in citrus groves within carriage, taxi-drive, or even walking distance [5 km.] from Soller, up a valley blessed with abundant running water. **Biniaritx** [3 km.] is another, snuggling under the heights of the mountains which culminate to the north in *Puig Mayor* (1,443 metres). The sloping terrain has dictated that these villages should have narrow and cobbled streets, sometimes stepped and devised for mule traffic, roofs set at angles and hidden patios which upon investigation are usually bright with flowers. Life is centred around the church, and of course in the evergreen orange groves. The district is one for walkers, as there is some level ground, as well as mountain tracks for the adventurous and fit.

Leave Soller by C.711, above the railway line. Except where the railway plunges underground, these two lines of communication remain in close proximity throughout the return trip to Palma.

[46 km.] **Coll de Soller.** The ascent to 400 metres above sea level is rapid, and achieved by innumerable hairpin bends cut through rocks and slopes covered with Mediterranean heath. A large *Gothic cross* stands at the top of the pass, also a café-restaurant. The descending road then curves rather than twists, making for easier driving. The views to the south embrace a fair proportion of the island, including the city of Palma and its bay.

[51 km.] **Alfabia.** Before reaching level ground there is a pull-in space for cars and coaches calling at this great house and garden. Jaime I granted the estate to Benhabet, the ousted Moorish governor of Pollensa and Inca who had victualled the Christian troops during the campaign of 1229 which preceded the capture of Palma. Since then the property has changed hands several times, but always among noble Christian families. However, the atmosphere of the gardens has remained distinctly Moorish, possibly because of the use of water and shade in its landscaping. The only very early features are the typical *watchtower* and the coffered ceiling of the *gatehouse*, which incorporates an Arabic inscription in praise of Allah.

An *avenue* of stately plane trees leads up to the mellow facade of the house; this supports a water cistern which is one key to the luxuriance of the gardens. A second ornamental front has been imposed on the western side; this incorporates the Gothic tower of the gatehouse mentioned above, and the Mauresque decoration, pierced by the arched passageway which, with its ceiling of inlaid woods, was executed by Moorish craftsmen employed by Christian masters. The *courtyard* has an enormous plane tree with a classical fountain and two doorways, one leading to the *piso principal* of the seventeenth-century residence.

The house is furnished throughout with typical Majorcan furniture, much of it made of local materials. These are not, in fact, the original contents of the house, though they have been carefully selected to be of the right period. There are also portraits of royalty, and many prints and engravings. Two special items to look out for are an oak chair carved with historical incidents, and made to order for Jaime IV, who did not live to enjoy it; and the patterned blue and white Majorcan handwoven cotton known as *lengue de Pollensa*, which is used as a wall-covering in one of the saloons. There is also a valuable *library*, and one is shown the *bedchamber* occupied by Queen Isabella IV when she came here to open the road to Soller over the mountains.

The *gardens* are at many different levels. The way round — or rather down and up — is traced by a system of arrows which lead beneath trellises of wistaria and jasmine, along paths and terraces bordered by channels of running water, some of which flow from large urns, and through patterns of light and shade. Vines, oranges and lemons then give way to an ordered wilderness of trees at lower levels. On the way, too, there is a kiosk selling fresh orange and lemon juice, squeezed to order.

[53 km.] *Alqueria d'Avail* to the right of the road is a seventeenth-century mansion with an interesting family chapel which has a gallery for use by the family's children. Unfortunately this is not open to the public. This is a neighbourhood of grand country houses, complementary to the *palacios* of Palma. All are slightly elevated, to look out over almond country, though many are so secluded as to be only identifiable by their gates and avenues.

[54 km.] **Buñola** is to the left of the road. It has a Baroque *church* on the south side of the town square. As is not unusual, the façade is seventeenth-century but the main fabric much older. A large *sanatorium* donated by Juan March, industrialist and banker, is on a dominating site just outside the town.

(It is feasible to drive for 12 km. along a rough road through the foothills to *Alaro*, via *Orient*, to emerge after a further 5 km. at *Consell* on the Palma-Inca road.)

[56 km.] **Raxa** is 5 km. to the right by a side road. This is a showplace comparable in many respects to Alfabia, so that there is an argument in favour of visiting it some other day, especially as Palma is only 12 km. away. The estate was given to the sacristan of Gerona cathedral in the period of resettlement after the Reconquest. In 1620 it came into the possession of the distinguished Despuig family, which ever since 1229 had been prominent in military and ecclesiastical circles. One member was created Count of Montenegro in the seventeenth century, but the best remembered must be Don Antonio Despuig y Dameto (1745–1812), who became a canon of Palma cathedral at the age of seventeen and a cardinal in 1803. He was a man of great culture who was responsible for the appearance of the house and grounds of Raxa as they are today.

The two principal features of the *garden* are an ornamental lake bordered by trees, and the monumental flight of steps modelled on those of the Villa d'Este near Rome. Lake water is channelled on either side, emerging at the head of the stairway from a fountain which features Apollo and his lyre in rustic surroundings. Originally the Cardinal used his garden as the setting for his collection of antique Roman statuary, much of which derived from excavations on the site of the Temple of Egeria near Albano, where he had a villa. Most of these have now been removed for safe keeping to the Museum of Mallorca in the Calle Llulia, Palma, though some are in Bellver Castle.

The house has the traditional courtyard (sometimes called a *clastre*, though the strict interpretation of that word is 'cloister'). The façade of the house is Italianate, while the rooms are fairly modest in proportion, with tiled floors, carved wooden rafters, and damask-lined walls, furnished with Majorcan craftsman-built tables, chairs and chests. It was here at Raxa that Santa Catalina Tomás worked for a while, until her reputation for saintliness drew her to a spiritual life, hastened by an encounter with the Devil attempting to distract her from her ascetic way of life. He departed, leaving sulphurous fumes in his wake.

[57 km.] Crossroads lead right to Esglaieta [4 km.] and left to Santa María [10 km.]

[63 km.] **Son Sardina**, where there is a station on the Soller railway line.

[68 km.] Junction with the Valldemosa road, on the outskirts of the city.

Route 3: Monastery of Lluch and La Calobra

This tour embraces the grandest of Majorca's mountain scenery and the highest pass through it; the Monastery of Lluch, the most famous of the island's places of pilgrimage; some typical hill towns, and a canyon of such splendid proportions that it has been likened to America's Grand Canyon. The destination is La Calobra, a creek of picture-postcard beauty at the mouth of the famous Torrente de Pareis. All these ingredients add up to a well-balanced sightseeing meal, with prospects not only of bathing and midday refreshments at La Calobra, but also of visiting inviting halting places on the return journey, after the descent to the plain at Inca.

However, distances are deceptive on mountain expeditions, and the operation requires time and stamina on the part of the driver; it might therefore be worth considering joining an organized coach trip.

Route Take the Palma to Alcudia-Pollensa (Route Exit E) road north-east as far as Inca (p. 221). Then head north through the hill towns of Selva and Caimari and continue into the mountains, with a short deviation for Lluch. Especially in its last sections, this road is truly tortuous. Because the views differ so greatly according to the direction one is travelling there is no hardship in returning by the outgoing route [71 km. one way]. However, an alternative exists in another scenic mountain road (C.710) through Soller [23 km.] and back to Palma (see Route 2, p. 204), though this may be considered to involve too high a proportion of mountain driving for comfort.
Bus For Lluch depart from railway station.
Restaurants Refectory in Monastery of Lluch, hotel and cafés at La Calobra.

The first section of this route, as far as Inca, is described under Route 4 (p. 218).

[29 km.] **Inca**. Leave the town by the Calle de Lluch, at the north-west corner of the market square.

[33·5 km.] **Selva**. This attractive hill town comes into view almost immediately, crowned by its old church, square-towered against the backdrop of high mountains, and with a line of windows supported by buttresses issuing from its roof like a well-proportioned arcade, and looking out over the falling ground. Closer inspection will show that these narrow windows have been blocked up and rose windows substituted. Like the market towns in the plain, Selva was founded by

Jaime II, and its Catalan-Gothic church dates from the beginning of the fourteenth century. A flight of forty steps bordered by cypresses leads up from the market square.

On certain afternoons of the week folk dancing is staged in this square by some of the most talented of the island's groups. If the weather is bad, they adjourn to a nearby hall.

[34·5 km.] **Caimari**. This smaller town appears to the left before the road swings down to its level. It is known for the production of olive oil. Soon the terraces where the olives grow become steeper, narrower and more irregular as they negotiate the contours; the road then climbs to an altitude where evergreen oaks take the place of olives, and after that there is only bare rock with the occasional pine. We defy anybody to count them, but there are reputedly one hundred and fifty hairpin bends on this road which winds upward over the *Col de Lluch* (540 metres) and the *Col de Calobra* (900 metres).

[44·5 km.] Past a cutting in the rockface, the terrain levels out temporarily at an altitude of 500 metres, and the road forks right for Pollensa [22 km.], skirting Mount Tomir (1,103 metres) to unfold a panorama of two bays and their promontories, backed by the horizontal plains and cultivations of central Majorca. The road to the monastery is left off the Pollensa road, very soon after the junction.

[47 km.] THE MONASTERY OF LLUCH

The complex of monastic buildings should ideally be first seen from a spot on the left-forking road slightly beyond the junction, where a *cross* has been erected and parking space provided. Now not only is the ground plan of the monastery exposed, but also the surrounding land, which has been reclaimed for cultivation of what are naturally barren, enfolding hillsides and wooded slopes.

One story goes that in 1258 a young shepherd named Lluch chanced upon the statue of a beautiful woman at some spot near the avenue of trees leading to the present monastery. When he led a monk from Escorca to the place they were greeted by a burst of celestial music and a vision of bright lights, proclaiming the statue to be that of the Blessed Virgin. A learned commission forthwith confirmed the validity of the experience, and the Knights Templar donated land for the erection of a commemorative shrine. An alternative theory more prosaically suggests that Lluch was founded here because it made a more convenient place of congregation than the church of San Pedro at Escorca, further into the mountains. We may choose which we prefer, but possibly will be swayed by the sight of the Black Virgin, La Morenata, which is to be seen, and revered, in the monastery's church. At any rate, by 1430 an Augustinian monastery was attached to the shrine, and its church took over the parish of Escorca. A choir school and seminary were added. The monastery has grown enormously since those days, and many of its buildings are modern, though pleasing to the eye in their quadrangular layout and rounded local roof tiles. They are occupied and administered by the Order of the Sacred Heart – a working community – and consist not only of scholastic and hospital buildings but also accommodation for visitors in converted cells, which are in reality self-contained apartments, as at Valldemosa. Other parts of the monastery open to the visiting public are the church and refectory (where cafeteria-type refreshments are available), part of the cloisters and the adjacent museum. Glimpses are obtained of the quadrangles and what were buildings for stabling and agricultural equipment.

The growth of Lluch as a pilgrimage centre, to which many thousands of people flock on the appropriate feast days and indeed throughout the year is, of course, attributable to the presence of the fabled and diminutive statue which stands in a place of honour in the side chapel adjoining the heavily decorated, red-marbled seventeenth-century *church*. Visitors are allowed to circulate close to the foot of the statue, and very lovely the Virgin is in her duskiness, set off by the golden haloes round the heads of both Mother and Child. Legend apart, there is documentary proof that this statue existed in 1417.

The *museum* is a treasure house of exhibits received as donations, and hence specialization has had to go by the board. Coins, flints, musical instruments, vestments, jewellery, primitive painted statues, ceramics, local costumes, tableaux of biblical scenes and of local life, a carved fourposter bed and many other disparate items are arranged, as far as possible in groups and in showcases. Perhaps their greatest significance lies in the exposition of many years of devotion.

Return to the fork and continue to the right past the cross, to embark upon another series of hairpin twists through wooded slopes which culminate in the *Coll de Lluch*.

[52 km.] **Escorca**. This tiny village, barely a hamlet, was settled soon after the Reconquest, and has two claims to fame, one magnificent, the other simple in the extreme. The ancient *chapel of San Pedro* is amongst those which claim to be the first to be built during the resettlement of the island. It attracted in the first place a nucleus of hermits and monks who remained there until its functions were eclipsed by the monastery of Lluch. The church's simplicity is of great appeal, and also its small size: no more than a rectangle measuring about 10 by 8 metres, divided into two by an arch, the one part containing the altar flanked by stone seating for the priests, and the other for the congregation. The roof is timbered and tiled, and capped by a small belfry.

The other sight is more imposing – even daunting: the canyon carved by the *Torrente de Pareis* over many centuries of seasonal spates of rushing mountain water, snow and ice. It can be viewed from here, far below. Incidentally, Escorca can be taken as the starting place for any hardy breed of pedestrian, climber or swimmer (there is need for all three skills) who may opt for that route to the sea. (Engage a guide, please, and above all do not undertake the adventure after rain.) Others will be satisfied by craning their necks to look down into the canyon from a *mirador* carved for that purpose on the brink of the steep slope which ends in the sheer walls of the watercourse. Not far from this point, on the upper side of the road, there is a café for wayfarers. Looking down upon the masses of rock of harsh metallic texture, one cannot help returning to the line incised to such a great depth that at its narrowest points no sun ever reaches the bottom. The phenomenon is hostile, more so perhaps than any moonscape, which after all has a certain tranquillity; no words can do justice to the grandeur of the sight. A comparable, though smaller-scaled appraisal of the canyon's sculptured shapes and colouring is to be obtained later, on the *torrente's* lower reaches.

[56 km.] After winding down to a lower level on a road cut into the fantastic rock shapes of Puig Mayor, and at one point tunnelling through the mountain, the Soller road comes in from the left, having rounded the mountain. This is the alternative route back to Palma, and runs through spectacular scenery, with changing aspects of Majorca's highest peak [Soller 23 km., Palma 53 km.]. Though there is not a great deal to choose between the two distances, the Soller alternative involves a greater proportion of mountain driving, so that an overnight stay there might be advisable.

Soon after this road junction, our route to La Calobra ascends once more in its familiar upward spiral, to traverse the highest coll of all.

Having negotiated this, the descent to sea level is so abrupt that the contortions of the road demand at one point that it loop back under itself. The levels of olive cultivation are reached, and then there are glimpses from above of tiny farms set in patches of cultivation. Otherwise for long stretches there is little vegetation, except for Mediterranean heath and colourful mosses and bracken. At one point a *mirador* provides the official viewpoint for La Calobra and the sea.

[69·5 km.] A new road leads left for 2 km. to the modern development of **Cala Tuent**.

[71 km.] **La Calobra**. There are no antiquities here – just a beautiful creek, with sandbanks and cliffs channelling water of a superb colour, especially after rain, when the sharp contrast between mountain and sea water is best seen. There is a hotel, and two café-bars with simple accommodation, as well as the inevitable souvenir shops; there is some space for bathing, but more for boating. The thing to do, however, is to remove one's shoes and paddle and scramble upstream as far as one wishes. Otherwise there is an ordered footway, cut into the rock in 1950, which is tunnelled and lighted. This leads upstream for an unhurried walk of about ten minutes each way, after which the explorer is thrown upon his own resources.

Route 4: Pollensa, Alcudia, Cape Formentor and the Central Plain

The straight road north-east from Palma parallels the mountains, and links thriving towns with the ancient settlements of Pollensa and Alcudia, each with Roman remains and two spacious bays, less crowded than those of the south coast. Cape Formentor, Majorca's Land's End, comes as a scenic climax. The return journey has been plotted to take in the strange Albufera marshes, famous for their wildfowl, and several of the fourteenth-century market towns, set in the unspoilt agricultural land which they were designed to serve.

There are numerous possible detours throughout this route, and if an attempt should be made to include them all it would be wise to convert this into a two-day trip, by staying overnight on the north coast: in fact, to take two bites at the cherry by assimilating, say, everything to the north and mountainous side of the main road on the first day and on the second, the lesser known inland districts.

Route Leave Palma by Calle de Aragón opposite Calle del Sindicato, three blocks south of the railway stations (Route Exit E). The straight highway (1) runs through stretches of almond orchards and links wine-making towns with the more industrialized, but still ancient town of Inca. This road continues in a direct line to a point 11 km. short of Pollensa, where a left turn leads to that attractive town and nearby places of interest. From here it is only 5 km. to Puerto de Pollensa and a good road along the mountain ridge to the sheltered bay short of Cape Formentor. Follow Pollensa Bay back towards Alcudia and its port, rounding a stretch of the larger bay before plunging into the marshes, to chart a homeward course by meandering secondary roads through La Puebla, Muro, Sineu and Lloret. This route reaches the Palma-Manacor road (p. 242) at a point immediately east of Algaida (p. 243). (Total distance 142 km.)
Bus For Puerto de Pollensa and Puerto de Alcudia depart from railway station.
Train To Inca, La Puebla and Sineu.
Museum Natural history museum at Santa María.

[5 km.] **Pont d'Inca** used to be the first village outside Palma, but nowadays can only be said to mark a point near the limit of the suburbs.

[6 km.] *Son Bonet Aeroclub*, on the site of the island's first airport.

[9 km.] *Son Veri*. This palatial country house stands back from the road at the right turning to La Cabaneta. It contains a valuable collection of paintings, fabrics, furniture and ceramics – most of them the work of Majorcan craftsmen.

[15 km.] **Santa María**. This old market town is thought to have been in existence many years before the Moorish occupation, since it is on the direct route from Roman Pollentia (present-day Alcudia) to Palmaria, as the capital was then named. This supposition is borne out by the discovery of the ground plan of an early Byzantine *basilica* near by. The chief manufactured products are wine and leather goods, similar to those of other towns along this route, though the town's prime function is as the centre of a prosperous agricultural district, where almond orchards undersown with cereal crops take pride of place. The rather sickly but evocative smell from a carob bean distillery hangs over the main square in late summer and autumn.

The most obvious stopping place is where the main street widens to become a market place. To the right there is a *bodega* occupying part of the old *Convent of Los Mínimos*. Its cloister adjoins the *Majorcan Museum*, which specializes in natural history. Another convent, dedicated to *Santa María de la Real*, also possesses a sixteenth-century cloister composed of low, rather countrified arches, and Baroque doors of a later style, which is similarly reflected in the architecture of the *Town Hall*. The *parish church* at the further end of the town is distinguished by the blue tiles set into its belfry. The interior is worth visiting, if only for a charming fifteenth-cenutry painting of the Madonna and the Child Jesus, who holds a goldfinch on a slender leash.

[19 km.] **Consell** is a not very exciting small town consisting of one long main street through which the highway runs. Its chief product used to be the manufacture of *alpargatas*, or sandals made from esparto grass, but nowadays there is a good output of wine and glass.

A reasonably good road leads left from here to **Alaro** [5 km.], a very old town distinguished by its red building materials and a contrasting grey stone church. Having gone as far as this off-course, it is well worth while continuing for two to three kilometres on the uphill road towards Orient to get a good view of the fifteenth-century *Alaro Castle* to the left, one of the strongholds built by the Majorcan kings. As this is in local stone it merges almost indistinguishably into its rocky foundations, and must have seemed impregnable. However this did not prove to be the case when Guillermo Cabrit and Guillermo Bassa made a last stand against the forces of Alfonso III of Aragon, and were roasted alive for their loyalty to the Majorcan reigning house. Alfonso was temporarily excommunicated for this act of cruelty. The footpath from the road up to the castle is very steep, and not recommended for people short either of time or of breath.

It is possible to get back to the main road by taking the Alaro-Lloseta road [7 km.], cutting out Binisalem and reaching Inca after a further 4·5 km.

[21 km.] A Museo Historico, newly created on stage-set lines, shows no prospect of blending into the landscape.

[22 km.] **Binisalem**. Though the country surrounding this busy little town is the heart of the almond-growing industry, it is also famous for its red wines, which are considered to be the best of the island's produce. The name of the town suggests that it could have once been the estate of a Moor named Selim, but all we know for sure is that it became one of eleven such market towns created by Jaime II. In fact, the *church* was originally built in 1364, though it was altered almost beyond recognition in the eighteenth century, and even more recently was heightened and provided with a spire. Nevertheless, it has been cited by experts as being one of the most successful blends of Gothic and Baroque architecture. Marble is used to excellent effect in its interior.

[24 km.] Here it is possible to turn left for **Lloseta** [3·5 km.], set amongst vineyards and close to the mountains. The town's most remarkable feature is the *Ayamans Palace*, traditionally the family seat of the Togores family, one member of which was ennobled in the sixteenth century. The property, which includes formal gardens and orchards, came into the possession of Juan March at the end of the Civil War. He and his family have spent a great deal of money in restoring the palace to its ancient grandeur. The palace and its terrace look out over the town square and towards the *church*, where the chief treasure is a thirteenth-century Madonna, which customarily is placed on the altar but covered by a painted curtain. This statue is assumed to have been hidden at the time of the Moorish invasion, and was lost for some time, until it was discovered by chance by a shepherd. In times of danger it is said to have acquired the habit of disappearing, only to be rediscovered unharmed in its original cache. Besides being a shoe-making town, Lloseta has an enviable reputation for wine and its consumption.

It is 4·5 km. by minor road to Inca.

[29 km.] **Inca**. The main road by-passes most of the town, so that to reach its centre it is necessary to branch left before reaching the railway bridge carrying the Manacor line. But even before that point there are showrooms attached to a factory, inviting passers-by to inspect the leather goods for which this town is famous. Textiles, too, are a local product. Less noticeably – except on Thursdays when an important local market operates in the town centre – Inca is crucial as the marketing point for extensive and prosperous farmlands. An index of change in such matters is that *Dijous Bou*, the annual agricultural show, is now turning over rapidly to demonstrations of farm machinery as an alternative to livestock or craftsmanship. Another recent trend is that many workers travel in by lorries from surrounding villages for work in the factories. The town is growing, and seems likely to overtake Manacor as the next largest and most important after Palma. It is also more sophisticated than others, and passers-by can find good class *bodegas* stocked with barrels of the wine of the country, as well as restaurants that maintain a reputation for presenting the best of local food, such as roast sucking pig. One inn, the *Son Fuster*, is very old indeed.

Most of the churches follow the familiar pattern of Majorcan Gothic imprinted with Baroque decoration, as instanced by the parish *church of Santa María la Mayor*. The first Christian church in the town was adapted promptly from a Moorish mosque, and later became the *Convent of San Bartolomé*. And the one-time *Convent of San Jeronimo* is the place to buy *concos d'Inca*, a very distinctive cake. The factory showrooms, the *bodegas*, and the weekly market are often crowded by tourists in search of bargains, souvenirs and subjects for photography.

From the centre of the town there is a road leading north through Selva (p. 214) to the Monastery of Lluch, and then on to La Calobra (see Route 3, p. 218). One short deviation which might please the unhurried traveller on the way to Pollensa is, after passing the town's outskirts, to take a turning to the right leading to the *oratory of Santa Magdalena* [2 km.] – a simple shrine on the *Puig d'Inca* from which there is a good view.

[35 km.] At this crossroads the right turn leads to Buger, the left to Campanet.

[38 km.] A left turn leads, in 2·5 km., to the church of San Miguel and the *Campanet Caves*. These limestone caverns, which were undiscovered until 1948, have now been fitted with electricity and generally made safe for escorted parties. The prescribed route through them, twisting and turning, measures 1,200 metres. If it were not that the series of caves on the east coast are more formidable, with even better formations, these would attract a great deal of attention. In effect, however, they can be omitted from the itinerary should there be the prospect of visiting the Caves of Drach, or Hams, or Artá on the opposite side of the island.

A famous glass-blowing factory is near by.

The little *church of San Miguel* is unique. It stands in fields, away from everything except its associated graveyard and the home of the custodian. The special quality of this little church lies in the fact that, though it has been restored, it has never been tampered with by succeeding generations, and remains very much as it was originally built: a simple rectangle made from primitive rubble, and ceilinged with wood, with two internal arches. The single nave has no side windows, and there is a plain, arcaded belfry, while the roof is made of local rounded tiles.

[39 km.] A right turn leads, in 3 km., to La Puebla.

[40·5 km.] Fork left off the main road which continues to Alcudia [12 km.].

[49·5 km.] Fork left away from the by-pass which continues towards Puerto de Pollensa. Near this fork a track leads off right up to the summit of the steep *Puig de María* (300 metres) and its tiny *convent*. The site was chosen by nuns in 1371, and they built their own quarters, from which, however, they were removed in the eighteenth century. Hermits then moved in to a site which might well have served as a fortress, and there they remained until the present century, when their successors were offered alternative basic accommodation on Mount Toro in Minorca, making it possible for the nuns to return. The western end of Minorca is visible from the Puig on a clear day. Refreshments are obtainable – and indeed almost mandatory – after a climb which takes about one hour.

[52 km.] **Pollensa**. Here again is a very old town, set inland from its port for the usual defensive reasons, and retaining much of its medieval atmosphere. In fact it has recently been described as 'fit for burghers' – an opinion based perhaps on its tall houses overshadowing narrow streets. Historically the town is known for its resistance to the conquering army of Pedro IV of Aragon shortly before the overthrow of the Majorcan line of kings, and also as the last refuge of insurgents during the rebellion of 1521. Then again the inhabitants successfully repelled a Moorish force which landed at Cala San Vicente in 1529 and the further raid of 1530 – the victory which is so exuberantly celebrated on its anniversary in June.

Pollensa is a pretty town in a beautiful situation, ringed by mountains on one side and agricultural land on the other. The northern quarter consists of modest, terraced houses laid out on a grid system, with cooling plane trees in the central plaza. But the best method of grasping its geography is to view it either from the dominating Puig de María or – more easily because there is a road up to it – from the *Calvary* to the north. Meanwhile, some of the things to look out for in or near the central plaza, are the parish *church of Our Lady of the Angels*, with the minimal lighting provided by an interesting rose window – and a pleasing view from its west front; a former Jesuit monastery converted to become the Town Hall; and the monastic *church of San Domingo*, south-east of the plaza, which is of interest for its barrel-vaulted ceiling and gilded and carved reredos, as well as pictures of local scenes, though these have suffered considerably from ageing. In the *cloister* attached to this church there is a plaque representing the death mask of Philip Newman, the Yorkshireman who died in 1966 and who will long be remembered for having instituted the international open-air Music Festival which draws many enthusiasts to Pollensa in July and August. A school of music occupies part of the cloister, while other quarters accommodate variously a school, a hospital and a home for the aged run by the Sisters of Charity.

It has been claimed by people who know the island well that Pollensa is the provincial town most versed in the arts. Certainly its citizens love to sing and dance, and the women work fine embroidery on linen. Apart from this, the streets and odd corners act as a magnet for painters.

The road to the heights of the *oratory of the Calvary* zigzags, presenting in rapid succession glorious views of coast, mountain and plain. For the energetic and the devout there is a straight flight of 365 stone steps, bordered by cypresses with the Stations of the Cross at appropriate intervals. The time to come here, for maximum effect, is for Good Friday's torchlight procession. The simple chapel at the summit has charm, as has the *church of Montesión* at the foot of the pilgrims' steps. This was built by Jesuits in 1765, not so many years before the expulsion of the order from the island.

Because of the scarcity of Roman remains in an area which must have been thoroughly settled by Quintus Cecilius Metullus, the little *Roman bridge* over the Torrente San Jordi, and just below the road coming in from Lluch, has interest as well as charm. Though not at all imposing, it is worth descending the bank to note the disparity of the two arches. Though the round one is typically Roman, the shallower of the two suggests that it was put in sometime in the fifteenth century, possibly as the result of flood damage.

[53 km.] On the outskirts of Pollensa, beyond the junction of the old road and the by-pass, the left turn is a recently much improved road to the north coast, and the two bays which constitute **Cala San Vicente** [4 kms.]. Despite the limitations imposed by the sheer mountains, and the height of the cliffs on either side, this pretty resort has been developed almost to capacity. However, the detour is well worth undertaking – unless it has been possible to arrange a sea-borne trip from either Puerto de Pollensa or Puerto de Soller. The *Castell del Rey*, to the west but on the far side of a spur of the mountains, is best reached by a minor road leading north from Pollensa from close to the foot of the Calvary, and for the most part following a valley studded with holm oaks [6 km.]. This castle is one of those built by Jaime I, and has stood up well to batterings by the various invasion forces that beset the island, though it has been spared onslaught by the sea, since it stands on a promontory 400 metres high. The garrison survived a long siege by the Aragonese in 1285 and surrendered in 1343 only when the cause of Jaime III became hopeless. These days the castle is the very image of what a Gothic ruin should be, with arches and battlements and above all the theatrical backdrop of sea and mountains, creating an impression that it is looking unblinkingly out towards the mainland of Spain.

[57 km.] **Puerto de Pollensa**. Until fairly recently this was essentially a fishing village, but it was inevitable that with the expansion of tourism hotels and apartment blocks should sprout up most of the way around the four kilometres of the sheltered bay. The planned route might take this as its turning point, but it is worth considering an extension to *Cape Formentor* and its *lighthouse* at the extreme north point of the island [20 km.]. Alternatively exploration of this majestic promontory can be done by boat from the port, while the Hotel Formentor – for many years the best in the land – operates its own shuttle service by sea.

The road to the headland at first follows the line of the bay, then opposite the promontory known as the *Punta de la Avanzada* cuts through the high ground to descend in a series of corkscrew twists to the north coast. There are several *miradores* for the convenience of motorists who wish to enjoy the splendid views which otherwise must escape the attention of the driver. The luxurious Hotel Formentor, on the sheltered south coast, to which the road swings back on its elaborate course, is in an idyllic situation, with its private beach. The road continues, following the ridge and offering on both sides magnificent views and accessible coves of fine sands with compellingly clear water. Near *Cala Murta* is a bust erected to the memory of the Majorcan poet, Miguel Costa y Lobera (1854–1932) whose works in the Catalan language are classics. The road then plunges for 200 metres through the *Es Fumat* mountain before descending to the *lighthouse*, on its rocky promontory, still 209 metres above sea level. Naturally this is a place for splendid views, even on a coast where these come at every turn.

Returning to the main route, the road from Puerto de Pollensa to Alcudia follows the shore of the bay for 8·5 km.

[65·5 km.] **Alcudia**. This walled town, the Pollentia of the Romans, occupies the site of a Phoenician settlement, and sits astride the neck of a promontory separating the two great bays, but looking towards Cape Formentor. After a devastating raid by Vandals in 426, when almost all the inhabitants were forced to flee inland to Pollensa, the town was completely deserted, on account of its vulnerability from two quarters. Later it was fortified by the Moors, and transformed into the Moorish stronghold of Al Kudia, or 'the hill'. Christian settlers reconstructed the Moorish town walls in the fourteenth and fifteenth centuries, but much of their work was destroyed when the stonework was sold by auction in 1871, leaving only two of the original gates standing. Even these have been heavily restored, in 1964–5, while the one original bastion going back to the reign of Philip III has now been incorporated into the structure of a large sports stadium. It is therefore not surprising that the existing walls and the gates with their square towers should have an unreal, theatrical look. However, it is to Alcudia that we must go for Majorca's principal Roman remains – at least those which have not been bulldozed in the interests of modern development. The centre of the Roman city – of which minimal traces survive – was outside the present walls, near the *church of San Jaime*, below the level of the road leading to the port. As for the rest, there is the charming Roman theatre to the right of that road. This site owes its existence in its present condition to the American Bryant Foundation, which occupies one of the old town houses and has converted it into an important archaeological museum.

In fact it is to the little town itself, cramped inside its own confines, that we must look for authenticity – though in connection with a period later than the Moorish. Its narrow streets of solid sixteenth to eighteenth-century architecture retain a medieval look, due largely to their Renaissance-influenced carved doorways and window frames. These houses have been much prized by resident artists and intellectuals. For lesser folk, Alcudia is a place for wandering and for taking photographs.

Two of the important sights are outside the town walls. The primitive *church of Santa Ana* is worth locating, just off the route to the port on what used to be the road linking both towns. It is immediately opposite the municipal cemetery. The church is unspoilt by restoration, and is almost undecorated − in fact faithful to the age when it was built, immediately following the Reconquest, when there was little time for extravagance. Proportionately, the single nave appears to be long and narrow, the only lighting coming from either side. The only details out of context are a tomb with armorial bearings dated 1730, and perhaps the stone figure of the Virgin Child above the west entrance. Her head was lost, but a replacement has been provided.

The *Roman Theatre's* attraction lies partly in its small dimensions; it is in fact the smallest of the twenty-three which have survived in Spain. It is reached by walking a short distance, following signposts, to the auditorium, which consists of eight tiers of seats carved out of the living rock and divided by two gangways. The benches for the leading citizens are in front. It is thought that the backstage rooms were constructed from earth and timber, and consequently they have been lost. But there are some caves behind and underneath the seating which may also have been used for that purpose. This description does not sound impressive, but the simplicity of this place is part of its charm, and its situation in what until recently was countrified reinforces this. Not much imagination is needed to repeople the theatre with actors and audiences of the past.

People with time to spare who have not yet had a surfeit of scenery might consider driving out along the inner (Bay of Pollensa) edge of the *Cape del Pinar*, with its pretty villas set among the pines of *Mal Pas*. Beyond this point the road deteriorates long before it reaches the tip of the headland [12 km.], so that it might be as well to aim no farther than the *Ermita de la Victoria*, 5 km. from Alcudia.

[67 km.] **Puerto de Alcudia**. Until recent times this port was little more than Alcudia's ancillary fishing and commercial harbour − from which, incidentally, steamers still leave on their regular service to Ciudadela in Minorca. Later it was chosen as the site of an enormous power station, which cannot help but be a disfigurement. The wide sweep of Alcudia Bay also proved irresistible to planners, so has now been thoroughly developed, subject only to the limitations imposed by an intractable hinterland. Even so, the quays have restaurants and bars, favourites with the citizens of Palma, from which the distance is no more than 53 km. by fast road, and visitors can spread themselves out further along the shore of the bay.

(The direct return route to Palma rejoins our outgoing route at the fork to Pollensa. However, the alternative cross-country exploration is to be recommended to those who have time.)

Follow the outline of Alcudia Bay, where an area of skyscrapers continues for about 4 km. until interrupted by the *Albufera marshes*. Attempts have been made to convert the outlets of the wetlands into a series of lagoons and canals to be known as La Ciudad de Los Lagos, but few of these plans have been realized, with the exception of the man-made Lago Esperanza which backs a portion of strip development nearer the shoreline. Yet it must be admitted that this huge sandy bay, continuing past *Ca'n Picafort*, and backed by dunes, provides some of the most popular bathing on the island, particularly as it is not hemmed in by mountains and therefore allows room for dispersal.

[71 km.] Turn right at the signpost for La Puebla. This road skirts the *Albufera marshes*, a region little known because of its resistance either to conversion into productive land or, latterly, to urbanization. First attempts were made by an Englishman in the mid-nineteenth century, in the hopes of growing several crops a year. Some canals and pumping stations were established at that time. Nevertheless, the project was abandoned in 1876. Recent threats have dismayed ecologists and naturalists, who regard the area as unique. It is said to harbour more than 200 species of birds – a large proportion of them migrants, making it a port of call midway between Europe and North Africa (see p. 61). Though much of the region's ecology must pass unnoticed by the traveller, this section of the containing road gives a rough idea of the solitude of the district, with its levees and cuttings going off at right-angles through high reeds. Finally the undrained area gives way first to rice fields, and then to rich horticultural land, studded with windmills connected with drainage.

[82 km.] **La Puebla** (in Mallorquin Sa Pobla). This is another of the market towns founded by Jaime II, the site being chosen for the arable land in its neighbourhood. The district in fact is one of the most fertile on the island, growing a succession of vegetable crops acceptable to the catering trade. The town represents one of the earliest attempts at township planning in units of a hundred hectares, each to consist of dwelling, orchard, vineyard and balance of pasture and arable land, with compulsory planting of trees. But the grid pattern does not appear to have regimented the people of La Puebla; they take great delight in their festivals. And though the area is comparatively wealthy, owing to the quality of the land, their women are kept busy weaving such things as hats, baskets, and mats from hemp and the rushes that are so near to hand. The 'Gothic' *church* in fact dates from the seventeenth and eighteenth centuries, and was little affected by the more sophisticated and ornate style of the period that was adopted in larger places.

Turn left in the centre of the town.

[87 km.] **Muró**. If a choice has to be made, this is easily one of the more interesting inland towns for a halt. The *church* on the main square demands some attention, with its tall, seven-storeyed belfry connected by a single arch to the body of the building. A beautiful eighteenth-century Madonna and Child seated in the tympanum over the south entrance is dated 1779. The simple interior is enlivened by a golden eighteenth-century altar. The church of St Francis, at the other end of the town, has recently had its peaceful cloister restored. Muró was one of the towns in which it was fashionable for wealthy persons to maintain town houses, away from their estates. And it is one of these, belonging to the Alomar family, which contains a most interesting *folk museum* which was presented to the nation in 1962. The museum contains much of local interest, with special sections for household effects, as well as a collection of agricultural implements, the most interesting of which is a *noria*, or waterwheel of Moorish invention, operated by a mule or a donkey, and in general use until fairly recently. Two smaller collections consist of pharmaceutical goods – of which the ceramic jars are the most decorative (and coveted) – and a collection of clay whistles, peculiar to Majorca.

Leave Muró by the road to the south, but fork right on the outskirts, away from the signposted road to Santa Margarita.

[96 km.]. Five roads come together (first right to Llubi, first left to Santa Margarita; second left to Santa María de la Salud, and straight on for Sineu). Carry straight on.

[103 km.] **Sineu**. As is typical of these towns of the plain, Sineu is

dominated by its great *church of Los Angeles*, very like the one at
Muró, with its almost free-standing bell tower, but having three
Gothic chapels in the apse. Jaime II favoured this among his new
towns by installing himself in a royal palace, which was used
occasionally by his successor, Sancho. It is here, too, that Jaime III
spent his last night before being killed in the battle of Lluchmayor. In
the sixteenth century the palace was presented to nuns, and is now the
Convent of the Conception. Nothing of the original palace is to be
seen.

A direct and conventional road to Palma continues [35 km.] but
passes through no places of present interest, so that an alternative
route slightly to the south is better. This goes through pretty,
untravelled country where soil colours vary contrastingly from
chalkish white to a dark red, reminiscent of parts of Devon.

[107·5 km.] **Lloret**.

[114·5 km.] **Pina**.

[120 km.] **Algaida** (see Route 8). Turn right for Palma.

Route 5: Foothills of the Sierras

Several shortish round trips in the lower levels of the *sierras* west and
north of Palma are feasible. These take in country which remains
virtually unexplored by the average visitor because they are away
from the coast and possess little sightseeing within the historical
context. We have selected one which follows the best minor roads of
that district nearest to Palma, bearing in mind that this is mountainous
country, and when steep gradients have to be negotiated repeatedly
there must be tortuous writhings and hairpin bends. As several
alternatives present themselves, these are indicated where they occur.

Attractive scenery begins with rising ground on the very outskirts
of the city, and we climb to typical hill villages, follow valleys incised
by water courses and wander through orchards and other pockets of
cultivation. We glimpse, too, many of the fine country houses built by
the Majorcan aristocracy to an architectural design which differs but
slightly from that of their town mansions or *palacios*. The important
difference is that here there has been greater space for the laying out

of formal gardens and landscaping. Most of these country houses are prefixed with the Catalan word *Son*, followed by the name of the owner of the estate, while those of lesser degree are prefixed *Ca'n*.

Route Leave Palma by Calle del General Riera (Route Exit G), which is signposted for Establiments. Fork left, following the course of the Riera *torrente*. After 2 km. take another fork right to the crossroads below Puigpuñent and Mount Galatzó. Return to this point after visiting Puigpuñent and continue, following the contours of the mountains to Galilea, from which a descent is made on the mountain road to Capdella and Calviá, before striking the coast at Palma Nova (p.198). Total distance 48 km.
Bus For Galilea depart from Archiduque Luis Salvador 50.

[6 km.] **Establiments**. A track to the right leads to *Son Berga* [1 km.], one of the grander country houses built in the eighteenth century. Its façade carries the date 1776, showing that it was one of the last of its period to be built. The grounds are particularly delightful with their palm trees, some of which are planted to form an avenue. The estate vineyards were once known for the high quality of their red wine – good enough to be exported to France until 1891, when they were decimated by phylloxera.

Fork left off the Esporlas road, immediately after the Son Berga turning. The main road proceeds north. Just before Esporlas a minor road, which has followed the Canet valley, comes in from Esglaieta. At La Granja (p. 202) a mountain road goes off to the left and follows the deserted upper slopes of *Mount Galatzó*, then rejoins our present route at Puigpuñent.

[8 km.] **Son Gual**, on the right.

[11 km.] Fork right, off the Calviá road.

[16 km.] Cross roads. Facing us is the entrance to *Son Nel*. Turn right for **Puigpuñent**, a delightful and simple agricultural community.

Just outside the village, to the left of the road which continues its climb towards La Granja, is the entrance to *Son Forteza*, one of the highest and most distinguished country houses. It was built by a family among the wealthiest in the land, who in the fifteenth century prefixed their name, making it 'Zaforteza' in order to distinguish themselves from the Huetas, or Jews who had adopted the surnames of those Christians who had befriended them in the events leading up to the mass 'conversions' of the fifteenth century. High on Mount Galatzo, this property has the benefit of several springs of water, some of which are the source of La Riera. Good use has been made of this supply in the provision not only of irrigation but of fountains, cascades and ornamental pools. The house, set on terraces, is more severe in style than some others, and looks down to valleys of almond trees punctuated by cypresses.

Return to the crossroads below Puigpuñent, and keep straight on, following the spur of the mountain.

[19 km.] **Galilea**. The village, just off the road to the right, is one of the most charming in this district, which is noted for its scattered, two-storeyed farmhouses, each set in an area of intense cultivation, with terraced orchards, and backed by pinewoods below the towering shape of the mountain. At this altitude the forbears of the local farmers obviously felt secure enough from invasion to spread themselves out over the workable land, instead of huddling into communities, as did the coastal dwellers. These days, when tourism has gained ascendancy over agriculture, some of these houses have been purchased by foreigners. The *church* is worth reconnoitring, both inside and out, and contains a fine, rather pagan-looking representation of the Virgin Mary.

[25 km.] **Capdella** (or Escapdello). The descent to this lower village is by a continuation of the mountain road, still travelling around the slopes of Mount Galatzó.

At Capdella there is a crossroads: the right turn reaches Andraitx below Son Mas [9 km.] (see p. 200); straight on is Playa de Paguera (p. 199); the left turn, for which we have opted, reaches the Bay of Palma some distance further east.

[29 km.] **Calviá**. This neighbourhood was one of the first to be settled after 1229 by feudal Christian overlords of whom the Bishop of Barcelona was the most important.

The road through the village goes over the *Sierra de Burguesa* by the *Col de Sa Creu* to Palma [15 km.], but the easier route strikes south to the coast, from the right turn in the village.

[31 km.] The right fork is a good road to Santa Ponsa (p. 198), but a corner may be cut by taking the alternative, though inferior, road to the left.

[34 km.] Palma Nova (p. 198). Turn left on to the coast road, described in reverse order in Route 1.

[48 km.] Palma.

Route 6: Monastery of Cura

This monastery, several kilometres from the sea on the summit of the hill of Randa, not only makes a platform for prospecting almost the entire south of the island but also allows one to renew acquaintance with the life and work of Ramón Llull, the medieval scholar and missionary, whom we have already encountered in wanderings around the old quarter of Palma and along the north-west coast.

The outgoing route can follow the shore of Palma Bay as far as El Arenal, giving the traveller the opportunity for viewing, *en passant*, the string of crowded resorts to the east of the city, without being obliged to pay too much attention to them, unless of course advantage is to be taken of their beach life.

Route Though the obvious road from Palma to Randa is by C.715 as far as Algaida [23 km.], the alternative coastal route may be preferred. This choice leaves the city by the Ronda Litoral, or joins it at the bottom of Avenida General Primo de Rivera, near the gasworks (Route Exit C). Keeping in close touch with the shore, a few smaller places are traversed before reaching Ca'n Pastilla, the first densely developed resort along the uninterrupted 4 km. seafront as far as El Arenal. Here leave the coast and swing inland for Lluchmayor, a historic and still thriving market town. A right turning off the Algaida road marks the beginning of the climb to the monastery and its two other places of pilgrimage.

Return to Palma through Algaida, to join C.715. Total distance 65 km. By turning right at Algaida a link with Route 7 (p. 238) is easily made.

Bus To El Arenal via Ca'n Pastilla depart from the railway station.

[1 km.] **Cala Portixol**. Originally this was a small fishing harbour with a horseshoe bay on the outskirts of the city, but nowadays it is too close for comfort. A second, smaller harbour accommodates the Club Maritimo de Levante.

[5 km.] **Cala Gamba**. This resort, backed by the Col d'en Rabassa on the more direct route to Ca'n Pastilla, was once popular because of its accessibility from Palma; but nowadays this militates against it, though its sheltered position is appreciated by owners of small boats, and is favourable for inshore fishing. However, this rocky section of the coast has been eclipsed by the wide beaches further east.

[8 km.] **Ca'n Pastilla**. As we round the headland, immediately to the south of the airport runway, the area of strip development is well and truly with us. Hotels, apartment blocks, shops and places of entertainment begin at the small promontory and overlook the 4 km.

sweep of the Playa de Palma. The buildings are all to the left of the road, and the beach with its ranks of South Sea Island type sun umbrellas is on the right, with a wide strip of promenade between. The main street of Ca'n Pastilla has managed to retain a little of a more old-fashioned atmosphere, though most side streets have a generous quota of bars and cafés geared to the taste of package-tour visitors from many lands.

[11 km.] **Las Maravillas**. This resort merges almost indistinguishably with Ca'n Pastilla and El Arenal. Nowhere along this coast does the development area go back very far into the rather dull country behind.

[12 km.] **El Arenal**. This is the best-known, and easily the most populous of the resorts on this side of Palma – which means that it has the largest hotels and is far from quiet, night or day, and its beach can become very crowded indeed, in spite of the space there is for dispersal. At the southern end there is a small harbour, as a reminder of a previous identity, though pleasure craft and the Club Marítimo have taken over from native fishermen. Just before reaching this point, the road swings inland by way of Calle Cristobal, making for Lluchmayor.

[24 km.] **Lluchmayor** is yet another of the market towns founded by Jaime II. It is built on rising chalky ground and is dominated by its ruddy-coloured *church* with an octagonal belfry, high above narrow streets with grey stone houses pressing in on either side. Most of the day the windows are shuttered, so presenting the illusion that they are uninhabited. With the help of irrigation the district specializes in orchards of peaches and apricots, which are used for jam-making or dried for export. The shoe-making industry is also well established.

Not only was this neighbourhood the scene of the battle which determined the fate of Majorca's monarchy, but it has also proved itself to be an area of prehistoric habitation (see Capicorp Vey, p. 255), the site of which is reached by a road forking back towards the coast to the south of the town.

The main road from Palma to Campos (C.717) cuts through the centre of the town. Our way continues by a left turn in the town centre northwards through pretty country, with the unmistakable hump of Mount Randa looming on the right.

[28 km.] Turn right at the signpost for the village of Randa, but before reaching it take another right turn to begin the ascent to the monastery. This involves a spiral course interspersed with sharp bends, which by the time the summit is reached has almost encircled the mountain.

[29·5 km.] During the ascent two buildings, both to the right of the road, are worth noting: first the small *oratory of San Honorato* in monastic grounds, and not much further on, but looking back towards Lluchmayor from the shelter of a huge outcrop of rock, the primitive hostelry and *oratory of Nuestra Señora de Gracia*. This was founded in the Middle Ages.

In the course of the drive up to a height of 548 metres there is an ever-changing view back towards Palma Bay, to Cabrera and the east coast, and, later towards the western *sierras*, past the whole sheet of cultivation in the plain. Almond country catches the eye: pink and white blossom in late winter and spring, and tender green leaves in summer. Twenty villages may be counted. If the weather is exceptionally clear, not only is the north coast outlined, but Ibiza can just be made out on the far horizon. Here on Mount Randa there is little vegetation to interfere with these wide views. Buzzards may be seen circling interminably above in search of prey.

[32 km.] **The Monastery of Nuestra Señora de Cura**. People arriving at the monastery will be welcomed and shown round by a member of the Third Order of Franciscans – those who wear the black habit rather than the more customary brown of the mendicant order. The friars from Cura maintain a close liaison with their brother house in the United States, so that it is likely that the cicerone will speak good English.

Though the greater part of the building is modern, this has been a place of pilgrimage since shortly after the Reconquest. Much of interest is to be seen, especially in the *library*, where the collections include old music books, missals and medieval manuscripts, housed in an elegant room with a domed ceiling incorporating the Star of David, in recognition of the Palestinian travels of the monastery's founder, the Blessed Ramón Llull. Near the entrance to the *eighteenth-century chapel* there has been set up the painted wooden *cross* which came from the Dominican monastery in Palma prior to its destruction. Outside there is a paved courtyard, and terraces acting as look-out posts, as well as clumps of pines, a spacious car park, and refreshment rooms. In fact this monastery, with its reputation for hospitality, can accommodate a fair number of pilgrims on special days, as well as a constant flow of sightseers during the season.

For the story of this important shrine we must go back to the founder, Ramón Llull, to whom reference has already been made in connection with the churches of Santa Eulalia (p. 176) and San Francisco (p. 166) in Palma, and Miramar (p. 207) on the far west coast.

He was born in Palma between 1232 and 1235 in a house which stood at one corner of the Plaza Mayor, his father being a knight-at-arms in the service of Jaime I, the Conqueror. As a youth Ramón served the king's younger son, who was to become Jaime II, and he appears to have thrown himself enthusiastically into court life, which was not noted for its morality. He married in 1257 and had two children, fatherhood seemingly not affecting his code of behaviour, which ended disastrously in the episode recounted on p. 177. But, as they say, good can come out of evil, and the result was Ramón Llull's total dedication to religion, scholarship and the evangelical life. Recognizing that he would not achieve maximum results in the non-Christian world by the penning of treatises and tracts in Catalan – for which he had developed considerable talent – he set himself to learn to read, write and speak Arabic. He subsequently founded colleges for the similar education of a band of missionaries who were to accompany him into the strongholds of the Islamic faith. After setting up a trust to guarantee the security of his family, he set out on the Feast of St Francis on a tour of holy shrines in Spain and France, during which he took time off for studies at the universities of Montpellier and Paris. This done, he returned to Majorca, where he took into his employ a Moorish slave from whom he learnt colloquial Arabic, and for this purpose he retired to the seclusion of the hilltop above Randa. In 1272 he was to embark upon the first of his prolific writings, *Ars Magna*. He eventually completed about 250 works, most of which were written in the Catalan language. He remained at Randa for about ten years.

Llull's scholarly endeavours came at last to the attention of Jaime II, and in 1282 he was invited to the court of his one-time employer at Montpellier. During the renewal of their friendship Llull was fortunate in being able to enlist the king's assistance in founding a monastic college at Miramar, with the express intention of equipping a body of friars for work in the North African missionary field. The principle upon which he worked was revolutionary: he believed that in order to convert people it was necessary to be in possession of a complete knowledge of their religion and way of life.

By this time Ramón Llull had entered the Franciscan order, much to the chagrin of the rival Dominicans who had hoped to make him one of their own. Having founded his school at Miramar and a hermitage at Randa, he and his band of friars set out, in the style of Paul, on travels which took them through Europe, in Asia as far as Tartary, and in Africa as far south as Abyssinia and the Sudan. In his spare time Ramón researched a variety of subjects, religious, scientific and philosophic, in many fields unrelated to religion. This mode of life was to continue for the remainder of his days, punctuated only by periodic visits to Majorca. It is believed (though never substantiated) that he was martyred in 1315 at Bougie in Algeria, and that his remains were brought back to Palma in a Genoese merchantman. These are in the catafalque in the church of San Francisco in Palma; and a statue has been erected to him at the lower end of Avenida Antonio Maura, west of the Almudaina Palace. The Blessed Ramón Llull is rated one of the foremost scholars in the Europe of his day.

[37 km.] Return to the fork where we left the Lluchmayor-Algaida road, and turn right.

[37·5 km.] A minor road forks off right to the *Ermita de la Pau*.

[42 km.] *Algaida* (p. 243). Turn left just outside the town.

[65 km.] Palma.

Route 7: Petra

Here is an expedition with a difference, in that it goes straight to a target, with nothing of terrific consequence on the way. It could, however, easily be combined with other routes, such as the one to Randa (see **Route 6**). As may be known to visitors from the United States, Petra is the birthplace of one of the greatest of eighteenth-century missionaries to venture into the New World, to whom is credited the foundation of the early missions on the West Coast and, incidentally, the creation of the State of California. However, it is more likely that the name of Fray Junipero Serra is unfamiliar to people of other nationalities; yet because his memory and his relics have been so lovingly preserved in this small town of his birth, and because there is ample to see within a small compass, the trip is well worth undertaking as a short expedition or, more cursorily, perhaps included in a brief detour on the way to the east coast by way of Manacor.

Route Leave Palma by Route Exit D, and follow the C.715 to a point 2·5 km. beyond Villafranca. A left turn here leads in 4·5 km. to Petra. Distance one way 45·5 km. A link with Route 6 could easily be made by turning left through Algaida and following Route 6 (p. 233) in reverse order.
Bus To Villafranca (Manacor bus) depart from opposite the railway station.
Train To Petra via Inca.

The route along the C.715 as far as Villafranca is described in detail in Route 8 (pp. 242–3).

[41 km.] Turn left. The *Bon Any sanctuary* on the hill is prominent. It is described as a detour which may be made on the return journey.

[45·5 km.] **Petra**. Perhaps because it was never favoured with a royal palace, as were Manacor and Muró, Petra existed as a backwater compared with its coeval market towns founded by Jaime II. It would doubtless have remained in obscurity had it not been the birthplace of Fray Junipero Serra, the Franciscan friar, who played such an important part in the settlement and Christianization of the Spanish colonies in North America. Some biographical details will not be out of place prior to a visit.

Miguel José Serra Ferre was born to humble and devout parents on November 24th 1713, and was baptized on that day, and later confirmed, in the parish church of San Pedro. He received his education in the church and monastery of San Bernardino in Petra, run by members of the Franciscan order. It was clear from an early age that the boy was predestined for the religious life. When he was fifteen he was sent to Palma for further education, and one year later was admitted into the Franciscan order, when he adopted the name of Junipero as a sign of his special devotion to one of the companions of St Francis. He specialized in philosophy and theology in the college attached to the monastery of San Francisco, and obtained a degree from the Majorcan Universidad Lluliana. While teaching for some years he developed a reputation as a preacher, and became a highly respected member of his order. However, his mind was set upon missionary work in the foreign field. He applied to missionary headquarters in Madrid for leave to be sent to the West Indies. This permission finally came through when he was engaged upon a spell of Lenten preaching at Petra. Following the annual pilgrimage to Bon Any, he and a companion left the island for Cadiz, where a party of thirty-three missionaries, including five from Majorca, were being assembled for embarkation. They set sail on August 30th, 1749, and after an uncomfortable passage landed at Puerto Rico in mid-October, and then, having survived a bad storm, arrived at Vera Cruz on December 7th.

From here Fray Junipero walked the 500 km. to Mexico City, reaching the church of the Apostolic College of San Fernando on New Year's Day. He volunteered for immediate work in the Sierra Gorda missions in Mexico, and remained for over eight years, during the course of which he was responsible for the building of the magnificent church in Jaipan. By 1758 the Spanish missionaries of New Spain were experiencing murder and extreme harassment, especially from the Comanche Indians, and Fray Junipero travelled the various dioceses making substantial conversions.

By that time Lower California had been won over to the Christians by the Jesuits, but when the order was disbanded by royal edict their work devolved upon the Franciscans. These were represented by fifteen missionaries, with Fray Junipero Serra as their superior. He arrived in the capital, Loreto, on April 1st, 1768. Politics now entered his life in the shape of orders from Carlos III, King of Spain, that Upper California must be won for Spain in order to prevent occupation by a foreign power. That power was Russia, who was showing interest in the potentialities of the western seaboard of the American continent. Colonization and conversion were now to run parallel. Accordingly, military expeditions set out for the north, by sea and by land − Fray Junipero accompanying the latter. His complement arrived at San Diego on July 1st, 1769, making rendezvous there with the sea-borne contingent, which by that time was in poor shape. Many men had died of scurvy. Fray Junipero planted a palm tree over their burial place, and this came to be known as the Serra Palm. It survived for 187 years.

While Fray Junipero remained at his base in San Diego, where he founded the first Upper Californian mission, an advance guard set off to locate and settle Monterey Bay, but failed in the attempt. For a while the entire colonization scheme was in jeopardy, and retreat was imminent. But Fray Junipero managed to negotiate a delay for a special period of intercession, during which relief by sea arrived. Strength of purpose returned, ending in a landing on Monterey Bay, and the foundation of the San Carlos Mission on June 3rd, 1770.

After this initial success, and reinforcement by a further band of missionaries, Fray Junipero continued his work among the Indians. It is claimed that his success was largely due to his inborn knowledge of rural life and agricultural skills, which identified him with Indian interests. The Mission of San Antonio de Padua was founded in June 1771, San Gabriel three months later, and San Luís Obispo in September 1772. There were setbacks so grievous, however, that it again appeared as though the Christian settlement of California would have to be abandoned. As the head of the missionaries, Fray Junipero set out on foot for the long slog back for consultation at headquarters in Mexico City. He arrived there, weak and exhausted, on February 6th, 1773.

As a direct result of his personal intervention, the Viceroy of New Spain changed his mind in determining to persevere with colonization, and to this end even went as far as sanctioning the foundation of new missions. At Fray Junipero's suggestion, he also planned expeditions further north – in effect, as far as Alaska.

The indomitable evangelist was then free to return to California, and arrived at San Diego in March 1774. Two months later he went on to Monterey. The following year the San Diego mission was burned by Indians and the incumbent martyred. Nothing daunted, Fray Junipero re-established that mission, and followed by founding that of San Juan de Capistrano.

By this time safe communications had been established between Mexico and Monterey, leading to the settlement of the bay and harbour of San Francisco. An open air Mass was said there on June 29th, 1776. This presaged the foundation of the mission named after the patron saint of the order, which had made itself responsible for all missionary functions in Upper California since those of Lower California had been handed over to the Dominicans.

In 1776 the first village settlement for Spaniards was established on the banks of the Guadalupe river; it was named San José, and provided with the Santa Clara mission. Four years later, in 1781, an even more important settlement came into being: the village of Nuestra Señora Reina de los Angeles de Porciuncula which, shortened, became Los Angeles. A bronze statue to Fray Junipero

Serra now stands in front of that mission's church.

Despite the outbreak of war between Spain and England in 1779, missionary work continued, resulting in the establishment of the San Buenventura mission in 1782, and eventually that of Santa Barbara, while the ageing Fray Junipero directed operations from San Carlos. There he died on August 26th, 1784, revered by his fellow workers and Indian converts alike. It is there that he was buried.

There are many memorials to this indomitable spirit in California within the context of the missions established by his labours, but it is more indicative of the respect and honour in which he was held that a statue, holding aloft a simple crucifix, is to be found in the Hall of Fame in the Capitol in Washington D.C., placed there in 1927.

The Serra family home at 48 Calle Botellas (known locally as Ca'l Pare Serra) was acquired by the city of San Francisco in 1932. Pruning of anachronistic features has left the simple period house, which is now endowed with household goods in general use in the early eighteenth century, including some authentic relics. The kitchen and small garden are of equal fascination.

(If not on the spot, the guardian of the house, and his keys, can be located in a house four doors away on the opposite side of the street.)

The Museum and Studies Centre, next door to the Serra house, was ordered to be specially built by 'the friends of Fray Junipero Serra' in traditional Majorcan style, so as to house material relevant to the missionary and his work.

The parish *church of San Pedro*: the foundation stone of this Gothic church was laid in 1582; the church contains the *font* in which the baby Miguel José Serra Ferre was christened, and the pulpit from which as a friar he preached some of his most famous sermons. In the sacristy there is a nineteenth-century portrait of Petra's most famous son.

The church of San Bernardino is the successor to an earlier seventeenth-century monastic church. This larger one was consecrated in 1672, and incorporated the school in which Fray Junipero was educated. Visiting Americans will be interested to note that the side chapels are dedicated to the various titular saints after whom the Californian missions were named – as, for instance, the chapel of Nuestra Señora de Los Angeles y la Purisma.

The market square contains a statue of Fray Junipero executed by a local sculptor in 1913 and erected to mark the second centenary of Fray Junipero's birth.

On the return journey to Palma, a visit to the *Sanctuary of Nuestra Señora de Bon Any* can easily be undertaken. Take the right fork on the outskirts of the town and proceed for 3 km. to the steep little hill upon which the oratory and hospice are built. This hill makes a classic site for such buildings as well as an irresistible grandstand from which to survey the quiet central districts of the island. The 317 metre summit is reached by motor road, and is additionally graced by an imposing stone cross, put there to mark the second centenary of the departure of Fray Junipero from Majorca, after he had preached his last sermon near this very spot.

Route 8: Porto Cristo and the Caves of Drach and Hams

The stupendous cave complexes of Drach and Hams, both of which are open to the public and well regulated for safety and maximum visual impact, are close to the small port and seaside resort of Porto Cristo. The Auto Safari Park, near the coast to the north, does its best to display exotic animals in something approaching their natural habitat. The Palma–Porto Cristo road passes through Manacor, the second largest town on the island, and the home of an interesting artificial pearl industry.

Route Take Calle Heroes, at its junction with Avenida General Primo de Rivera (Route Exit D). This develops into C.715, which passes north of the airport, and drives a straight line east past Algaida, Montuiri and Villafranca to Manacor, and from there to the coast at Porto Cristo. The Auto Safari park is 5 km. to the north, off the Artá road which runs parallel to the east coast.
    A round trip, circling either north or south may be contrived by linking with our Routes 9 or 10, but the majority of motorists based in or around Palma might find that a simple there-and-back trip is enough for one day. Distance one way, 60 km.
Bus To Porto Cristo via Manacor, depart from the railway station.
Train To Manacor.

[8 km.] Our route passes to the north of the modern airport.

[9 km.] **Casa Blanca**, a village from which there is a right turn leading back to the main entrance to the airport [2 km.] and Ca'n Pastilla [5 km.].

The route continues without much incident except for the presence of disused windmills – which signify irrigated land – towards low hills rising from the *huertas*, or orchard-farms, where almonds, figs and carob trees are interplanted with catch-crops.

[21 km.] **Algaïda** is by-passed. This market town, lying close to the south of the road, is old, and has an attractive *church* of mixed styles, with a charming primitive Mother and Child presiding over the main door. It is at this point that a road comes in from the direction of Randa and the Monastery of Cura [10 km.], the destination of Route 6 (p. 235). Other roads converge from the inland districts to the north.

[28 km.] **Montuiri** also can be by-passed, and most tourists do just that, apparently satisfied with its outward aspect of lines of old stone-built windmills along its ridge – most of them in such disrepair, and bereft of their sails, that they look like ruined fortifications. As it happens, closer inspection will reveal some traces of *ramparts* and a medieval *convent*. The *church* is dignified by a very small dome.

On the level with the town there is a right turning for Randa [8 km.] and in the town itself a left turn for the small agricultural town of San Juan [6 km.], passing the *Ermita de la Consolación* en route.

[29·5 km.] A minor road leads right to Porreras [6 km.] and Campos [16 km.]. Most of the neighbourhood is given over to cereal crops.

[30 km.] A steep track left leads up to the *Ermita de San Miguel*.

[38·5 km.] **Villafranca de Bonany** comes into sight from some distance away, since it is effectively pinpointed by a domed *church* surmounted by an oversized statue of Christ. The road leads straight through the town and the single main street carries one rapidly out of the built-up area. Incidentally, this town is of importance as the centre of a melon-growing neighbourhood.

[41 km.] A left turn goes to Petra [4·5 km.] and the Sanctuary of Nuestra Señora de Bon Any [7·5 km.]. (See Route 7.)

[48 km.] **Manacor**. Evidence of industrial activity in the form of tile and furniture factories and timberyards herald Majorca's second largest town, while hoardings proclaim its identification with the manufacture of artificial pearls. The demonstration areas and sales counters of the factories concerned do business with coach parties so effectively that many people are brainwashed into supposing that these are all that is to be seen in Manacor. However, a sally into the true centre of the town proves otherwise. It is built of stone of rather a forbidding dark colour, while its urban architecture retains something of the quality of the fortified dwellings which in medieval times were a necessary part of the life style of baronial families residing within reach of a vulnerable coast with no intervening natural barriers.

Manacor was of such great importance amongst those towns founded by Jaime II as part of his scheme to provide agricultural districts with outlets for their produce that he built himself an *Alcazar*, or palace, here. It was also used by his successor, King Sancho. One of its towers, the *Torre de Palau*, at the rear of the church in Plaza del Rector Rubi, is easily located, for its two rooms house a small *museum* containing exhibits which reflect the very long history of the locality. They begin with artefacts of clay and bronze from prehistoric cave dwellings found in the hills to the east and north-east of the town, and are followed, chronologically, by some Roman remains, Visigoth metalwork and Moorish ceramics. But the greatest interest lies in a collection of discoveries from the fourth-century triple-naved *basilica of Son Pereto*, about 5 km. along the Artá road. The mosaics, sarcophagi and other monumental Christian remains have been allocated a room to themselves. Since everything portable has been removed from the site, it is unprofitable to search out this source.

The neo-Gothic *church* distinguished by its tall bell towers, is visible from a great distance across flat, cultivated country, and the seventeenth- and eighteenth-century *convent of San Domingo*, with its two-tiered cloister, has attractive Baroque decoration. Besides the remains of the Alcazar there are two further towers of the same period, and other fragments of outer defenses crop up here and there. Both of the towers, the *Torre de Ses Puntas* and the *Torre del Anagistas* are within easy reach of the main square, though of course they originally were part of the perimeter of the town.

Whatever may be thought of coerced sightseeing, the pearl factories are worth visiting. At both of the main factories a glassed-in walk has been contrived to follow the production line. The material is shaped into thin, taper-like rods which are then melted into globules of the correct size and weight by the flame of a blowlamp, while being twiddled by hand to achieve perfection. The final stages are grading and polishing. There is a great degree of craftsmanship involved, but one of the fascinations is that though the composition of the basic material is said to be secret, rumour has it that the principal ingredient is pulverized fish scales. Whatever the truth, the result is impressive, and these iridescent Majorcan 'pearls' find their way to high-class jewellers in most European cities, both unset and threaded and twisted and arranged into all manner of designs.

The main road (C.715) to Artá has left Manacor to its right. Drive straight through the town centre on the Porto Cristo road.

[60 km.] On the heights above the harbour of Porto Cristo are signposts for the Caves of Hams to the right and the Auto Safari Park to the left. Directions for reaching these follow (pp. 247, 248).

[61 km.] **Porto Cristo**. This was one of the first resorts to be developed for visitors, but it had an importance of its own in relation to Manacor, for fish and for sea-borne trade. It has a pretty harbour, with fishermen's houses built up around a winding inlet. It is only recently that the upper levels have been developed. There is a small sandy beach inside the sheltered area, and visitors need go no further than the quays for their angling. The *Aquarium* overlooking the harbour from the west, was opened in 1975, and is of high standing in the world of marine biology. Twentieth-century history is recalled by the *fighter plane* mounted to overlook the harbour. Porto Cristo saw the island's only severe fighting during the Civil War, when in August 1936 a Republican force some 12,500 strong, and backed by naval units, landed close by after the occupation of Ibiza. A front was established between here and Artá, but when the Nationalists counter-attacked with Italian air support, the invading force retreated with heavy losses, after three weeks' fighting.

Holiday life at Porto Cristo would be more peaceful were it not for the exploitation of two vast complexes of limestone caverns which draw crowds and make demands upon parking space, as well as promoting a proliferation of bars, eating places and souvenir shops. It is as though Cornwall's St Ives and the Cheddar Caves coincided, with a strain on both. Yet it would be foolish to allow this perhaps unfortunate circumstance to deter one from experiencing the scenic pleasures of the place, and particularly the caves, which may be something new to the British experience.

The Caves of Drach lie about a kilometre south of the port. The existence of the Dragon Caves, to give them their translated allegorical name, was known for many years before the end of the nineteenth century, when they became famous as a result of the questing curiosity of the great Archduke Luís Salvador, then resident at Miramar (pp. 207–8). It was he who commissioned the noted French geologist, Professor E. A. Martel, to explore and survey them, following a preliminary and almost fatal attempt in 1878. The more scientific operation began in the second week of September 1896, with the participation of two Majorcan enthusiasts. As far as the present-day public is concerned, the result has been to provide access to a well-regulated underground route consisting of platforms and flights of steps, up and down, which continue for 1·2 km.; though the total extent of the labyrinth has been calculated as at least 2 km. The prescribed route takes about one hour – longer when there are crowds, as may happen on Sundays and holidays and at the height of the summer season. Concealed electric lighting not only makes the experience safe, but also enhances the beautiful and in some cases grotesque shapes and colours of the rock formations and the more regularly fluted stalactites and stalagmites. The effective lighting is the work of the Catalan expert, Buigas, who acted as consultant following his success in floodlighting the great fountains of Barcelona as part of the 1929 International Exposition. He has paid special attention to reflections in the still waters of the underground lakes, where reality and mirrored image merge mysteriously. It may be remarked here that much of the blackening of the roofs has been caused by the smoke from torches carried by visitors previous to the installation of electricity.

For convenience, the connecting caverns may be divided into 'suites' of rooms, each having attracted some descriptive name. The principal among them are known as *La Cueva de los Franceses* (the Frenchmen's), the *Cueva de Luís Salvador* – in honour of the nineteenth-century patron – the *Cueva Blanca* and the *Cueva Negra*. While the caverns themselves have comparatively staid names, the same cannot be said for individual formations: the *Image of San Antonio*, the *Venus de Milo*, the *Indian Pagoda*, and many others. The truth is that centuries of slow-dripping water has produced calcium carbonate 'statuary' of all imaginable shapes. We can make what we will of such abstractions, some being beguiled by a ceiling composed of porcupine quills, or fish scales, ferns or other naturalistic shapes, some by formations resembling giant fossils, and some by imaginary phantasmagoric tableaux.

Much of the magic of the caves can be attributed to the presence of underground water in pools and channels, and in one large lagoon, known as the Martel Lake, which is overlooked from an auditorium that can seat some 3,000 people. Here, as the finale to the tour of the caves, visitors are treated to a water pageant of *son et lumière* performed by singers arriving in a torchlit procession of decorated rowing boats. Barcarolles, most suitably, take precedence on the programme.

For the inquiring visitor, *Lake Martel*, which was named after its discoverer in 1896, is said to be the largest underground lake in Europe. Its extent is about 177 by 40 metres, and in places it is 14 metres deep. It is of scientific interest that this measurement varies, not so much seasonally or even tidally (though there is connection with the sea) but as it is affected by the barometric pressure of the outside world. However, shreds of mystery remain in the advancement of another theory, that some of this variation is caused by seismic underground movement which has not yet been explained. Visitors must be prepared for an air temperature which remains constant, winter and summer, at about 20°C – and this, combined with some exertion may make for claustrophobic conditions. Neither photography nor smoking is allowed.

The exit seems to come suddenly and without much of a climb. A few visitors are lucky enough to secure a boat trip on the way out.

The Caves of Hams

These are reached from the left turn off the Manacor road, on the ridge above the town, and near the Castel del Hams Parador. Since they are so close to each other, comparison with the Drach Caves cannot be avoided. To begin with, those of Hams are smaller, less magnificent, but for this reason perhaps prettier, and the colour of the rocks and formations has not been affected by smoke, for although the caves were discovered in 1906, they have only recently been organized for mass sightseeing, and consequently have never known other than electric lighting. Many of the stalactites are whitish, and almost transparent, which gives the effect of marble. Others, due to the presence of ochres and iron oxide, provide a contrast. The prescribed route is plotted and hewn to include seven grottoes, all of which have been endowed with appropriate but fanciful names, such as *The Enchanted Villa*, *Paradise Lost*, *The Madonna of Montserrat*, *La Crèche* and *The Angel's Dream*, and each with items or 'exhibits' similarly labelled; though, again, some visitors prefer to make their own interpretations. One point of interest lies in the word 'Hams' itself; this is derived from a Majorcan word meaning 'fisherman' – its significance here being that some of the stalactites take an upward turn, and resemble the barbs of fish-hooks.

Neither is this set of caverns without water. A trickling underground river at one point forms 'The Venetian Lagoon'. One feature here is a breed of aquatic creatures, not unlike centipedes though they live under water and swim, and are classified as fish rather than insects. However still and clear the lagoon water, they are too small to be easily located in their natural habitat, so live specimens have been collected and put into a glass tank for inspection.

The route through these caves is physically less exacting than that through Drach. Parties tend not to be so large, and therefore are not over-organized.

The Auto Safari Park. From the Caves of Hams it is necessary to turn back a little way towards Porto Cristo in order to get on to the secondary road to Artá, which parallels the east coast at a distance of about 1 km. Yellow signs blazon the way to the park, so that no mistake can be made on the way north past *Cala Morlanda* and *Cala Moreya* – two of the many coves which are characteristic of the east coast. Upon nearing the entrance to the park, 5 km. from Porto Cristo, a display of such things as assegais and shields made of zebra skins leave us in no doubt of our arrival. As at Longleat and other wildlife parks, only wheeled traffic is allowed, and for their own sakes – chiefly to foil the mischievous proclivities of apes – visitors are advised to keep car and coach windows closed. There are no carnivores, and therefore little personal danger, though the monkey tribe are apt to make free with human possessions and have been over-encouraged by constant feeding. Ostriches, exotic breeds of deer, pelicans, marabous, flamingoes, peacocks, gnus, oryx, antelope, zebras, rhinoceros and giraffes are among the denizens, some in their own enclosures. All can be viewed at snail's pace, following a winding arrowed route which makes the most of the available space and the effort of the promoters to reflect the African image, in the midst of which the animals appear to be more bored than melancholy.

The easiest way back to Manacor is by the outward route via Porto Cristo.

Route 9: Artá, its caves and the north coast

This route heads for the north-east corner of the island, south of the wild headland of Cape Farruch – the nearest point to Minorca. It ends at Cala Ratjada, a fishing village recently developed for tourism on the rocky, pinewooded coast, with smaller sandy coves near at hand. On the outgoing journey a visit is made to the magnificent caves of Artá, east of the medieval castle of Cañamel. The way back is through the fortified village of Capdepera, and the still-medieval town of Artá, continuing by way of the north-east coast with its vestiges of ancient civilizations contrasting with the more obtrusive new coastal developments. After skirting the Albufera marshes (p. 228) on the edge of Alcudia Bay, a straight road, the best in the island, leads back to Palma, parallel to the mountains (pp. 219–21).

Route Leaving Palma by Route Exit D, take C.715 as far as Manacor [48 km.] as on Route 8 (pp. 242–3) and continue along it as it swings north-east towards Artá. Digress by turning right at San Lorenzo [57 km.] for Son Servera [65 km.], which offers a possible detour to the east coast resorts of Cala Millor and Cala Bona [7·5 km.]. Two km. further along the Cala Ratjada road there is another right turning, leading to Port Vey [3 km.] and Costa de los Pinos, a further 3 km., both resorts typical of the east coast. From Son Servera it is 6 km. to the Caves of Artá, and the nearby Castle of Cañamel. The Son Servera road continues for 4 km. to Capdepera [75 km.] at the junction with C.715 from Manacor and its continuation to Cala Ratjada and the headland of Punta de S'Olla.

The return journey follows the shoreline from Ca'n Picafort to Alcudia, and back to Palma on the direct road through Inca (pp. 219–21).

Bus To Cala Ratjada depart from opposite the railway station.

Train To Manacor and Artá, via Inca.

[48 km.] **Manacor** (p. 243). The main Artá road by-passes the town on the right.

[57 km.] **San Lorenzo**. Turn right, passing a side road which comes in from Porto Cristo and various small seaside places between there and *Punta de Amer*, such as *Cala Moreya* and *Cala Morlanda* (p. 248).

[66 km.] **Son Servera**. A short detour may be made from here to the sea at **Cala Millor** [2 km.], a modern resort spreading along an extensive bay, with a seafront of hotels lining a promenade which is largely traffic-free. The development has spread to the older **Cala Bona**, 1·5 km. to the north and centred around a small harbour.

[68 km.] A second diversion to the east coast leads to **Port Vey** [3 km.] and the picturesque *Cap de los Pinos* [3 km.] – a name which speaks for itself.

[74 km.] Turn right here for the *Cuevas de Artá*. To the right on low-lying ground, you will see the *Torre de Cañamel*, a medieval keep standing four-square as a key position in the defence of the island against Saracen raiders. Besides their primary function as defences, such towers acted as early-warning systems – the signal of imminent danger being relayed by fires of brushwood kept ready for that purpose. Though outwardly picturesque, this castle compares unfavourably with that of Capdepera, further along the route.

[79 km.] **The Caves of Artá**. When it nears the sea, the road has to climb several hundred feet before reaching the entrance to the caves and the parking place overlooking a precipitous drop. A many-stepped ramp leads up to the cavernous antechamber to the caves, where visitors wait to be sorted out into groups. This gives an opportunity not only to peer forward towards what is to come, but also for backward glances at the sea framed by rocky portals in striking contrasts of light and shade. Despite the grille which at first inhibits passage into the underworld, the approach is more magical than that of either Drach or Hams (pp. 246, 247), but there is the same attention to safety, discreet and artistic illumination, and relayed Wagnerian music provided when the magnificence of the changing scene and natural 'props' demand it. On the whole, these caves are more impressive in their grandeur, though – to balance the account – the underground water which can be assumed to have formed them, no longer exists.

This cave system has been known since the thirteenth century to contain one of several individual caves believed to have been used by more than a thousand Moors taking refuge from Jaime I and his conquistadors, until they were forced to surrender by a smoking-out operation such is nowadays used for the stupefaction of bees. The Artá Caves are also reputed to have inspired Jules Verne to write his *Voyage au Centre de la Terre* in 1864. The caves penetrate the headland for 310 metres, and most are noted for their great height. One, the *Hall of Standards*, where the formations resemble partially furled flags, reaches to 45 metres. Others of particular note include the *Hall of Columns*, where one pillar of fused stalactites and stalagmites stands 17 metres high. Some of the columns are slender, and when tapped by the guide emit definite notes, which echo and re-echo into the distance. The *Devil's Hall*, 45 metres below the surface, is particularly infernal in aspect on account of its proliferation of rough columns, like the encroaching boles of palm trees. This is matched by the *Paradise Hall*, with patterned formations reminiscent of the pipes of a giant church organ.

Return to the Son Servera–Capdepera road, and turn right where a cross-country road cuts across to Artá.

[88 km.] **Capdepera**, standing above the Cala Ratjada road, is one of the oldest and most picturesque of Majorca's fortified villages. The inhabitants were originally concentrated within the walls, but they tended to spread beyond these limits as soon as the threat of piracy diminished. The ruins of the castle, standing guard above the village, preserve its original outline; the crenellated walls, some 400 metres in circumference and equipped with four towers and a main gate, were built in the fourteenth century by order of King Sancho, who endowed the fortress with a Gothic oratory in a sheltered position dedicated to *L'Esperanza* (Our Lady of Good Hope). The nearby *windmill* is of course later, but is of importance as evidence of the water supply which contributed to the castle's potentiality to withstand siege. The castle is reached by steps; the best place to park is in the main square of the village.

To the north of Capdepera there is a virtually untamed headland jutting out in the direction of Minorca. It is from here that Jaime II perpetrated his confidence trick in persuading the occupying forces of Minorca that he was heading an invincible army, whereas he had at his disposal no more than six knights and a handful of courtiers. He did this by lighting a long line of fires along these high places, arguing massive troop concentrations, and so gained the Moorish capitulation without bloodshed.

A roughish road leads north from Capdepera to **Cala Mezquida** [6 km.] – an isolated bay laid out by British interests as a holiday village.

[90·5 km.] **Cala Ratjada**, in the shelter of the *Punta des Farayos* the most easterly Majorcan headland, was a fishing village long before its attractive situation brought visitors to what is also the furthest seaside place from Palma. It attracts many sailing devotees, while the best bathing beaches are at *Son Mol* to the south and **Cala Guya**, 1 km. north of the *Punta de S'Olla* with its watchtower and lighthouse.

Locally caught fish is an added attraction, as are the painted boats still used by the locals.

Return on C.715, and continue past Capdepera and the junction with the side road from Son Servera.

[110 km.] **Artá**. Because of its inland situation, Artá has managed to remain virtually unaffected by the revolution wrought by tourism. There is a distinct likelihood that the town was settled by the Greeks and Phoenicians, and it certainly was by the Moors, who named it Jartan, and are thought to have had a castle on the site of the present *hermitage*. This is of ancient foundation, its original purpose being to enshrine a miraculous image of the Virgin Mary which accompanied the conquistadors in 1229. The hermitage stood until 1820, when it was demolished as a measure to counteract contagion from a plague which in that year was killing many thousands of people. Between 1825 and 1832 it was rebuilt and surrounded by the present castellated wall.

The town itself remains distinctly medieval in atmosphere, with neat terraced houses once owned by grandees lining the winding, paved streets leading up to the ancient stronghold on the ridge above. Some of these houses still have coats of arms in their façades, and black marble doorposts and lintels. The single-naved *church of San Salvador* is an example of pure Catalan-Gothic architecture, and is reached by steps.

A great deal of interest is provided by the neighbourhood of Artá. It contains several prehistoric sites, a few of which are maintained in sufficient order to impress the visitor. The easiest to reach is the *Talayot de Ses Paisses*, just outside the town to the left of the road to Manacor, near the railway line. *Sa Canova*, 10 km. along the road to Alcudia, is another. Many of the finds from these ancient sites are on view in Artá's *archaeological museum*. Tourists more interested in scenery might prefer to explore the neighbourhood to the north, starting with the hills which culminate in *Mount Morey* (560 metres) near Cape Farruch. Much of this wild corner of the island is uninhabited, though it may be explored on an unsurfaced road leading from Artá to the *Hermitage of Betlen* and its hospice [10 km.] or the more difficult track to the watchtower called the *Atalaya de Morey*, from which there is the best of all possible views across Alcudia Bay in the direction of Minorca, which is often visible on the horizon. On the lower ground around Artá dwarf palm trees are a feature; they form the basis of a cottage industry which produces matting, hats, and many shapes and sizes of containers.

Take the C.712 leading west.

[118 km.] A road leads north, past the prehistoric village and megalithic monuments of *Sa Canova* to the *Colonia de San Pedro* [5 km.] on the east side of Alcudia Bay, but comes to an abrupt end about 1 km. later.

[120 km.] A minor road to the left goes south to Manacor [18 km.].

[122 km.] On the far side of the *Torrente na Borga*, another country road leads to Petra (p. 238) [14 km.].

[124 km.] **Son Serra**. A road to the right negotiates sand dunes, to reach the shore at *Colonia de Son Serra*.

[126 km.] After another bridge over a 'torrent' there is a road left for the old market town of **Santa Margarita**, known locally as Santa Margalida [12 km.].

[129 km.] **Son Real**. The site of a *Phoenician necropolis*, the contents of which are to be seen in the archaeological museum in Alcudia.

[132 km.] **Ca'n Picafort** is at the centre of a major chain of developments planned to take advantage of the Bay of Alcudia, which is backed by dunes and pines. The beaches are of grey sand. To the east, near *Son Baulo*, strong currents can be a hazard to swimmers.

[134 km.] The road which has been built to serve Ca'n Picafort's related developments comes in from the right, while one to the left goes back to Santa Margarita, and also forks to skirt the *Albufera marshes* (p. 228), leading eventually to Muró (p. 229) [11 km.] and La Puebla (p. 228) [12·5 km.].

The Alcudia road continues along the coast with a line of dunes between it and the sea, and marshlands to landward. The route crosses the main drainage canal of the marshes, and reaches a development area at Lago Esperanza (see Route 4).

[145 km.] **Puerto de Alcudia** (p. 227). Turn left at the harbour.

[148 km.] **Alcudia** (p. 226). Turn left on to the main road to Palma.

[150 km.] The Pollensa road (p. 223) comes in on the right. The route from here back to Palma is covered in Route 4 (pp. 218–23).

[201 km.] Palma.

Route 10: South-east coast

The scenery changes abruptly beyond El Arenal. The coast becomes wild, and its shore is reached with difficulty, while the hinterland is almost featureless until the south-eastern tip of the island is rounded. Until then the few seaside places are patronized mainly by families with modest requirements. In making as close as possible a tour of this neglected part of the island, we pass within easy reach of Capicorp Vey, one of the most complete prehistoric settlements in the Balearics, and one which not only has been well documented, with literature in several languages available on the spot, but is maintained by the authorities in good order, so that the megalithic remains can be identified and speculated upon.

The excursion embraces as many as possible of the seaside places which begin to proliferate within a succession of headlands as soon as the east coast proper is reached. Many of these can be visited on short there-and-back deviations from the inland linking road. This also passes within easy reach of such inland centres as Campos, Santañy, Porreras and Felanitx. Just beyond the last of these there is the opportunity to drive up to the Sanctuary of San Salvador, a most exciting place 500 metres above sea level, which surveys wide tracts of hills and vineyards farmed by people thoroughly preoccupied with traditional day-to-day life. A visit to Santueri Castle might also be considered.

Route Taking Route Exit C, follow the built-up shoreline east of Palma as far as El Arenal (pp. 233–4). Then, instead of cutting inland to Lluchmayor, turn right beyond the yacht basin and continue along the coast as far as Cape Blanco, after which the road runs some 5 km. inland, passing Capicorp Vey, and offering side-trips to Vallgornera, La Rápita, Puerto de Campos and other small places. The route described is the inland one by way of Santañy − eventually reaching the coast at Porto Colom (p. 258). Total distance 142 km.
Bus For Cala d'Or depart from Av. Alejandro Roselló 97.

[12 km.] **El Arenal** (p. 234).

[15 km.] **Cala Blava**. This urbanization consists mainly of villas and chalets, surrounded by maquis, but affording one of the last points of access to the sea for some distance. The route follows the outline of the clifftops, but at some distance from the edge, so that only occasional glimpses of the shore, some 100 metres below, occur. Much of this desolate, unproductive land is sequestrated for military purposes.

[30·5 km.] **Cape Blanco**. An excellent viewpoint and lighthouse, where the road turns inland.

[36·5 km.] **Capicorp Vey** (or Capocorp Vell, one of several alternative spellings) is one of the most important prehistoric sites in the Balearic group. It is thought that the settlement may have been inhabited some 1,000 years before Roman times. Its fame — if not knowledge of its existence — may be attributed to the indefatigable Archduke Luís Salvador, though systematic excavations were not undertaken until 1918, under the direction of the Institute of Catalan Studies, after which the site was designated a national monument.

The place is easily found because the way to the entrance is signposted. The custodian lives in a farmhouse on the corner of the road opposite, and will unlock the gates for visitors. The features most easily identifiable, after the climb over megalithic blocks, are two square towers or *talayot*s possessing internal chambers, in conjunction with an outer wall which contains a great many chambers constructed of drystone and with foundations going deep into the red earth. Two outer towers are circular. Cursory exploration may prove baffling, but assistance is at hand in the form of the official pamphlet obtainable from the custodian. It sets out the bare facts in French, German and English and, more fully, in Spanish, and has a map.

Various objects found during excavation, for instance pins made of bone, pottery and grindstones, as well as other objects of later date — running up perhaps to the time of the Roman occupation of the island, have been removed for safe keeping to the Barcelona archaeological museum.

Part of the magic of this place can be attributed to its lonely situation in the midst of wasteland. This may also furnish a reason for the site having remained undisturbed by agriculture or the demand for building material during the course of possibly 3,000 years.

From here there is a road leading back to the coast, to the first development beyond Cala Blava. **Cala Pi** [3 km.] is built on the edge of a beautiful creek, and the neighbouring newer resort of *Vallgornera* [1 km.] is patronized particularly by French visitors.

[43 km.] A left turn leads to Lluchmayor [13 km.] and a right turn to the coast at **Estanyol** [4 km.] from where there is a coastal road to **La Rápita** [4 km.], a small seaside place without much character.

[50 km.] At the crossroads the left turn is for Campos [5 km.] and the right for La Rápita. [5 km.]

[54·5 km.] Turn right to pass on the right the saltpans known as *Las Salinas de Levante*, and on the left the Balneario or spa hotel associated with the thermal springs of *San Juan de Campos*. This is strange but attractive country, and a happy hunting ground for ornithologists, especially those interested in waders and migrants.

[59 km.] The Santañy road comes in on the left.

[61 km.] **Puerto de Campos** is an attractive fishing village, with a modern church presented by a member of the March family. *Colonia San Jordi* opposite has furnished evidence that a Roman settlement or trading centre may have existed here. If so, use would have been made of the thermal springs. However, salt is nowadays a prime factor here, even for the development of the village, since it has to cope with the demands of that industry for housing, etc. There are plans for further development. Boating expeditions to the *island of Cabrera* (p. 259) may be arranged from here. It is twelve sea miles away, and is clearly visible on most days of the year. There are also excellent views of this almost unspoilt coast back as far as Cape Blanco.

Return 2 km. to where the road forks right.

[66 km.] **Ses Salines** village.

[69 km.] A track goes off south through strange level country to *Cape Salinas* [9 km.] and its lighthouse.

[70 km.] **Llombarts**.

[74·5 km.] **Santañy**. Here our route converges with the main road from Palma [51 km.]. This ancient fortified town is devoted to agriculture, and is set in charming wooded country. It was largely rebuilt in the sixteenth century, following a Saracen raid which laid waste to it and the neighbourhood. A gate and portions of ramparts have survived.

It is from this district that the famous Santañy yellow stone was quarried, to be transported for the construction of so many of the medieval buildings of Palma, and even to be shipped as far afield as Naples. The *church* is a dominating landmark, and should be visited, if only for a sight of the enormous church organ which was brought here after the closure of the Dominican convent in Palma.

At this point of the excursion the touring visitor may want to take stock of further possibilities. The map will show that a good secondary road runs north-east for 33 km. to Porto Cristo, (p. 245) the first place where it reaches the sea. However, there remains an almost bewildering choice of alternatives, each ending at some point in the fretwork of creeks and coves for which the east coast of Majorca is remarkable. **Cala Santañy**, **Cala Llombarts** [3 km.] and **Cala Figuera** [5 km.] are the furthest south – the last named being to many minds the most picturesque, though swimming is from platforms, as the beaches are a short distance away. According to taste, a decision may be reached to cut further inland, over the not very high mountains which run parallel to the east coast. This road, C.714, goes to Felanitx [16·5 km.] and passes within reach of the medieval *castle of Santueri*, once the most important of its period, whose function it was to guard the east coast ports and inland towns. It withstood many a siege in the Middle Ages.

We opt to describe the more easterly route, indicating side trips to the coast where these occur, until, level with Porto Colom, we turn inland for Felanitx and the *San Salvador Sanctuary*. The continuation of the road north from Porto Colom leads from 3 to 5 km. inland of the sequence of small coves known as the *Calas de Mallorca*, a rocky stretch from *Cala Murada* to *Porto Cristo.*

[79·5 km.] **Alqueria Blanca**. At the further end of the village there is a right turn for **Cala Modrago** [7 km.] and the road goes straight on to **Porto Petro** [6 km.]. This is a delightful fishing harbour built on the edge of a typical creek, which does not so far appear to have been over-developed. Turn left at the crossroads in Alqueria Blanca.

[83·5 km.] **Calonge**. A right turn goes to **Cala d'Or**, a relatively new development, with low-lying villas built into rocky headlands thick with pines. This resort may be recommended to underwater enthusiasts. A network of smaller places based on narrow creeks is to the north, with a second road leading back 2 km. to S'Horta. From Calonge a minor road goes into the mountains, south of Santueri Castle, and after 5·5 km. joins the Santañy-Felanitx route.

[85·5 km.] **S'Horta** A right turn provides an alternative route (see above) to the **Playa d'Or** resorts.

[89·5 km.] Turn right for **Porto Colom**, an old port at the end of a broad but shallow harbour overlooked by quays where old boathouses have been converted for modern occupation.

[90 km.] Second turning for Porto Colom.

[91 km.] Fork left for Felanitx, cutting through the hills. The Sanctuary and its huge cross act as a direction post pointing the way not only to Felanitx but, more fancifully, to the upward haul towards heaven.

[96 km.] Turn left on to the steep, twisting but well-graded road leading up to the sanctuary.

The Sanctuary of San Salvador [6 km.] This is visually the most exciting of all comparable holy places on the island. The tortuous ascent gives a panoramic preview of the surrounding country – which can be fully enjoyed from a spacious terrace 500 metres above sea level. The medieval hermitage was enlarged in the seventeenth century, and is now additionally equipped with a hostelry and refectory for the visiting public. The special works of art to seek out in the *chapel* include a beautiful Gothic sculptured reredos, and a Madonna, also in stone. Baroque, garlanded columns contribute to the feeling of richness. Outside there is an enormous statue of the Sacred Heart under a canopy reminiscent of Kensington Gardens' Albert Memorial, while on the north side a huge cross set up on a flanking hill towers over the carpet-like landscape below.

[93 km.] **Felanitx**. Turn left when the road from Manacor is reached. Felanitx is one of the most important market towns in the south-east and was founded, like many others, soon after the Reconquest. Today it trades principally in white wine, almonds and pottery. The *church*, unduly large for present needs, was restored in the seventeenth century, and is approached by a flight of shallow steps. The façade, pierced by a rose window, and with a Baroque entrance surmounted by an elaborate pediment, is otherwise plain, and the whole is of

Santañy stone, such as was used by Guillermo Sagrera for Palma cathedral. This is his birthplace.

Take a secondary road leading north-west past Mount Mola towards Porreras.

[94 km.] Fork left away from the Villafranca road.

[107 km.] **Porreras** is another town with a history as a market centre. It was built in the thirteenth century to accommodate Catalan settlers. The district around specializes in cereal crops, and grows the best milling wheat, to the quantity of which, at least, the windmills of the neighbourhood testify.

Cross the Villafranca-Lluchmayor road, and carry on north-east.

[114 km.] **Montuiri** (p. 243). Turn left onto C.715.

[142 km.] Palma.

Route 11: Island of Cabrera

This island, lying 17 km. off the south-eastern tip of Majorca, does not feature on the tourist map because it is short of water, there being only one spring. Its vegetation has been substantially depleted by the depredations of wild goats, leaving it all the more dry and bared to its rocky skeleton, which is crowned by the Puig de la Guardia (172 metres) — a name which gives a clue to the island's historical significance in the days of manned watchtowers, and to its present function, with the keepers of two lighthouses and their families, doubling up as marginal farmers, as its sole inhabitants.

Route The 51 km. trip by sea from Palma by scheduled service takes about three hours, but the expeditions by motor cruiser operated through tourist agencies are more convenient, and include circumnavigation of the island as well as a visit to the Cova Blava. These operate in the summer season only. It is also possible to arrange outings from one or two of the fishing harbours between Puerto de Campos and Porto Colom. (p. 256 and p. 258). There are no restaurant facilities on the island, so that packed lunches are the order of the day.

During the early seventh century Cabrera was of sufficient consequence to have its own bishop and religious community, but these did not survive the Vandals, or the Islamic invasion. The island only became re-populated in the fourteenth century as a military outpost of the Christian kingdom. The fourteenth-century *castle*, built upon a rock and standing high above the entrance to the harbour was several times captured by Corsairs, to be used by them as a base from which to launch more profitable raids against the Majorcan coast.

Later the whole island was to become a prison-fortress for criminals and political offenders – a sort of mini-Devil's Island – most notoriously in the early nineteenth-century after the battle of Bailén in southern Spain when Napoleon's army surrendered to the Spaniards. Initially, prisoners of war, numbering about 19,000, were force-marched to Cadiz and kept in prison hulks under conditions so desperate that almost three-quarters of them perished. At that stage survivors were transported to Cabrera, where conditions were scarcely better, due not only to the chronic water shortage but also to the difficulty of victualling the island across a channel beset by currents and prone to winter storms. Very few managed to escape, and though eventually officers and non-commissioned officers were transferred to England, other ranks were reduced to about 2,000 in number, until, in fact, a viable prison population was reached. Even so, it is on record that this was achieved by murder, mayhem, disease and even cannibalism. The last few hundred survivors were finally carried off by a French transport in 1814, putting an end to a dreadful experience which had lasted five years. In 1849 a memorial was erected, overlooking the small port, to honour those who had died in captivity.

Cabrera is the centre of a small group of rocky islets, of which *Conejera* is the second largest. The total area of the island is no more than 1,800 hectares, most of which consist of cliff and barren rock. At its greatest stretch it measures no more than 7 km. from north-east to south-west, or from west to south-east – though most of the latter measurement consists of a tongue of protective land south of the fine natural harbour, which is of sufficient depth to accommodate ships of substantial draught. Such tracks as there are on the island cover easy walking distances, though there is little level ground.

Besides the castle and the sea views the other interesting feature is the grotto or *Cova Blava*. This is inaccessible except by small boat – and even then landings are dangerous. The secret of its beauty is deep water overlying white sand, resulting in reflections comparable to those of Capri's well-sung tourist attraction.

MINORCA

INTRODUCTION TO MINORCA

Some of the natural philosophy of Minorcans seems to communicate itself to the island's visitors, in that they seldom feel an urge to do too much, too quickly, or beyond what is necessary to enrich the period of their stay. Even sightseeing need hardly be planned, and certainly not over-organized; interesting things to be seen, heard and tasted will occur in the normal course of events, and according to personal inclination.

The two capitals, one harking back to the eighteenth century, and the other to earlier, more exotic days, and linked by an excellent highway which forms a mini-grandstand raised above much of the interior, reveal the essentials of this pleasantly relaxed island, while the coastal villages, and even the newer built-up resorts rely for their charm on natural resources: scenery, food and drink and the basic activities peculiar to beach and bay. Both Mahón and Ciudadela are compact and easily assimilated, while the island's most original monuments, the *taulas*, *talayots* and *navetas*, present themselves not only unexpectedly in country districts, but also alongside roads which are in everyday use.

TRANSPORT ON THE ISLAND

Buses

There is no railway. A regular bus service runs between Mahón and Ciudadela at two-hour intervals in the winter and more frequently in the summer. Most of the popular seaside resorts in the east of the island are served by buses from Mahón, and those in the west from Ciudadela. These services are operated by

Mahón: Transportes Menorca S.A., Plaza Miranda 17.
Ciudadela: Transportes Torres, Calvo Sotelo 42.
Fornells: Autocares Fornells s/n.

A comprehensive timetable is available from Tourist Offices, and hotels also supply the necessary information.

Taxis

These are the best means of making round trips, especially if four people can share. Lists of official fares are displayed in hotels, but where some diversion is to be made a price should be discussed beforehand, and allowance made for waiting time. Minorcan taxi-drivers have a reputation for honesty.

Guided tours by coach and boat

Excursions to all the resorts, as well as trips around the harbours may be made from Mahón and Ciudadela – and passengers may be picked up at their hotels. Leaflets are to be found at hotel desks, where bookings may also be made. Otherwise visitors should contact one of the local travel agencies licensed to operate these services; among those in Mahón are:

Viajes Iberia, Calle General Goded 39.
Viajes Universal, Plaza José Antonio 21.
Thos Cook and Son, Plaza Generalísimo 10.

Car Hire

Travellers are advised to make prior arrangements through their tour operators, paying in sterling. Otherwise, well-established firms have offices in Mahón.

It is also possible to hire motor scooters, but bicycles are more difficult, and the most likely place to find them is in Villa Carlos, adjacent to the church.

Maps

The official map issued by the Tourist Office is overall rather too simplified when compared with the Firestone Balearics one (p. 23). However, its street plans of Mahón and Ciudadela are excellent and easy to follow.

HOTELS AND HOSTALES

Because new hotels appear most years, or have changes made to them, the best guide to accommodation must be the official leaflet issued annually by the Tourist Information Office in Mahón, or by the Spanish Tourist Board in London (see p. 25). At the time of going to press there are only four four-star hotels, the most individual being the long-established Port Mahón on the Paseo Marítimo overlooking the water, and away from dense building.

The Mahón leaflet also gives a short list of small restaurants (*fondas*) with basic accommodation, and guest houses (*casas huespedes*). There are no camping sites.

In the following list, telephone numbers are given in brackets.

Mahón
HOTELS
Four star: *Port Mahón*, Paseo Marítimo, (362600). (Swimming pool).

Two star: *Capri*, San Esteban 8.

HOSTALES
Two star: *El Paso*, Cos de Gracia 157.

One star: *Orsi*, Infanta 19.
                    La Perdiz, Mahón 14.
                    Reynes, Comercio 26.
                    Roca, Sta Catalina 4.
                    Sa Roqueta, San Juan 62.

Cala'n Porter
HOTELS
One star: *Aquarium*, Playa.
                    Playa Azul, Apartado 130.

HOSTALES
One star: *Castillo Sancho Panza*, Urb. Cala'n Porter.
                    La Paysa, Via Principal.
                    S'Acantilat, Calle W. Parcela 37.

Ciudadela
HOTELS
Three star: *Almirante Farragut*, Urb. Los Delfines, (382800). (Swimming pool, tennis).
                    Cala'n Bosch, Urb. Tamarinda, (380600). (Swimming pool).
                    Cala Blanca, Urb. Cala Blanca, (380450).
                    Eleycon, Paseo San Nicolás, (380250). (Swimming pool, tennis).

Two star: *Cala Galdana*, Cala Sta Galdana, (373000).
                    Cala'n Blanes, (382497).
                    Los Delfines, Urb. Los Delfines, (382450). (Swimming pool, tennis)
                    Ses Voltes, Cala Santandria, (380400).

One star: *Cala Bona*, Urb. Son Oleo, (380016).

HOSTALES

| Two star: | *Mar Blava*, Urb. Son Oleo. |
| | *Menurka*, Domingo Sarria 6. |

One star:	*Alhambra*, Trav. Calvo Sotelo.
	Bahía, Playa Santandria.
	Madrid, Calle Madrid.
	Oasis, San Isidro 33.

HOLIDAY CAMP

| Three star: | *Club Siestamarinda*, Urb. Tamarinda (380550). |

Cala Galdana

HOTELS

| Four star: | *Audax*, Cala Galdana, (373125). (Swimming pool) |

| Three star: | *Los Gavilanes*, Cala Galdana, (373175). (Swimming pool) |

Fornells

HOSTALES

| Two star: | *Port Fornells*, Ses Salinas, (375073). |
| | *S'Algaret*, Plaza Generalísimo 7, (375174). |

Arenal d'en Castell

HOTELS

| Four star: | *Castell Playa*, (371450). |

| Three star: | *Aguamarina*, (371276). (Swimming pool) |

| Two star: | *Topacio*, (371301). (Swimming pool) |

Santo Tomás

HOTELS

| Four star: | *Santo Tomás* , (370025). (Swimming pool, tennis) |

| Three star: | *Lord Nelson*, (370125). |
| | *Los Buhos*, Playa (370050). |

| Two star: | *Vistamar*, Urb. Santo Tomás, (373000).(Swimming pool, tennis) |

San Luís

HOTELS

| Three star: | *S'Algar*, Urb. S'Algar, (361704). (Swimming pool) |
| | *San Luís*, (361750). (Swimming pool, tennis) |

| One star: | *Pueblo Menorca*, Punta Prima, (361850). (Swimming pool) |

Sur Menorca, Urb. Biniancolla, (361800). (Swimming pool, tennis)
Xaloc, Playa Punta Prima, (361922). (Swimming pool, tennis)

HOSTALES
Two star: *Son Rusiñol*, Ctra. Binibeca, (361824).
              Xuroy, Cala Alcaufar, (361820).

One star: *Mar Blava*, Playa Punta Prima.
              Playa Punta Prima.

Son Bou
HOTELS
Three star: *Laguna Playa,* (371075). (Swimming pool, tennis)
              Tamo, Urbanización, (371175). (Swimming pool, tennis)

Villacarlos
HOTELS
Three star: *Agamenon*, Paraje Fontanillas, (362150). (Swimming pool)
              Rey Carlos III, Miranda de Cala Corp, (363100). (Swimming pool)

Two star: *Hamilton*, Paseo de Santa Agueda 6, (362050). (Swimming pool)

HOSTALES
Two star: *Miramar*, Fonduco, (362900).
              Rocamar, Cala Fonduco, (365601).

One star: *Toni*, Castillo 3, (365999).

TOURIST INFORMATION

Though a wide range of tourist literature is obtainable from the Spanish Tourist Office in London (see p. 28), specific local information is obtainable on the spot at the two addresses in Mahón listed on p. 266.

HEALTH

The advice on vaccination given on p. 31 is equally applicable to Minorca.

The addresses and telephone numbers of hospitals are listed under the sections on Mahón and Ciudadela. In Mahón there is always one chemist remaining open twenty-four hours a day, while others take it in turns to open on Sundays and feast days. The duty chemist's address is to be found in the current local newspaper.

MAHÓN

Population 20,000

Air and sea connections
Mahón's airport, San Clemente is 5 km. from the town centre.
Terminal Plaza Explanada.
Reservations Aviaco: Plaza Explanada 59.
Shipping Berths immediately below the city.
Reservations Compañía Trasmediterránea, Calle General Goded 27.

Buses
To Alayor, Mercadal, Ferrerias and Ciudadela: C. José M. Quadrado.
To San Clemente, San Luís, Punta Prima, Alcaufar and Cala'n
Porter: Plaza Explanada.
To Villa Carlos: Plaza San Roque.
To Fornells: Plaza España.
To San Cristobal: Plaza Bastión.

Taxis
Plaza España (tel. 362891).
Plaza Explanada (tel. 361283).
Plaza Miranda (tel. 363113).

Hotels See p. 263

Information
Oficina de Información y Turismo, Plaza del Generalísimo 13.
Delagación Insular del Ministerio de Información y Turismo, Plaza Explanada 48 (*Map* **7**).

Post and telegraph office
Calle de Buen'Aire 15. (Hours 09·00–13·00, 18·00–19·00).
Twenty-four hour service at the telegraph section (*Map* **6**).

Telephone exchange Calle Calvo Sotelo 4.

Medical services
Hospital Municipal, Cos de Gracia 26.
Residencia Sanitaria, Calle Bellavista.
Red Cross, Cos de Gracia 26 (tel. 361180).

Police *Traffic Police* Calle Concepción 1 (tel. 363712).

Consulates
British British affairs handled by the British Consul in Palma, Majorca.
French Calle Iglesia 2.
Netherlands Calle de la Infanta 3.
Italy Calle Norte 2.
Greece Calle General Sanjurjo 24.

Banks include:
Banco Central, Calle General Goded 39.
Banco Español de Credito, P. Generalísimo Franco 11.
Banco Hispano Americano, Calle Deyá 5.
Hours 09·00—12·00 Monday — Friday.

Theatre Principal, Calle Deyá (*Map* **12**).

Cinemas Salon Alcazar; Actualides.

Clubs
Club Marítimo, Calle Andén de Levante (*Map* **13**).
Tennis club: Pistas Talayot.

Lost property Plaza del Generalísimo Franco 1.

HISTORY

Where sightseeing is concerned, history may be taken as beginning in the eighteenth century, from which almost all of the town's architecture springs. However, this rather easy assumption is contradicted by Mahón's site, at the head of a secure deepwater inlet which dictated its use by the Mediterranean powers for many centuries before the warring interests of Spain, France, Austria and Great Britain brought it into strategic prominence, and the occupying power eventually designated it the capital of the island.

The Carthaginians and the Moors both had strongholds here, but during the Middle Ages, when Palma was experiencing a trade boom, the neighbouring island remained isolated and uncompetitive. History had consisted principally of fierce and predatory Arab raids, as in 1534 when Khair ed Din, otherwise known as Barbarossa, sacked the town to devastating effect. Improved systems of defence were subsequently created on either side of the entrance to the harbour, which meant that though the eighteenth-century town was out of range, it was subjected to several sieges – the most important being in 1756, when the Duc de Richelieu mounted an effective blockade.

THE OLD TOWN

This presents no problems to the sightseer, who would be well advised to park his car, if that is the means by which he has arrived, since everything of importance is within easy walking distance from the town centre, which may be taken to be the *Plaza de la Conquista*. Arrival and departure points for country buses, which serve different quarters of the island, are logically distributed, and they are situated not far from this point, a few blocks away in the direction they serve. Though all the inner streets are narrow and somewhat similar − so narrow as to be one-way − and not arranged in any geometric pattern, one cannot be lost for long, as the northern edge of the town is defined by a cliff overlooking the quays that border the inner harbour. Respite may be had there before plunging anew from sunlight into overshadowed darkness. From the edge of the town it may be seen that though Mahón is 5 km. from the sea it is unmistakably a seaport.

There is very little modern building in the town; developments have been restricted to the suburbs, so that the inner streets have a timeless quality which transmits the feeling of preoccupation with traditional trade and craftsmanship and does not pander unduly to outside influences, such as gimcrack impulse buys, though local products, many of them destined for everyday use, are well in

---

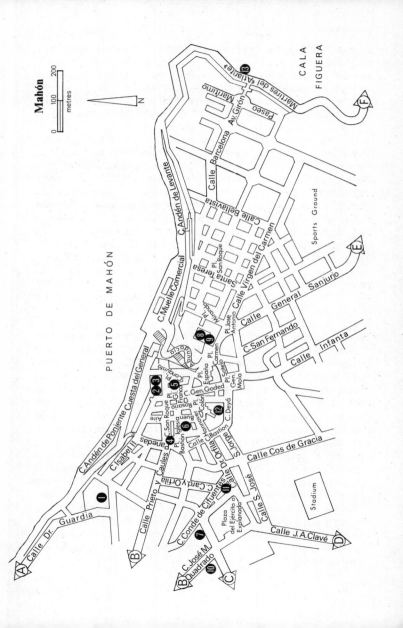

Mahón

metres
0   100   200

N

PUERTO DE MAHÓN

CALA FIGUERA

Calle Dr. Guardia

Calle Prieto y Calles

C. Andén de Poniente Cuesta del General

C. Isabel II

C. Muelle Comercial

C. Andén de Levante

Calle Barcelona

Av. Girón

Paseo Marítimo

Martínes del Atalaie»

Calle Bellavista

Calle Virgen del Carmen

Santa Teresa

Pl. San Roque

Pl. Miranda

Pl. José Antonio

Calle   General   Sanjurjo

C. San Fernando

Calle   Infanta

Sports Ground

Calle Cos de Gracia

Calle S. José

Calle J. A. Clavé

Stadium

Plaza del Ejército o Explanada

C. Conde de Cifuentes

Card. y Orfila

Calle Dr. Orfila

Calle S. Jorge

C. Deyá

Pl. Gen. Mola

Pl. Colón

Pl. Sotelo

Pl. Carmen

Pl. España

C. Gen. Goded

Pl. Rosario

Calle Chamor

C. Bastión

Calle del Carmen

Calle Iglesia

C. San Roque

C. del Aire

Penedes

Pl. Franco

Pl. Constitución

Garcia

C. José M. Quadrado

A
B
C
D
E
F

evidence. The citizens of Mahón are friendly, and make up in their helpfulness for the characteristic (and perhaps commendable?) absence of identification of the various buildings and institutions which the stranger may wish to visit. Small and intimate shops make loitering a pleasure and there is an excellent choice of cafés and bars, such as the American Bar in the Plaza General Mola, which has a reputation as a rendezvous for all comers.

Let us pretend an arrival by sea, when the first view of the town will be cliffs topped by white houses and dominated by the outlines of three important churches. Between them there is a great flight of steps leading up to town level, in relation to which a serpentine carriageway, delightfully named *Calle Abundacia*, ascends to the Plaza de España, not far south of the Plaza de la Conquista, our point of reference. Here we come upon the *church of Santa María* (*Map* 5) and, close by, the most important museum on the island, as well as the elegant *Town Hall* (Ayuntamiento or Casa Consistorial, *Map* 2). There is also a *statue of Alfonso III of Aragon*, Minorca's own conquistador, and an arch through which there is a particularly photogenic view of the harbour. Not far to the east is the *Carmelite church* (*Map* 9), the cloisters of which have been converted into a *market* (*Map* 8). The separate fish market is hard by.

But to see the most concentrated area of seventeenth- and eighteenth-century streets one should wander further west, preferably by way of Calle San Roque, to see the sole extant remains of ancient fortifications and then north-west, by way of the old-world Calle Isabel II with its splendid array of eighteenth-century town houses. This street leads to the *church of San Francisco* (*Map* 1), at the outer limit of what may interest the sightseer, and presents a further fascinating view of the harbour, without which none of this would ever have come into being. The town houses may present impassively plain faces to the street, but their proportions are fine, and most of them have courtyards and a cliff-hanging prospect of the harbour from their rear. One is supposed to be able to detect English influences in the Mahonese architecture, as well as in furniture design, but these appear to have mellowed by now into something distinctly Minorcan.

For the rest, the enormous *Plaza de la Explanada* brings one into the neighbourhood of useful addresses, not only the principal Tourist Office, some bus stops and a choice of eating-places, but also, near by, the central bus depot and Calle Cordova y Orfila with its banks and travel agencies.

PRINCIPAL SIGHTS

Church of Santa María
Plaza de la Conquista; Map **5**.

Though this church was founded by Alfonso III in 1287, the year after he overcame Arab resistance in the island, its present neo-classic form owes itself completely to reconstruction between 1766 and 1772, a period when Minorca was governed by the British. Its impressive single nave with Gothic roof is lit by arcaded windows set high in the walls. The fabric of the interior is local stone, while the *altar* is framed in red marble with an elaborate heavy canopy, and flanked by Solomonic or barley-sugar pillars. The orientation is paradoxically from north to south, the high altar being at the north end. Much of the detail, especially in the side chapels – some of which were crowded out by the dimensions of the altar, and the remainder inserted between buttresses – is distinctly Baroque in style. But for many people the most interesting feature of all will be the *monumental organ* which occupies the gallery over the main or south door. This was built by an Austrian, Johannes Kiburz, in 1810, and is rated one of the most important in Europe. It is noteworthy that its transportation from the Continent was effected at the height of the Napoleonic Wars, and great credit must be given to Admiral Lord Collingwood for interesting himself in the project. The relevant correspondence and documentation is filed away among the archives of the Casa Cultura Library. Apart from the very obvious beauty of the instrument, and the materials from which it is made, its size and scope cannot fail to impress, comprising as it does four keyboards, fifty-one registers and over three thousand pipes. And, as a reminder of the troublous days of that and an earlier period, when the fate of the island swung like a pendulum, the church also contains memorial tablets to two of the French governors who ruled Minorca between 1756 and 1763.

Ayuntamiento or Casa Consistorial (Town Hall)
Plaza del Generalísimo Franco; Map **2**.

The traditional seventeenth-century building was thoroughly restored in 1788, when its façade was provided with attractive arcades and balconies furnished with the wrought iron of the period. Another distinctive feature is the English-made clock, presented to the town by Sir Richard Kane. The entrance hall contains the British coat of arms brought from Fort San Felipe after its defences were demolished. The (literally) plushy reception hall is hung with portraits of civic dignitaries, past and present, amongst whom is Dr Mateo Orfila, a Mahonese who won international repute as a pharmacologist.

At a lower level, entered from the street, there is a small vaulted room displaying the island's saleable handicrafts, including the model ships which are a speciality of the craftsman who has set up his workshop in the town of San Luís.

Church of San Francisco
Calle Isabel II; *Map* **1**.

This church dominates the western end of the old city, as it does the roadstead, though buildings have encroached upon it so that there is inadequate space in Plaza San Francisco for a long view of its lovely façade, the chief ornamentation of which is a Romanesque and therefore anachronistic doorway; nothing however, is lost from that fact – indeed it makes an aesthetic link between the plain stone of the church's front and its ornamental parapet and belfry. The church, attached to the adjoining Monastery of San Francisco, was built in the seventeenth and eighteenth centuries, following the destruction of the town by Barbarossa's Corsairs. Definite dates have been ascribed to one side chapel (1738) and the apse (1791). The interior consists of a single nave without aisles, though there are five side chapels on each side. The roof is in six sections. Contrary to general practice it is entered from the east end, and the high altar, accordingly, is to the west. This was dictated by the exigencies of the site. The *high altar* is a splendid one, flanked by Solomonic pillars in gold and brown, entwined with carved flowers and foliage, and with rather more sober pictorial panels. But probably the more striking feature here is the large *octagonal chapel* on the north side. It is lit by a lantern-topped dome supported by those attractive twisted Solomonic pillars, all garlanded in vines and roses, and usually attributed to Franciso Herrera, who worked for ten years in Minorca before being summoned to undertake his major work on Palma's cathedral.

Though badly damaged in the Spanish Civil War of 1936–9, the church has been well restored. The ancillary monastic buildings near the entrance were originally dormitories and service rooms for the friars, but they have been turned over long since to become a school, orphanage and youth centre, and are therefore not open to the general public.

OTHER SIGHTS

Carmelite church
Plaza del Carmen; *Map* **9**.
In former times this domed eighteenth-century church, with its enormous interior, was attached to the Carmelite convent. Nowadays the adjoining cloisters have been adapted to form the town's principal covered market, which has an attraction all its own, though the transformation may be initially shocking. The Baroque west front of the church is plain, and bears the date 1751. Evidence in the form of small objects found on the site seems to argue that it could have been a Roman cemetery, but it has yet to be excavated.

Statue of Alfonso III
Plaza de la Conquista.
The square of la Conquista is graced by the Aragonese king, represented as a young man. It was the gift of Dr Francisco Franco y Bahemonde, better known to us as General Franco.

San Roque Arch
Map **4**.
This medieval gateway, with its supporting towers, was built in the reign of Pedro IV of Aragon, and straddles the *calle* of the same name; it is the sole surviving fragment of the town's medieval defence system.

MUSEUMS

Museo Provincial de Bellas Artes de Mahón or Casa de Cultura
Plaza de la Conquista; *Map* **3**.
Originally this was a *palacio* owned by a noble family, and though the date, June 16th, 1761, appears on its entrance arch, the interior is older. The museum sets out to display a cross-section of the island's history − one of its prides being a mosaic pavement from the Isla del Rey, one of the harbour's islands. A place has also been found for some Mayan and Aztec artefacts transported from the New World. The museum occupies the ground floor of the palace. On the higher level there is an excellent library of ancient books and documents, and a room containing portraits of our George III and Queen Charlotte. Other rooms house material relevant to the port and harbour,

including charts, models of ships and interesting pictures and prints, while a separate collection of eighteenth-century books, other publications and MSS throw light on the British occupation.

(The whole of this cultural complex has been pronounced structurally unstable, and therefore has been temporarily closed to the public. So far plans for its rehabilitation, or the re-housing of its contents have not been promulgated.)

Ateneo Museum
Calle Conde de Cifuentes; *Map* **11**.
The proper name of this institution is the Ateneo Científico, Literario y Artístico – which gives a clue to the manifold functions of the society to which it belongs. On entering what was once a smallish private town house, one finds reading rooms and a library, and a great variety of miscellaneous objects, such as stuffed birds and seashells, but all relating to natural history. The boast is that this inconspicuous building houses the most comprehensive collection of seaweeds in southern Europe.

Teatro Principal
Calle Deyá; *Map* **12**.
A gem of its kind, this once-glamorous building has been relegated to being used as a cinema. When it was designed in 1824 the intention was that it should be an opera house, to replace the garrison theatre which was demolished when the British forces were evacuated from Minorca, and indeed it served as such until the outbreak of the Spanish Civil War. The concierge may be contacted 'out of hours', and will show people over for a small tip. Incidentally, contemporary scores and playbills are to be unearthed from among the archives in the Casa de Cultura.

SIGHTSEEING ITINERARY

When setting out from Plaza de la Conquista, it will assist one's orientation first to walk the short-distance to the head of the flights of steps descending to the harbour, in order to overlook the port installations, the deep water channel, inner islands and opposite shore. Then, returning, the *church of Santa María* (*Map* **5**, p. 271) is dominant on its island site on the west side of the plaza. North of this point we see the archway, a relic of old fortifications, close by the

Casa Cultura, or principal museum, (*Map* **3**, p. 273) and the adjacent
Ayuntamiento (*Map* **2**, p. 271).

From this point Calle Generalísimo Franco and Calle General
Goded lead southwards away from the sea to Plaza General Mola;
from one corner of this square Calle Sotelo slants back to Plaza
Carmen, to the church of that name (*Map* **9**, p. 273) and the *market*
(*Map* **8**) in its cloisters.

Returning to Plaza de la Conquista through Plaza de España, walk
along Calle San Roque to the *San Roque Arch* (*Map* **4**, p. 273), which
effectively blocks the street to heavy traffic. Plaza Bastión, at this
point, is on the edge of a maze of streets for shoppers and happy
wanderers, though the dedicated sightseer may prefer to persevere in
the opposite direction by way of Calle Panedas and Calle Isabel II to
the *church of San Francisco* (*Map* **1**, p. 272), the western limit of this
itinerary.

Though everything of prime importance has by this time been
taken in, the return journey might be varied by heading for Plaza
Explanada, where the Tourist Office (*Map* **7**) is located, and Calle
Conde de Cifuentes, at a tangent to the north-west side of the plaza,
for the *Ateneo Museum* (*Map* **11**, p. 274), Calle Dr Orfila, Calle Bastión
and Calle Deyá (for the *Theatre*, *Map* **12**, p. 274). Then skirt the most
interesting shopping quarter, to return to Plaza General Mola and the
already explored district around Plaza de la Conquista.

ROUTES ON MINORCA

Minorca's road system makes round tours difficult to plan or usually unfeasible to attempt. With one central highway, from which minor roads slant north and south to the coasts, and without links between, it is advisable to return from one destination to some initial point of deviation from the Mahón-Ciudadela road before setting off at a tangent for another. This is because the terrain allows for very few coastal roads. Our routes have accordingly been charted as beginning not only from Mahón and Ciudadela – obvious choices – but also from Alayor, Mercadal and Ferrerías – the three market towns which straddle the road between the two cities. These are not, however, intended to be overnight stopping places, for there is little accommodation for tourists, since they are intrinsically agricultural centres. The diversions could of course be treated as optional detours from the main route, but it seems more sensible to describe them individually, since it should be remembered that a large proportion of visitors to Minorca install themselves at small seaside places – north, south, east and west – rather than in Mahón or Ciudadela. Hence their approach to various coastal places is likely to be from any given direction. The Chart of Excursions (pp. 12–13) gives distances as the shortest one-way route from Mahón.

It may be added that though travel by country bus cannot be wholly ruled out, Minorca is the one of the principal Balearic islands where use of car or taxi is especially to be recommended if the island is to be explored more than superficially.

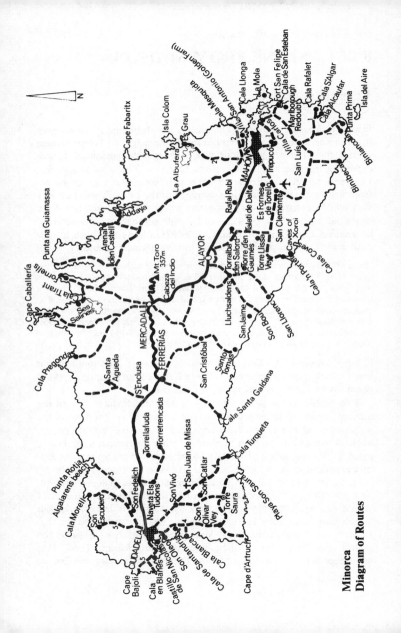

Minorca
Diagram of Routes

EXCURSIONS FROM MAHÓN

1: South coast

Instead of keeping compulsively close to the shore and its views over the harbour, those people who are interested might be better advised to visit the Trepucó megalithic site, a short distance inland, before exploring the two small but historic towns of Villa Carlos and San Luís, and the various seaside resorts which have sprung up, or grown from fishing harbours, within easy reach of the town. These last, in a way which is characteristic of Minorca where the conformation of the shore admits of few coastal roads, will present a succession of alternatives consisting of, usually, a diversion there and back from a road which closely parallels the sea but is definitely inland.

Route The most attractive route out of Mahón to the south-east is by way of the quays (Exit F), starting at the commercial dock and rounding Cala Figuera on which the town's principal and long-established Port Mahón hotel sits in a commanding position. Here too is the Club Marítimo, which is of great social as well as nautical importance. An alternative way out of the town is by Calle General Sanjurjo (Exit E), bearing left towards Villa Carlos but taking, almost immediately, a right turn on a consistently signposted but narrow road to Trepucó, passing en route the new Horizonte *urbanización*.

[2 km.] **Trepucó**. At the end of what has become little more than a track which leaves a cemetery to the left, there is an adequate parking place for cars, but no supervision of the site.

This prehistoric settlement has as its principal features two of the ancient types of structure for which Minorca is famous in the archaeological world. The *taula* consists of a massive central upright, about 4 metres high, which supports another laid across it, making a giant 'T'. It is the tallest of its kind. Diagonal chisel marks may be seen on the central stone, which is set in a groove so as to provide stability. As is usual, a series of smaller standing stones are grouped around. The associated *talayot*, a solid tapering monument, the purpose of which has never been defined to the satisfaction of all experts, but which may have been a watchtower, is certainly well sited for that function. It overlooks not only Mahón and its harbour but also the inland districts as far as their highest point, Mount Toro. This advantage was not overlooked by the French commander, the Duc de

Crillon, in his command of the island between 1781 and 1782. He mounted guns on the summit of the *talayot*, and at the same time assembled many of the scattered stones on the site to make a star-shaped surrounding wall. This disturbance has placed difficulties in the way of research into the design of the settlement, but work on the site is well documented in accounts of the Cambridge Museum of Ethnology's excavations of 1932–4, which are presented in readable form in Margaret Murray's autobiography, *My First Hundred Years* (see p. 353).

[3 km.] **Villa Carlos**. The fascination of this town is due to its distinctive style and period. At the time when it was built by the British in the 1770s it was called Georgetown – in honour of George III – and served as a garrison for troops manning the island and, in particular, the forts at the entrance to the harbour. The chief survival from those days is a gigantic parade ground lined by barrack buildings. In fact, the whole town is planned with a precision which is patently military, and English at that, with doorways with fan-lights, windows with sashes, and iron door-furniture – all of which are commonplace in English towns, but outlandish in this context – to be found in side streets.

The seafront, which follows several indentations, has picturesque bars and simple eating places set into arches which may double up as boathouses. The bathing here is not to be recommended, except in hotel swimming pools, of which there are several. The most attractive, but by no means the biggest of these hotels is El Fonduco (otherwise known as the Hotel Almirante) on the road back towards Mahón. This was a private house occupied by Admiral Lord Collingwood after the battle of Trafalgar, and its public rooms contain some excellent prints as well as British and Spanish uniforms of the period. Like the Port Mahón hotel its exterior is painted a Venetian (or Georgian) red – again a most unusual, and therefore evocative colour for this part of the world. The hotel looks back towards Cala Figuera, which is now a depot containing oil storage tanks, but which was once the point of intake of fresh water for the British fleet.

Being so close to Mahón, Villa Carlos is nowadays virtually a suburb, with developments spreading inland, and it provides some night-life, which is in short supply in Mahón itself. From here one can continue above the shore in the direction of the fortifications at the mouth of the harbour.

[4·5 km.] **Cala de San Esteban**. The road to this cove facing the entrance to the harbour deteriorates as it passes the site of Fort San Felipe, the strongpoint demolished by the Spanish authorities in 1807, a short time before the French invasion of the Iberian peninsula. Above we can see the Marlborough Redoubt (p. 285), which can be visited, although part of the area is still a prohibited military zone. The top of the Redoubt provides an excellent view of the opposite shore and its twinned fortifications on La Mola.

San Esteban has made use of some of its natural caves by converting them into houses for the summer season.

[7·5 km.] **San Luís.** The inland town is reached by taking a road to the left, a short distance back in the direction of Mahón. Whereas Villa Carlos has a claim to being 'English', San Luís is distinctly 'French' in some of its aspects. In other respects it has earned its nickname of La Ciudad Blanca (the White Town) by reason of the plain, white-washed and windowless fronts many of the houses present to the street – as much Moorish as Spanish. In fact, San Luís was built by the Duc de Richelieu between 1756 and 1763 for the accommodation of the Breton sailors who sailed under his command.

San Luís is on the way to a string of small but growing seaside places, and traffic is considerable enough for it to be by-passed. However the main street, flanked by parallel and mainly residential streets, is of obvious consequence. The *church*, which is dedicated to St Louis, King of France, stands centrally amongst neat, terraced houses. Opposite there is a friendly square, graced by an obelisk and stone seats. The church is simple, with a single nave and four side chapels. Inside there is very little decoration beyond the 'marbling' of some of the stonework. Outside, the west front displays the French royal coat of arms, and those of two of the early administrators of the island.

In what may be interpreted as surviving traces of Gallic exuberance, there are several lively places of entertainment, including restaurants and night spots, which attract the patronage of visitors staying in neighbouring resorts, as well as the inhabitants of Mahón, which is only 4·5 km. away by the direct road.

From this point all pretence of an orderly circular tour has to be abandoned.

Cala Alcaufar is reached by driving for 4 km. through a horticultural district divided into small fields by stone walls. It is mainly residential, and serves as a quiet summer retreat without losing its identity as a fishing village. Two more populous resorts are slightly to the north: **Cala S'Algar** (where the bathing is from rocks) and **Cala Rafalet**, with a small creek.

Punta Prima is 4·5 km. south from San Luís, at the extreme south-east corner of the island. This is one of the few characterless resorts, with an assortment of new hotels facing level sands, and the beach is very popular with Mahonese townspeople, so it can become crowded. Biniancolla is near by, opposite the Isla del Aire.

Take the road leading south from San Luís, heading for the sea.

[11 km.] **Binibeca** is a source of pride to the planning authorities. Feeling a need for a picturesque fishing village on this section of the coast, if possible with a medieval and Hispano-Moorish atmosphere, and not finding one ready to hand, the developers started from scratch. The result is surprisingly successful. Typical fishermen's dwellings line the quays and alleys, and these white houses are built into each other at different levels and provided with authentically styled trimmings in the way of ironwork, stone steps and arches. The only comparable neighbourhood is in Ciudadela, where, as it happens, almost all the architecture is genuine. This is indeed a compliment to the designers of Binibeca.

Return inland, then turn left and westwards. After about 2 km. the road turns north in a right angle to skirt the airport.

[17 km.] **San Clemente**. This is where we join the road from Mahón to Cala'n Porter (see p. 303).

Just before entering the city, initiative combined with perseverance may bring a bonus. To the left of our road, and not far south of the Mahón-Ciudadela road, there is the site of an early Christian basilica, *Es Fornes de Torello*, so called for lack of identification under the name of a saint. The mosaic pavement and scant remains of an altar are all that remain, but it is worth searching out by a lane that is difficult to negotiate, followed by further effort across trackless ground. Look for a plain corrugated iron roof erected to protect the mosaics from weather, and make for this landmark on foot. The mosaics are 16 by 5 metres, and depict beautiful and almost pagan representations of birds, flowers and the classic geometric patterns.

Further points of reference for what has the makings of a treasure hunt are the town's refuse dump and a quarry.

[23 km.] **Mahón**.

2 : North shore

Exploration of the northern shore of Mahón harbour is not quite as rewarding as of the southern, except that it offers different views of the town from those already described. Near at hand, however, there are features which tend to crop up in local history, the best known of which is Golden Farm, where Lord Nelson is believed to have lodged, if only for a few nights. Continuation as far as La Mola [7 km.], the northern headland guarding the mouth of the channel immediately opposite Fort San Felipe, is not particularly interesting because the fortifications and barracks, now largely in disuse, are part of a prohibited military area, and the surrounding terrain is somewhat bleak and windswept. One feature to the left of the road is a memorial cross set up in commemoration of the execution of Nationalist partisans in the Civil War. Some effort has been made to create an *urbanización* at Cala Llonga, which is immediately opposite the Isla del Rey.

The country and coast slightly further north, approached by other roads as indicated, are more enjoyable but do not have the views.

Route Leave Mahón by the Fornells road (Exit A), which follows the south shore of the harbour to the west of the church of San Francisco. Distances are from Mahón.

[0·5 km.] Branch off to the right, still keeping close to the shoreline.

[1 km.] Fork back right, leaving the road to Cala Mesquida on the left, and continue for 2 km. to *Villa San Antonio* (Golden Farm). This attractive house (in private ownership and only open to members of the public by arrangement) stands to the right of the road high above the harbour, and therefore facing Cala Figuera, and hence Admiral Lord Collingwood's headquarters of El Fonduco (p. 279). One must resist the notion that had Nelson stayed at Villa San Antonio in 1799 the two famous sailors would have been able to chat to each other across the water by semaphore. The timing is wrong for such a romantic idea – as indeed for the well-fostered myth that Lady Hamilton visited Golden Farm when her lover was in occupation. Apart from all this, the classical architecture of the house, with its pediment and balcony over the main entrance, coloured white on its lower storey and a rich Venetian red above, repays even a glimpse, as does the terraced garden falling away downhill and planted with palm trees. Those people who are fortunate enough to be admitted to the house will find that its contents are in the most perfect taste, and include collections of Georgian furniture and porcelain, as well as interesting relics of Lord Nelson and the period of British dominion of the island.

Close by, and immediately opposite the Isla del Rey, walled (and probably locked) as well as tumbling down the hillside towards a creek, there is a small cemetery which has all the sad charm of such places. Here were buried many British and American seamen who served in these waters. The best-known to us (though not all that well-known) is one Edward Gaynor Fry, a Quaker who acted as Nelson's major-domo until the hero's death at Trafalgar, after which he retired to Mahón, where he worked in a dual capacity as lay preacher and ship's chandler. Even if the graveyard happens to be locked, the slope of the ground allows one to see over the white-washed walls.

[7 km.] **Cala Mesquida**. Return to the road fork 1 km. from Mahón, mentioned above and take the left fork. The bay of Cala Mesquida was the scene of one prong of the invasion by the French under the command of the Duc de Crillon in 1781. A landing effected here was followed by the siege of Fort San Felipe. A ruined fortress stood on the edge of the sea, as is usual at all strategic points in the Balearic island group. This resort is one of the most open and easily reached from Mahón, its one disadvantage being that it gets very hot in summer as there is little shade.

[8 km.] **Es Grau**. Return to the Cala Mesquida fork, as above, and drive for less than 0·5 km. along the Fornells road before turning right on to a good new road running almost due north. Es Grau is a comparatively new development, and has an excellent beach and a choice of modern attractions. One attractive natural feature is the uninhabited and rocky *Isla Colom* (Pigeon Island) which can be reached by rowing boat. It has two excellent bathing beaches, as well as grotesque rock formations and the remains of an eighteenth-century British copper mine. Another attraction of the neighbourhood is inland, the salt marshlands known, as in Majorca, as the *Albufera*. This provides a distinct change from the coastal grandeur of much of the rest of the island, as well as being a place of particular interest to naturalists and ornithologists, and to humbler birdwatchers and ordinary walkers.

As usual, we are out on a limb here, and have no alternative but to return by the outgoing road from Mahón.

3: By boat around the harbour

It could be argued that Mahón's roadstead is its most important feature, and it is true that the town would have been of less importance, especially in relation to Ciudadela, if such superior harbourage had not existed, or if the English had not realized the possibility of developing a string of strong points and depots at the mouth of the inlet, as well as on the strategically situated islands in the deepwater channel which reaches inland for almost 5 km.

Port Mahón was capable of accommodating and maintaining an entire fleet, though its reputation for impregnability was damaged late in the thirteenth century when Alfonso III wrested it from the Arab usurpers, and also much later, in 1756, when the French captured the town – albeit from the landward side. But when European power politics shifted away from the Mediterranean after the War of the Spanish Succession, the Seven Years' War and the Peninsular War, Mahón's strategic importance declined, and the town was left stranded on its cliff, with its quays moving over to commerce – though a Spanish naval station has survived on one of the islands nearest the town.

Though it is possible to survey the whole extent of the channel and its historic islands and fortifications from either shoreline, the most enjoyable plan is to take to the water, either on one of the organized tours by launch – some of which include a visit to Mahón's most famous gin distillery – or independently. Both courses inevitably recall eighteenth-century history, and the naval involvement of Britain in the politics of that period.

Approaching from the sea, would-be invaders would initially have been confronted by the northern cape known as *La Mola* – a natural vantage point 80 metres above sea level, and capable of carrying heavy armament. On the opposite side of the shore stood Fort San Felipe, a strongpoint fortified in the sixteenth century by Charles V and refitted by the British two centuries later at the then astonishing cost of £1½m. It is now dismantled and in ruins. A secret tunnel connected the fort with *Fort Marlborough* (or the Marlborough Redoubt) above the Cala de San Esteban. This second fortress is in better repair, and sightseeing launches are permitted to land passengers who wish to make a closer inspection. It is of interest while standing here to remember that these waters were the scene of the Duc de Richelieu's blockade of Mahón, which was followed by the disembarkation of his troops at the opposite end of the island. Strange as chance is, head-on confrontation with the English at the mouth of the channel, which could have led to stalemate, had been precluded by the fact that, so the rumour goes, the French were not equipped with the charts of this locality, and so had to switch their landing to the west, resulting in Mahón being attacked from its landward, vulnerable side. Though a naval force commanded by Admiral Lord Byng was sent in relief, as soon as he was intercepted by the enemy he turned tail and sailed away, a notorious act of cowardice which resulted in his eventual court martial and death by firing squad.

As we enter the harbour, the islands become the focus of attention when the forts on either side of the channel have been passed. *New Quarantine Island* or *Lazaretto Island* – a leper colony – the first to be reached, was also given over from time to time to victims of the plague. High walls were built around it in the ingenuous belief that these would prevent wind-borne infection being carried back to Mahón. Not unnaturally there remains a sense of macabre uneasiness in this place. But to those visitors who are successful in obtaining a permit to land – a protracted procedure to be played out with the Department of Sanitation – the rewards go beyond the atmospheric, in that they can see historical details such as the Spanish flag carved over the entrance (removed here from Fort San Felipe) and a most curious *chapel*, purpose-designed. This is circular and open to the sky, with a central altar, and as substitute for pews there is a circle of individual cells, each equipped with a grille, for isolation of the unfortunates. High-walled windowless corridors connect the various quarters of what was more of a prison or concentration camp than a hospital. Those lepers who perished were buried in unmarked graves, since the scale of epidemics, when they occurred, outstripped all possibility of formal burial.

The second island to come into view is the smaller *Old Quarantine Island*, now the *Isla Plana*, the chief interest of which lies in its having been leased at the beginning of the nineteenth century to the Mediterranean Squadron of the United States Navy, the forerunner of the Sixth Fleet. It became the training ground for many of the midshipmen who were to win fame as admirals during the American Civil War. The practice ended in 1845 with the founding of the United States Naval Academy at Annapolis.

The boat trip up this fiord-like stretch of water leaves Villa Carlos on the port shore. This town, 3 km. from Mahón, is well worth visiting (see p. 279). The next island to be reached is the *Isla del Rey*, where Alfonso III landed in 1287. Its naval hospital was built by the British, and conditions there were so rough that it came to be known as Bloody Island. After having been leased to the French for a short time in 1830, the island and hospital were returned to Spanish hands. Permission to visit may be obtained from the Military Commander at Port Mahón.

By this time we are close to the quays, lined by fishermen's houses and backed by the cliff, above which rears the skyline of this interesting town ornamented by the silhouettes of its churches and reached by either the imposing flight of steps or the zigzag carriageway. From here one may look back at the inner harbour, commercial docks and naval base which has been built out upon another island – this being man-made. Here the barracks are graced by a typically English Georgian clock. One can look further, too, to the opposite shore, where it is claimed that Nelson for a short time took up quarters.

MAHÓN TO CIUDADELA

The key to Minorca lies in its central highway, which runs with almost Roman precision across the centre of the island, effectively linking Mahón and Ciudadela at the two extremes, and passing through the three traditional but small market towns of Alayor, Mercadal and Ferrerías. In one way this works well for the tourist, in other respects not so well.

No one should travel this way without sparing a thought for Sir Richard Kane, the first British Governor of Minorca who officiated from 1713–20, and subsequently from 1730 until his death in 1736. He was the prime mover in the construction of the road between the two capitals, as well as in many other enlightened public works, in the field of agriculture in particular, and the island economy in general. He is still remembered by the islanders with respect and gratitude. A statue has been erected to Sir Richard's memory on the outskirts of Mahón, appropriately overlooking the beginning of the road which was his brainchild, and the first section of which now lies, overgrown, slightly to the north of the modern one on the way to Mercadal, after which the two merge. Construction costs for the old road were partially offset by a tax on alcohol.

By now it is largely forgotten that Sir Richard fell foul of the ecclesiastical authorities by dint of his use of some Catholic churches by Protestant British troops. This explains the hiatus between his stints as Lieutenant Governor. His career in the army and in the administrative service earned him a mausoleum in Westminster Abbey incorporating a bust which reinforces our impression of his having a kindly but strong and resilient nature.

Route Leave Mahón by Calle Prieto y Caulas (Exit B), which runs through an industrial quarter of the town. The main road, C. 721 passes to the north of the lanes which eventually lead to the basilica of Torello (p. 281). Continue to Mercadal where the C. 721 branches left to reach Ciudadela via Ferrerías. Total distance 45 km.
Bus For Ciudadela depart from Calle José María Quadrado.

Open agricultural land soon presents the pleasant and evocative sight of grazing black and white cattle, no doubt distant kindred of those introduced by Sir Richard Kane. The road follows a low ridge, which because it is central can almost be described as a plateau, overlooking arable and pasture land to the north, and rockier terrain to the south.

The farmhouses, usually set back some distance from the road, are Georgian in appearance, ochre or terracotta in colour, and often with a shallow pediment. But usually it is the vast quantity of stones littering the land which is most striking, and it can be guessed that they have been gathered together as much to get them out of the way as to be used for enclosure. The result is a network of small fields of irregular pattern, so typical of this part of the island.

[4 km.] *Talati de Dalt*. A small turning to the left leads 0.5 km. towards a field distinguishable by a low clump of trees and an important *talayot*. Its two associated *taulas* are surrounded by an area of scattered stones which once must have composed the material of a prehistoric settlement, but which is now partially overgrown by scrub. These hazards – fallen stones and prickly bushes – make investigation difficult, but it is possible to identify a so-called hypostyle court, a cave-like structure which may have been a human habitation.

Return to the main road by keeping right at the hamlet of Algendar.

[6 km.] **Rafal Rubi**. Two *navetas*, one of which has been restored, can be seen to the north of the highway, a short distance back in the direction of Mahón.

[12 km.] **Alayor**. Just before a bridge on the outskirts of the town, a minor road to the left slants back towards Mahón, but in fact soon turns south near the *Torralba d'en Salord* to join the Mahón-Cala'n Porter road west of San Clemente (p. 303).

Alayor, one of the original market towns founded after the Reconquest of the island, seems from its approaches to be composed of white cubes, with splashes of terracotta. With a population of 5,200 it is really little more than a large village, but gives out an air of prosperity which is largely maintained by two local industries, both of which owe their existence to cattle. Shoe-making is the senior craft, and as well as turning out excellent factory-made articles, there is at least one craftsman whose handmade footwear has found its way into the expensive shops and even palaces of European capitals. The manufacture of ice cream is a later and equally logical development of the dairying industry, the local product being of such excellence as to compare favourably with the Neapolitan ices that have set the standard of perfection in this branch of gastronomy.

There are *two churches* in the town, *Santa Eulalia* and *San Diego*, the latter having been badly damaged during the Civil War. Its cloister is distinctly Spanish – or reminiscent of the early Californian missions. The streets of the town are so narrow that a by-pass has been constructed. A good road from the centre of the town goes to the south coast, forking after 4 km. for San Llorenc and Son Bou (p. 303).

Continuing along the Ciudadela road *Mount Toro*, the central feature of the island, and at 357 metres its highest point, comes into view.

[15 km.] A road to the left meets the San Llorenc and Son Bou roads, which come in more directly from Alayor.

[16·5 km.] Another road to the left leads through pretty country to the inland village of San Cristobal (p. 304). Much of the soil in these parts is of a Devonshire redness, and the pockets of land are good for grazing, the growing of wheat and strikingly verdant lucerne crops, though it is difficult to get away from stone and rocks in the form of knobbly outcrops where small pines flourish.

[19·5 km.] Our road takes a northerly turn, to ascend through a defile known as the *Cabeza del Indio*.

[23 km.] **Mercadal**. Though by no means large (population 3,000), this market town has from its beginnings contributed greatly to the island's economy, chiefly on account of its central position, from which roads radiate in all directions towards the coasts (pp. 304–5). Yet there are few survivals of historical importance, and the town relies for its charm upon a general impression of provincial prosperity enhanced by the whitewash of its houses and small factories. It is here that the cheap shoes known as *albarcas típicas menorquinas* are made. Their uppers are of rough cowhide, their soles of used tyres, and they are said to carry a guarantee for 8,000 km., after which they may be given a retread service! These shoes are a must for energetic walkers on rough coastal paths.

The *Sanctuary of Mount Toro* is reached by a short diversion of 2 km. to the east, and fully compensates for the dearth of sightseeing in Mercadal. Nowadays there is a serpentine motor road to the top of what is in effect a grandstand 357 metres high, from which to view more than half the island. The ascent is steep, so that a car or taxi ride is preferable, though the walk down can be exciting and more revealing. The name of the hill and the sanctuary with which it is crowned, has misguidedly led people to associate it with Cretan culture, but nowadays, more prosaically, the ascription is to the

Moorish *El Tor*, meaning a high place (Devonians please note). Throughout history the site has been occupied by a monastery or nunnery, though interesting early remains are overshadowed by a modern Christ figure commemorating the fallen of the Civil War. Recent history recounts that the site was occupied in 1969 by hermits who had previously made their home in the Puig de María, near Pollensa in Majorca, but they have now departed, and nuns have returned. This means that the seventeenth-century sanctuary and its church are maintained in apple-pie order, and visitors are welcomed.

The road leading west from Mercadal soon climbs gradually into wooded country, before descending to the third of the central market towns. This is built on sloping ground that has dictated a terraced layout.

[29 km.] **Ferrerías**. Most of this small town (population 2,100) is built into the angle made by the main road and another which slants back to San Cristobal (p. 304); it is also connected by another road to Santa Galdana, one of the most flourishing resorts of the south coast (p. 306). Again, there is little of historical importance preserved here, if one excepts the small Baroque church; and as much of the town has, as it were, trickled down into a hollow, there are few views. In fact the one remarkable feature of this town is said to be its fecundity, for there are reckoned to be more children to each family, and to the square metre, than in any other town or village on the island.

The westward road passes south of the small hill of S'Inclusa (274 metres).

[31 km.] A roughish road leads off to Santa Agueda (p. 306) and stops short of the sea's edge. It is noticeable that in this part of the island most of the farmhouses have been built on whatever small hilltops there are, in positions aimed at surveying their domains.

[39 km.] A new building, a mock-up of some imaginative medieval concept, has been built to the right of the road for the benefit of touristic wayfarers.

[41 km.] The *Naveta of Els Tudons* on the left is well signposted and is less than 2 km. to the south. As well as being one of the most accessible of the Minorcan *navetas* or *naus*, it is the best documented of its kind, and was restored in 1960, since when it has been in the care of the March Foundation. The name *naveta* is explained by its shape, which is that of an upturned boat. There are many more scattered at random around the island, at least ten being in fair condition. Their function as funerary buildings is not in dispute and, like this one, they usually consist of a ground level entrance to a small hall (here on the west side) leading to two larger chambers built one above the other.

Two other prehistoric monuments can be reached from here by carrying on for 3 km. along this minor parallel road, away from Ciudadela. *Torre Llafuda* and *Torre Trencada* are closer to the pattern of prehistoric settlements.

[45 km.] **Ciudadela**. The main road begins to descend, and the sight of the ancient capital, though marred by rather unfortunate and higgledy-piggledy factory development on its outskirts, cannot fail to stimulate the sightseeing appetite. Even from a distance it can be observed that the city owes nothing to the British occupying powers of the eighteenth century, and little to the French. Spanish and Moorish blend to make it essentially Minorcan. The old part of the town is reached beyond the Plaza Alfonso III at the end of Calle Calvo Sotelo.

CIUDADELA

Population 14,573.
Air and sea connections
   Air reservations: Aviaco, Calle Calvo Sotelo 5.
   Sea reservations: Compañiá Trasmediterránea, Santa Clara 31.
Buses The depot is in Calle Calvo Sotelo.
To Cala en Blanés, Santandria, Cala Blanca and Cape d'Artruch: Plaza Cabrisas.
Taxis
   Plaza Alfonso III (tel. 509).
   Calle Obispo Comes 7 (tel. 382335).
   Calle Calvo Sotelo 112 (tel. 380442).
   Calle Conquistador 52 (tel. 382290).
Hotels See p. 263.
Post and telegraph Office Plaza Generalísimo 5 (*Map* 12).
Telephone exchange Plaza Rosario 4.
Medical services
   Hospital Municipal Plaza San Antonio (tel. 381914) (*Map* 1).
   Clinica S.O.E. Av. Republica Argentina 96 (tel. 380687).
Police Plaza Generalísimo 1 (*Map* 10).
Viceconsulate *France* Calle 9 Julio 13.
Bank Banco Central, Calle Pio XII 5.
Yacht Club Club Náutico, Paseo Puerto (*Map* 13).

Ciudadela

0   100   200
metres

INTRODUCTION

This town is small, with a well-defined old quarter untouched and (hopefully) untouchable by the worst aspects of modernity. For practical purposes, let us assume that one plunges into the Hispano-Moorish precincts from Plaza Alfonso III. From there onwards narrow paved streets – some with thick white-washed arches known as *voltas* inset with Aladdin's caves turned boutiques and others overshadowed by town houses retaining much of their noble grandeur – lead in an irregular pattern towards a splendid square, officially Plaza del Generalísimo, but familiarly El Borne. Here are to be found the Ayuntamiento or Town Hall, several *palacios* of note, an enthralling view over the harbour (which is so much more narrow and tricky to negotiate than Mahón's), a fine church and the post office and police station. A long avenue, which begins as Paseo de San Nicolás, goes south-westward through newer developments parallel to the shoreline, to become Plaza Almirante Ferragut and then Paseo Marítimo, where hotels are sited to overlook the open sea.

HISTORY

In the catalogue of historical events shared between Minorca's two principal towns, Ciudadela's entries are more numerous, and reach back more consistently into the past. Various survivals of the *talayot* period are on display in the museum section of the Ayuntamiento. Pliny refers to the settlement as the Carthaginian Jamno, the meaning of which in a Semitic language would have been 'city of the west'. Then, under Muslim rule it became Medina Minurka, which gives a clue to the present name of the island. Better authenticated history then begins with the arrival of the army of King Alfonso III of Aragon in 1287, when the principal mosque was forthwith converted to Christian usage and dedicated to the Blessed Virgin Mary. Other city mosques underwent similar transformation. The entry of the Aragonese king on January 17th into the city is commemorated annually on the Feast of St Anthony, who became the patron saint of the island. After the taking of the city, which was at that time the sole urban concentration on the island, the houses of Muslim notabilities were made over to such of the king's followers who were prepared to establish themselves on the island, while much of the neighbouring land went to members of the monastic orders who had accompanied the fighting forces, amongst them Franciscans and Clares. A Saturday market was established.

Unfortunately almost all the city's documents were lost at the time of the Turkish invasion of 1558, but it is known that Ciudadela incurred the envy of the rest of the island owing to the privileges the city's Universidad accorded itself. On more than one occasion in the early fifteenth century, outsiders from Catalonia had to be brought in to keep the peace. Nevertheless, Ciudadela rendered assistance to Mahón in 1535 when that town was captured by Barbarossa.

Already, even before the British occupation, Mahón was improving its position in relation to its rival. In general Ciudadela opposed the British regime, and in particular was affronted by discrimination against herself. Ancient jealousies flared. So when the logical transfer of the seat of government took place in 1722 it was wisely decided that the older city should remain as the ecclesiastical capital of the island. The two roles were confirmed in 1782 by the Spanish authorities. In 1795 when the Pope, petitioned by Charles IV of Spain, proclaimed Minorca an independent bishopric – for the first time for 1,200 years, in fact since a bishop named Makarios disappeared in Carthage and presumably was put to death by the Vandals – few arguments were advanced to take the honour of being the cathedral city from Ciudadela.

Almost the last occasion when Ciudadela was to see enemy action was in 1798, when it was besieged for three days by British troops during their takeover of the island as a precaution against Napoleon's spread of power in the Mediterranean. One is occasionally reminded, however, of the damage done to the city in the course of the Civil War, when Republican extremists are said to have run riot through the cathedral, destroying much in its interior, including the choir. This bitter period of comparatively recent history is indicated by the fact that many of the city's churches were never returned to religious use following their desecration.

PRINCIPAL SIGHTS

Cathedral
Plaza Pío XII; *Map* **6**.
The church of Santa María was given the status of cathedral in 1795, as seat of the bishopric which had been in abeyance since 484. It is

built in the familiar fourteenth century Catalan-Gothic style, with neo-classical additions. The outer walls rise to a substantial height without fenestration. These walls – possibly defensive in intention – probably date from repair work following the Turkish raid of 1558. The tower to the north shows traces of stonework belonging to the original Muslim minaret which existed on the site at the time of Alfonso's conquest of the island. The building's Christianization was completed in 1362. Various restoration work went ahead between 1558 and 1719, at which date the alterations and repairs were judged complete enough to warrant a special consecration service. Work continued, however, in neo-classical style now, resulting most signally in the west front, built in matching local stone, which was added in 1813. The size of the single nave is enhanced by light filtering down from a height – principally from five narrow windows at the east end – and by an absence of decoration which can be attributed to Republican action during the 1936–9 Civil War. Items of interest which escaped, however, include the doorway known as the *Puerta de Luz*, in which heraldic animals display the coats of arms of the city of Ciudadela and the kingdom of Aragon.

Bishop's Palace
Calle Obispo Torres; Map **5**.
Situated to the north, close to the cathedral, not much of the building can be seen except the entrance giving on to a classical courtyard planted with flowering shrubs, on the far side of which there is a grand stairway leading to the *piso principal*. The best view is obtained from Calle San Sebastian, round the corner to the right.

Ayuntamiento
Plaza del Generalísimo; Map **8**.
The Town Hall, on the site of the Moorish Alcazar, is not the most successful of civic buildings, and certainly does not compete aesthetically with the various town houses or *palacios*, some of which are in the same plaza. The medieval building which stood on this site was destroyed in the 1558 raid. It now consists of three storeys with a not very imposing tower and clock. A modest *museum* is maintained in the building which also houses the mayor's office and is the seat of local government. The most important exhibit (kept in the mayoral office) is the *Llibre Vermell* or Red Book, which records grants made to his adherents by Alfonso III immediately after the capture of the

island, and also the standard that was carried on the invasion. In the museum itself there are one or two perhaps incongruous items associated with British rule, as well as whatever memorabilia have been gleaned to remind visiting Americans that the father of Admiral David Farragut was a citizen of Ciudadela. As the Ayuntamiento consists primarily of offices, the museum opens only after working hours, that is between 18·00 and 20·00 on weekdays and from 12·00 to 13·00 on Saturdays.

El Borne
Plaza del Generalísimo

If it has not proved possible to ascend to the Ayuntamiento's roof, from which the best view of the harbour is obtained, the next best place to make for is the north side of the square, which has a balustrade overlooking the narrow harbour and its shipping. Proudly, this harbour, estuarial in appearance, is listed in the Blue Book of Monaco's Yacht Club – an honour achieved by few. The wall above which we stand constitutes the remains of the city's original ramparts, which succumbed to the 1558 Turkish assault, were then rebuilt, but finally almost totally dismantled in 1868 to allow for the growth of the city. The *obelisk* in the Borne is commemorative of the resistance to the invasion. Beyond the Borne a road descends to the quay with its berths for coastal shipping and the passenger boat from Majorca.

OTHER SIGHTS

The Palace of Torre-Saura (*Map* 7), facing the Ayuntamiento, is one of three in the Borne which were built in the early nineteenth century at a time when the plaza began to acquire a new look. The loggia, the stone-arched entrance to the courtyard with its wooden door surmounted by the family's coat of arms, is built entirely in the traditional style, despite its comparatively recent date. It is said that it contains a very fine and large reception room, and watercolours and engravings from the time of British rule.

Other palaces. The majority of these are still owned and inhabited, at least seasonally, by descendants of the Spanish nobility. Those deeper and more hidden are worth seeking out, especially in view of their greater age. The *Saura Palace* in Calle del Santissimo, (*Map* 11,) has beautiful windows with wrought ironwork forming balconies. It was built towards the end of the seventeenth century, though its great flight of steps leading up to the *piso principal* is dated 1718. The *Martorell Palace* which is in the same street is plainer, as is the palace owned by the Barons de Lluriach, members of a very old Minorcan family. This is in Calle de Santa Clara, nearly opposite the convent of that name, which was founded for the Clares almost immediately after Alfonso III's arrival in the city. Opposite the main entrance to the cathedral is to be found the *Olives Palace*, which contains a great many treasures, among them an English-built harmonium, together with Minorcan-made Georgian furniture and French eighteenth-century furniture acquired during the French regime. Another Saura mansion in Calle Obispo Vila is now a bank. Then there is the Squella town-house (*Map* 4) near the cathedral, owned by the Marqués de Menas Albas, and of special interest because of its association with one of the heroes of American history.

David Glasgow Farragut's father, Jorge, a native of Ciudadela, emigrated to Tennessee before the outbreak of the War of Independence. There he married an American girl, and their son was born in 1801. Following a distinguished career, David was promoted Vice-Admiral in 1864 and Admiral eighteen months later. When given command of the United States European Squadron he put into Mahón in December 1867 and took the opportunity to visit his father's birthplace. Here he was acclaimed as a native and given a civic reception. He was put up for the night in the grand house belonging to Señor Don Gabriel Squella, where he was able to get away from the enthusiastic crowds who pressed upon him during his sightseeing. The bed and bedroom where the Admiral slept are kept sacrosanct to commemorate this overnight visit.

Churches. One would expect to find such a city as this full of churches, and indeed many can be located. But the sad fact is that several suffered considerably at the time of the Civil War and were never returned to ecclesiastical use. One to escape such treatment is the *church of San Francisco* on the south-east corner of El Borne (*Map* 9). As usual, much of the structure is fourteenth-century Gothic, while the east end and the dome are seventeenth-century. There is also a gem of a chapel in Calle Obispo Vila, which was thoughtfully restored to commemorate its tricentenary in 1967, and the *chapel of Santo Cristo* is pure and extravagant Baroque. Besides taking in the general beauty of this intimate building, one should look for the wood carvings on the north side of the altar. The *church of Our Lady of the Rosary* in Calle Rosario near the south side of the cathedral is capable of restoration, but this has not so far been put in hand. It originally belonged to the Dominicans, but was later transformed into a church for the use of British troops – a most unpopular move.

EXCURSIONS FROM CIUDADELA

Sightseeing in Ciudadela being finished, there are few historic sites to be visited in the immediate neighbourhood, the obvious exceptions being the *naveta* of *Els Tudons* and the prehistoric settlement of *Torre Llafuda*, both of which are located a short distance away, off the road to Mahón (p. 290). In fact, the usual coastal watchtowers and the very often unmapped and unremarkable groups of stones are of less importance than the scenery into which developments – hotels and villas – have been fitted. As usual on this island, the road system is not conducive to round trips.

4 : South of the City.

[0·75 km.] CASTILLO DE SAN NICOLÁS
The direct road from El Borne runs straight as a die on high ground towards the open sea and the nearest of the resorts which grew up to compensate Ciudadela for its understandable shortage of accommodation. Alternatively, and without adding significantly to the distance, it is possible to drive or walk along the quays, collectively known as Paseo del Puerto.

As the two roads converge to become first Paseo Almirante Farragut and then Paso Marítimo, it is reassuring to notice that modern building has been restricted to the landward side. The octagonal castle stands isolated on its rocky foundations, a reminder of the importance of Ciudadela's strategic position at the head of its narrow inlet, though far more vulnerable to weather and enemy attack than Mahón's harbour. The Eleycon Hotel, with its three stars, immediately opposite, is the best that Ciudadela has to offer.

CAPE D'ARTRUCH

The route to Ciudadela's nearest and longest established watering-places leads directly south by way of Calle Mallorca from Plaza Colón and El Borne (Exit B). The ground is level, and built over in an unplanned fashion.

[1 km.] **Son Oleo**, on the south shore of the first small cove to be reached, consists substantially of villas used either as second homes for Ciudadela's citizens, or as permanent quarters for commuters.

[3 km.] **Cala de Santandria.** This resort is so close to built-up areas that it inevitably becomes crowded in summer on account of its sandy beach. Its hotels are likely to appeal to visitors who wish to be within easy range – even walking distance – of Ciudadela. A new *urbanización*, Son Carrio, on the way to Cala Blanca is taking shape.

[3·5 km.] **Cala Blanca.** The chief developments are centred around a small cove, with rock-strewn flat country behind, where the small fields are enclosed by the stone walls so typical of the Minorcan landscape. The hotels are at the sea's edge.

The road now leaves the coast, to run about 1 km. inland.

[7 km.] **Son Olivar Vey**. A minor road to the left goes to *Torre Saura*, inland of a small stretch of the southern coast which has no easy access to the water's edge.

[9 km.] **Cape d'Artruch**. This headland with its lighthouse is known indiscriminately by the Spanish and Catalan versions of its name. The coast here is rocky, but there is good bathing from Playa Bosch, a short distance to the east. The Tamarindo *urbanización* is on a fairly large scale for these parts.

CALA TURQUETA

Another inland road, running through unspoilt country, leaves Ciudadela by the Camino San Juan. (Exit C).

[3 km.] **Son Vivo**. By forking right here it is possible to visit *Torre Saura* [6 km.] after passing the megaliths of *Son Catlar* [2 km.]. The watchtower from which this small settlement gets its name presides over a stretch of coast which has proved intractable to development, though there is a lateral road linking up with Son Olivar Vey, 3 km. to the west, and Playa Son Saura, 1·5 km. to the east. This beach is the most westerly on the south coast and demonstrates the usual Minorcan pattern of a stream cutting through the land and emerging by way of a creek and cove which are adaptable to holiday requirements.

[4 km.] To the left of the road is the small wayside church of San Juan de Missa.

[10 km.] **Cala Turqueta**, beyond the tiny hamlets of Marjal Veya and Marjal Nova, is one of the newer development areas, and makes the most of pinewoods.

5: North and West of the City

The extreme north-west coast is more rugged. Several roads fan towards it from Ciudadela, but they are mostly of secondary standard or lower, and not all manage to descend to the water's edge – and why should they, since settlements are so few? This corner of the island is distinctly one for energetic and sure-footed walkers.

CAPE BAJOLI (or Cape Minorca)

The north side of Ciudadela harbour has more indentations than the south, and is steeper, so that the road to the westerly headland (Exit A) is forced into a slightly inland course. Paseo de la Colonia de la Asunción rounds the bay known as the Racó des Frares.

[2 km.] **Cala en Blanés**, situated beyond the lighthouse which guides shipping approaching the harbour, is the nearest to an extrovert playground that this part of the island can produce. In these parts, where deep water and rocks prevail over beaches, much has had to be contrived. The Los Delfines *urbanización*, just to the west and above Cala'n Forcat, consists mainly of new villas which look as though they have been fixed with studs into the slopes.

[4 km.] **Bajoli Lighthouse**. Predictably this makes an excellent scenic viewpoint, as well as a starting-place for walks, long or short, along the clifftops. The *Torre de Ram*, not far inland, similarly holds a commanding position.

CALA MORELL AND CALA ALGAIARENS

Leave the city by the road which runs north, (Exit E) passing the Municipal Hospital in Plaza San Antonio.

[0·5 km.] A road branches off left to Son Escudero (5 km.), but comes to an end before reaching the north coast.

[1·5 km.] **Son Fedelich**. Fork left.

[8 km.] **Cala Morell**, the first development on the north coast, is famous for the clear waters of its sea. Prehistoric cave dwellings some 100 metres from the beach and a zone scheduled for villa development are the main attractions. In winter this section of the north coast gets the full force of gales.

There being no coastal road either to east or west, it will be necessary to return almost to Ciudadela before forking back in a north-easterly direction, to strike the coast once more at the growing, but still fairly secluded Algaierens beach and the wider bay protected on one side by the Punta Rotja, 9 km. from Ciudadela.

Though in contrast to the cliff scenery the countryside is far from dramatic, it has a great deal of charm, not least of all in its portrayal of a rural life which has continued without major interruption for many centuries.

The Coasts from the centre of the island

FROM ALAYOR

To Cala'n Porter.

A road leading south from the eastern outskirts of Alayor slants back in the direction of Mahón. This way to Cala'n Porter (in preference to the more direct route from Mahón by way of the airport and San Clemente) has the advantage of passing close to megalithic sites.

[2 km.] *Torralba d'en Salord* is counted as one of the largest of Minorca's prehistoric settlements. The *talayot* first comes into view, on the left of the first pronounced bend in the road. Near by there is a hypostyle chamber and evidence of a large well or crater, some 46 metres deep, in addition to other rather less identifiable features. The *taula* is on the opposite (or west) side of the road, which now follows a winding course south, leaving on the right another, though minor site, the *Torre Llissa*.

[4·5 km.] Turn right, away from San Clemente on the main Mahón road to Cala'n Porter.

[7 km.] **Cala'n Porter**. In the opinion of many discriminating visitors this is the ideal seaside place. Its shape has been determined by the seasonal stream which has cut its way through the cliffs, and has thereby discouraged building on either side of the inlet. Development has been concentrated in the hinterland, mainly in the area known as Son Vitamine del Mar, which forms a sun-trap. This resort has a pleasant but not roomy beach, and is patronized by visitors to the ancient *Caves of Xoroi* above the bay, one of which has been converted into a discothèque and bar.

Several other such troglodyte cave dwellings in the area to the east can be reached by road, but more easily by boat. They are spread over a cliff area known as *Calas Coves*.

To Cala San Llorenc and Playa de Son Bou
Take the south-westerly road from the centre of the town. This winds its way lazily in the direction of the coast.

[4 km.] Road junction at the hamlet of Lluchsaldens. (A turning right here would lead back in another 4 km. to the main Mahón-Ciudadela road, though a second turn right just over 1 km. further runs down to the coast at Son Bou for San Jaime.)

[5·5 km.] **Torre d'en Gaumés**. A signpost points to a lane on the left of the road. This leads immediately to the masses of stone which are the remains of a Bronze Age settlement. This site contains three *talayots* situated close together, a hypostyle chamber and various indeterminate but generally roofless circular buildings thought to have been habitations. The village was built on elevated ground, so there is a fine view of the sea and the surrounding country.

[8 km.] **San Llorenc**. This small village, a short distance from the sea, serves the two pleasant coves of *Cala Llucari* and *Cala San Llorenc*.

Alternative route to the Playa de Son Bou
Another road leads, as previously indicated, from the road fork north of the Torre d'en Gaumés to a point on the coast further west, and the

Playa de Son Bou, behind which a new resort named after San Jaime has grown up. This is a stretch of shore provided with pleasant beaches, hotels, villas and the usual amenities.

A short distance to the west of the development area clifftop walkers can locate the remains of a simple early Christian *basilica* known as the church of San Jaime Mediterráneo. Its walls are knee-high, and define three naves with two central lines of pillars which supported the roof. The sanctuary has the usual semi-circular apse, with a sacristy and a baptistry on either side. There are no signs of mosaics in the floor. These either never existed or have disintegrated from exposure to wind and weather.

FROM MERCADAL

To Santo Tomás
The road south from Mercadal goes through undulating country of some charm, but it is not as fertile as that to the north.

[3 km.] Another road comes in from the left – actually from a point midway between Mercadal and Alayor.

[5 km.] **San Cristobal** is not a very old village, but its efforts have earned an island-wide reputation for folk dancing and singing. From here a third road leads back to reach the main highway at Ferrerías [6 km.].

[11 km.] The beaches of white sand at **Santo Tomás** are among the best in an island famous for such things. There has been considerable but largely enlightened development, particularly to the west, to bring into use the sequence of bays stretching for as much as 7 km., and including San Adeodato.

To Fornells
Unlike Alayor and Ferrerías, Mercadal has good communications with the north coast.

A drive almost due north goes through pleasant agricultural land on a road dignified with official numbering (C.723), and leads to a point where it is joined by the road from Mahón [22 km.] From it there are turnings to the newer resorts of the east coast such as Arenal d'en Castell, Addaya and the lesser developed sequence of inlets which end at the lighthouse of Cape Fabaritx. This road continues inland of the Albufera (p. 284) and El Grau before reaching the capital.

[9 km.] **Fornells**. Were it not for the superiority of Port Mahón this fiord-like inlet would have assumed even greater historical importance than came its way. As it is, it was in constant use by the barbaric Corsairs of the seventeenth century, who were a recurrent threat to its population of fishing people. A fortress constructed to the north of the town did little to save them from these incursions. Later another was built by the British on the opposite side of the water as a defence against the French.

Today Fornells is a truly lovely, indeed idyllic place, with breakwater, palm trees, terraced white houses – many with green woodwork – and excellent provision for the parking, which became necessary when the charm of the traditional fishing village, combined with good restaurants, attracted many day visitors. The local shellfish, especially lobsters, are famous – so much so that it is advisable to order them in advance by telephone.

In winter, this being the north coast, the neighbourhood is windswept, which explains the dearth of vegetation here. But in summer it comes into its own; and though there are minor roads to Cala Tirant, 3 km. north of the salt lake of Ses Salines, and also to the easternmost headland of Punta na Guiamassa [11 km.], the holiday spirit encourages us to take to boats for exploration of the islands and tiny bays within the shelter of the fiord.

To Cape Caballería and Cala Pregonda

There are two other possible routes to the north coast from Mercadal: to *Cape Caballería* [12 km.], passing through Casa Novas at the corner of Ses Salines; and a more picturesque drive which leaves the first road on a level with the hill called Montenegro to continue in a more westerly direction to the newly developing resort of Cala Pregonda. Though this north coast has been receiving a good measure of attention in recent years, it is far from catching up in development with the *urbanizaciones* of the more hospitable south.

Walkers should take note that there is a *sendero* or footpath which follows the clifftops round the north-west corner of the island to within reach of Ciudadela.

FROM FERRERÍAS

The classic communications of Ferrerías are with the south coast.

To Cala Santa Galdana
The direct route to this bay is 8 km. long; there a mammoth de luxe hotel has been built, which most unusually has been allowed to dwarf the scenery. The beach is excellent, and one extra pleasure is a freshwater stream which flows mainly in springtime, and contributes to the beauty of the landscape. The *Barrenca de Algendar*, in fact, is the finest of the ravines that are a recurring distinguishing feature of the south coast, and which, incidentally, have done so much to deter road builders from linking up the various southern resorts.

Santo Tomás and San Adeodato via San Cristobal
This route is described from Mercadal (p.304).

To Santa Agueda
The one road north from near Ferrerías has been more used and is therefore better kept than it was, now that the north coast is being opened up. Turn right off the Ferrerías–Ciudadela road after 2 km., and then continue towards the small bare hill of Santa Agueda (264 metres), on the top of which there once stood a Roman fortress, and later a Moorish one. Now farm buildings have taken over the sparse remains of these fortifications, but they still provide a splendid look-out post over one of the wildest sections of Minorca's coastline.

IBIZA AND FORMENTERA

INTRODUCTION TO IBIZA

Everything is on a small scale – made to measure, as it were, for relaxation and pleasure. No distance by road is great. There are no daunting mountains, just an infinity of beaches dispersed around the greater part of the island's coastline. The climate is temperate: snow is rare enough to be talked about for months; rain is absorbed by lush growth; temperatures are reliable: equable in winter and making for drowsy appreciation at the height of summer. Add to this a theatrical, almost picture postcard beauty and it will be understood why this small island, only 83 km. from the Spanish mainland and 220 km. from North Africa, attracts not only seasonal visitors but lovers of an easygoing way of life who have discovered cottages, small farms, villas and apartments where they can hole-up and ignore the pressures of more crowded lives.

Development came late to Ibiza and, by accident as much as design, has been concentrated principally around San Antonio Abad on the opposite side of the island to the capital of Ibiza, where a natural acropolis, walled, densely populated and surmounted by historic buildings, has for hundreds of years defied innovation.

The beaches to either side of the beautiful harbour have attracted as much tourist development as they can bear, but this in no way detracts from the fascination of the Dalt Vila or Old Town. Most of the other resorts are intimate places, providing what is required for relaxation, sport and entertainment, no more and no less. Because of the short distances involved, exploration can be expressed in terms of happy wandering.

TRANSPORT ON IBIZA

Buses

Timetables are available at the Tourist Information Office and at hotel reception desks. Bus routes operate from Ibiza Town to:

San Antonio Abad
Santa Eulalia del Río
Portinatx
Figueretas and Playa d'en Bossa

Talamanca
San Miguel
San José
San Juan and
Cala San Vicente

A frequent local bus service also links San Antonio and Port des Turrent – a boon to bathers.

Taxis
Fares between Ibiza, San Antonio, Santa Eulalia and other important places are listed in an official tariff. There are no extras except for waiting time and baggage. A mileage charge is made for unscheduled journeys. In that case the Tourist Information Office in Ibiza Town will be helpful in advising on the correct price.

Car hire
Local firms specializing in car hire and self-drive have offices in Ibiza, San Antonio and Santa Eulalia. *Autos Ibiza* also has branches in several smaller places, such as Es Caná, Portinatx, Cala Tarida and Cala Vadella. The international firm of Hertz has an office at the airport.

Boat
There are regular launch services to neighbouring beaches from San Antonio Abad.

Maps
Apart from the Firestone map recommended for all the Balearic Islands (p. 23), the contour map of Ibiza and Formentera which is sold in local newsagents and through the Tourist Information Office is perfectly adequate, since it includes plans not only for Ibiza Town itself, but also San Antonio and Santa Eulalia (scale 1 km. to 1 cm.). The legend indicates natural features of importance as well as hotels, restaurants, hospitals and chemists, sports centres, etc.

GETTING TO FORMENTERA

Since this tiny island has no airport, the only way of getting there is from Ibiza by ferry or launch. Boats leave Ibiza from the quay almost opposite Plaza Marino Riquer, and land at La Sabina, Formentera's only viable harbour. On average there are four ferry crossings from Ibiza on weekdays and two on Sundays. This frequency increases in the high season. The boats can carry about fifty passengers and take about one hour to make the trip.

Transport on Formentera
The local bus meets the ferry boats, and follows the main road through the centre of the island. Hotels also provide transport for expected visitors. Otherwise it is possible to hire a self-drive car from Autos Ibiza in La Sabina (tel. 320031). Mopeds and bicycles may also be hired at La Sabina.

HOTELS AND HOSTALES

For general information on categories and prices see p. 25.

It should be realized that though Ibiza Town is the capital of its island, it has very limited accommodation and relies on its outlying neighbourhoods, Figueretas, Playa d'en Bossa and Talamanca, to cater for visitors choosing to stay in this part of this island. As it happens, San Antonio Abad boasts more hotels and other accommodation than the remainder of the island put together. The municipal districts of Santa Eulalia del Río, Cala Llonga, Playa Es Caná and San Juan Bautista have a good choice in all categories.

There are holiday camps at Punta Arabi, near Santa Eulalia and at Cala Portinatx, and camping sites at San Antonio, Cala Bassa, and Punta Arabi, Santa Eulalia.

Formentera's best hotels, though few, are concentrated around Playa de Mitjorn and Playa es Pujols – though there are also *hostales* and pensions at these and other places. The coast, naturally, takes preference over inland San Francisco Javier.

In the following list, telephone numbers are in brackets.

Ibiza Town
HOTELS

Four star:	*Los Molinos*, Ramón Muntaner 60 (302250). (Swimming pool)
Three star:	*Ibiza Playa*, Playa Figueretas (302804). (Swimming pool)
Two star:	*Cenit*, Archiduque Luís Salvador (301404). *Copacabana*, Ramón Muntaner (301458).

Don Quijote, Alava 10 (301869).
Nautico Ebeso, Ramón Muntaner 44 (302300). (Swimming pool)

One star: *Figueretas*, Playa Figueretas (301243).
Marigna, Al Sabini 18 (301450).
Marítimo, Ramón Muntaner 48 (302708).
Palau, Galicia 12 (302350).

HOSTALES
Two star: *El Corsario*, Poniente (301248).
Estrella del Mar, Felipe II (303509).
Es Vive, Barrio es Vive (301902).
Internacional, Ctra. San Juan (302492).
Montesol, Vara de Rey (301104).
Parque, Cayetano Soler (301358).
Pitiusa, Galicia (301905).
Ursa, Galicia (301982).

One star: *Comercio*, Olozaga.
Costa, Barrio Escandell (301562).
Dalt Mar, Los Molinos (301974).
Ebusitania, Obispo Huix.
Espana, B. V. Ramón (301209).
Europa, Aragón (303428).
Juanito, Juan de Austria (301910).
Las Nieves, Juan de Austria (301910).
Marblau, Los Molinos (301284).
Marina, Olozaga (301151).
Muntaner, Ramón Muntaner (302043).
Ripoll, Vicente Cuervo (301428).
Sol y Brisa, B. V. Ramón.

Cala Llonga
HOTELS
Three star: *Cala Llonga*, (330050).
Playa Imperial, (330287).

Two star: *Playa Dorada*, (330010). (Swimming pool)

One star: *El Pinar*.

Playa d'en Bossa
HOTELS
Four star: *Torre del Mar*, (303050).

Three star: *Algarb*, (301904).

	Tres Carabelas, (302416). (Swimming pool)
	Don Toni, (302954).
	Goleta, (302158). (Swimming pool)
	Playa d'en Bossa, (302100).
One star:	*Mare Nostrum*, (302662).

HOSTALES
Two star: *Ca'n Bossa*, (301446).

Cala Moli
HOSTAL
Three star: *Club Cala Moli*.

Cala San Vicente
HOTELS
Four star: *Cala San Vicente*, (33021).
          Imperio Playa, (333055). (Swimming pool)

Na Xamena
HOTEL
Four star: *Hacienda Na Xamena*, (33046).

Playa Es Caná
HOTELS
Three star: *Miami*, (3302010).
          Panorama, (330000).

Two star: *Anfora Playa*, (330176). (Swimming pool)
          Atlantic, (330175). (Swimming pool)
          Caribe, (330252).
          Cala Nova Playa, (330300).
          Coral Playa, (330177).
          Es Caná Playa, (330152).

One star: *Ereso*, (330099).
          Pinomar, (330099).

HOSTALES
Two star: *Flamingo*, (330717).
          Las Arenas, (330790).
          Mar y Huerta, (330787).
          Perla.

One star: *Casa Pepe*, (330256).
                 Es Alocs.
                 Los Pinos.
                 Vistamar.

Playa Las Salinas
HOSTALES
One star: *Mar y Sol.*
                 Sa Palmera.

Playa Portinatx
HOTELS
Two star: *El Greco*, (333048). (Swimming pool)
                 Presidente Playa, (333014). (Swimming pool)

One star: *Ciguena Playa*, (333044).

HOSTALES
Two star: *Ca's Mallorquin*, (333067).
                 Oasis (333070).

One star: *La Ciguena.*
                 Portinatx, (33043).
                 Se Vinye.

Puerto San Miguel
HOTELS
Three star: *Cartago*, (333024). (Swimming pool, tennis)
                 Galeon, (333019).

Two star: *San Miguel*, (333041).

Sa Caleta
HOSTAL
One star: *Codolar.*

San Antonio Abad
(There are nearly one hundred hotels and *hostales* in and around this
very popular resort. The following list contains a wide selection.)

HOTELS
Four star: *Nautilus*, Carretera Port des Tuent (340400). (Swimming pool)
                 Palmyra, Av. Dr Fléming (340354). (Swimming pool)

Three star: *Abrat*, Es Caló del Moro (341286).
            Acor, Camino de Cala Gracio (340851). (Swimming pool, tennis)
            Arenal, Playa de San Antonio (340112). (Swimming pool, tennis)
            Bellamar, Playa es Puet (340104).
            Cala Gracio, Playa de Cala Gracio (340862).
            Els Pins, Cala Bou, (340301).
            Helios, Playa S'Estanyol (340500).
            Milord, Bahía de San Antonio (341227).
            Pinet Playa, Bahía de San Antonio (340250). (Swimming pool)
            San Remo, Playa S'Estanol (341150).
            Tampico, Cala Bou (340662).
            Tropical, (340050). (Swimming pool)

Two star: *Brisa*, Valencia 21 (341216). (Swimming pool)
            Es Pla, Ctra. Ibiza-San Antonio (341154).
            Gran Sol, Es Caló des Moro (341108). (Swimming pool)
            Pacific, Ctra. San Antonio (341162).
            Piscis Park, Miramar (34065). (Swimming pool)
            Ses Sevines, Playa San Antonio (340066). (Tennis)

One star: *Don Juan*, Santa Ines 7 (341212).
            Excelsior, Vara de Rey 17 (340185).
            Galfi, Av. Dr Fléming (340912).
            March, Ctra. Ibiza-San Antonio (340062). (Swimming pool)
            Mitjorn, Camino del Faro 10 (340900)
            Orosol, Ramón y Cajal (340712).
            Vedra, Del Mar 13 (340150).

HOSTALES

Three star: *Osiris*, Playa Es Puet (340916). (Swimming pool)
            Reco des Sol, Pinar den Frit (341104). (Swimming pool)
            Ses Alameres, Ctra. San Antonio (340200).

Two star: *Cervantes*, Cervantes 34 (340571).
            Fleming, Av. Dr Fléming 67 (340021).
            Norte, Barcelona 7 (340127).
            Roca, San Mateo 13 (340067).
            Rumani, Mosen Ribas (340056).
            Tarba, Ramón y Cajal (340216).
            Valencia, Valencia (341035).

One star: *Alicante*, Alicante (340277).
            Cisne, Vara de Rey 13 (340093).
            Florenco, Soledad 44 (340723).
            Horizonte, Progreso 62 (340333).
            La Sirena, Vedra (340718).

> *Mari*, Progreso 36 (340124).
> *Rita*, Mallorca 5 (340168).
> *Sala*, Soledad 18.
> *Vall Puig*, Progreso (341106).
> *Vista Alegre*, Ramón y Cajal.

San Juan Bautista

HOSTAL
One star: *Ses Arcades*, Ctra. Ibiza-San Juan (332002).

HOLIDAY CAMP
One star: *Cuidad Mar*, Cala Portinatx (333077).

Santa Eulalia del Río

HOTELS
Four star: *Fenicia*, Ca'n Fita (330101). (Swimming pool, tennis)

Three star: *Augusta*, Urb. S'Argamassa (330077). (Swimming pool)
                       Don Carlos, Urb. Siesta (330128). (Swimming pool)
                       Los Loros, Ses Estaques (330350). (Swimming pool)
                       S'Argamassa, Urb. S'Argamassa (330075). (Swimming pool,
                       tennis)
                       Ses Estaques, Ses Estagris (330200).
                       Siesta, Urb. Siesta (330275). (Swimming pool)
                       Tres Torres, Ses Estaques (330326). (Swimming pool)

Two star: *Riomar*, Playa des Pins (330327).

One star: *La Cala*, San Jaime (330009). (Swimming pool)
                       Mediterráneo, Camino de Misa (330015).
                       Ses Roques, Del Mar (330100).

HOSTALES
Two star: *Buenavista*, San Jaime (330003).
                       Es Pujolet, Del Mar (330025).
                       Giros, San Jaime (330707).
                       March, San Lorenzo (330023).
                       Marsol, Playa des Pins (330108).
                       Mayol, Av. General Franco (330282).
                       Rey, San Jaime, (330210).
                       Santa Eulalia, San Jaime (330807).
                       Yevisah, Paseo Generalísimo (330160).

One star: *Central*, San Vicente (330943).
                       Jerez, Del Mar (330232).
                       La Pilarica, Av. General Franco.

Los Hermanos, San Vicente (330043).
Sa Rota, San Vicente (330022).

HOLIDAY CAMP
Two star: Punta Arabi, (330085).

Talamanca
HOTELS
Three star: Argos, Playa de Talamanca (301066). (Swimming pool)
                El Corso, Playa de Talamanca (302062). (Swimming pool)
                Playa Real, Ses Figueres (300900). (Swimming pool)
                Simbad, Ses Figueres (302262).

Two star: Victoria, Ses Figueres (302512).

One star: Benjamin, Ila Plana (302512).
                Isla, Playa de Talamanca (302123).
                Ses Figueres, Barriada de Ses Figueres (301362).

HOSTALES
Two star: Rocamar, Talamanca (300690).
                Talamanca, Playa de Talamanca (302093).

Formentera
HOTELS
Four star: Club La Mola, La Mola (320050).

Three star: Formentera Playa, Playa Mitjorn (320000).

One star: Rocabella, Playa Es Pujols.

HOSTALES
Two star: Cala Sahona, Cala Sahona (320030).
                Calma, Playa Es Pujols.
                Casbah Mitjorn, Playa Mitjorn.
                Entrepinos, Es Caló.
                Roca Plana, Playa Es Pujols (320163).
                Tahiti, Playa Es Pujols (320122).
                Voramar, Playa Es Pujols (320121).

One star: Alemania, Playa Es Pujols.
                Bahía, La Sabina (320106).
                Bellavista, La Sabina.
                Cala Es Pujols, Playa Es Pujols.
                Camari, Playa Mitjorn (320180).
                Capri, Playa Es Pujols (320121).
                Costa Azul, Playa Mitjorn.

Italia, Playa Mitjorn.
Lago Dorado, La Sabina (320196).
Lago y Playa, Es Pujols.
Levante, Es Pujols (320183).
Los Rosales, Es Pujols (320123).
Mayans, Es Pujols.
Maysi, Playa Es Arends.
Pepe, San Fernando (320033).
Pascual, Es Caló.
Rosamar, Es Pujols.
Santi, Playa Mitjorn.
Sa Roqueta, Playa Pujols.
Sol y Mar, Playa Mitjorn (320180).

TOURIST INFORMATION

To supplement the tourist literature and advice available at Spanish Tourist Offices in European capital cities (for London see p. 28) an excellent local service is provided by the Oficina de Información y Turismo, Vara de Rey 13, on Ibiza Town's principal boulevard.

The local English language newspaper, *Insight*, is of use in locating current events and entertainments.

Information about Formentera and its facilities are available at the Vara de Rey Tourist Office.

IBIZA TOWN

Population 20,000.
Air and sea connections The island's airport is 6 km. to the south-west of the town.
Reservations: Iberia, Paseo Vara de Rey 15 and at the airport.
Aviaco: Av. Bartolomé Vicente Ramón 1.
Shipping offices
Compañía Trasmediterránea, Av. Bartolomé Vicente Ramón 2.
Naviera Formentera, Av. Bartolomé Vicente Ramón 8.
Naviera Mallorquina, Edificio Bahía.
Buses Bus Station: Av. Bartolomé de Rosello and Av. Isidoro Macabich.
Taxis
Paseo Vara de Rey (tel. 301794).
Playa de Figueretas (tel. 301676).
Hotels See p. 309.
Information Oficina de Información y Turismo, Vara de Rey 13 (*Map* **23**).
Open 09·30–13·00, 17·00–19·30 Monday to Friday.
09·30–13·00 Saturday.
Post and telegraph office Calle Madrid (*Map* **22**).
Post office hours: 09·00–13·00, 16·00–17·00 weekdays.
09·00–11·00 Sundays and holidays.
Central telephone exchange Calle Aragón, off Av. España.
Medical Services
Emergency Service: Paseo Vara de Rey 18 (tel. 303131).
Clinics: Alcantara, Av. Ignacio Wallis 10.
Villangomez, Av. España.
Policlinica Nuestra Senora del Rosario, Via Romana.
Nuestra Señora de la Paz, de la Paz.
Police Calle Madrid (tel. 301131). Office hours: 09·00–12·00.
Vice Consulates
U.K. Av. Bartolomé Rosello 24 (9th floor) (tel. 301818).
Hours 09·30–14·00 Monday–Friday
09·30–13·00 Saturday.
France Av. España 1
Holland Via Punica 2B.
Italy Av. Bartolomé Vicente Ramón 32.
Banks There are many banks in the centre of the new town, among them
Banca March Av. Bartolomé Roselló.
Credito Balear Av. España 1.
Hours 09·00–14·00 Monday–Saturday.
Clubs
Yacht club, Club Náutico, Astilleros.
Pigeon shooting Sociedad Colombófila, Conde Roselló 3.
Shooting Sociedad de Cazadores, José Antonio 5.
Tennis club Av. España.

Sport and Entertainment
> **The** *bullring* is off the Av. Ignacio Wallis (route to San Antonio) on the right.
> The *racecourse* (*Hipódromo*) is 2 km. from the town centre on the same road.
> The *football ground* is behind the tennis club.

Cinemas
> *Cartago*, Via Punica.
> *Serra*, Paseo Vara de Rey.
> *Central*, Cayetano Soler.
> *Pereira*, Conde Roselló.
> *Salon Ibiza*, Av. España.

Chiefly because it consists of four distinct quarters which fit closely into one another, this is an intimate town, making for easy sightseeing. At the same time it must be recognized that the beaches, and hence most of the hotels, are a few kilometres on either side of the harbour – a fact which not only allows them more space but also a cleaner sea (see p. 329). Ibiza was granted the title of city by royal charter in 1783.

THE WATERFRONT

This is picturesque and functional, as all such places should be, combining the old and the new in the form of a marina. It is here that passenger ships from the mainland and Majorca as well as the Formentera ferries dock; diverse marine activities – cargo vessels, trawlers and all manner of pleasure craft – are also dispersed in recognized areas within the sheltering arms of the harbour. The quays are lively, with a full quota of bars, cafés and restaurants – none of which make too great a concession to sophistication because, though they attract many visitors, they show few signs of having been appropriated by any of the élite. People who visit Ibiza evidently wish to participate in the life of the town rather than to skim the surface in search of a sophistication which does not come naturally to it.

The *obelisk* (*Map* **1**), at the centre of the quay which runs from west to east, and immediately opposite the Compañía Trasmediterránea's berth, was erected in 1906 to commemorate the exploits of Ibiza's own Corsairs – notably one Antonio Riquer – who paid back the North African raiders of the seventeenth and eighteenth centuries in their own coin; plunder was levied in terms of men and goods – with no greater resource than the daring sailing of their *zebecs*, tough vessels constructed of native pine. One of the most intrepid exploits was the taking of the vastly superior and better armed British brig

Felicity in 1806, after a glorious and bloody engagement conducted in full view of Ibiza's citizens, who no doubt cheered its progress from the ramparts high above the port.

Behind the quays and palm-lined waterfront, and sandwiched below the massive walls of the Old Town, a maze of little streets which becomes more intricate towards the east and the fishermen's quarter of Sa Peña, is full of small shops, music bars and cafés patronized by the cosmopolitan young. *San Telmo church*, (*Map* 2), inland from the obelisk, is the traditional church of local fisherman, and when attending Mass some of the older women may still be seen wearing their native costume complete with ornate jewellery. This was one of the old fortified churches, and presents a plain face to the world. It has recently been restored.

SA PEÑA QUARTER

Sa Peña may be taken as running from level with the obelisk as far as the eastern mole, where the shore tapers to an acute point, extending upwards and backwards as far as the foot of the outer wall of the old city. From the end of the quay it is possible to continue on foot around the corner. The map is misleading: it shows long parallel streets leading back to the new parts of the town, but though these exist as narrow alleys they form only a part of a confused but fascinating district of cobbled lanes and uneven flights of steps twisting in all directions to other levels but always rising up towards the walls. It is obvious that motor traffic is out of the question. The dazzlingly white houses, fitted together like pieces of a jigsaw puzzle, are simply built for occupation by fishermen and allied craftsmen; some have storehouses at ground level, but all are picturesque, resplendent with the colour of paint and pot plants and alive with the song of cagebirds. Expatriates have infiltrated here and live simply in a style which does not depart far from that of the fishermen and their families, who still form such a distinct section of the citizenry of this town. This is a part of Ibiza for rambling and allowing oneself to get lost, sure in the knowledge that the quarter is defined by the sea on one side and the walls on the other, so that it is impossible to stray far from one or other of the straighter streets, such as Calle Mayor, which point back towards recognizable landmarks and a part of the town where there is provision for wheeled traffic.

Ibiza Town

Waterfront:
1 Obelisk (p. 318)
2 San Telmo church (p. 319)
3 Market (p. 322)

Dalt Vila:
4 Santa Lucia Bastion (p. 323)
5 San Juan Bastion (p. 322)
6 Il Sirto Postern Gate (p. 326)
7 Portal de las Tablas (p. 322)
8 Museum of Contemporary Art (p. 326)
9 Church of San Domingo (p. 323)
10 Portal Nou Bastion (p. 326)
11 Town Hall (Ayuntamiento) (p. 323)
12 Archaeological Museum (p. 325)
13 Sa Portella Arch (p. 323)
14 Cathedral and Museum (p. 324)
15 Episcopal Palace (p. 325)
16 Castle (p. 325)
17 San Bernardo Bastion (p. 325)
18 San Jorge Bastion (p. 325)
19 Santiago Bastion (p. 325)

New Town:
20 Plaza de Toros and Taurino Museum (p. 329)
21 Bus station
22 Post and telegraph office
23 Information office
24 Hospital
25 Puig des Molins Archaeological
    Museum (p. 328)
26 Punic Necropolis (p. 327)
27 Observatory

A route to Talamanca, Santa
   Eulalia del Rio
B route to Hippodrome,
   Talamanca, San Antonio
   Abad
C route to Playa d'en Bossa,
   Airport, San José

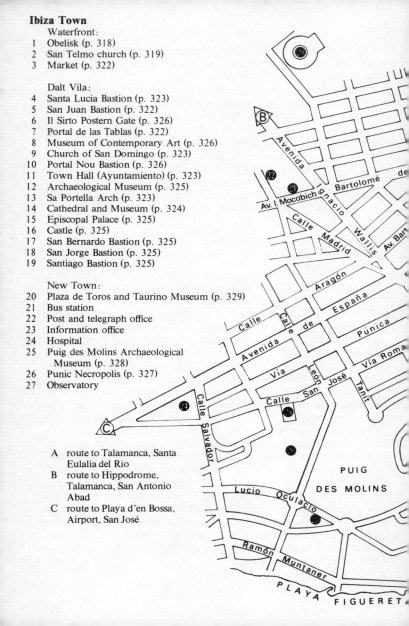

PORT

San Juan

selló

Avenida   Andenes

Eugenio   Molina   Pl.
                             Jose Pidal

Vicente Ramón   A. Primo de Rivera   Obispo   Cardona   S. Telmo   Calle   Mayor

Rey   Avda. Ramón Tur   Con Roselló   Pl.
                                                    Canalejas

Caetano   Soler   Pedrera

tara de   SA   PEÑA

Pl.
Desamparados   Av. Gen. Franco

Pedro Tur

Conquista   Juan Romaní   C. Santa Maria   Av. Gen. Balanzat   Pl. España

Obispo   Torres   Pl.
                       Catedral

PUNTA
RATJADA

Military
Barracks

PUNTA
MALLORCA

DALT VILA OR OLD TOWN

Nowhere in the town can one be unaware of the fortress looming high above with its series of walls and striking buildings on the summit, overlooking the approaches to the harbour as well as large areas of the island. Not surprisingly, this imposing fortress features in every range of picture postcard and on many an artist's canvas. There are three entrances: Portal de las Tablas is the main one, from which the one road suitable for cars – known as Sa Carrossa, or otherwise Avenida Generalísimo Franco – ascends in serpentine twists as far as the cathedral square. But more is to be seen by travellers on foot using the more direct, but consequently steeper, route which takes short cuts and allows for loitering in odd corners made by houses piled one above the other, in fact fitting in to one another on the perpendicular as well as the horizontal plane.

The massive containing walls of the Dalt Vila with their seven bastions have been described as 'new'. They are indeed the last of a series of lines of fortification, and were put in hand by the Holy Roman Emperor Charles V in 1554, one year before his abdication in favour of retirement to the monastic life. It was left to his son, Philip II, to carry on the work to the design of the famous architect and military engineer, Juan Bautista Calvi, who came from Rome, and was also responsible for such important fortresses as Cadiz and Perpignan and, nearer to hand, Fort San Felipe in Minorca. These outer walls have two other entrances in addition to the Portal de las Tablas, both of them comparatively modern, the second in importance being Portal Nou at the south-western bastion, and the third at the west corner of the San Juan Bastion. Both of these are for pedestrian traffic only.

Portal de las Tablas – on the east side of the San Juan Bastion – is reached most conveniently from the harbour by plunging inland from the obelisk. A few hundred metres of walking south leads, not absolutely directly but easily enough, by way of the produce market and its adjacent fish market in Plaza Mercado (*Map* 3), to the broad ramp which takes the place of the original wooden drawbridge operated by wheels, remains of which have been preserved. Flanking the imposing gateway are two marble Roman statues, much disfigured, their headlessness doubtless attributable to the Vandals – the original species with a capital 'V'. One is of Juno, and the other of an anonymous warrior. These are two of a trio that were discovered during the course of roadworks in the lower city. Above the gateway there is a huge carved coat of arms of the kingdom of Aragon and Castile, and an inscription which commemorates the completion of the defences by the 'invincible and Catholic Philip II'. It was he, incidentally, who contracted a fateful marriage with England's Bloody Mary, wooed Elizabeth I, and whose Armada was routed by a combination of Sir Francis Drake and foul weather.

Once inside the portal, the steepness of the town is demonstrated by a second high wall. Into this are set a series of arched recesses, occupied by booths displaying and selling representative arts and crafts of the island. The carriage road swings first right and then left inside the line of the walls, emerging near the ramparts and the Santa Lucia Bastion, from which there is a good view over the Sa Peña quarter, and beyond the harbour in the direction of Formentera. From this point onwards the foot-slogger would be advised to leave the main road where it continues the ascent by turning first south, then west, then east again before arriving in the cathedral square. Whichever way one goes, however, there are fascinating glimpses of a historic and ancient town which continues to be lived in to the full, with alleys, steps, cobbles, corners, patios, flowers, and even trees planted wherever there is room for them.

By continuing on foot – the only way when few passing-places for cars exist, and practically none where one can be parked – the first feature of architectural importance is the small *church of San Domingo*, which was built in the sixteenth century but, in a manner not unusual in these islands, embellished in the Baroque style some two centuries later. Its three tiled domes are delightfully 'Byzantine'. The adjacent building with its entrance on Plaza España originated as the Dominican monastery attached to the church, but in 1838 it was converted into the *Ayuntamiento* (Town Hall) when the original civic building was removed from the heights opposite the cathedral. Its storerooms are said to be the repository of many ancient documents, some of which have yet to be classified. Plaza España, which has a *mirador* overlooking the sea, is the point at which Sa Carrossa goes off in search of easier gradients. Otherwise, by various ups and downs, but chiefly following Calle Santa María, the more unconventional climber may continue above this better ordered road, to enter the second line of walls through the dark tunnel of the *Sa Portella arch*. (Take heed, the beguiling doorway above Plaza España leads not into the interior fastness, but by that postern known as Il Sorto out on to a cliff walk, wild and sloping steeply to the shore.

Whichever upward course one chooses, the inevitable destination must be the cathedral square, with its fine buildings which contribute enormously to its charm and to the various bird's-eye views it presents.

PRINCIPAL SIGHTS

The Cathedral
Map 14.

Dedicated to Santa María la Mayor, the cathedral is believed to have been built on the site of a mosque 90 metres above sea level, where once a Roman temple, and earlier still, a Punic shrine may have stood. In a time sequence to which the visitor to Balearic churches rapidly becomes accustomed, the original Christian church was late fourteenth-century, and then was revamped in Baroque. The one salient feature of the earliest period to survive is the rectangular bell tower, in the style which has come to be known as Catalan-Gothic, while far the greater part of the remainder is early eighteenth-century. The building was not dedicated as a cathedral until 1782. Because of the exigencies of the site, it has had to manage without an imposing west entrance; instead a charming doorway on the north side is set into a plain rough-stone face overlooking the square. This doorway contains a modern statue of the Virgin and Child. It will be seen from here that there would never have been space for a west doorway, because of the juxtaposition with the Moorish Almudaina. Another unusual feature of the cathedral is the line of six buttresses (seven on the opposite, south side) rising from well above the height of the doorway, and providing space for the side chapels of the interior. Both the roof and the copings of the buttresses are tiled.

Inside there is a single nave without either aisles or transepts. The interior is singularly uncluttered – perhaps because the church was never richly endowed. Two important pictures of saints – Santiago (St James) and San Mateo – are on either side of the high altar. They were specially commissioned from the Spanish painter, Valentin Montoliu, in the fifteenth century. One striking feature is a memorial to those men who died at the hands of Republicans in the 1936–9 Civil War. The *sacristy* contains an interesting collection of treasures, especially vestments and sacred pictures, many of which were executed by well-known painters of the Majorcan school; a number of these have been assembled to form a separate small museum.

Cathedral Museum
Hours *Summer* 10·00–19·00. *Winter* 10·00–16·00, both weekdays only.
Entrance 20 pesetas.

Archaeological Museum (*Map* **12**)
Hours *Summer* 10·00–14·00; 16·00–20·00, weekdays only.
      Winter 09·30–13·30; 16·00–18·00, weekdays only.
Entrance 25 pesetas.

This occupies two rooms of a small building across the square from
the north wall of the cathedral. One of these was originally a chapel,
the other the assembly place of the Universidad or town council. The
fourteenth-century *chapel of the Redeemer* was special to fishermen,
and was not appropriated by the Universidad until 1702. The civic
functionaries moved their Ayuntamiento downhill to the Dominican
monastery in 1838.

Both of the chambers house discoveries from the present site,
including a beautiful and excruciatingly thin figure of the crucified
Christ; but many of the exhibits have been gathered in from various
parts of the island. Among them are Carthaginian, Greek, Roman and
Muslim relics, though it must be borne in mind that the Carthaginian
remains from Ibiza's necropolis at the foot of the Dalt Vila, the best of
their kind, are concentrated in the specialized Puig des Molins
museum. There is also evidence here that in times gone by this church
building contained or was built over an ossuary.

The episcopal palace on the upper side of the cathedral square is not
at the highest level; it is possible to climb further to reach the remains
of the *castle*. Little remains of the building except a platform on the
San Bernardo Bastion, but this still demonstrates the raking field of
fire commanded from its dominating position.

Though the ramparts may be followed downhill as far as the San
Jorge and Santiago Bastions and Portal Nou, it is preferable (after one
long last look at the view from the parapets of the square) to set out on
the descent by way of Sa Carrossa, but without keeping slavishly to it.
One may yield to many a temptation to dart off at angles by way of
steps and cracks between buildings, leading beguilingly to studios,
eating places and secretive houses, whether grand and old or
ramshackle and old. With luck one will come across the derelict
Hospitallers' church, in Calle Conquista, immediately below the first
hairpin bend of Sa Carrossa. Around here much of the quarter is the
purlieu of gypsies. Portal Nou is to be found below, but don't expect

ordered streets, or anything but cobbles and flights of steps.

The third breach in the walls occurs to the east, where a narrow gateway opens into the arcaded Calle Conde Roselló, which runs straight to one corner of the harbour. If map-reading has failed in this pilgrim's progress from the heights, all one has to do is continue always downhill to hit one or other of the three gates. And if this happens to be Portal de las Tablas, one can make a point of visiting the **Museo Arte Contemporáneo**, which is in the Armoury in Plaza Desemparados (*Map* **8**). (**Hours** 10·00–13·00; 18·00–20·00, weekdays only. **Entrance** Free.)

NEW TOWN

Modern Ibiza lies below the Dalt Vila, at sea level except where the south-west slope known as the *Puig des Molins* intervenes between it and the shore. This 'the Hill of the Windmills', is the place where formerly the corn from Formentera was brought to be ground into flour. In archaeological terms this is the most interesting district of the town, though the major part of its remains are either buried or have been dispersed irretrievably. It is quite fair to say that there is nothing very distinguished about the rest of the town, though a possible exception might be made for Paseo Vara de Rey, which is put to full use by visitors and citizens alike. As is usual, this main boulevard, which is as long as Palma's El Borne, has wide pavements, and the one-way traffic runs either side of a broad central island well suited for the traditional evening parade. A rumbustious band plays there on Sunday mornings. The north side, being both sheltered and sunny, has the fuller complement of pavement cafés for floating or sedentary patrons, whereas functional public buildings and offices are located opposite. The north-east corner, occupied by the Montesol Hotel and its spread of tables and chairs, is something of a rallying point for the young of many nationalities, though the central focus was intended to be the flamboyant statue of the Ibizan-born general after whom the *paseo* is named. It was unveiled by King Alfonso XIII in 1904.

Vara de Rey distinguished himself in the Hispano-American War which followed the blowing up of the United States warship *Maine* in Havana harbour in the year 1898. Hostilities lasted only from May to August, by which time Vara de Rey had been killed in battle. When peace was declared, Cuba was granted independence and Puerto Rico and the Philippines came under the governance of the United States.

Most of the new town is very new indeed, having been rapidly built in a grid pattern punctuated by apartment blocks rising from ugly, colourless buildings which somehow transmit a feeling of neglect, or at least lack of care. For the history of early times we must go back to Via Romana, which runs from near Portal Nou on a parallel separated by two blocks from Avenida España, the continuation of Paseo Vara de Rey leading to the airport, San José and the south-eastern corner of the island.

PRINCIPAL SIGHTS

The Punic necropolis

Much of the Puig des Molins is riddled with the underground tombs that formed an extensive Punic burial ground, to which in Carthaginian times and as late as the Roman era, bodies were brought from far afield for interment in what was believed to be soil free from corruptive elements. Thousands of graves have been counted, and it is possible that as many again exist, though even from the very earliest days they were the prey of marauders, not only in the years of Arab domination of the island, but regrettably up till comparatively recent times, before the area was declared a national monument. Burials are known to have taken place from about the seventh century B.C. well into the third century A.D. The necropolis is the concern of the Ibizan Archaeological Society, founded in 1903, though their task has not been an easy one, since they have been in confrontation with property developers fully cognizant of the possibilities of the site, as well as what may be termed professional treasure seekers conversant with the collectors' market. On the face of it, it would appear that the battle has been a losing one. The hill is unkempt; except for 'show' chambers the tombs are not only empty but likely to be unsafe even if they are possible to locate, and the interested visitor may soon lose whatever enthusiasm he arrived with. The saving grace, however, is the well-ordered specialist museum adjacent to the site.

Puig des Molins Archaeological Museum (Map 25)

Hours *Summer* 10·00–14·00; 16·00–20·00, weekdays only.
Winter 09·30–13·30; 16·00–18·00, weekdays only.
Entrance 25 pesetas (tickets also valid for the other branch of the archaeological museum in the cathedral square). Tickets may also be obtained here for the necropolis.

This museum was built early in the present century in order to house whatever had been, and could be, reclaimed from the necropolis. As distinct from the other branch of the archaeological museum in the Dalt Vila, it concentrates entirely upon the funerary remains from the site immediately behind it, together with those from a contemporary shrine, the cave sanctuary of the Punic goddess Tanit, at the opposite corner of the island. It follows that those visitors who may have been disillusioned had they expected to be led by candlelight through labyrinthine passages as in many catacombs, will at least – and without danger of claustrophobia – be afforded the consolation of seeing well-arranged collections of Punic material, including reconstructions of typical burials, such as existed in their thousands so very close at hand.

The average grave was sunk from 2 to 2½ metres deep at the bottom of a shaft, the entrance to which was eventually covered by a stone slab. The burial chamber was usually roomy enough to contain six sarcophagi as well as space for amphorae and a fair sample of the possessions of the deceased, such as jewellery, cosmetics, domestic utensils and votive objects. In spite of the wholesale pillage which occurred throughout history, a great deal has been salvaged for exhibition – far more, in fact, than ever came to light in Carthage itself, the metropolis of the Punic empire.

The museum is a sturdy building on two floors. Steps lead up to the main vestibule, where one is introduced to the subject by an archaeological map of Ibiza and a model of a section of the necropolis to illustrate the layout of the hillside tombs. This is presided over by a bust of the goddess Tanit, the most important deity of the Punic cult; she has been equated with the Greek Demeter. The first room contains a great deal of early material, including funerary urns, charming zoomorphic votary statuettes, ritual vessels, Punic and Greek lamps, and strangest of all, painted ostrich eggs, which were presumably valued as fertility symbols, and would certainly have originated from some distance inside North Africa. Other rooms specialize in ceramics, terracotta masks, figurines and jewellery ranging through a wide spectrum of well-used objects, even down to everyday fish-hooks. Though outside influences are apparent, beginning with the Assyrian style of art from early Phoenician times, through the Hellenistic period into the Roman era, almost everything is imprinted with a definite Carthaginian significance. Upstairs there is a Roman room, and one devoted principally to coins.

Museo Taurino
Plaza de Toros; *Map* **20**.

Hours 11·00–13·00; 17·00–19·00, daily.
Entrance 25 pesetas.

The exhibits in this museum demonstrate the history and ceremonial of bullfighting.

BEACHES

Ibiza Town's bathing beaches and playgrounds lie on either side, a few kilometres distant, and are easily reached on foot, by bus or by water.

Figueretas (2 km. to the west) is served by frequent buses which leave from the Hotel Montesol end of Paseo Vara de Rey. The alternative is a ten minute walk, either over the Puig des Molins or, keeping to more level ground, by way of Avenida España, turning left at the hospital.

Though there are a good many residential villas, most of Figueretas is a mushroom development, with hotels of various categories, restaurants, discothèques and the usual holiday ingredients, and though its beach is by no means the best in the island, this resort caters well for visitors wishing to stay near but not actually in Ibiza Town.

Playa d'en Bossa 1 km. further along the coast, has hotels, numerous café-restaurants and a better beach. It can be reached from Figueretas or by turning off the airport road before San Jorge. The bus service operates from 09·00 to 19·30.

Talamanca has been built around level strips of sand sheltered by the promontory formed by Isla Plana. Walking there by way of Ibiza's marina could take about half an hour, and many visitors prefer to use the hourly ferry which operates from the town's waterfront. By road, leave the town on the Santa Eulalia route (Exit A) and fork right less than 1 km from the town centre. As with Figueretas, this makes an excellent dormitory for visitors wishing to enjoy the usual amenities of a seaside resort and yet be within easy reach of the picturesque town across the bay, and its network of communications.

ROUTES ON IBIZA

Though the greatest proportion of visitors to Ibiza stay at San Antonio Abad, or scattered amongst the smaller resorts – that is to say not in Ibiza Town itself – a glance at the map will show that the roads spread out from the capital like the struts of a fan. This is why Ibiza is used as base and departure point, bearing in mind that the crossroads at San Rafael make a suitable taking-off point for people from the San Antonio neighbourhood who wish to explore the north and east coasts. In that case distances will not usually be affected, because San Rafael is almost exactly midway between the two towns.

Excursions from Ibiza Town

1: SAN ANTONIO ABAD (DIRECT ROUTE) AND SANTA INÉS

Though the more interesting way of getting to San Antonio Abad is circuitously through San José [28 km.] (see pp. 338–41), the direct road makes a saving of some 13 km. It describes an obtuse angle at the village of San Rafael at the centre of the island, and from this hub of the island's communications it is more practical to set out for the village of Santa Inés [12 km.] rather than try a cross-country route from San Antonio. It should be appreciated that the north coast of the island is wild and cliff-bound, and for the most part lacking in accessible beaches. In fact, no coastal road exists between San Antonio and Puerto San Miguel, nor further east, though a few indifferent tracks adequate for the use of farming communities connect various hamlets in those parts. Though many of these are worth a visit, if only for their unspoilt atmosphere and some delightful old parish churches, the tourist is recommended to approach each separately from San Rafael by better maintained roads rather than attempt the short cuts that appear on maps.

Route Leave Ibiza Town by Av. Ignacio Wallis (Exit B), which becomes C.731. Continue on this road beyond San Rafael to San Antonio [15 km.] or fork right in San Rafael for Santa Inés [20 km.].

[1·5 km.] The *Hipódromo* is on the left.

[4·5 km.] A track on the right circles the small hill of Monte Cristo.

[8 km.] **San Rafael** can be seen from some distance, marked by its hilltop church. At its foot is the Club San Rafael, where there is also a restaurant. The *church* nestles securely behind a long containing wall and terrace from which there is a panoramic view of the island, particularly exciting in the direction of Ibiza Town and its harbour. The impression given by San Rafael's church and immediate surroundings is one of combined simplicity and strength, owing to the dazzling whiteness and sturdy construction in which buttresses are an important feature. Parochial notices are displayed in the arcades around the church and the self-contained complex includes the priest's house, garnished with songbirds in cages when last viewed by the author.

Beyond San Rafael the San Antonio road descends to a lower level near the Europark pleasure centre and children's amusement ground on the left, then runs with what could well be Roman-inspired straightness to San Antonio's harbour and the new buildings that line the bay.

Detour to Santa Inés
The farmlands between San Rafael and the tiny village of Santa Inés are of red earth which yields field crops punctuated by carob, olive and fruit trees; figs, propped up against both weather and ageing by crutchlike supports, are also a feature. In the last 5 km. the road crosses a ridge of hills with, to the right, Puig Serra (256 metres) and, to the left, Juanot (276 metres).

[12 km.] The *church of Santa Inés* stands on the edge of an open space which could be termed a village green if there were sufficient houses to describe a square or rectangle. It is distinguished, if that is the word, for its functional and plain architecture, completely in accord with the agricultural district it serves.

A minor road leads west from here towards Cape Negret [2·5 km.] to end short of Cape Nonó (p. 336), which can be approached more closely though circuitously by taking another indifferent road branching south to San Antonio [7·5 km.]. An easterly continuation of the transverse Cape Negret road goes from Santa Inés to San Mateo. To the north the cliffs are so sheer that they allow no access to the shore; hence no development has been possible.

[15 km.] **San Antonio Abad** (by the direct route).

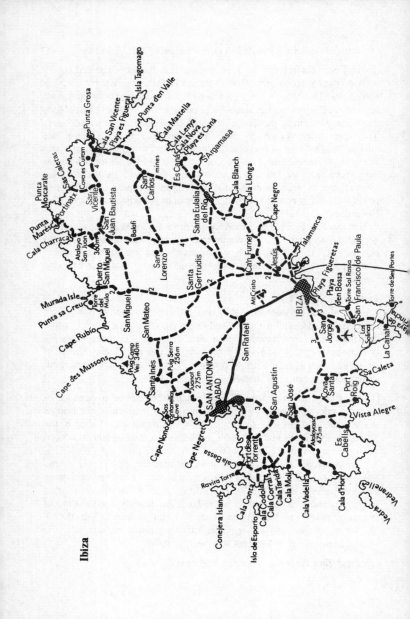

Ibiza

Formentera

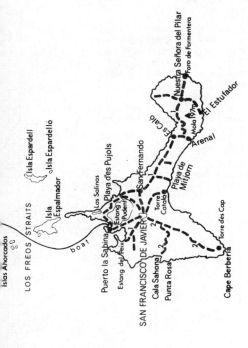

Islas Ahorcados

LOS FREOS STRAITS

Isla Espardell
Isla Espardelló

Isla Espalmador

Los Salinos
Puerto la Sabina
Playa des Pujols

Estang (Pudent)
Estang del Peix

San Fernando

SAN FRANCISCO DE JAVIER

Torre
Cala Sahona   Catalá
Punta Rosa

Playa de
Mitjorn

Torre des Cap

Cape Berberia

Es Caló

Mola 197m

El Estufador

Arenal

Nuestra Señora del Pilar
Faro de Formentera

boat

N

Diagram of Routes

SAN ANTONIO ABAD

Population 8,000.
Buses Bus station on quay at the bottom of Calle San Vicente.
Taxis Ranks near coach station, and at bottom of Calle Ramón y Cajala.
Hotels See p. 312.
Post and telegraph office Calle del Mar.
Telephone exchange Calle Obispo Cardona.
Medical service Red Cross, Calle Obispo Cardona.
Police Calle San Vicente.
Town Hall (Ayuntamiento) and Law Courts: Calle Miramar.
Vice Consulate *USA* Edificio Porto Maguo.
Banks
   Banco Bilbao Calle del Faro 2.
   Banco March Calle Obispo Torres.
   Banco Exterior de España Calle San Vicente 14.
   Creditó Balear Av. Dr Fléming.
Sports *Stadium (tennis, football, etc.)* off Calle Ramón y Cajala.
   Riding Playa de San Antonio.
   Mini-golf off Av. Dr Fléming.
Camping Campo San Antonio (between San Antonio road and the Av. Dr Fléming).
Museum Ethnic Museum, Calle Santa Inés.
Cinemas
   Reggio, Calle Barcelona.
   Torres, Calle Obispo Torres.
Beaches served by ferries and launches:
   Playa Calagrassio
   Port d'es Torrent (water skiing)
   Hotel Columbus and Milord
   Cala de Bou
   Punta Serral
   Playa S'Estanyol
   Playa d'es Puet (water skiing)
There are also boat trips around Isla Conejera to Cala Conta and Cala Tarida.

This is the most popular and populous tourist resort on the island, patronized predominantly by British and German visitors. In itself it is not large, having originally been a fishing village related to safe harbourage, but is now extended, though to no great depth, with high-rise hotels and apartment blocks rearing themselves around the entire sweep of the bay. Consequently pleasure craft far outnumber fishing boats. In fact, this is the nearest approach to a Costa Brava that the island can produce.

Neither architecturally nor historically is there much to see. The sheltered anchorage won the town the name of Portus Magnus in the days of the Romans; the Arabs changed this to Portmany – from which is derived the Ibizan dialect name of Purmany. The most important historical events were incursions by raiding parties, such as the Saracen landing of 1343, when nineteen inhabitants were carried off as captives. This brings into focus the fourteenth-century *church of San Antonio Abad*, after which the village came to be renamed when it was elevated from the status of a chapel to parish church. Its two towers were fortified and capable of mounting cannon in protection of the harbour. Except for the east tower, which is of plain native sandstone, the exterior is lime-washed white (as are so many Ibizan houses), and this treatment includes the unusual double-arched belfry over the south entrance to the church's courtyard. The interior consists of a single nave with four side chapels, one of which has been opened to form a south entrance. The ceiling is eighteenth-century. One special feature is a well underneath the nave, and its existence, in conjunction with the courtyard, points again to those days when the whole population was able to take refuge there against attack, and so survive some length of time unscathed. Most Corsair attacks were tip-and-run, or burn-and-loot affairs.

Any surviving old buildings in the form of traditional dwellings are grouped around the busy Plaza de la Iglesia. The quays are colourful, and alive with holiday activity, thus compensating for the lack of a good town beach other than the mere 200-metre stretch on the eastern edge of the harbour; the ferries do good business taking visitors to their choice of nearby pleasure spots, as well as on longer cruises along the coast in both directions.

Other sights

The *Cueva Santa (Holy Cave) of Santa Inés*, east of the Atalaya San Antonio on the northern outskirts of the town, is reached in 2 km. by way of the secondary Calle Santa Inés.

Sas Fontanellas. This natural cavern with possible (but debatable) Bronze Age rock paintings is near Cape Nonó, 6 km. distant; however, it is not easy to reach by the approaching rough track, and when located apt to be disappointing.

2: SAN MATEO AND SAN MIGUEL

The attractive hamlets of San Mateo and the more important San Miguel, with its famous church, make an attractive excursion across the centre of the island to within sight and sound of the north coast, returning halfway to the road fork at Santa Gertrudis instead of undertaking a round trip.

Route Leave Ibiza by skirting the Marina (Exit A), but instead of continuing to Talamanca fork left on to C.733 immediately opposite the eastern arm of the harbour. At 6 km. fork left for Santa Gertrudis; continue straight on for San Miguel [17 km.] or, fork left for San Mateo [18 km.].

[2 km.] The road from Jesús and the east coast comes in on the right.

[6 km.] Fork left away from the San Juan Bautista road.

[8 km.] Cross the highway between San Rafael and Santa Eulalia del Río.

[11 km.] **Santa Gertrudis** village is situated on the left fork leading to San Mateo. Its *church* was built in the traditional style at a period when fortifications were an essential part of life, and is a typical example of an Ibizan chapel which eventually acquired the dignity of a parish church. There is something very satisfying about its shape, narrow windows and tiled roof. The belfry is off-centre on the west side. The interior consists of a single nave with two side chapels, one of which contains seats placed so as to face the main altar. Square-faced pillars support the barrel-vaulted roof.

The road to San Mateo travels through country graced by terraced hills and pinewoods, well off the tourist map. There are some vineyards, though viticulture has declined since the days when San Mateo wine was plentiful enough to be exported; nowadays it can only be obtained locally, if at all.

[18 km.] **San Mateo's** *church* dates from the eighteenth century. The village marks the end of the secondary road, though it is possible to proceed a further 2 km. (with care) nearer to the coast beneath the shadow of Camp Vei, a headland 340 metres high.

Return to Santa Gertrudis, and turn left for San Miguel. The road north follows the eastern slopes of a line of hills.

[17 km.] **San Miguel.** As in the case of Santa Inés and San Mateo the village is little more than a hamlet, though the *church* – once the seat of a bishop – is of a size and importance enough to serve a prosperous farming district. It stands high above the road and is reached by a steep street. In a pattern to which we have become accustomed, it was built in the fourteenth century, but was greatly added to and embellished in the eighteenth. The spacious courtyard, large enough to harbour the entire community, is entered through archways and a timbered portico supported by white-washed pillars. Rather surprisingly this entrance admits us to the middle of the church on its south side. The interior – larger than many others – is T-shaped, and is provided with a gallery. It will be observed that the priest's house is incorporated in the fabric of the church, making in all an imposing, aesthetically satisfying group. It is of some interest to know that until 1782 these country places of worship were designated chapels, and not churches. Their chaplains were not resident except in the Lenten period; at other times they lived in Ibiza and officiated in the church of Santa María la Mayor, which was elevated to the status of a cathedral in that same year (1782), when the country parishes were created and allotted their churches and resident priests. Most of the exterior of the church of San Miguel is of untreated sandstone, without lime-wash.

[22 km.] It is possible to continue further north along the road which winds down to the sea at **Puerto San Miguel**, where the harbour is flanked by steep slopes. Behind the hotels, which have been squeezed into a constricted space, a road services the modern development area and produces excellent views looking towards Punta Sa Creu, which is crowned by the *atalaya* known as the *Torre del Mula*, with the island of Murada at its foot.

Though a cross-country road goes east to San Juan Bautista and the east coast, the recommendation once again is that all but the most intrepid should return to the crossroads 3 km. south of Santa Gertrudis should they wish to explore further east and north on this same trip. However, it is usually better to incorporate San Juan in a tour embracing the north-eastern corner of the island, as indicated in Excursion 4.

3: SOUTH-WEST CORNER

Though this is not the most direct route to San Antonio Abad, it is full of incident, including lovely scenery, and giving choices of access to the shoreline. It can therefore be recommended to motorists with time in hand, especially those favouring a round trip. As we can see, no distances are great, and the only delays are likely to be caused by compulsive stops and the occasional diversion on to an indifferently maintained road. Detours are especially recommended to Las Salinas and the approach to San Antonio by way of Port d'es Torrent, as well as one or other of the recently developed beaches of the extreme west. Otherwise the most important place of call is San José, an inland village which attracts a great deal of attention.

Route Leave Ibiza Town by Avenida España (Exit C), as though for the airport. At 2 km. fork left for a detour to Las Salinas [8 km.]. Return to San José road. At 8·5 km. a left turn leads, in 2 km., to the Cova Santa. Continue on the main route through San José; at 14·5 km. a left fork leads, in 6 km., to Cala Vadella, or in 4·5 km. to Cala Moli. Back on the main route fork left at San Agustín for Cala Bassa, where a right turn leads along the coast to San Antonio [32 km.]. The round trip back to Ibiza via the C.731 makes a total distance of 47 km.

The road towards the airport leads to abundantly fertile land known as Ses Feixes, which owing to surviving Moorish irrigation systems has been profitably used for market gardening for many centuries. One noticeable feature consists of the vines which are trained over the channels, fulfilling the dual purpose of keeping the water cool and drawing sustenance for their own crops. Owing to the vicinity of the airport very few high-rise buildings have been permitted on the nearby shore. One built in contravention of this restriction was blown up, and its shell is still to be seen.

[2 km.] A left fork leads to Las Salinas. Taking this fork one comes, in 2 km., to **San Jorge** *church* on the right of the road. It was built late in the fourteenth or early in the fifteenth century, and is of extreme simplicity, lime-washed, with a single nave, two side chapels and a belfry over the west entrance. Two features are of special interest: a covered porch tied to the west front – suggesting that this area is likely to have functioned as a market – and the castellated roof, which argues beyond doubt that the church was fortified and acted as a refuge for the local population in times of danger from raiding Corsairs. Just beyond San Jorge the right fork goes to the airport [3 km.].

San Francisco de Paula *church*, 5 km. from the main route, was built primarily for the use of local salt workers and is equally simple, though really only distinguished by the fact that it has no burial ground attached. The reason is that the brackish content of the earth would pickle bodies indefinitely – a paradox when set against the Carthaginian high esteem of Ibizan soil for its preservative qualities, for which the dead and dying were brought from far afield to this island for burial.

Here the saltpans, *Las Salinas*, begin, coming into sight first on the right of the road, then on both sides. They lie below sea level, so that the salt water is introduced through sluices which are then closed to allow for evaporation by the sun. The dazzling pyramids of harvested salt are at their maximum towards the end of summer, when the drying out process has been completed and the salt awaits shipment. Some statistics indicate the scope of an industry which has existed here since pre-Roman times. There are more than forty salt pans occupying a space something in excess of 500 hectares, from which evaporation has been estimated as 1,200 litres per square metre annually, involving production of more than 100,000 tonnes. Originally the industry was state-owned, and was most profitable, but then it was sold in 1871 to a foreign company, resulting in substantial loss to the island's economy.

A minor road leads left from the village of San Francisco to the shore below the watchtower of *Sal Rossa*, south of Playa d'en Bossa where there is good bathing. The southward road continues, keeping the principal saltpans on its right, while pine-speckled hills intervene between it and the sea on the left; the road accompanies the charming Heath Robinson railway, which is used for transport of the salt to its *cargadores*, or loading points, both traversing a short causeway between two sets of pans. *La Canal*, 8 km. from the main route at the end of the road, has been enlarged and deepened to accommodate cargo boats. The *Playa de San Trincha*, which has simple accommodation in *hostales*, faces south, only 6 km. from the island of Formentera. Return to the San José road, 2 km. beyond San Jorge, then fork left.

The straight road west leaves level ground behind after passing the Club de Camp (holiday camp) on its right, and then winds into the hills.

[8·5 km.] Turn left for a detour to the *Cova Santa* [2 km.]. This is a set of caverns in the hillside, likely to have been inhabited at an early period, but now transformed into a holy shrine and equipped with an altar furnished with what in pagan days would have been regarded as votive objects. Apart from its 'peasant' simplicity, the cave is in no way comparable to the limestone caverns found elsewhere in the Balearics. (A continuation of this road goes to the shore at *Sa Caleta* [3 km.] and comes to a dead end.) Return to the San José road. The Sierra de San José on the left is now at its highest, and the Atalayasa (476 metres) rises ahead, appearing disproportionately high because Ibiza reaches no exceptional altitudes.

[9 km.] Another track on the left goes to the sea at Port Roig [5 km.].

[14 km.] **San José** is a substantial village by Ibizan standards, and has made a name for itself by the cultivation of folklore expressed in singing and dancing by troupes wearing traditional costumes and jewellery. Much of the community's pristine simplicity has therefore been lost, especially by its becoming a halting place for coach trips bringing in tourists expressly to watch performances and dally in the several souvenir shops.

The white eighteenth-century *church of San José* is very attractive, with a belfry built over the west entrance. Inside, at the west end, there is a gallery, and throughout a wealth of Baroque is represented by a gilded reredos, a painted octagonal pulpit, and many sacred pictures and statues. The most valuable of these is a representation of San José (St Joseph) in an alcove central to the reredos which is believed to have survived from an earlier church that existed on this same site.

(A secondary road goes south from here to the Hermitage of Ez Cabells – or Escubells – and the nearby beach of the same name [6 km.] and links with Vista Alegre and, more circuitously, with Port Roig on the east.)

The San Antonio road now winds higher into the hills, and where it loops right [15 km.] before beginning to descend, another road branches off left to the sea, beyond a track which goes to the summit of the Atalayasa, from which there is an unsurpassed view of this corner of the island. This side road forks again after 1 km., leading left to the attractive and newly developed areas at *Cala Vadella* [6 km.] and right for *Cala Moli* [4·5 km.] and, at the same distance yet another fork to *Cala Tarida*. Any minor roads or tracks which go to the coast produce rugged cliff scenery, views of the sheer rocky island outpost of *Vedra* and its attendant *Isla Vedranell*, both the haunt of seabirds and wild goats, and possibly glimpses too of the islands of Conejera and De Esparto further north. All these islands can be circumnavigated from San Antonio Abad. The best view of Vedra from the land, showing it to rise to a height of 382 metres, is obtained from *Cala d'Hort*, which is reached by a 3 km. track branching left from the Cala Vedella road.

There is no coast road, so that a return must be made once again to the main road 1 km. above San José.

[16·5 km.] **San Agustín**, a small village, shows up on the right above the road. It has a plain white-washed church such as is typical of so many Ibizan villages. This makes a pleasant, off-the-road halting place for a survey of San Antonio Abad and its sweeping bay, guarded to the west by Isla Conejera. Incidentally, the San Agustín wine has a good reputation, though it is not produced in sufficient quantities to be sold outside its own neighbourhood.

From the road fork below the village the distance to San Antonio is no more than 4 km. on the direct route, but a much more interesting indirect route forks down left to the sea at this point.

[20·5 km.] A left turn here heads for Cala Corral [6 km.], Cala Codola [6 km.] and Cala Conta [7 km.]; it links with a country road to the limit of San Antonio bay at Cala Bassa, from where there is a track to *Punta Sa Torre* and the Ravira watchtower immediately opposite the channel which separates Conejera from the main island. It might, however, be easier to turn left for Cala Bassa some 3 km. further on.

[24 km.] Turn right for San Antonio Abad, to reach the sea at *Port d'es Torrent*, one of the most popular of San Antonio's beaches, which is served by ferries. The main road then runs slightly inland of the shore of the bay, with hotels and high-rise apartment blocks intervening between it and the sea, and joins up with the San José highway to approach the town by Avenida Dr Fléming.

[32 km.] San Antonio Abad.

4: NORTH-EAST AND EAST COASTS

In spite of difficulty in planning comprehensive round trips in an island where there are very few coastal roads, the opportunity to quarter the island, taking in the whole of the north-eastern region, fits well into the required pattern. Beginning by heading north-east from Ibiza in order to descend to sea level at Portinatx, then branching off east through the village of San Juan Bautista and visiting its church, one strikes the coast again at Cala San Vicente. From there it is worth exploring some of the beaches that have lent themselves to more recent development, before reaching Santa Eulalia del Río and its famous church on the Puig de Missa and resuming an exploratory route back to the capital, with the church of Jesús as a bonne-bouche.

Route Leave Ibiza on C.733 (Exit A), as in the San Miguel excursion. At 6 km. fork right on this main road and continue to the north coast at Portinatx. Return to the fork just before San Juan Bautista and continue through this village to the east coast at Cala San Vicente [30 km.]. From here a rough road leads south to San Carlos, where an asphalted road continues south to Santa Eulalia del Río, and then follows the coast, only one or two kilometres inland, to rejoin the C.733 just outside Ibiza. Total distance (excluding detours) 56 km.

The road north from Ibiza passes, for its first 6 km., through the fertile plain which is distinguished by traditional irrigation systems based on *norias*, or waterwheels, which have remained unchanged since the days of Moorish occupation. Much of the land is divided into smallholdings – a practice resorted to by Catalan overlords after the Reconquest, the intention being to prevent any challenge to their power by landowners. The farmers raise market garden crops for Ibiza and the various seaside resorts.

[6 km.] Fork right, following the main road.

[8·5 km.] The San Rafael-Santa Eulalia road crosses here, just before the bridge over the Santa Eulalia river, which can boast to be the only permanently running water in the Balearics, and so has won the epithet of *único*. The soil in these parts is of an almost Devonshire redness, and the fig trees are propped up into characteristic umbrella-like shapes.

[16 km.] A turning off the ascending road leads right to San Carlos and left to **San Lorenzo** [1·5 km.], a typical isolated hamlet; a short distance to the left of the main road in the same parish one can view the antique *Balafi* settlement, astride a rocky ridge, and distinguishable by two earth-coloured defence towers in which the early inhabitants used to take refuge in times of peril, climbing up to them by means of ropes and ladders in a manner reminiscent of the Celtic round towers of Ireland. This hilly region is exclusively rural, grazed by flocks of sheep tended often by women engaged in knitting or spinning, to while away what must be tedious hours.

[21 km.] For the time being ignore the right turning to San Juan Bautista, a short distance after the cross-country road from San Miguel comes in on the left. Soon after passing these two road forks, the route breasts the ridge below Atalaya San Juan (360 metres) and produces the first of several spectacular views of the north coast with its intractable cliffs and foaming sea far below; the heights above Cala Charraca and Cala Chucla, both of which are accessible by boat, provide similar views a little further on.

Portinatx village, 8 km. from the forks, is just before the end of the descending road, soon after a left turn leading to the headland of *Punta Mares* [1 km.]. Its harbour acquired ephemeral fame when Alfonso XIII visited it in 1929 while viewing naval exercises. For a brief time his landing place was known as Puerto del Rey, but this is now forgotten. *Cala Portinatx* has proved itself to be an ideal site for a small, self-contained resort, where holiday occupations include skin-diving in exceptionally clear water, sailing, water skiing, riding and dancing. The hotels are in two groups, with access to two small, sandy, rockbound beaches which do not lend themselves to major development. All the same, enough has been fitted in to make this a favourite spot for long-stay visitors, as well as day tourists from the more populous coastal resorts. Public transport is limited, so that crowds are avoided, and indeed there would be little room for them. A discothèque, an 'English pub' and some shops selling well-chosen souvenirs, such as goods made of shell or sheepskin – both local products – and such things as fishing tackle, contribute to the permanent amenities of this pleasant, rather remote place.

The coastline to the east, north of Cala San Vicente, is accessible by one track only, and this has to approach the area from the south.

[21·5 km.] **San Juan Bautista** shows few signs of once having been the centre of the most important country parish on the island. Even its church, however attractive, is by no means the most interesting from either a historical or even an architectural point of view. Nevertheless its 'Byzantine' dome and eighteenth-century proportions, to which newer red roofing tiles and a belfry have been added, give an air of pastoral simplicity which attracts quite a number of visitors.

The road now cuts through the hills, running east in a series of ascending hairpin bends.

[27 km.] **San Vicente** is a small village containing a newish (nine-teenth-century) church and, more strangely if it survives, a cinema. It is from here that the minor road runs north to Sas Caletas [3·5 km.].

[29 km.] It was on the hillside above the road, to the left, that the archaeologically important Punic sanctuary dedicated to the goddess Tanit, and known as the *Cave of es Cuiram*, was discovered in 1907. However, the site itself is hardly worth exploring by the casual visitor, as its contents have long since been removed to be worthily housed in the Puig des Molins museum in Ibiza Town (see pp. 328–9).

[30 km.] **Cala San Vicente**. This fishing village, the furthest from Ibiza Town, was not developed as a pleasure resort until 1965. This coincided with what some people consider to have been a period of hasty and unplanned building, and its few hotels are somewhat obtrusively out of scale with their environment. However, the place has the advantage of a wonderful sweep of bay, though much of this is shingle. A short continuation of the road ends abruptly at the *urbanización* above *Punta Grosa* and its limestone caverns, from which there is a fine view across the bay to the uninhabited island of *Tagomago*, in part of the sea noted for its fish, amongst which the bass-like grouper is much prized.

More conventional motorists may now opt for resuming their tour by returning to San Juan Bautista, so as to get on to the main Ibiza road, off which there is a turning to Santa Eulalia, as mentioned above – a distance of about 25 km. There is, however, a much more direct route from Cala San Vicente to San Carlos [approximately 6 km.] after which there is a 6 km. stretch of asphalt road south. Nevertheless, this short cut should not be embarked upon without the benefit of local advice because weather hazards such as heavy rainfall occasionally make some of the first section impassable.

[36 km.] **San Carlos**, inland below the range of hills known as the Sierra de San Vicente, is an ordinary rather sleepy village, offering a few facilities for the traveller, as well as being the meeting-place of small roads leading east to Playa es Figueral on San Vicente Bay [4 km.], the *Punta d'en Valle* with its watchtower opposite Tagomago [5 km.] and various secluded beaches further south: Cala Mastella, Cala Lenya and Cala Nova. The larger Playa es Caná is more conveniently reached from Santa Eulalia, as is the development area known as S'Argamassa. The parish church serves a district of scattered *fincas*, and is simple and white, its design including the priest's house, over which bougainvillaea rampages.

[40 km.] **Santa Eulalia del Río** is approached through a valley that was for many centuries noted for its lead mines – traces of which may be seen to the left, soon after leaving San Carlos. The town (and one is tempted to call it that in preference to 'resort') is laid out on the grid system, and has an old-fashioned, rather Edwardian atmosphere with its long main street – Calle de San Jaime – running at right angles to the formal Paseo del Generalísimo (taxi rank here) and Plaza España overlooked by the Ayuntamiento. The statue outside the Town Hall was erected to commemorate the part played by the citizens of Santa Eulalia in rescuing the crew and passengers of the S.S. *Mallorca* when it was shipwrecked near by in 1913. Santa Eulalia has hotels and *hostales* and, above all, good restaurants. But more modern excitements, including bigger hotels and apartment blocks, as well as better beaches, are located at S'Argamassa (3 km.) and Es Caná (4 km.) to the north-east.

The name of this idiosyncratic little town derives from that of a Catalan girl-saint, St Eulalia of Meridá, who defied the Roman Emperor Diocletian by adhering to the Christian faith, and in fact courting martyrdom. When she was burnt at the stake it is believed that white doves issued from her mouth at the moment of death.

The beautiful little *church*, built in 1577, for which Santa Eulalia del Río is famous, crowns a small but steep hill known as the Puig de Missa, which is reached from Calle de la Iglesia on the inland boundary of the town. The approach is through a paved forecourt surrounded by wide horseshoe-shaped arches. The enclave would variously have functioned as a place of refuge in times of danger and for buying and selling local produce, as well as for parochial activities in peacetime. This example of an Ibizan fortified church would have replaced the main body of a medieval watchtower, and incorporates the older semicircular bastion at its east end. Certainly this could have produced no more commanding site both for defence and observation. Another part of the fabric is obviously that of a mosque, where it is said that Christian services were celebrated until architectural 'conversion' was propitious. The ancient church shows no trace of having been set on fire after a landing by Republican forces in 1936, unless this is indicated by the lack of flamboyant Baroque decoration. Yet the interior has much of interest to offer, and such treasures as are displayed are offset by plain white-washed walls and a barrel-vaulted ceiling. Features to look out for are a beautiful and simple wooden altar, the Stations of the Cross depicted in tiled alcoves, and life-size statues reflecting a simple taste. The side chapel to the south is surmounted by a well-proportioned tiled dome.

But perhaps the perimeter of the buildings will provide the most lasting memories, as a look-out post across the gardens and over the quaint chimneys of traditional small houses, many of which have attracted writers and artists, making this place slightly reminiscent of such hilltops as that at Cagnes, near Nice, though on a smaller scale. Santa Eulalia del Río was in fact the retreat of Barrau, whose name figures among the most important of Catalan painters, and whose pictures are on permanent exhibition in the small art gallery near the entrance to the church. It is interesting also to notice how well the priest's house has been fitted in to one side of the great bastion, following complete destruction in 1936. Another feature which is touching for its simplicity is the walled cemetery beyond. Through its gate it is possible to view the alcoves into which the dead are laid to rest in tiers, amid lavish votive offerings, flowers and commemorative plaques. It will be discovered that there is a path below the outer walls. This is rather pretentiously named Paseo de Maroves de Lozoya, but it will be found to be rocky and partially overgrown with wild fennel, prickly pears with leaves scratched with lovers' names, and many sweet smelling herbs which are likely to invoke the memory of this charming place in greyer days to come.

There is no great advantage in taking the inland route back to Ibiza [13 km.] which links with the Portinatx road 6 km. from the town. The more scenic way, with frequent access to the coast, is only some 3 km. longer. It is necessary, however, first to follow the main road from Santa Eulalia for a short distance in order to cross the river, before forking sharp left past areas which have been imaginatively developed, as in the La Siesta *urbanización*, around which, incidentally, there is a minor road through Cala Blanch to the resort of Cala Llonga, both more accessible by our route.

[43 km.] A side road left leads to *Cala Blanch* [2·5 km.].

[45 km.] The left turning goes to Cala Llonga [1 km.], the white houses of which occupy the floor of the valley. This resort has something reminiscent of a rockbound Cornish seaside place such as Newquay, though the hotels and apartment blocks built into its cliffs and slopes are on a larger scale.

[48 km.] A minor road forks left for *Cape Negro*, and a fork off it continues by way of Jesús to Ibiza, though this is not recommended except to motorists in an exploratory mood.

[50 km.] To the right there is the inland development centred around the village of *C'an Furnet*, not far from which a new golf course has been laid out.

[53 km.] **Jesús**. Where the road comes in on the left from Cape Martinet by way of this village, there stands what on external evidence seems to be just another of Ibiza's simple sixteenth-century country churches. However, the *church of Nuestra Señora de Jesús*, which is approached by a short lane, far exceeds the ordinary, for the reason that it enshrines one of the most beautiful ecclesiastical treasures to be found on the island, and with the benefit that it has not been removed from its proper position behind the church's altar. This is the unique Gothic retable comprising painted panels executed by the fifteenth- to sixteenth-century artist Rodrigo de Osona. (An example of his work may also be seen in London's National Gallery.)

The buildings consist of three units, which functioned as monastic premises, priest's house and the church itself, all fused together. Originally this was a Franciscan monastery, later to be taken over by the Dominican order. The church is sixteenth-century, and is entered through a round arch, with three windows above and a simple belfry. The famous retable fills the area at the east end behind the altar, reaching to the ceiling. The central panel portrays the Virgin enthroned, nursing the Holy child, and supported on either side by three angels. Others play musical instruments at her feet. Pictures of the Apostles and incidents in the Virgin's life appear above and on either side, while below in the section known as the predella, smaller pictures carry a wealth of incident. The influence of the Italian Renaissance is obvious. As it happens, the church is apt to be kept locked when services are not in progress. This is both because of the value of the retable, and for the reason that in the past some objection has been made to sightseers who fail to bear in mind that the object they have come to view is a sacred one and not an exhibit such as is found in museums or art galleries. However, no one should be discouraged from a visit, because if located at his house, or otherwise found through the good offices of the local café-bar, the parish priest should be happy to admit visitors. It would be no more than a fitting gesture to leave a donation in the church's collecting box.

[54 km.] Junction with the Ibiza-Portinatx road.

[56 km.] Reach Ibiza Town by way of the southern side of the harbour.

INTRODUCTION TO FORMENTERA

Islands beyond islands exercise a most potent allure, and Formentera is no exeption. This small outpost, with few salient characteristics, is very close to Ibiza's south coast, and yet paradoxically feels totally removed from the larger island's sphere of influence.

Boats for La Sabina, Formentera's only viable harbour, leave Ibiza from the quay almost opposite Plaza Marino Riquer. The course taken varies according to weather conditions, but in the first stages the magic silhouette of the Dalt Vila must be the focus of all eyes and cameras. The boats sail south – on the same course initially as the steamers bound for Valencia and Alicante, but not for Palma and Barcelona – roughly parallel with the Ibizan coast east of San Francisco de Paula and Las Salinas, past the Torre de ses Portes, then through the narrows known as Los Freos, passing between Isla Ahorcados and the northern tip of Isla Espalmador. The former is 'the island of the hanged men', where prisoners condemned to death were brought for execution, to prevent the violence of their deaths defiling Ibizan soil. Espalmador has happier connotations. It is partly cultivated, and has an ancient defence tower as well as a lighthouse, while a movement is afoot to declare it a nature reserve. The tideless sea between it and Formentera is so shallow that it may be reached by wading over sandbanks. Amongst the other islets, which are so low-lying that in heavy seas they are apt to be completely shrouded in spray, are Isla Espardell and Isla Espardelló to the east. Warning must be issued to intending visitors to Formentera that, owing to a complexity of currents, the short and seemingly insignificant crossing from Ibiza can be very rough – at which times all but the most seasoned of sailors would be justified in deferring the trip. Very occasionally the service itself has to be delayed, or even postponed until the following day, so that visitors may find themselves marooned. But Formentera is by no means a desert island, so that such a fate need not be calamitous.

Routes on Formentera

1: ACROSS THE ISLAND FROM WEST TO EAST

Puerto La Sabina on first sight presents a passable likeness to the South Seas: crystal clear sea, palms, lagoons, shoal waters and no glaring modernity in its installations. Besides the normal activities of a small port which is little more than a wharf, there are some salt silos. Easily the most interesting physical features, however, are the two stretches of inland water on either side. The *Estang del Peix* opens to the sea, though too narrowly to admit any but small boats, so that it is now largely given over to water skiing and dinghy sailing; but some traditional fish farming is still carried on, as is instanced by the sight of fish, hung out rather incongruously on trees to dry. The larger *Estang Pudent* immediately to the south-east of the harbour contains dead landlocked water. Hence its name, which is translated as 'the stinking lake'. A minor road, mainly used in connection with the salt industry, runs along the foreshore of Cala Sabina, then turns south to run between the edge of the lagoon and the saltpans, *Las Salinas*, continuing to San Francisco Javier [7 km.] and passing the *Playa d'es Pujols*, where the most ambitious as well as the first of the island's tourist developments came into being. (A not very good road goes from Playa d'es Pujols to San Fernando village in 2 km.)

La Sabina, sometimes called Puerto de Sabina, though a modest place, has conditioned itself to the reception of travellers – at least in all but the provision of high-class hotel accommodation. There are two *hostales*, however. The main holiday attraction might be said to be the Club la Sabina, on the western lagoon, which is patronized by the water sports and sailing fraternities. Cars, motor scooters and bicycles may be hired upon arrival at the quay, though in the busy season it is advisable to make arrangements in advance. The island's bus service coincides with arrival and departure times of the steamers, and hotels look after their own customers.

[3 km.] **San Francisco de Javier**, built on a slight slope, stands at the junction of the island's road system, forming as it were the central point of a spider's web. As the capital of the island it possesses the basic requirements: post office, telegraph office (hours 16·00–17·00), two banks (hours 09·00–13· 00; 16·00–18·00), small shops, and a chemist's and doctor's surgery at the Centro Rural de Higiene on the Sabina side of the little town. More important from a traditional point of view must be the *church* on the central square. As might be expected its designers made provision for fortification, and in fact cannon were once mounted on its roof, even though building did not begin until 1719 and the dedication ceremony took place seven years later. As usual, the outside is white-washed. It is even plainer than the majority of Ibizan churches, having a completely unadorned west front. The interior is small, but enshrines a work of great interest: a painted mural immediately behind the altar, giving the impression of a tapestry.

From here there is a route to the *Playa de Mitjorn* and its watchtower, the *Torre Catala* [4 km.] by forking right from the main road in the town. The Playa de Mitjorn is the longest and best beach, of sand backed by dunes and then by pinewoods, extending for as much as 6 km., being broken only occasionally by rocks, which lend it character. The inevitable development is spread from *Arenal* in the east (south of Es Caló) to the Torre Catala, which allows for the dispersal of visitors, who may thus pursue their own interests undisturbed.

[5 km.] **San Fernando** village, to the east of San Francisco Javier, is the next stop on the tarmac road which runs the length of the island. It is a straggling place, without much of interest, except that it provides shops selling basic requirements. A track comes in from Playa d'es Pujols to the north.

[6 km.] A right turn goes to the Playa de Mitjorn, reaching it east of the previous one [1½ km.].

[8 km.] Another right turn, for the centre and so far undeveloped part of the Playa de Mitjorn [1½ km.].

[11 km.] The road has kept within touch also of the wide north-eastern bay as far as *Es Caló*, with pasture and arable land alternating with pinewoods, before the dunes bordering the Playa de Mitjorn appear. Es Caló possesses a primitive natural harbour, and makes a good place for a simple family holiday or outing, with options of beach life and walks in the rising ground to the east.

Immediately after leaving Es Caló the main road takes a right-angled turn south, ready to breast the eastern slopes culminating in *La Mola* or Atalayasa (197 metres) which, after many bends have negotiated the rising ground, is left to the south.

[16 km.] **Nuestra Señora del Pilar** is the farthest east of Formentera's small settlements. Its dazzling white church, of no great antiquity, serves the scattered farming families of the district. At this point there is a track going north for 3 km., to end abruptly 132 metres above the sea, where there is an excellent though not unique view of Ibiza. Another track goes south to the cliffs of El Estufador [2·5 km.] but there is no beach.

[18 km.] Continuing eastward, the main road traverses what has become a plateau, where livestock are put out to graze, and both field crops and vines flourish. The road ends without any substantial descent to the sea, at the high cliff-edge lighthouse called (pragmatically) the *Faro de Formentera*. Though there is no way down to the shore, the views amply justify the drive. In fact, it is claimed that on clear days Majorca may be seen on the horizon.

2: SOUTH AND WEST FROM SAN FRANCISCO JAVIER

The country on these two sides of San Francisco Javier contrasts with the centre of the island in being wilder and partly undeveloped, even for agriculture. The roads, too, are rougher. Ignoring the by-road back to the Estang del Peix, and the fork from it which ends in the hills, head south-west, making for Cape Berbería [8 km.], taking the opportunity to make a detour to Cala Sahona.

At first the road keeps to low ground at the foot of the hills.

[2 km.] Crossroads lead right to **Cala Sahona** [3 km.]. This attractive beach, sheltered behind the dominating Punta Rosa, is well worth searching out, with the added advantage that it has a good but small restaurant attached to a *hostal*. Unless recent improvements have been made to the road, care should be exercised. (The track to the left reaches the sloping green shoreline [2 km.] and low cliffs which stretch without interruption from the roadless western end of the Playa de Mitjorn to Cape Berbería.)

The inland road continues in a southerly direction, crossing the hilly ground which forms a peninsula and comes to a point at the Torre Catalá, or Torre d'es Cap.

[8 km.] **Cape Berbería** In the words of old map-makers: here be views.

SELECTED BIBLIOGRAPHY

Bidwell, C. T., *Balearic Islands* (Sampson Low, 1876).

Byne and Stapley, *Majorcan Houses and Gardens* (New York, 1928).

Cleugh, Eric, *Viva Mallorca* (Cassell, 1963).

Colas, Jean Louis, *The Balearics, Isles of Enchantment*, trans. by Christine Trollope (Allen and Unwin, 1967).

Dameto and Mut, *Ancient and Modern History of the Balearic Isles*, trans. by Colin Campbell (London, 1716).

Foss, Arthur, *Majorca* (Faber and Faber, 1972).

Graves, Robert and Hogarth, Paul, *Majorca Observed* (Cassell, 1965).

Hemp, W. J., 'Some Rockcut Tombs and Habitation Caves' (*Archaeologia* Vol. 76, 1927).

Hervey, Augustus, *Journal*, ed. by David Erskine (Kimber, 1953).

Isaacs, A. Lionel, *The Jews of Majorca* (Methuen, 1936).

James I, King of Aragon, *The Chronicle*, trans. by John Forster (Chapman and Hall, 1883).

Murray, Margaret A., *My First Hundred Years* (Kimber, 1963).

Ripoll, Luis, *Son Marriog and the Archduke Louis Salvador*, trans. by Renate von Wangenheim (Palma).

Sand, George, *Winter in Majorca*, trans. and annotated by Robert Graves, with José Quadrano's 'Refutation of George Sand' (Cassell, 1956).

INDEX